RAISED from the RUINS

For Alistair

Published in 2021 by Unicorn
an imprint of Unicorn Publishing Group LLP
5 Newburgh Street
London
W1F 7RG
www.unicornpublishing.org

ISBN 978-1-913491-91-8

10 9 8 7 6 5 4 3 2 1

Designed by Stephen Morris www.stephen-morris.co.uk smc@freeuk.com
Printed in Turkcy by FineTone Ltd

RAISED from the RUINS:

MONASTIC HOUSES AFTER THE DISSOLUTION

Jane Whitaker

UNICORN

I do love these ancient ruins.
We never tread upon them but we set
Our foot upon some reverend history;
And, questionless, here in this open court,
Which now lies naked to the injuries
Of stormy weather, some men lie interr'd
Lov'd the church so well, and gave so largely to 't,
They thought it should have canopied their bones
Till dooms-day. But all things have their end;

John Webster, *The Duchess of Malfi*, Act V Scene III

Contents

1 *Portrait of Henry VIII*, Hans Holbein the Younger, *c.*1537

Introduction

In 1535, there were around 850 monastic houses in England and Wales. Five years later there were none. In the late summer of 1535, as Thomas Cromwell's commissioners rode through the English countryside, life in the monasteries was continuing as it had done for centuries. Monks and nuns, in their black or white habits, walked through cloisters; bells still rang to Mattins and Mass. Five years later, the monks and nuns were gone, and the bells were silent. The Dissolution of the Monasteries under Henry VIII transformed English society. Henry had severed links with the pope and the Catholic Church in Rome and declared himself Supreme Head of the Church of England (*1*). His intention in destroying the monastic system was to reap its wealth for his own coffers and to suppress opposition to his newly claimed position as head of the church. The monasteries he took over between 1536 and 1540 had been home to about 11,000 monks, nuns, friars and canons. A few monks who resisted suppression were executed, but the majority were paid or pensioned off, leaving their former homes deserted.

In these four short years all was swept away, the vast wealth of the monasteries transferred to the Crown and their lands and buildings converted to secular use. Some former monastic churches survived as cathedrals or parish churches; a few monastic buildings became colleges at the universities; some were left to fall to ruin. But many monastic sites and buildings were sold to men who saw an opportunity to benefit from the sudden availability of land and the wealth and position it would bring them. By background, these men ranged from great aristocrats to intimate members of the king's inner circle, from administrators and royal servants to local gentry. Some of these new owners, including the king himself, chose to convert the monastic buildings for their own use as impressive new houses. Saved from total destruction, the buildings were reconfigured in many imaginative ways. The churches and cloisters, abandoned and empty, were transformed to create extraordinary new houses, raised from the monastic ruins.

The Dissolution of the Monasteries during these four years represented a sudden and complete transformation of English social and religious life. It was, in essence, an act of resumption, a restoration to secular uses of property provided over many centuries, for the support of monastic houses.[1] It was primarily a revolution in land ownership on a scale which had happened only twice before. The first occasion was the seizure of Anglo-Saxon estates by the Normans after the Conquest, in which the majority of English lands changed hands. Soon after, there began another, more gradual, transfer over the next four hundred years – the granting of substantial lands to the Church by the Crown and aristocracy.[2] This created a mediaeval landscape comprising great estates owned by the Crown, the aristocracy and the Church. As a result, by 1500 the monasteries had accumulated great wealth in the form of bequests of land, estimated to be around a quarter of all the cultivated land in the kingdom.[3]

The origins of the Dissolution of the Monasteries lay in the 'King's Great Matter', Henry VIII's desire for a divorce from Katherine of Aragon to enable him to marry Anne Boleyn. By early 1527 Henry, having no male heirs, had come to the conclusion that his marriage was contrary to scripture and must be ended. He looked to the pope, Clement VII, to declare it invalid, and did not anticipate any difficulties – popes usually gave a sympathetic hearing to princely petitioners.[4] But Clement was reluctant to reach a verdict – he did not want to offend Henry, but he even less wanted to offend the Emperor Charles V, Katherine's nephew. A legatine court hearing the case in 1529 did not reach a final judgement. Henry's response was quick: Parliament was summoned, and a series of measures enacted over the next three years to put pres-sure on the Church and persuade Clement to be more accommodating. But these measures failed to alter the papal position.

The tempo changed significantly in 1533, with the secret marriage of Henry and Anne in January, Anne's pregnancy, and the appointment of Thomas Cranmer as Arch-bishop of Canterbury in April. Cranmer held a special court in May to pronounce on the king's first marriage and, having declared it invalid, the way was open for Anne to be crowned Queen on 1 June 1533. Her daughter Elizabeth was then born on 7 September.

Following these events, Parliament enacted a series of statutes which set out, elaborated and justified the ideas which from the beginning of the king's quest for a divorce had underpinned his actions.[5] The Act of Appeals dealt directly with the divorce, preventing any appeal to the pope. The Act of Succession declared the king's issue by Anne his lawful children and heirs. However, two acts more than any others began the process which would lead, less than three years later, to the Dissolution of the Monasteries: the Act of Supremacy and the Act of First Fruits and Tenths. On 3 November 1534 Parliament passed the Act of Supremacy, which defined the right of Henry VIII to be Supreme Head on Earth of the Church of England. This severed all ecclesiastical links with Rome and marked the beginning of the Reformation. It began a process which, in less than two years, led to the suppression of the first monasteries.

It had been the custom since 1320 that the first year's income of episcopal sees after a voidancy, known as the first fruits, should go to the papal treasury. Shortly after the Act of Supremacy, and directly resulting from it, a bill passed through Parliament securing the first fruits of all spiritual and temporal bene-fices and offices to the Crown, instead of the

2 *Portrait of Thomas Cromwell*, attributed to Hans Holbein the Younger, 1532. Cromwell was Henry VIII's chief minister throughout the Dissolution

pope. It also imposed a new annual tax of ten percent of the net incomes of all spiritual and temporal benefices to take effect from 1 January 1535.[6] This act came to be known as the Act of First Fruits and Tenths. The author of the policy was Thomas Cromwell (*2*), Chancellor of the Exchequer and Master of the Rolls.

In order to assess this new tax properly, a survey of all church property and revenues was essential, and on 30 January 1535 commissioners were appointed across the country to conduct the survey. The result was the collection and summary of returns known as the *Valor Ecclesiasticus*, which for the first time gave the king a full understanding of the wealth of the church as a whole, and especially

the monasteries. Superiors and officials of each monastery were bound to appear before the commissioners with full information to be given on oath. Detailed instructions were provided to the commissioners regarding the inspection of books and records, and the taking of evidence. From this evidence, a list was to be prepared of all income for each religious house, including both spiritual and temporal revenues. After all the returns had been made, a book for every diocese was to be compiled and returned to London.[7]

The commissioners were a group of men who had long been used as agents for government. The commission was always headed by the bishop, supported by mayors, sheriffs, justices of the peace, official auditors and local

3 Detail of the title page of the *Valor Ecclesiasticus*, 1535. The illumination shows an enthroned Henry surrounded by his courtiers

gentry. The final lists were in the hands of the Exchequer early in 1536. Most of them still exist, in twenty-two volumes and three portfolios held at the National Archives. Of these volumes, two are known officially as the *Liber Regis*, made for the king. They are written in Latin on vellum, and beautifully illuminated (3).[8] It had been the custom throughout the history of the monasteries that episcopal visitations were made from time to time as a basis for correction, remedial punishment and injunctions, though some, notably the Cistercians, Observants, Gilbertines, Premonstratians and Cluniacs, had been exempt.[9] The Act of Supremacy gave the king the right to conduct

visitations of all religious houses, including those previously exempt. Thomas Cromwell was appointed on 21 January 1535 as vice regent in spirituals, for the purpose of undertaking these ecclesiastical visitations. It was important to assert and demonstrate the new authority – ultimately the royal supremacy – over the monasteries.[10] Following behind the commissioners for the *Valor*, the visitors carried with them two documents. The first, a list of 'instructions', was a long questionnaire to be asked of each of the religious. The second was a set of injunctions to be issued at the end of the visitation in which the wish to exert the king's new authority was crucial.

The questionnaire differed little from those which had been used for centuries by bishops. It covered the whole range of duties of the religious life as well as questions dealing with the abbot or prior and his administration. The questions were, on the whole, reasonable and not unduly inquisitorial.[11] However, the injunctions differed from those previously used, with no opportunity lost of emphasising to the religious their obligations to the new regime.[12] They began by reminding the abbot and community of the two oaths they had recently taken regarding the Acts of Succession and Supremacy. The other injunctions dealt with the daily life of the house, including 'that no monk or brother of this monastery by any means go forth of the precincts of the same' and 'that women … be utterly excluded'.[13] These were probably intended to re-assert what was already law, but additional articles were added towards reform including that relics were not to be exhibited for 'increase of lucre' and, if pilgrims wished to donate to the shrine, the money was to go to the poor. There was also an obligation on priests to remember Queen Anne daily in their Mass.[14]

The visitors began work in July 1535 and were on the road for six months.[15] They moved with speed as it was important that Cromwell should be seen to be exercising his new powers by as many people as possible without delay.[16] Richard Layton, a Cumberland man and one of the most energetic visitors, wrote to Cromwell that 'There can be no better way to beat the King's authority into the heads of the rude people of the North than to show them that the King intends reformation and correction of religion.'[17] There is no clear evidence that Cromwell or the king had decided upon total or partial suppression of the monasteries before the visitations began,

but rather that strong reform was intended.

However, the visitors' reports led to a change of policy which shortly resulted in the suppression of the smaller monasteries. Certainly, there were many reports of abuses: Layton wrote to Cromwell of the abbot of Bisham selling his house's goods 'for white wyne, sugar, burage leaves and seke [sack] whereof he sippes nightly in his chamber tyll mydnight'.[18] Of Shulbrede Priory in West Sussex, Layton wrote that: 'The prior of Shelbrede, the bearer, has seven [women], and his monks four or five each.'[19] At Maiden Bradley Priory in Wiltshire, Layton found: 'a holy father prior, with but six children, and but one daughter married yet. His sons be tall men waiting on him; and he thanks God he never meddled with married women, but all with maidens, and always married them right well.'[20] Conversely, the visitors not infrequently commended whole communities to Cromwell, and certainly did not paint a picture of unrelieved villainy.[21] Layton's main colleague in the north was Thomas Legh, a Cheshire man. The two other principal visitors were John ap Rice, a lawyer from an ancient Welsh family, and John Tregonwell, a Cornishman. They both later created houses for themselves in ex-monastic buildings; ap Rice at Brecon and Tregonwell at Milton Abbas.[22]

Immediately following the visitations of 1535 a few monasteries, where the visitors had been especially critical, were closed. Beyond that, all the reports did was to confirm and amplify long-held convictions that the monasteries were generally in need of reform. Since there was a tradition of reform by suppressing smaller, weaker monasteries, it made sense for the government to respond to further evidence by dissolving such houses.[23]

The *Valor* and the visitations together therefore led almost immediately into the first stage of suppression of the smaller houses. Parliament met on 4 February 1536 and received a digest of the *Valor*. Towards the end of the month a bill for the dissolution of the lesser monasteries was passed. The act was entitled, 'An Acte wherby all Relygeous Houses of Monkes, Chanons, and Nonnes, whiche may dyspend Manors, Landes, Tenementes, and Heredytamentes, above the clere yerly value of ij. c. li. [£200] are geven to the Kinges Highnes, his heires and Successours, for ever'.[24] It is now known as the Suppression of Religious Houses Act 1535, also referred to as the Act for the Dissolution of the Lesser Monasteries.

The preamble to the act describes the corruption prevailing in communities of less than twelve, a number which had for centuries been the traditional minimum number of a perfect community, with the abbot as the thirteenth:

> Forasmoche as manifest synne, vicious, carnall, and abhomynable lyvyng, is dayly usyd and commytted amonges the lytell and smale Abbeys, Pryoryes, and other Relygyous Houses of Monkes, Chanons, and Nonnes, where the congregacion of suche Relygyous persones is under the number of xij. Persones […] soe that without suche small Houses be utterly suppressed, and the Relygyous persons therin commytted to greate and honorable Monasteries of Relygyon in this realme, where thei maye be compelled to lyve relygyously for Reformacion of ther lyves, ther canne elles be noo Reformacion in this behalf.[25]

At this time, the larger monasteries did not have their full complement of monks, and it was considered that the religious from smaller houses could be relocated to the larger monasteries, where they could 'be compellyd to reforme ther lyves'.[26] The financial measure adopted for selecting these smaller monasteries was a net income of less than £200 per year, as recorded in the *Valor*. In return, pensions were to be paid to the monks, or they were to be permitted to travel abroad, or they could move to larger monasteries, which were required to take them in. The aggregate income of all the smaller houses was about £19,000, less than a fifth of the total monastic income. The act was swiftly implemented and on 24 April 1536 instructions were issued to a commission in each county to visit the smaller houses. There the superior and officials were put on oath to answer a questionnaire specifying the number of religious, their 'conversation' (moral repute) and their choice between going to another house or 'taking capacities', that is accepting dispensation from their vows of poverty and obedience. They were also required to state the number of servants, the value of lead and bells, and the amount of valuables, stores and stock. They were to make a new assessment of the revenues including the value of the demesne and woodlands, and to send in their report to the newly established Court of Augmentations.[27]

Within a few weeks of the Suppression of Religious Houses Act, and as a direct consequence, Parliament also passed an act establishing a new body for the purpose of administering the property which would shortly come into Crown hands, 'to be called the Courte of Thaugmentacions of the Revenues of the Kinges Crowne'.[28] The title, as well as the creation of this new body, suggests that it was intended to retain the greater part of the monastic property coming from the dissolution of the smaller monasteries, towards the permanent augmentation of the Crown's resources.[29]

The Court of Augmentations had four

principal officers: a chancellor (also *ex officio* a member of the Privy Council), a treasurer, an attorney and a solicitor, and all of these had been appointed by the end of April 1536. The first chancellor was Sir Richard Rich, who later benefitted from the Dissolution, building himself a new house at Leez Priory. The act also provided for ten auditors and seventeen receivers, as well as other functions such as clerk and messenger. The auditors and receivers were regionally based, covering groups of counties, and in the case of the receivers were drawn from local men with knowledge of local society and conditions. All these appointments were made by the middle of May 1536, and the Court set to work.

The monastic property for which the Court was now to be responsible was comprised largely of manors or collections of rents, most of them well organised as a *rentier* estate and provided with bailiffs or rent collectors. This entire existing structure was taken over by the Court, with accounts presented to the auditor and monies due to the receiver. The information regarding all rents and other income was drawn in the main from the *Valor,* or if available a valuation made at the time of the Dissolution.[30] Where the demesne land of the monastery was in hand, it was let out, as specified by the act, on a twenty-one-year term. In most cases no value was ascribed to the monastic buildings themselves, except for movable goods, bells and lead, which were reserved to the Crown, as were woods. The general policy applied by the Court seems to have been to avoid raising rents, to protect existing tenancies, and to favour local men in letting monastic properties, a business-as-usual approach which might best reconcile laymen to what had taken place.[31]

The act establishing the Court of Augmentations also allowed for the possible alienation of monastic property by gift or sale. Such grants began almost immediately, and by the time Henry died in 1547 over half of the monastic estates had been alienated by the Crown. However, very few were by outright gift to favoured courtiers, the great majority being sold at commercial rates. In the first few years these might be the complete property of a religious house, including its site and buildings. As time went by, and when the larger monasteries were suppressed, most were sold at the level of individual manors or groups of manors. The process was that no property was ever put up for sale: a prospective purchaser had to approach the Court asking to buy (or be given) a certain property. If the Court was willing to sell, the appropriate auditor would prepare (at the applicant's cost) a valuation of current income. The Crown would then reserve a tenth of this as a continuing rent, and reserve tenurial rights (i.e. holding by knight's service) to protect feudal income, such as rights of wardship. The remaining ninety percent of annual income was multiplied by twenty to arrive at a sale price.[32] This approach meant there was little opportunity for haggling.

Following the rapid suppression of the smaller monasteries during 1536-7, a new policy soon developed by which wealthier monasteries, excluded from the 1536 act, were surrendered voluntarily to the king. On 11 November 1537, the Priory of Lewes in East Sussex surrendered, and Castle Acre Priory in Norfolk followed on 22 November. The surviving ruins of Castle Acre were atmospherically illustrated by the Bucks' engraving of 1738 (*4*). A few days later, the Abbey of Titchfield in Hampshire was surrendered by its abbot, followed almost immediately by Warden Abbey in Bedfordshire.[33]

This policy was clearly seen to be effective,

To the R.^t Hon:^{ble} M.ARGARET Lady Baroneſs Clifford
Wife of the R.^t Hon:^{ble} Sr THOMAS COKE Lord Lovel & one of the Daughters
& Coheirs of the late Thomas Earl of Thanet ———
This Proſpect is gratefully Inſcrib'd by ———
Her Ladyships most Obed.^t Serv.^{ts} ———
Saml & Nathl Buck.

4 *The East View of Castle-Acre Priory in the County of Norfolk*, engraved by Samuel and Nathaniel Buck, 1738

RY, IN THE COUNTY OF NORFOLK.

THIS Priory was founded by W.m Warren Earl of Surry, A.º 1090. It was Subordinate to Lewis in Sussex. Herbert B.p of Norwich constituted the Church & Monastery, and placed therein Cluniac Monks, under the Rule of S.t Benedict. It was seis'd as an Alien Priory 24.th Edn.d I. but in the 34.th Year of his Reign proof being made that it was in no respect Subject to the Power or assessments of any foreign King or Monastery, except only when the Abbot of Clugny some times came into England he used to visit in this Priory, it was restored to it's former Priviledges & Possessions. The present Proprietor is the R.t Hon.ble the Lord Lovel.

An. Val. 306. 11. 4 ½ Dug: 324. 17. 5 ¼ Speed.

S. & N. Buck. del: et Sculp: Publish'd according to Act of Parliam.t Mar. 25.th 1738

since early in the new year of 1538, pressure was increased to obtain surrenders 'voluntarily'. To achieve this, commissioners again toured the country. Their task was to persuade abbey superiors to surrender. Because of the uncertainty over the legality of their actions, the commissioners endeavoured to obtain 'voluntary' confessions. For example, the monks at St Andrew's, Northampton, expressed 'contrition for the enormities of their past living'.[34] Failing this, the superiors might be tempted with promises of an office or pension in case of compliance and threats of poverty and deprivation in case of refusal. There were those who resisted: in December 1538, the abbot of St Albans wrote that he would 'rather choyse to begge his bredde all the days of his lif than consent to any surrender', although he did in fact accept a pension when he was finally removed.[35] At other abbeys, the monks were keen to leave: when the commissioners arrived at Beauvale, they 'founde the prior of the Charterhouse in hys short gowen and velvytt cappe, redy befor our commyng'.[36] At Bisham, the monks were ready to leave, so that 'whan we were making sale of the olde vestments within the chapitre house, they [the monks] creyede a newe marte in the cloister; every man bringing his cowle caste upon his nec to be solde'.[37]

At the same time as these surrenders were taking place, commissioners were sent to rifle some of the wealthiest shrines. At Bury St Edmunds, the shrine of St Edmund was defaced and 5,000 marks worth of gold and silver as well as precious stones were removed. In September, the 'disgarnishing' of St Thomas Becket's shrine at Canterbury provided the king with several wagonloads of jewels and precious metals. From there, the commissioners went on to Winchester, where they dismantled the shrine of St Swithun.[38]

In May 1539 Parliament passed an act, later called the Second Dissolution Act, which declared that the preceding 'voluntary' surrenders were entirely legal, and that all leases made by abbots should be treated as continuing in force. Although sometimes interpreted that way, the act did not of itself authorise the dissolution of any monasteries.[39] The principal reason for securing the act was that the legality of induced surrender was highly dubious. The act, therefore, simply stated that all preceding voluntary surrenders of lands and possessions to the king 'by their sufficient writings of record under their convent and common seals' shall be for the king, his heirs and successors forever to 'have, hold, possess and enjoy'.[40] The act also declared that other monasteries 'which hereafter shall happen to be dissolved, suppressed, renounced, relinquished, forfeited, given up or by any other means come unto the King's highness' would similarly have assured title.[41] All future dissolutions were thereby made legally sound, by whatever means they were achieved.

The parliamentary session of April to June 1539, which saw the passage of the Second Dissolution Act, brought a temporary halt to further dissolutions. It was not until July that the commissioners recommenced operations, taking voluntary surrenders of larger monasteries as well as the dozen or so smaller houses which had escaped dissolution in 1536-7.[42] By early autumn the last great onslaught got under way, with around thirty commissioners involved in three main groups, dealing with the western counties, the north and the east. Twelve of the commissioners were officers of the Court of Augmentations, while the rest were largely lawyers and experienced royal servants. Almost all surrenders were voluntary, albeit under pressure, though there was a hard core of abbots who resolutely refused to surrender, at Glastonbury, Colchester and Reading. These three were arrested and executed for treason – denial of the royal supremacy – at the end of 1539, and their houses taken by attainder.[43] Formally, the very last abbey to be dissolved was Waltham, on 23 March 1540, but this surrender must have been delayed for some reason, since for all practical purposes the surrender of Evesham Abbey on 27 January 1540 brought the Dissolution to an end.[44]

For the vast majority of the monasteries dissolved between 1536 and 1540, apart from the few which became cathedrals or colleges, the process of converting the buildings into cash for the king's coffers began swiftly after their surrender. Firstly, any remaining plate and jewels were sent to the royal treasury, together with a few books that might be suitable for the royal library. Next, everything moveable was auctioned in the cloister or chapter house, including all the church and domestic furniture, the altar, pulpit, tables, cupboards, benches, candlesticks, pans and vestments, as well as paving stones, glass, bricks and tiles. Everything that could be moved was put up for sale.[45]

The buildings, which were regarded as largely superfluous because the main value lay in the land, were stripped of woodwork and locks. The valuable lead was removed from the roofs and melted down on site, together with the bells. The official instructions were that the commissioners should 'pull down to the ground all the walls of the churches, stepulls, cloysters, fraterys, dorters, chapter howsys'.[46] Sometimes this was done where the materials could be easily transported away, but more often the commissioners found that the cost of demolition was prohibitive. In Lincolnshire John Freman, given the task of pulling down all the monastic churches in the county, estimated that the total cost would be at least £1,000. He proposed instead the 'defacing' of the churches and making the buildings uninhabitable by removing roofs and stairs. The ruins could then be leased as a quarry.[47] This proved a successful strategy for demolition but means that the county, which originally had more monasteries for its area than any other in England, now has few remains.[48] When the commissioners themselves did not destroy the church and main buildings, one of the conditions of lease or sale was usually that the new owner or occupier should demolish them within a certain period of time. This was designed to ensure that there was no possibility of the monks returning – as a new owner put it, 'The nest had been destroyed lest the birds should build there again.'[49] Most monastic churches were destroyed, wholly or in part, both for religious reasons and as a source of valuable building materials. From the abbey churches at Bisham and Chertsey, materials were shipped downriver on the Thames to use in the building of Oatlands Palace.

Some monasteries avoided this complete demolition and survive today as magnificent ruins. At Tintern (5), Fountains and Whitby (6) the walls of the abbey churches still stand, reaching high into the sky as skeletal remains of the monasteries they served.

Those monastic buildings that survived did so because there was a ready alternative use for them. Some were retained for educational purposes and became colleges at the universities. There were only two English universities in the Tudor period – Oxford and Cambridge. By the sixteenth century, both had existed as seats of learning for several centuries, at Oxford in some form since 1096 and at Cambridge since 1209. Whereas earlier founders of colleges had royal or aristocratic

6 The surviving east end of the Church of
Whitby Abbey, Yorkshire

5 The ruins of the Great East Window of Tintern Abbey,
Monmouthshire

connections, those who established new colleges on monastic sites were largely royal servants, such as Cardinal Wolsey and Sir Thomas Audley. Whilst all had educational goals, they sometimes had very different religious objectives for their new foundations. Sir Thomas White, at St John's College Oxford, was a conservative Catholic, while Sir Walter Mildmay at Emmanuel College Cambridge was a Puritan. Some, such as Audley at Magdalene College Cambridge, simply took over the monastic buildings, while Wolsey at Christ Church College Oxford initiated an extensive building programme.

Some monastic churches were retained to be used as a parish church for their local communities, after the claustral buildings had been demolished. These include Tewkesbury Abbey, Great Malvern Priory and Malmesbury Abbey, which all remain in use as parish churches. Malvern was saved by the local parishioners, who petitioned the king and succeeded in purchasing the church for £20. They had no money to remove the mediaeval glass, and so it survives. Malmesbury Abbey was bought by a wealthy clothier, William Stumpe, who donated the church to the parish (7). At Tewkesbury, the parish paid the Crown the very large sum of over £700 to buy the abbatial church for use as a parish church.

Some monasteries were converted into secular cathedrals after their suppression.

7 Malmesbury Abbey, Wiltshire, now the Abbey Church of St Mary and St Aldhelm, occupying the six surviving bays of the nave

8 View from the monastic Chapter House through one of the surviving cloister walks at Lacock Abbey, Wiltshire

There were eight monastic cathedrals with existing dioceses which were re-constituted under canons as secular cathedrals, while six abbey churches became secular cathedrals of newly created dioceses. These cathedrals have all survived and are as close as it is possible to come today to knowing what a great mediaeval monastery was like. A particularly fine example is Gloucester Cathedral, where the church, precinct and many of the mediaeval buildings can still be seen.

Other monastic buildings survived because they had value when converted into domestic residences. Their new owners ranged from the king and his most favoured courtiers to merchants and local gentry, all of whom saw this as an unprecedented opportunity to create a new, often magnificent house for themselves. Some, like Richard Rich and Thomas Wriothesley, were closely involved with the Dissolution process. Henry VIII himself acquired and converted more monastic sites than anyone else – eleven in total. In some cases, he simply took over the existing buildings with little change, as at Reading Abbey. At other sites, he spent a great deal of money to build impressive new houses, converted from the monastic buildings. Henry also had both the resources and the organisation to carry out his conversions in a very short period of time. However, unlike those of most of his subjects, Henry's conversions were never his principal residence and he rarely visited them.

The other new owners, whatever their background, took a wide variety of different approaches to the problem of physically converting monastic buildings to domestic use. The result was a wide variety of architectural styles, individually designed and adapted to the requirements of their new ownership. In many cases the monastic buildings are hard to discern or have subsequently been further adapted in later periods. Others have fallen to ruin. But in some instances, parts of the monastic buildings reveal themselves as architectural features in the present day (8). This book is about the houses created from monasteries after the Dissolution, and the men who built them.

St Peter's Abbey (Gloucester Cathedral)

The most striking and best-preserved remains of the former monasteries are the fourteen which were converted into secular cathedrals after the Dissolution. Eight monastic cathedrals with existing dioceses were re-constituted under canons as secular cathedrals: Canterbury, Rochester, Winchester, Durham, Norwich, Worcester, Ely and Carlisle. The six abbey churches of Bristol, Chester, Gloucester, Oxford, Westminster and Peterborough became secular cathedrals of newly created dioceses. These cathedrals are as close as it is possible to come today to knowing what a great mediaeval monastery was like.

The structure of English dioceses had remained unchanged for four centuries, although by the early sixteenth century there was increasing concern that reform was necessary. Immediately before the Dissolution there were seventeen dioceses and nineteen cathedrals in England. Ten of these cathedrals were monastic foundations and nine were secular, headed by a dean and chapter. Two of the monastic cathedrals did not survive the Dissolution: Bath Abbey, which was one of two cathedrals in the diocese of Bath and Wells, was defaced and allowed to fall into disrepair, with Wells becoming the sole cathedral in the see; similarly, Coventry Cathedral fell into ruin after the seat of the diocese transferred to Lichfield. After the suppression of the smaller monasteries in 1536 there was concern that the wealth of English monasticism should not be wasted but should be used for educational and social ends. To assuage these concerns, on the same day as the Second Dissolution Act was passed in May 1539, Parliament passed the Bishoprics Act, which empowered the king to create any new bishoprics he judged necessary. By this, the king proclaimed numerous good causes to which monastic wealth was to be applied and promised to endow them.[1]

Initially, plans were made to create thirteen new dioceses endowed with the wealth of twenty large abbeys.[2] In the event only five dioceses

9 View of the tower at Gloucester Cathedral

were founded in 1541: Gloucester, Oxford, Chester, Peterborough and Westminster. Gloucester, which had been formed from the division of the diocese of Worcester, was itself divided by the foundation of the diocese of Bristol in 1542. Each of these new dioceses was endowed only with the wealth of a single abbey.[3] However, though much watered down compared with the original intent, the fact that as many as six new dioceses were established might be seen as a substantial reform.[4]

The new dioceses in every case took the monastic church as their cathedral and the precinct buildings to provide for the requirements of a new bishop, dean and chapter. All these cathedral churches remain in use today, together with other associated buildings from the monastic period that have survived. As a result, their precincts include some of the best-preserved remains of mediaeval monasteries. Remarkably, at Gloucester, most of the fabric of the great Abbey Church survives, as does the precinct, which enclosed approximately thirteen acres of the north-western sector of the town.[5] Unusually, many of the conventual buildings have also survived, adapted to new uses. Consequently, Gloucester can give a unique insight as to how such great monasteries appeared and functioned at the time of the Dissolution.

The Cathedral Church of St Peter and the Holy and Indivisible Trinity, Gloucester is a magnificent mediaeval survival in the heart of the city. It is one of a group of Benedictine monasteries which were founded over nine hundred years ago on the banks of the River Severn and its tributaries, and the first in order along the river. The others in the series are Tewkesbury, Pershore, Evesham, Malvern, Worcester and Shrewsbury. The pale stone tower of Gloucester Cathedral (**9**), visible from a considerable distance across the Severn

Vale, would have been a landmark for pilgrims visiting the tomb of Edward II. John Leland visited just before the monastery was dissolved and described 'the exceedinge faire and square tower in the midst of the church. This tower is a pharos to all partes about from the hilles.'[6] A nunnery was the first foundation at Gloucester, established by Osric, ruler of the Anglo-Saxon Hwicce, in 678-9 AD in honour of St Peter and St Paul. In the eighth century the nuns dispersed and were replaced by a body of secular priests. In 1022 the Bishop of Worcester introduced the Benedictine rule and re-established the monastery as it was to be for the next 500 years, but at the time of the Norman Conquest the abbey was not wealthy. In 1072 it consisted of only two monks and eight novices; Abbot Wilstan had gone on a pilgrimage to Jerusalem.[7] That year, William the Conqueror appointed Serlo, a monk from Mont Saint Michel, to be abbot. By the acquisition of extensive lands and with the aid of the king, Serlo was able to begin building the Abbey Church and expanding the abbey. King William kept Christmas in Gloucester in 1085 and this was the occasion when he ordered the compilation of the Domesday Book. The foundation stone of the new church was laid by the Bishop of Hereford on 29 June 1089, and the building was dedicated on 13 July 1100, by which time there were more than sixty monks in residence.[8] It is from this point that the abbey, as it was at the Dissolution, began to emerge.

Building work continued for more than two centuries under a series of abbots, developing both the Abbey Church and the claustral buildings. But the fortunes of the abbey were transformed when, on 21 September 1327, King Edward II was murdered while imprisoned at Berkeley Castle. The monasteries of Bristol, Kingswood and Malmesbury

10 The tomb of Edward II at Gloucester Cathedral, near the high altar

had refused to receive the royal corpse, but Abbot Thokey of Gloucester brought the body back with great ceremony in a hearse decorated with golden leopards and accompanied by a procession of monks.[9] A grand state funeral, deliberately made an event of political significance by the new young king Edward III, was held at St Peter's Abbey that December and a magnificent shrine-like monument was later erected over the tomb of the king (*10*). Royal patronage and popular devotion led to funds flowing into the abbey, and these enabled the remodelling of the eastern end of the church in the new style of architecture later known as Perpendicular. The royal tomb became a focus for visiting pilgrims who brought further wealth to the abbey and the city, extending the building programme into the early sixteenth century.

In 1539 Abbot Malvern, who was to be the last abbot, died. The history of the abbey ended on 2 January 1540, when the monastery with its cells was surrendered and the prior, who was temporarily at the head of the abbey, was discharged with a pension of £20. The clear yearly value of the property of the monastery in the *Valor* of 1535 amounted to just over £1,430.[10] St Peter's was, therefore, among the wealthiest abbeys in England. On 3 September 1541 Gloucester diocese was created out of the mediaeval diocese of Worcester. The Abbey Church became the Cathedral of the new diocese and its dedication was altered from St Peter to the Holy and Indivisible Trinity. The Letters Patent reconstituting the monastery at the same time gave the designation of city to

11 Harold Brakspear's conjectural view of Fountains Abbey, Yorkshire, showing
the extent of the precinct and its range of buildings

the town of Gloucester.[11] No longer a community of monks, the Cathedral was to be led by
a dean and a chapter of six canons. The Abbot
of Gloucester having died, the former Abbot
of Tewkesbury, John Wakeman, was made
bishop, and the Prior of St Oswald, Gloucester, became dean. The possessions of the
former abbey were divided as the endowments
of the bishopric and of the dean and chapter.[12]

The Abbey Church and conventual buildings in the precinct at Gloucester consequently
survived the Dissolution and were adapted to
new uses to suit the requirements of a secular
Cathedral. The mediaeval buildings conformed
to a conventional layout, common to most
monasteries. The Church, aligned east-west,
was at the heart of the precinct, with the
square Cloister extending from the transept to
the west end of the nave. The Cloister was

usually on the south side of the nave of the
Church, but sometimes, as at Gloucester, on
the north. It was probably built on this side to
take advantage of the water supply in the Full-
brook which ran through the precinct. The
entire precinct, of around thirteen acres, was
enclosed by a high wall, entered through a
gateway from the town.

This typical layout is illustrated on a drawing by Harold Brakspear of Fountains Abbey,
which shows the monastic precinct and many
associated buildings, enclosed by walls with an
imposing gatehouse (*11*). A river runs beside
the abbey, used by the monks for the supply of
fresh water and disposal of waste. The monastic Church and Cloister, central to the life of
the abbey, are at the heart of the precinct.

All the religious orders, though differing in
customs and dress, were founded on a princi-

12 A plan of Gloucester Cathedral, giving the principal features of both the Abbey Church and Cloister

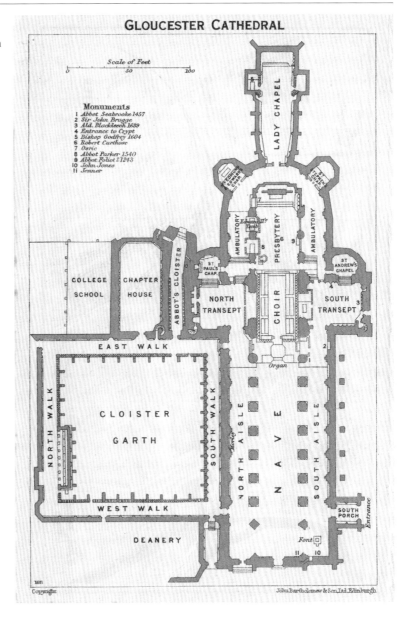

ple in which the daily services of the church, the recitation of the canonical hours and the celebration of Mass for the souls of benefactors, were the prime duties of the convent. The Church was, therefore, at the centre of monastic life and was generally cruciform in plan, with north and south transepts and a tower above the crossing. The choir was usually at the crossing and was divided from the eastern bay of the nave by a screen. The western end of the nave was, in most orders, open to the laity. The eastern end was in many cases enlarged and lengthened to make more room for altars and sometimes a shrine.

At Gloucester, the Abbey Church remained intact after the Dissolution, though the ornaments and jewels which had enriched its interior were removed for the king's use, and

14 The south walk of the Cloister, with the carrels used by the monks for study

13 The Great East Window, a triumph of the Perpendicular style

later many of its fittings were lost, particularly perhaps under John Hooper, Bishop of Gloucester between 1551 and 1554, who went further than most of his contemporaries in ordering the removal of effigies, rood screens, and other such survivals.[13] However, most of the fabric remains, and most of the usual features can still be seen in the present day Cathedral floor plan (*12*). The east end of the Abbey Church, with the choir and high altar, was re-modelled in the Perpendicular style after 1337, with intricate lierne vaulting giving an impression of soaring height. The Great East Window, made between 1337 and 1365, was at the time the largest window in mediae-

val Europe (*13*).[14] Using only white, blue, yellow and red glass, the window is filled with tiers of full-length figures filling the long Perpendicular panels. The subject of the window is the Coronation of the Virgin, who is attended by the apostles and saints as well as by the founders of the Abbey.[15] The choir stalls of around 1350 also mostly survive from this period. The Lady Chapel, built between 1457 and 1499, extends eastward from the choir and presbytery.

As well as the church, the other centre of monastic life, which existed at all monasteries, was the cloister. This was a square enclosure surrounded by buildings and a covered walk,

15 The *Lavatorium* adjoining the north walk of the Cloister, near the door to the Frater

with a garth, or garden, in the centre. At Gloucester, the Great Cloister has been preserved intact, and is one of the best examples in England. The east walk has the earliest fan-vaulting known in England, dated to between 1351 and 1377. The other walks were vaulted between 1381 and 1412. All the walks have fine leaded windows towards the central garth, creating a light airy space, with sunlight filtering through the coloured glass. For the monks, much of the time between services was spent in the cloister walks, and in the south walk the side facing the garth is divided into twenty carrels, each with its own window (*14*), used by the monks for their study.[16]

In all monasteries the east range of the cloister was in line with the north or south transept of the church, and contained a chapter house, where the convent met daily for the discussion of business, a vestry and possibly a library. There might also be a common house or warming house containing the main, or only, fireplace in the monastery. There was usually a vaulted passage leading through the east range to the cemetery and used as a parlour or *locutorium* where necessary conversation was allowed at times when in the cloister it was normally forbidden. All these features can be seen at Gloucester. In the east walk, next to the Cathedral is the East Slype, originally the passage through which the monks accessed their cemetery. It has an arcade of Early Norman arches on each side. Above this passage are the Vestry and the Library, which were enlarged in the fourteenth century. To the north of the Slype on the east walk is the Chapter House, where a structure existed as early as 1080. This continued to be used by the new dean and chapter. In most monasteries the monks' dorter, or dormitory, was on the first floor of the east range, giving direct access to the church, but at Gloucester it was at right-angles to the east range, running east-west. However, at Gloucester the Dorter was one of the few conventual buildings demolished after the Dissolution.[17]

The range of claustral buildings opposite and parallel to the church usually contained the monks' frater, or refectory, where the convent took communal meals. At Gloucester, the doorway at the west end of the north walk, now filled with a nineteenth-century window, was the entrance to the Frater, beneath which was a cellar. The north walk has an extremely well-preserved *Lavatorium* near this doorway (*15*), where the monks could wash before meals, which was supplied with water from a lead tank. The kitchen was on the north-west corner of the Frater and was briefly retained after the Dissolution, being known as the Common Kitchen. It was converted into a house in the late sixteenth century and the remains are now incorporated into 3 Millers Green.[18] With the monks replaced by a smaller number of secular priests, who did not eat communally, the Frater was later demolished.

At the east end of the north walk is a doorway into the Infirmary Slype, a passage which led to the Infirmary, used for elderly and infirm monks as well as those who were ill. In all monasteries the infirmary was near to, but separate from, the cloister. At Gloucester, as at most monasteries, the Infirmary was a large hall that ran east to west, built like a church nave, with beds on either side; there would have been a chapel at the east end. Only the west end and six arches of the thirteenth-century arcade survive. A building east of the Infirmary (now incorporated into Dulverton House, part of King's School), was the monastic Infirmarer's Lodging. After 1541 it was remodelled as a prebendal house assigned to the Prebendary of the Third Stall.[19]

Between the Frater and the Infirmary is the Little Cloister, which survives and would have provided a garden for medicinal herbs for use in the Infirmary. On the west side of Little Cloister is Little Cloister House, which contains the remains of the monks' Misericord, or place of indulgence, where they were allowed to eat meat and other more delicate foods than in the common diet. Now part of King's School, this was also among those buildings adapted as the houses of prebendaries after the Dissolution.[20]

The west range of the Cloister was used for different purposes. In most monasteries the ground floor was the great cellar or storeroom, though in Cistercian houses it accommodated the lay brothers. In houses of other orders, the upper floor was often the lodging of the abbot or prior, and contained his guest hall, great chamber and chapel. At Gloucester, this was originally the case, but after a new Abbot's Lodging was built it then became the Prior's Lodging. To the west of College Green and connected with the west walk of the Cloister by two doorways, the Prior's Lodging was a substantial building. The mediaeval passage nearest to the nave, which runs beneath part

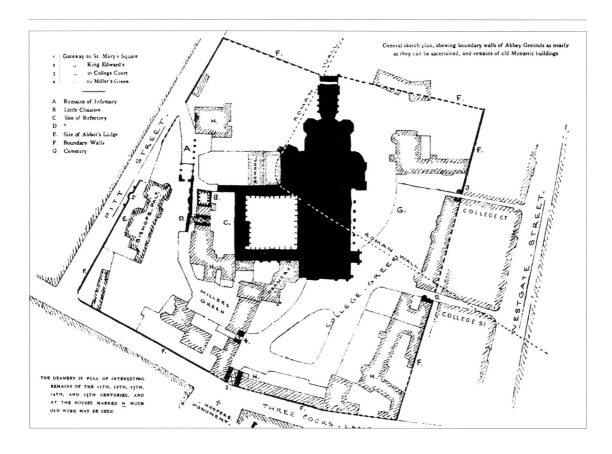

1 | Gateway to St. Mary's Square
2 | „ King Edward's
3 | „ in College Court
4 | „ to Miller's Green

A | Remains of Infirmary
B | Little Cloisters
C | Site of Refectory
D | ?
E | Site of Abbot's Lodge
F | Boundary Walls
G | Cemetery

THE DEANERY IS FULL OF INTERESTING REMAINS OF THE 11TH, 12TH, 13TH, 14TH, AND 15TH CENTURIES, AND AT THE HOUSES MARKED H MUCH OLD WORK MAY BE SEEN.

16 A plan of Gloucester Cathedral and precinct made in 1905 showing all the buildings surviving from the Dissolution

of this lodging, served as an outer parlour where monks could talk to lay visitors.[21] The rooms in the Prior's Lodging include the Henry Room, traditionally used by Henry VIII and Anne Boleyn in 1535, which contains a stone Tudor fireplace. To the north of this and set at right angles is a thirteenth-century building with a fifteenth-century upper storey, known as the Parliament Room. It is thought that this may have been the Hall of the Prior's Lodging.[22]

In large monasteries, abbots' lodgings often grew into considerable houses, separate from the cloister, and this was the case at Gloucester. Immediately to the north of the Great Cloister and within the precinct wall was the Abbot's Lodging, built in the early fourteenth century. After the Dissolution this house was assigned to the bishop as his palace and provided substantial accommodation, though on a much smaller scale than the palaces at long-established cathedrals such as Winchester. Part of the original palace wall can be seen in Pitt Street.[23] The Bishop's Palace was largely destroyed by fire in 1849 and re-built in 1861; King's School now occupies the site. The remainder of the precinct and the other buildings went to the dean and chapter. The Prior's Lodging became the Deanery and is now called Church House; others were assigned as residences of the six prebendaries (or principal canons), the minor canons, the choristers, the masters of the College school run by the chapter, the almspersons maintained by it under its statutes of 1544, and other members of the establishment.[24]

The precinct of a monastery was always enclosed by a wall or hedge or ditch, with a gatehouse giving access. At Gloucester, the precinct, which enclosed approximately thirteen acres of the north-western sector of the town, survived relatively intact.[25] The layout is shown in the plan of the precinct (*16*). The main entrance to the precinct was from the west, through the thirteenth-century Great Gate, or St Mary's Gate, which led into the outer court. This would have contained the main offices such as brewhouse, bakehouse and granary, and often a guest house for the reception of visitors who claimed hospitality. After the Dissolution, this outer court was re-named College Green. The Inner Gate led from the outer court to the inner court, now Miller's Green. This inner court gave access to the Cloister, the Abbot's Lodging and the Infirmary. These gatehouses survive, as does a large part of the west wall of the precinct.[26] The early fifteenth-century building south of St Mary's Gate (now number 14 College Green) was the monastic Almonry, where daily distributions of food were made and poor visitors seeking charity might be lodged. After the Dissolution it became the house of the Prebendary of the Sixth Stall.[27] Other prebendal residences were also in the outer court, in buildings adjoining the south wall. The house of the Prebendary of the First Stall (now 7-8 College Green) re-used a fifteenth-century monastic building.[28]

The College school, now called King's School, is one of thirteen abbey schools established or re-endowed and re-named by Henry VIII between 1540 and 1545. Gloucester, along with Bristol, Westminster, Oxford, Chester and Peterborough, were in newly created cathedrals with new dioceses. Six of these schools continue under the King's name, six under other names, and one, Carlisle, has closed. Some of these, even after over 500 years, still occupy, at least in part, the monastic site. At Gloucester the former fourteenth-century Abbey Library, at the top of the east range of the Great Cloister between the Chapter House and north transept, became the schoolroom of the College school.[29]

The Colleges

In the sixteenth century Oxford and Cambridge were the only universities in England, and by the time of the Dissolution the majority of the colleges were long established. There is no clear date of foundation for Oxford University, although teaching existed from 1096, with students living in lodgings or together in halls. The first colleges – University, Balliol and Merton – were founded between 1249 and 1264, followed by four others in the fourteenth century and three more in the fifteenth. The last college founded before the Dissolution was Corpus Christi in 1517. Cambridge University was established in 1209 by scholars from Oxford who initially lived in lodgings in the town. The first residential college, Peterhouse, was founded in 1284, followed by seven others in the fourteenth century, and six more in the fifteenth century. The last college to be founded before the Dissolution was St John's in 1511. As well as the colleges, there were many religious establishments in both towns including friaries, monastic hospitals, abbeys and priories.

There was a long tradition at both universities of the foundation of colleges primarily for the training of priests and canon and civil lawyers. By the beginning of the sixteenth century, humanists saw the main task of the universities as the provision of facilities for clerical education. John Fisher, Bishop of Rochester and Chancellor of Cambridge University, was a leading prelate who saw it as essential to reform the church from within by raising the educational standards of the clergy, and he influenced Lady Margaret Beaufort, mother of Henry VII, in the foundation of Christ's College and St John's College in Cambridge.[1]

At the same time, the most striking expression of concern over the condition of the monasteries was the widespread conviction that it would be better if smaller and decayed monastic houses were suppressed and their revenues, instead of supporting monks and nuns, were diverted to more relevant purposes, namely the education, in grammar schools and

17 The Gatehouse at Jesus College, Cambridge, with a statue of the founder, Bishop Alcock, above the gate

at new colleges, of men who would serve, not in enclosed orders, but in the community as parish priests.[2] It was also perceived that the monastic sites and buildings themselves might be adapted to secular use. This was the background against which Cardinal Wolsey sought to create a grammar school at Ipswich and Cardinal College at Oxford, founded in 1525. After the Dissolution, more new colleges were founded on monastic sites and in some cases, remains of monastic buildings survive in present-day colleges.

The first college to reuse a monastic site and buildings for an educational purpose, and in fact the first secular adaptation before any residential conversions, was Jesus College, Cambridge (*17*). This was founded in 1496 by John Alcock, Bishop of Ely, on the site of the dissolved Priory of St Radegund, a small nunnery reduced to only two nuns. The dilapidated buildings proved in sufficiently good condition to allow their repair and modification for college use.[3] The alterations included transforming the nuns' Frater into the college Hall,[4] and the interiors of all the buildings in the east and west ranges of the Cloister were remodelled to conform to the college staircase plan. The Priory Church, which took about a century to build and was completed around 1245, was considerably reduced in size but continued as the college Chapel and is the oldest building in Cambridge still in use.

Queens' College, Cambridge, also acquired a monastic site but, unlike at Jesus, the monastic buildings were entirely demolished. The site adjacent to the college was a Carmelite Priory, also known as the Whitefriars, which had been founded in 1290. When the Priory was dissolved in August 1538, the college was eager to acquire its site, but it initially remained in possession of the Crown and between September 1538 and 1540 was largely

dismantled. On 28 November 1541 the Court of Augmentations sold all the building material of the Carmelites' house which 'at this prsens standithe and remaynyth' including 'stone, slate, tyle, tymber, yorne [iron] and glasse' to Dr May, President of Queens', for £20.[5] In April 1542 the king granted May a lease of the site for twenty-one years, except for a part already granted to King's College.[6] Then in November 1544 May bought the site outright, with college money, to secure the property for Queens' in the longer term.[7] With the completed demolition of the Carmelite buildings, the college began to lay out new gardens on the site. Walls were erected to subdivide the newly acquired land into four squares, either in 1544 or shortly afterwards. The plot attached to the President's Lodge became the President's Garden which was, and still is, overlooked by the windows of the gallery of the Lodge. The plot beyond it became a Fellows' Garden around 1553, and within this a bowling green was laid out before 1608.[8] Both these gardens remain in their original location.

Trinity College, Oxford, was founded on a monastic site and made use of the existing buildings. Trinity had its origins in Durham College, established in 1291 as a cell of Durham Cathedral Priory so that monks could be educated at Oxford. From 1381 it was fully endowed by the will of Thomas Hatfield, Bishop of Durham. As a result, between 1400 and 1421 the buildings of the college were much enlarged.[9] An inventory taken in 1428 shows that the buildings then comprised a chapel, vestry, hall, buttery, kitchen, treasury, parlour or *loquitorium* and warden's chamber, plus twelve other chambers mostly with fireplaces and studies, and stables.[10]

After the Dissolution, the site and build-

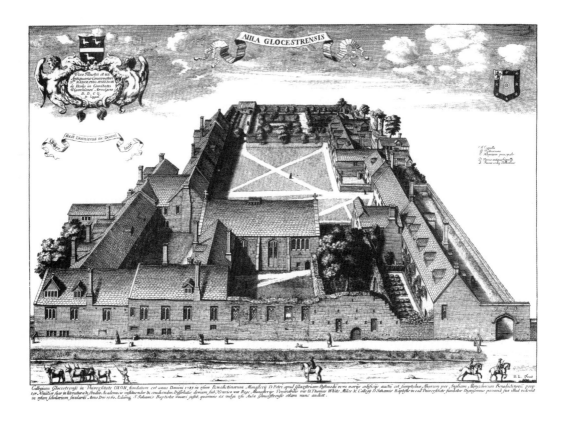

18 *Gloucester Hall, Oxford*, engraved by David Loggan, 1675

ings of Durham College passed to the Crown, and in 1554 were bought by Sir Thomas Pope, formerly Treasurer of the Court of Augmentations and a privy councillor under Queen Mary, for his foundation of Trinity College. Pope's new college was intended for the education of Catholic priests. No new buildings were initially erected, but in 1573 attics were built over the chambers at the south and north of the hall, and over the north range in 1577 in order to provide additional accommodation.[11] In the east range of Durham Quad are survivals of the monastic buildings, essentially those built in 1417-21.

Worcester College, Oxford, also made use of monastic buildings. It had its origins in Gloucester College, founded in 1283 as a Benedictine priory where monks from abbeys of the Canterbury province could live and study in Oxford. Each abbey contributed to shared buildings such as the Chapel, as well as building tenements, or *camerae*, for their own monks.[12] With the Dissolution the site passed to the Crown, and then through various hands until by 1559 many buildings had been demolished and the remainder were 'sore decayed'.[13] In 1560 the site and remaining buildings were conveyed to St John's College in return for 'a certain sum of money' paid by Sir Thomas White, the founder of St John's, for use as an

19 The *camerae*, or tenements, of the monasteries at Worcester College

academic hall. This can be seen in David Loggan's view from *Oxonia Illustrata* of 1675 (**18**); by then it was known as Gloucester Hall. A substantial part of the monastic buildings remains within Worcester College (**19**), which was founded in 1714 on the site. These are principally the original *camerae* of individual monasteries. There are coats of arms above some doorways which identify Glastonbury, Malmesbury, St Augustine's, Canterbury and Pershore. The original kitchen, built in 1423, also survives.[14]

Painted by Hans Holbein.

Engraved by P.W. Tomkins

AUDLEY, LORD CHANCELLOR.

Henry, VIII.

From the Original in the Possession of Lord Howard, at Audley End.

London Pub. Feb. 1 1792. by E. Harding Fleet St.

Magdalene College Cambridge

Overlooking the River Cam on its north bank, at the foot of Castle Hill, Magdalene College, Cambridge, now possesses the longest river frontage of any Cambridge college. Under the patronage of the Lord Chancellor, Thomas Audley, 1st Baron Audley of Walden (*20*), the college was re-founded after the Dissolution as the College of St Mary Magdalene, in 1542. The coat of arms of the College, its motto *Garde ta Foy* (Keep Faith) and the crest of the mythic wyvern, all derive from Audley. To this day, this small college is one of Cambridge's gems and First Court is an excellent surviving example of a mediaeval college.

The origins of Magdalene College lie in the fifteenth century, when, by the Constitutions of Pope Benedict XII, issued in 1337, every Benedictine monastery was bound to send one monk for every twenty members of their convent to a *studium generale* or university. At Cambridge such monastic students were initially scattered in lay hostels.[15] In 1426 John Sudbury, then prior of the students, complained at a general chapter of the Benedictine Order of the harm which arose from this arrangement.[16] It was represented to Henry VI that some of the monks were sent to Cambridge to study canon law and theology, but as there was no hostel for the Benedictine Order, they were compelled to lodge with seculars.[17]

As a result, on 7 July 1428, licence was given by the king for Abbot Litlyngton of Crowland Abbey in Lincolnshire to acquire two messuages in the parish of St Giles, called 'lez pondyards', for which he paid 18d to the town treasurer in 1432.[18] The site embraced the principal portion of the present Magdalene College, and here a new hostel was established where Benedictines studying could live together. This was probably initially in pre-existing houses on the site. Because it was the only hostel on the northern side of the River Cam, the monastic scholars were removed from the temptations of the town which had so concerned Sudbury. However, the community housed in this hostel was probably

20 Thomas Audley, 1st Baron Audley, the founder of Magdalene College

always small, as most monasteries seem to have sent their scholars to Oxford.[19] A condition of the licence was that other Benedictine houses should be able to build rooms for their monks.[20] Three Benedictine houses of East Anglia – Ely, Ramsey, and Walden – all took a share, though as late as 1534 the college was still considered a cell of Crowland.[21]

It was on this land in 1476 that the Abbot of Crowland, John de Wisbech, erected buildings which form a considerable part of the present First Court of Magdalene College.[22] In common with other colleges, the buildings enclose a square courtyard in a similar style to a monastic cloister, with access through a gatehouse from Magdalene Street, shown in David Loggan's engraving from *Cantabrigia Illustrata* of 1690 (*21*). The east, south and north ranges are all pre-Dissolution in date. The south range was built in the late fifteenth century, though much altered since. Nonetheless, it retains in part the original arrangement of rooms. The north range primarily features the Chapel, built shortly after 1476 by Abbot Wisbech. It was later altered and restored, but the eight-bay roof is original and there is some late fifteenth-century and sixteenth-century heraldic glass. The Hall, which dominates the east range, was built in 1519. To this day it has no electricity and is lit purely by candlelight.

The west range to the street was substantially completed by 1574, as shown on the Lyne map, *Oppidum Cantabrigiae* (*22*), but it must have been begun much earlier as it included the monastic staircase of Ely Cathedral Priory. The individual staircases, of two storeys, are thought to have been built by the four Benedictine houses that sent students up to the college; the coats of arms above the doorways indicate what is conjectured to have been the contribution of each.[23] Three of these are in the south range. The 'monks' rooms in stair-

case E are perhaps the most intact mediaeval scholars' rooms in either Oxford or Cambridge.[24]

In a deed of 1472 the house is mentioned as 'the Hostel called Monkis place', but from 1483 it was given the name Buckingham College, assumed to be in commemoration of benefactions from Henry, 2nd Duke of Buckingham, or possibly from his grandfather Humphrey, 1st Duke. These benefactions probably financed much of the building work in the 1470s and 1480s. Edward Stafford, 3rd Duke of Buckingham, who had in 1519 built the College Hall (*23*), was probably ready to endow Magdalene handsomely but, like his father, he was executed in 1521 for treason. The college was still operational up to the Dissolution, the last prior being appointed in 1535. Royal Injunctions that year included Buckingham College amongst those which were to maintain one Greek and one Latin public lecture each day.[25] However, sometime in the late fifteenth century, students who were not monks were admitted. Such lay students would have paid rent to the host abbey whose rooms they occupied. Thomas Cranmer, later Archbishop of Canterbury, was appointed a lecturer at Magdalene in 1515.

On 4 December 1539, Cromwell's commissioners arrived at Crowland, and the surrender was signed by the abbot and 28 monks. Probably for his compliance, the last abbot, John Bridges, was awarded the large pension of £133 6s 8d, and the rest of the monks received sums varying from £5 to £10 a year. The income of Crowland in the *Valor* in 1535 amounted to just over £1,093.[26] The history of Buckingham College at the Dissolution is murky, but it evidently ceased to exist as a corporate body when its parent abbeys were suppressed. On 3 April 1542 the king granted the site and buildings of the college to Thomas Audley for the establishment of his new foun-

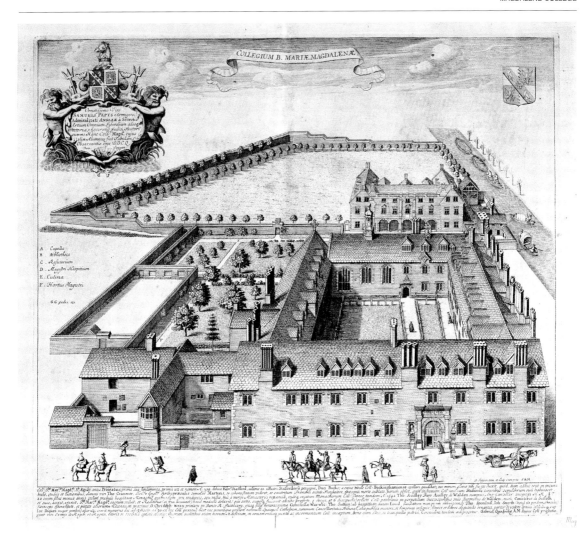

21 *Magdalene College, Cambridge* engraved by David Loggan, 1690

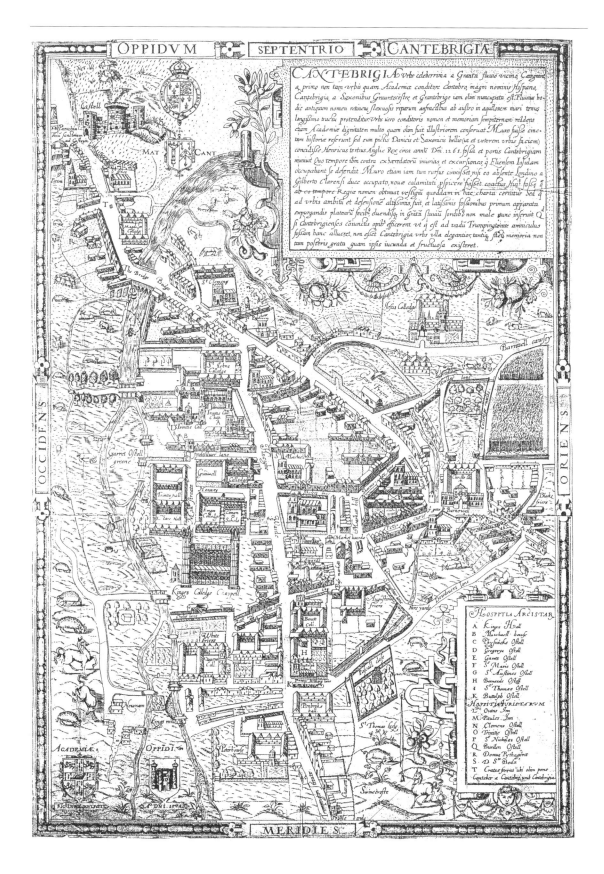

22 *Oppidum Cantabrigiae* engraved by Richard Lyne, 1574, showing Magdalene
College beside the Cam in the upper left directly above the bridge

dation, the College of St Mary Magdalene:

> College of St. Mary Magdalen, Cambridge.
> Establishment, at the suit of lord Chancellor
> Audeley, of a college in honor of St. Mary
> Magdalen, upon the site of the place lately
> called Bukkyngham College, in the University
> of Cambridge, with a master and eight fellows,
> to be nominated by the said lord Chancellor,
> his heirs and assigns. Also grant to it of the
> place called Bukkingham College, with its
> buildings and two gardens or parcels of land
> with ponds in them, called 'two pounde
> yardes'; with licence to the master and fellows
> to acquire lands to the yearly value of 100l.[27]

Audley is thought to have studied at Buckingham College as a lay student, before he later
re-established it as Magdalene College, so that
may have played a part in his wish to found
the new college.

The Dissolution was of great personal benefit to Audley, enabling him, a man of modest
origins, to build up a substantial landed estate
worth about £800 a year by 1540. In 1534 he
was granted Holy Trinity, Aldgate, which became his London house, and in 1542 he was

given the Priory of Colchester and the Abbey
of Tilty in Essex. The most valued of his
monastic acquisitions was Walden Abbey, the
source of his title, which was granted to him in
March 1538, and renamed Audley End in
1616.[28] When Audley re-founded Magdalene,
he gave the college seven acres of his property
at Aldgate, although this property was perma-
nently alienated to the Crown in 1574. Magdalene was never a richly endowed college,
but immediately after its re-foundation it was
the poorest of all the Cambridge colleges, with
an annual income of just over £42. However, a
royal commission into finances in 1546 found
that it was one of the few whose income was
greater than its expenditure.[29]

It was perhaps because of this relative
poverty that little building work took place
during the sixteenth century and the college
relied on the existing monastic buildings. At
the time of the Dissolution, the west range, on
the street front, was unfinished.[30] This was
finally completed in the 1580s thanks to the
generosity of Sir Christopher Wray, Chief
Justice of the Queen's Bench.

23 The Front Court of Magdalene College, with the Hall in the east range
on the right and the Chapel in the north range on the left

St John's College, Oxford

The entrance to St John's College, Oxford, on the east side of St Giles, has a forecourt enclosed by a low wall; the only remaining example of this once common feature on St Giles. The wall was built in 1579 and encloses a garden planted with trees between the college entrance and the street.[31] Beyond the forecourt, the west range of Front Quad has an impressive central tower containing the Gatehouse, hung with the original fifteenth-century gates. Above the gates is an oriel window surrounded by three niches for statues: at the top is St Bernard, and below him are statues of Henry Chichele, Archbishop of Canterbury, and Sir Thomas White (*24*). These three men embody the foundation and early history of the college. The Front Quad of St John's still comprises the original buildings of its predecessor, St Bernard's College.

In 1433 it was reported at the general chapter of the Cistercian Order at Cîteaux that Archbishop Chichele proposed to build a college at Oxford for Cistercian scholars. Four of the Cistercian abbots in England were charged with the duty of collecting £80 a year from the Cistercian abbeys for the construction and in March 1437 Chichele obtained royal licence to erect the *notabile mansum collegiale* in the parish of St Mary Magdalen on the east side of Northgate Street (now St Giles), outside the town walls.[32] The new college was named in honour of St Mary and St Bernard and became known as St Bernard's College. The Cistercian students had been known as St Bernard's College even when they had no central buildings and lived scattered in different lodgings.[33] But building work on the new college proceeded swiftly and by February 1438 it was ready for occupation and the first prior, or provisor, had been appointed.[34] In view of the short time between the granting of the royal licence and the installation of the first monks, it seems likely that Chichele's original building was a temporary timber-framed structure.[35] In 1449 the Abbot of Morimond, commissioned by the general chapter of the Cistercians to

24 Sir Thomas White, the founder of St John's College, Oxford

25 The Gatehouse of St John's College, with its original fifteenth-century gates

hold a visitation 'of the college of our order', gave certain injunctions to 'the college of St. Bernard near Oxford': none but Cistercians were to stay in the college; the seniors were not to have more than one servant apiece; there was to be reading at meal times; and the gates of the college were to be shut early.[36]

The accounts record that buildings on the south side of the quadrangle were also begun in 1438, but thereafter work proceeded extremely slowly.[37] It was with difficulty that the abbeys could be persuaded to pay their share of the cost, and out of the small funds raised some had to be devoted to maintaining the provisor and other necessary expenses.

For example, of £64 3s 4d collected in 1478, only £30 6s 1½d was expended on the building.[38] Of this, £16 9s 4d was spent on the purchase of stone, timber and slates and £11 12s 4d on the wages of the masons, carpenters and labourers.[39] A sum of £2 9s 7d was spent on 'new gates of the college' which are probably those which still hang beneath the tower.[40] The following year, the Abbot of Woburn reported that 'so far as the buildings are concerned the college is not yet half finished'.[41] In 1482, further efforts were made to raise funds. That year, the chapter of the Cistercians decreed that in every monastery of twelve monks one was to be sent to the college of St

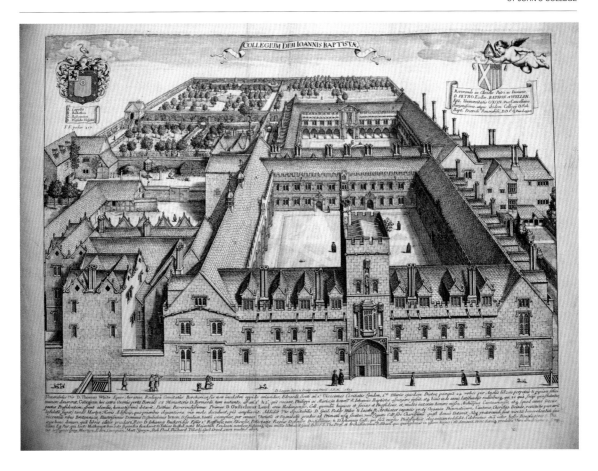

26 *St John's College, Oxford*, engraved by David Loggan, 1675

Bernard; if there were twenty-six monks, then two were to be sent. Monasteries with two or three monks were to unite so as to make up the necessary allowance for one scholar.[42]

Some progress must have been made because on 2 December 1483, Richard III wrote in a letter to all Cistercian abbots that when he was last in Oxford the college 'proceeded right well in buylding'.[43] However, by 1489 the buildings were still incomplete and the Abbot of Fountains wrote that the inside was still hardly begun and complained of the disgrace the unfinished building was bringing on the order.[44] In 1502 an effort was made to complete the college by Marmaduke

Huby, then Abbot of Fountains, who entered an agreement with Master William Orchard, a leading Oxford mason and quarry owner, for a supply of Headington stone. He was then able to report to the Abbot of Cîteaux that the college buildings were 'rising and increasing from day to day to the no small credit of the order'.[45] The quad is built entirely of limestone from Headington, two miles east of the city.[46]

By April 1517 the Abbot of Rievaulx reported that the Abbot of Fountains had 'built the hall and chapel very splendidly with glass in the windows' and had 'provided chalices, books, vestments, copes and other ornaments for the chapel', which must have been struc-

27 The Front Quad of St John's College, with the north range containing the Hall and Chapel on the left

turally complete by then although it was not consecrated until 1530.[47] In May 1530, permission was given by the Bishop of Lincoln that Robert, Bishop of Rheon, should consecrate the chapel in Bernard College.[48]

The west range, which is the façade on St Giles, built probably in the 1490s, consists of a pair of two-storey residential blocks flanking the tall, battlemented gatehouse (*25*), similar to that at All Souls College, which was also founded by Archbishop Chichele one year later, in 1438.[49] The dormer windows, which can be seen in the west range in David Loggan's view from *Oxonia Illustrata* (*26*) are a later addition of 1616.[50] The Gatehouse has a two-

bay vault with diagonal and ridge-ribs.[51] The south range consists of further residential blocks, which were already being constructed in 1438.[52] The north range has the Chapel and Hall (*27*), which structurally date from the early sixteenth century.[53] The Chapel has some later external modifications, but internally is entirely nineteenth century.[54] The east range was unfinished when St Bernard's was dissolved and St John's was founded, but it was soon completed. Whilst there were some later additions, such as the battlements around the inner face of the quadrangle, which were added in 1616-17, what is visible today in Front Quad is in essence the buildings as they were at the Dissolution.[55]

St Bernard's College was dissolved in 1540, along with the larger Cistercian abbeys, passing into the hands of the king. The site was granted by him to Christ Church in 1546.[56] A survey of it, made probably about May 1546 at the time it was transferred, records that the east side was nearly finished but lacked its roof; the rest of the quadrangle was complete.[57] The survey provides a description of the still unfinished buildings left by the Cistercians. It describes a 'Quadrauntt' 117 feet square 'in the suburbes of Oxford withowt the northe gate'.[58] On the west side of the quadrangle was the main gate with four chambers on either side, two above and two below. The south side of the quadrangle contained ten more chambers, 'fyve above and fyve bynethe'.[59] The survey records that each of these chambers contained two studies and was thus intended to accommodate at least two students.[60] On the north side of the quadrangle there was a 'fayre haull' with a large chamber above, a 'fayre kechyn' and 'a fayre chapele … withe iij aullters and vij wyndowes, and every windowe six lighttes well glased, and a grete windowe on thc cest ende behynde the high aulltour'.[61] The east side of the quadrangle was still incomplete, consisting as yet only of walls 'buyllded rough high, purposing a library and chambers'.[62]

St John's College was founded on the site of St Bernard's in 1557 by Sir Thomas White. In December 1554 he obtained from Christ Church, practically as a gift, the site and buildings of St Bernard's, presumably as described in the 1546 survey, on condition that within three years he would found a college there, which he quickly proceeded to do.[63] White was in all likelihood born in Reading in 1495 to William White, a clothier of Rickmansworth, Hertfordshire. At the age of

nine he was apprenticed to Hugh Acton, a prominent member of the Merchant Taylors' Company in London. Acton provided the capital upon which White's own trading ventures were initially founded, and with a bequest of £100 from his late master, combined with an inheritance from his father, who died that year, he was able to set up his own business in the cloth trade in 1523. He prospered in that trade, and was elected to various posts in the Merchant Taylors', culminating in master in 1535.[64]

During the 1540s White began to make large charitable donations, principally directed at assisting young men to establish themselves, especially in the cloth trade, by making interest-free loans. These were perhaps an acknowledgement of his own debt to Hugh Acton's charity and support. At the same time, he advanced in the City of London, being elected an alderman in 1544, Sheriff in 1547 and Lord Mayor in 1553. He was a loyal supporter of Queen Mary, both as a financier and as Lord Mayor. It is likely that White had Catholic sympathies, although this did not preclude his involvement in the establishment of the Merchant Taylors' School (in association with the Puritan Richard Hills) in 1561, which had a decidedly reforming emphasis.[65]

Perhaps it was because White never had any children of his own that his benefactions to others were so extensive. The most ambitious of these entailed his foundation of St John's. Although he had expanded the scope of his business interests as one of the London merchants responsible for opening up trade with Russia in 1553, and consequently as one of the promoters of the Muscovy Company of merchant adventurers, subsequently his fortunes declined. Suffering diminishing returns from the cloth trade, White was unable to endow his college sufficiently in its

28 Map of Oxford by Ralph Agas, 1578, showing St John's College and its gardens at the lower right

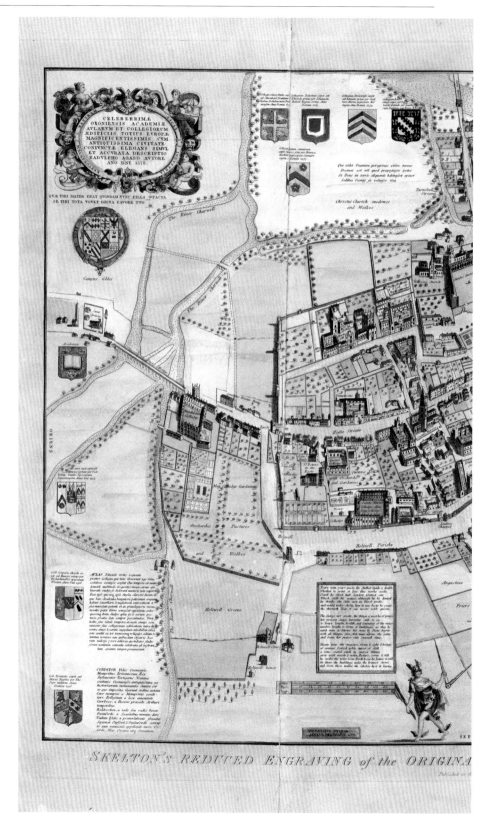

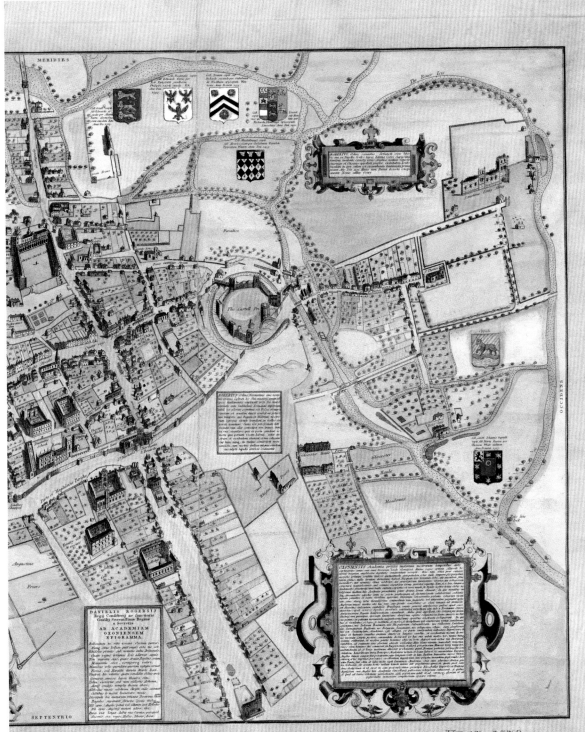

GINAL PLAN of OXFORD TAKEN by RALPH AGAS in the YEAR 1578.

early years. He died on 12 February 1567 at his house in Size Lane, London. As requested in his will, he was buried on 24 or 25 February in St John's College Chapel.[66]

The object of White's foundation of St John's College was to 'strengthen the orthodox faith, in so far as it is weakened by the damage of time and the malice of men' and especially 'to help theology, much afflicted of late, as we see with sorrow and grief'.[67] The college was to provide educated clergy who could hold their own in argument with Lutherans and Calvinists. This was with the encouragement of Cardinal Pole, who saw that the long-term health of the Catholic church, re-established in England under Mary, required improvements in the education of clergy.[68]

The college, which was under the patronage of St John the Baptist, the patron saint of tailors, began at Michaelmas 1557 with twenty members. The founder aimed for fifty members but the funds of the college for its first fifteen years were so deficient that they could not maintain more than half the intended number, and it was not until 1583 that the college was filled. Besides the fellows, there were commoners; by the statutes they were limited to sixteen in number, and the founder in a letter of autumn 1566 ordered that there should be no more than twelve. However, at Michaelmas 1568, when the bursars' accounts begin, they were more than forty. As a result, the buildings were very crowded, and many of the rooms contained three or four men. Those under sixteen years old slept two in a bed. In the years 1570 to 1573 the top storey was added on two sides of the quadrangle to provide more space.[69]

Because the buildings of St Bernard's College were comparatively recent, when St John's acquired the site it was relatively easy to adapt them for the use of the new college. The buildings were occupied by workmen between 1555 and 1557, but it appears from comparison with the survey of 1546 that no changes were made to the south range, which continued in use as residential accommodation.[70] The west range was also left unchanged. However, there were considerable changes required to the north range, where the small monastic Hall was inadequate. The building to the west of the Chapel, which had been the kitchen of St Bernard's, was made the new Hall, while the earlier Hall was converted into a pantry and buttery, and the room above was partitioned into chambers.[71] The original cellar beneath the Buttery was retained and is now the best-preserved fifteenth-century work in the college.[72] To replace the former kitchen, a new one was constructed outside the north wall of the college.[73]

According to the survey of 1546 the east range was unfinished by the Cistercians, but was intended to comprise a library above with rooms below.[74] This purpose was changed by White, so that the northern half of the range, on both floors, was to be the President's Lodging, which it remains. The other half seems to have consisted of two rooms on the ground floor, that on the south being a library, and next to it a bursar's room; on the floor above was the 'gallery' (*superius ambulacrum* in the statutes), a sort of common room for the fellows.[75] This would have overlooked the gardens to the east, illustrated in the Ralph Agas map of 1578 (*28*). These changes were completed by the early 1560s.[76]

The college has always been famed for its garden, which in part dates back to the monastic period. The southern half of it was originally part of the grounds of Durham College (which later became Trinity College), but when Durham College and St Bernard's College were in the hands of the king, he assigned half the garden to St Bernard's, which then passed to St John's. About 1558 a wall was built which stands between Trinity College and St John's, separating the two gardens.[77] The garden was the location of another building erected by White, the pigeon-house. Its position is indicated by the terms of the agreement between St John's and Trinity concerning the wall between the colleges, where it is stated that a tenement next but one to the college on the south side extended at its east end to 'a little dove-house appertaining to the College of St. John's'.[78] This is probably the small building set in the garden, shown in the Agas map. The surviving bursars' accounts for 1568-90 mention each year the purchase of barley for the pigeons, and when the finances of the college had improved there was a salary of '6s 8d or a load of wood' for the keeper of the pigeons, who was generally one of the younger fellows. But by the end of the sixteenth century the pigeon-house was 'now for want of pigeons unprofitable and otherwise very ruinous' and in February 1599 the college decided to pull it down.[79]

Part of the original Elizabethan garden lay on the site of what is now Canterbury Quad, and beyond this was the Grove, stretching to the east as shown in the Agas map. In 1600 four acres to the north were acquired by the College and enclosed, together with the original Grove, by a stone wall built in 1613 with money left by a former fellow, Edward Sprott. A stretch of Sprott's Wall survives today. With the building of Canterbury Quad between 1631 and 1636 the enlarged Grove was laid out as three distinct gardens: the President's Garden, the Masters' Garden or outer grove (the original Grove) and the Bachelors' Garden, or inner grove.[80] Only the Masters' Garden remains on the site of the original sixteenth-century garden.

Christ Church, Oxford

Christ Church is one of the largest and wealthiest colleges in Oxford. In 1524, at the height of his power, Cardinal Thomas Wolsey (*29*) suppressed the Priory of St Frideswide in the centre of Oxford and founded Cardinal College on the site. The college was later re-founded in 1546 by Henry VIII as Christ Church. Entering from St Aldate's Street, beneath Tom Tower, the Great Quadrangle known as Tom Quad is an impressive size, enclosed largely by Wolsey's buildings. Behind the Quad rises the tower of Christ Church Cathedral, built at the end of the twelfth century, which is one of the oldest buildings in Oxford.

Christ Church remains a testament to the work of Wolsey, while his other major educational project, Cardinal School in Ipswich, did not survive his downfall. Both are remembered by Shakespeare in *Henry VIII*:

> Those twins / Of learning that he [Wolsey] raised in you,
> Ipswich and Oxford! one of which fell with him,
> Unwilling to outlive the good that did it;
> The other, though unfinish'd, yet so famous,
> So excellent in art, and still so rising,
> That Christendom shall ever speak his virtue.[81]

St Frideswide was a noble Saxon lady who established a nunnery for herself and twelve virgin ladies, despite being pursued relentlessly for her hand in marriage by Algar, Prince of Leicester. Frideswide, now patron saint of both the university and the city, died in 727, and the nunnery became a monastery soon after her death.[82] The Domesday Book records that there were secular canons at St Frideswide's in 1086. But in 1122 an Augustinian priory was established by Gwymund, a royal chaplain, and Henry I confirmed the site to the regular canons. The priory was close to the ford across the Thames, and the city wall ran around the south and

29 Portrait of Thomas Wolsey, Cardinal Archbishop of York, Sampson Strong, 1526

west sides of the precinct. Before 1130 the priory had the advowsons of seven of the churches of Oxford, while the king gave the churches of Headington, Marston, Elsfield and Binsey, and permission to hold a fair for a week beginning on the vigil of the Translation of St Benedict.[83] Between 1135 and 1140 King Stephen granted the canons their gate in the town wall, with permission to build over the wall itself.[84]

By the time Prior Philip left an account of the translation of the bones of St Frideswide, on 12 February 1180 in the presence of the Archbishop of Canterbury, the original church had probably been completed. But in 1190 it burnt down, along with the other priory buildings. Money for the rebuilding was being collected in 1194 and evidence of the resultant work survives in the present day Cathedral, which is probably dated between 1190 and 1210.[85] The Church was completed first, and its crossing tower is Norman, with shafted pinnacles at the corners, the spire rising between them.[86] The Lady Chapel was added later to the north of the north choir aisle, and beyond this the Latin Chapel was built in about 1320 or 1330. The watching loft in the Lady Chapel served to watch St Frideswide's Shrine, and may date from around 1500.[87] In the south transept, the east window in St Lucy's Chapel has the original fourteenth-century stained glass.[88]

The Chapter House dates mainly from the second quarter of the thirteenth century, and the Dorter is much altered but probably also of thirteenth-century date, though with a fifteenth-century doorway.[89] In 1423 the Bishop of Lincoln ordered a new house to be built for strangers and laymen, formerly lodged in the Infirmary. The Cloister (30) was rebuilt in the late fifteenth century and a large new Prior's Lodging added south of the

Dorter.[90] The Frater on the upper floor of the south side of the Cloister was rebuilt about 1490, and it became the college library about 1613.[91] At the visitation of 1520 the Priory had nine resident monks, while six more were absent serving other churches. When St Frideswide's was suppressed the prior was made Abbot of Osney.[92]

In 1519 Cardinal Wolsey was appointed by the pope, together with Cardinal Campeggio, as papal legates for the reformation of the monasteries. His authority was renewed in 1521 and 1524.[93] There is evidence that the king himself supported Wolsey and other reforming bishops.[94] As late as May 1529, shortly before his fall, Wolsey was granted sweeping powers by the pope to convert abbacies into bishoprics, create new dioceses, suppress smaller monasteries and unite those with less than twelve inmates into larger houses.[95] That Wolsey should dissolve no fewer than twenty religious houses between April 1524 and December 1525 in order to found Cardinal College was simply an early manifestation of this reforming drive, which was to lead to the Dissolution in the following decade. Most of the suppressed houses were small, though their aggregate annual income was £1,913, equivalent to a single very large and wealthy abbey.[96] However, more than half this sum came from just five houses: St Frideswide's, Bayham, Daventry, Lesnes and Tonbridge.[97] St Frideswide's, as well as providing the site for the new college, had an annual income of over £284, while at the other end of the scale Tiptree's income was less than £23.[98] The suppression took place on 19 April 1524, in accordance with Wolsey's scheme for the erection upon its site of a great college, authorised by Pope Clement VII and Henry VIII.[99] On 1 July 1525, Wolsey was formally granted by the king the site and lands of the suppressed

30 Christ Church Cathedral Cloister, originally the Cloister of St Frideswide's Priory

priory. On 13 July, Henry granted him licence to found a college on the site, and endow the same to the annual value of £2,000.[100] Wolsey's foundation charter was signed at Westminster, 15 July 1525.[101] After the suppression, to make way for the college, much of the priory including the west end of the Church was demolished. Wolsey also demolished the west walk of the Cloister, even though it had been rebuilt only twenty-five years earlier. The rest of the Cloister survived, as did the Chapter House on the east side, the Frater on the south, and the Dorter to the south-east. The Prior's Lodging became the east range of the Chaplain's Quadrangle but was removed later. Wolsey also demolished the kitchen, which lay west of the Frater.[102]

The first Dean of Cardinal College was John Higden, who had previously been President of Magdalen College, and whose brother was Wolsey's vicar-general at York. As Dean, he was head of the whole institution, and had total authority.[103] Higdon's book of accounts from 28 January to 1 July 1525 concerning the building of Cardinal College was rediscovered in a chest of old papers in 1928.[104] In those few months, there are expenses itemised for tools, stone quarrying and the carriage of stone from the quarry. Slaters were paid from May 1525 and the wages of masons and labourers for hewing stone and setting walls amounted to £177 19s. Wood was obtained from the Abbot of Abingdon, and the cost of tree felling and squaring the timber was £42 10s 8d. The total expenditure up to 1 July was £403 18s 9 ½d. Carvers were paid from March and carriage-loads of wainscot and glass were bought from April, while in July payment was made for 100 trees of timber.[105] Some wood was brought from Cumnor, from where shipping charges by water to the bridge at Oxford were 8d a load, while carriage by road cost 10d a load, reflecting the poor condition of the roads.[106]

Wolsey wasted no time in beginning his building work, and by 1 July the number of workmen involved in the project included thirty-two masons, sixteen rough-layers and sixty-four labourers.[107] In July 1525, Wolsey wrote with instructions to Robert Cartar, Laurence Stubbes and Nicholas Townley touching his college:

> They are to call the Dean and others before them, and inform them that Wolsey intends this summer to set forth the buildings of his college … They shall arrange with the owners of certain houses belonging to the late monastery of St. Frideswide's, and others belonging to Bayly (Balliol) college and Godstowe monastery, for pulling the same down, and clearing the site. He has ordered his chaplains by his power legatine to take down the parish church of St. Michael, and annex it to that of St. Aldacte adjoining … That the burying ground of St. Frideswide's shall be now taken in for the buildings of the college … The masons and others are to set forth the ground, for which he appoints a surveyor, Sir Nich. Townley and Rowland Mesanger, not forgetting this summer to cause timber and stone to be conveyed to the ground in convenient abundance … As warrant has been delivered to Sir Nich. Townley by the King's liberal grant to take such trees as are necessary from the park of Bekley and Shotover wood, they are to see that no waste is made.[108]

31 Tom Quad, with Wolsey's Great Hall on the right and the spire of
Christ Church Cathedral in the background

The Great Quadrangle, known as Tom Quad, was largely constructed between 1525 and 1529 (*31*). By the time of Wolsey's death the south side was complete and the east and west were almost finished. The first buildings to be completed were the Hall and the Kitchen, which was ready for Christmas dinner in 1526.[109] To support this there were a range of ancillary buildings described by the Warden of New College as 'larder houses, pastry houses, lodgings for common servants, slaughter and fish houses … substantially and goodly done in such manner as no two of the best colleges in Oxford have rooms so goodly and convenient'.[110]

In 1530 Wolsey was charged with praemunire and lost most of his lands and titles. The future of Cardinal College was in grave doubt. The Cardinal deeply regretted the loss of his college and in July 1530 he wrote to Thomas Cromwell that he was:

> much indisposed, and put from his sleep and meat, in consequence of the news of the dissolution of his colleges, and the small hope he has of being relieved by the King. Cannot write for weeping and sorrow. Thanks him for all the pains he has taken, and will requite him when he can. Recommends his estate and his colleges to his help. Asks him to consider whether he deserves that they should be turned to other profane uses. Looks for redress to the Prince's most merciful [consideration]. Thus, with wepyng terys, I byd [you]. [111]

A few days later, Wolsey wrote to Stephen Gardiner, the king's secretary, pleading for his college:

> Begs the continuance of his favor, and that his poor estate may be remembered. Specially entreats him in behalf of the college of Oxford, that it may not be dissolved or dismembered. He knows the whole history of their foundation, and to destroy them entirely would be great pity.[112]

But Wolsey's pleadings were to no avail and after his fall Cardinal College ceased to exist, with most of its endowment of lands and revenues taken by the Crown. However, by December 1531 the king provided 600 marks (£400) for the creation of a new college, using the same site, which was formally established in July 1532 as a foundation of a dean and twelve canons. This new college was to be called King Henry VIII College, and in addition to the canons to have eight priests, eight chaplains, eight clerks and ten choristers.[113] This was a small number compared with that envisaged for Cardinal College, but the college was not impoverished. According to the *Valor* its income in 1535 was £666, with a surplus of £450.[114] Though many of the buildings were unfinished and barely habitable at the time of Wolsey's fall, it seems likely that with these new resources the parts of Cardinal College nearing completion were finished and used to provide accommodation for the new college, along with the remaining buildings of St Frideswide's Priory.[115] St Frideswide's shrine was destroyed around 1538.[116] Initially the Priory Church would have been used as the college Chapel.

The new diocese of Oxford, created in 1542, had as its cathedral the former Abbey of Osney. This was endowed with an annual income of around £600, about the same as King Henry VIII's College, and it was concluded that by amalgamating the two, revenue could be released to the Crown.[117] Plans were developed during 1545 for this amalgamation and it was decided to move the cathedral from Osney to the college church.

The prominent spire can be seen in the detail in the upper left of Strong's portrait of Cardinal Wolsey. The new combined college and Cathedral was formally founded on 4 November 1546 as the Cathedral Church of Christ in Oxford of the Foundation of King Henry VIII. Both college and Cathedral were uniquely under the Dean and Chapter as governing body.[118]

The scale of the new establishment was close to that of Cardinal College and, in spite of the original intention to economise, the endowment provided an annual revenue of £2,273 3s 3d.[119] With such expanded numbers work began in 1545 to repair and furnish the buildings and prepare the Church for its new role as the Cathedral. The king had granted to the dean and canons all the stone, timber, iron, bells, glass and lead at Osney. The sides and stalls of the choir were dismantled and reinstalled at the college, and the Great Tom bell was moved and reinstalled in the bell tower. A large workforce was employed and payments fall into regular blocks which suggest that at this time there were about thirty masons, a slater and his boy, a glazier, two sawyers, a plumber, a chief labourer and thirty-six others, three joiners, and perhaps eleven carpenters. By Michaelmas 1546 the wage bill included only between four and five joiners, five to seven carpenters, two or three slaters, five to six sawyers, and no more than eight labourers.[120] Such a workforce suggests a great deal of work was carried out on the buildings, both the new Cathedral and the residential, though exactly what is not entirely clear. Timber was purchased from Sugworth and Abingdon and recycled from Osney, plus over 72 fothers of lead recovered from Osney.[121] After this no further building work was undertaken until the seventeenth century.

The new college received a most eminent guest when Elizabeth I visited in 1566. The east side of the Great Quadrangle was made into a residence for her, with direct access created to the Hall.[122] The buildings must have been completed to a high enough standard for a royal visitor. She arrived with her retinue from Woodstock and as she approached the University was met with an oration given by the mayor and presented with a gift of a silver-gilt cup containing £40 of gold.[123] She rode into the City in a rich chariot, about five or six o'clock in the evening. Scholars, Bachelors and Masters crying 'Vivat Regina' lined the streets and the Quadrangle of Christ Church, where another oration was spoken by Mr Kingsmyll, Orator of the University, at the Hall door.[124] After this, she entered the Church, where the Dean said prayers of thanksgiving for her safe arrival and the anthem Te Deum was sung to cornets.[125] On the Sunday of her visit there were sermons in Christ Church Cathedral, where a platform was erected for her at a considerable height, just opposite the pulpit.[126] The Queen's visit lasted a week, during which she listened to disputations and herself gave a Latin oration. On the last day there was a Convocation at which twelve of her courtiers were created Master of Arts, including William Cecil, her Secretary of State; Edward de Vere, Earl of Oxford; and Ambrose Dudley, Earl of Warwick. The Convocation was held in the Refectory of Christ Church, in the presence of Robert Dudley, Earl of Leicester, who was Chancellor of the University, after which they took their oath in Christ Church Hall, followed by a Latin Sermon in the Cathedral.[127]

GUALTERUS MILDMAY. *Eq Aur.* Coll: Emanuel.s *Fund.*

A.o *Dni* 1584

Hanc Effigiem Rev.do Viro Joh.s Balderston. *S.T.P. et istius*

Coll: Magistro. *a Tabula in Suis Ædibus*

asservata factam. *Summa cum* Humil. & Observantia *D.D.D. J. Faber* A.

Emmanuel College, Cambridge

Later in the sixteenth century new use continued to be made of former monastic buildings within the university towns. Emmanuel College, Cambridge, had its origins in the Dominican priory which had stood for over 300 years at the time it was dissolved in 1538. When Sir Walter Mildmay (*32*) founded Emmanuel College on the Dominican site in 1584, he was at pains that his 'spearhead of puritanism' should preserve as few traces as possible of the former priory, and in particular that the Chapel should not stand upon the site of the friars' Church. Considerable remains of the foundations of that church are, however, incorporated in the present buttery.

The Dominicans, or Order of Preachers, were founded by Saint Dominic in Toulouse in 1215. They were known as Black Friars, because of the black cloak worn over their white habits. Governed by The Rule of St Augustine, they focused on study and preaching, and the order is known for its intellectual tradition. Every Dominican priory contained a 'school' where there were daily lectures on the Bible. Because of their role in preaching to the laity, Dominican priories were always located in towns. Some, like Cambridge, were established near universities and by 1260 several friars were lectors in the university's Theology Faculty.

Thirteen Dominican friars had first arrived in England in 1221 and they opened some eighteen houses in major English towns during the next twenty years. The priory in Cambridge, dedicated to the Holy Trinity, was founded either in or shortly before 1238, since in that year King Henry III gave three oak trees to build the Chapel.[128] The friars settled on a site beyond the Barnwell gate, away from what was then the town centre. Based on historical accounts and archaeological investigations, the buildings of the priory then had three main phases of expansion: following its founding around 1238; at the time of Alice de Vere's grant around 1285; and during the second half of the fourteenth century, probably associated

32 Sir Walter Mildmay, the founder of Emmanuel College

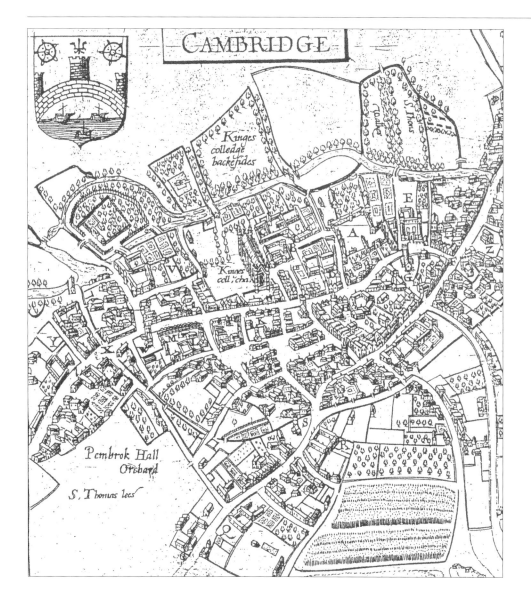

with the 1388 Parliament.[129]

Building works on the Priory Church began early with gifts from Henry III. In 1242 the king gave five marks to buy timber and twenty marks for the fabric of the church; six tree-trunks were sent from Weybridge forest. In 1244, six more oaks, with fallen wood, were given for the same purpose, and by November 1248 the work had got as far as the choir, for which a further six oaks were granted.[130] The Church was on an east-west orientation, and formed the north range of what is now the Front Court of Emmanuel College. It is not known whether the claustral buildings were positioned to the north of the Church or to the south. Of fifteen examples in England, eight Dominican priories had the church to the north of the cloister, six to the south and one to the east.[131] There is traditional and some archaeological support for the Cloister

33 A detail from John Speed's map of Cambridge, 1612, showing the
newly founded Emmanuel College marked as 'Q' at the lower left

being sited to the north of the Church at
Cambridge. However, architectural observa-
tions have led to the suggestion that it may
have been to the south.[132]

Whether to the north or south of the
Church, the east range of the Cloister would
have contained the Chapter House and the
Dorter above. A Cloister to the north of the
Church might therefore imply the Frater was
in the north range, abutting what is now
Emmanuel Street and was earlier called
Preachers Lane. In 1285 the Black Friars
received a generous donation from Alice, wife
of Robert de Vere, Earl of Oxford. About this
time, they enlarged their site, and the Church
was so far finished by 1286 that it was consecrated by William de Fresney, titular Bishop of
Edessa.[133] A further two acres were acquired
in 1293 and in total the Dominicans acquired
surrounding properties to create a site covering some ten acres.

There was also a substantial two-storey
stone building, with a finely finished exterior,
to the immediate north-east of the Church,
which excavated floor tiles date to the second
part of the fourteenth century.[134] This may
have been the Guest House and may have
been associated with October 1388, when the
only Parliament ever held in Cambridge sat at
the priory. To the east of that building, Speed's
1612 map from *The Theatre of the Empire of*

Greate Britaine (**33**) shows gardens and
orchards, and since in 1539 the Crown leased
'lez Blak Freres' with gardens, orchards and
dovecotes to William Shirwood for twenty-
one years, it is likely that these were from the
monastic period rather than newly laid out for
the college. The rectangular pond shown on
the map (and the site of a pool still in the
grounds of Emmanuel College) is probably
the fishpond of the friars.[135]

By the early sixteenth century, the image of
Our Lady of Grace drew great crowds to the
Priory Church and on 30 August 1538 Prior
Gregory Dodds approached Cromwell with
the request that he might remove the image
from the people's sight, because he could not
well bear 'syche ydolatrye' and large numbers
of pilgrims were still coming to her shrine. At
the same time Dodds asked that his house
might be taken into the king's hand 'to be put
to such use as his grace should think best', and
shortly afterwards the priory was surrendered.
When the commissioners arrived, they found
that the 'religious persons' and servants were
'dispersed and gone'. Sixteen friars signed the
surrender and Prior Dodds was given the
living of Smarden in Kent: he became Dean of
Exeter in 1560 and died about 1570.[136]

After passing through several hands, the
former priory and its remaining buildings
were purchased for £550 in June 1583 to be

the site of the new college, founded the following year by Sir Walter Mildmay, Chancellor of the Exchequer and a privy councillor under Elizabeth I.[137] Mildmay was a Puritan, and his main aim in establishing the college was to provide a perpetual supply of educated clergy for the reformed church.[138] The statutes were designed to promote a spartan and disciplined regimen, and the only studies permitted besides theology were Latin and Greek.

Walter Mildmay was born in 1520 or 1521, the youngest son of Thomas Mildmay, a mercer of Chelmsford. By 1538 he was at Christ's College, Cambridge, where he remained for two years, but he did not take a degree. In 1540 he joined the Court of Augmentations, and by 1547 he was appointed one of two surveyors of the new Court, a post second only in importance to the Chancellor, Sir Edward North. He was also knighted. At about this time, in May 1546, he married Mary Walsingham; Sir Francis Walsingham, Elizabeth I's future Secretary of State, became his brother-in-law.[139]

By 1549 Mildmay's reputation as a financial expert was well established among privy councillors, and his talents made him indispensable under Edward VI. As an ardent Protestant, his career under Mary received a slight check, but with the accession of Elizabeth on 17 November 1558, Mildmay's fortunes and career revived. On 5 February 1559, at the urging of William Paulet, Marquess of Winchester and Lord Treasurer, Mildmay was appointed Chancellor of the Exchequer. In 1566 he became a privy councillor and in January 1567 was named Under Treasurer of the Exchequer. He is generally credited, along with Winchester, with masterminding the exchequer reforms of the latter part of the sixteenth century, and he also took over the day-to-day duties of the senior exche-

34 The Front Court of Emmanuel College with the Hall and Combination Room in the north range on the left

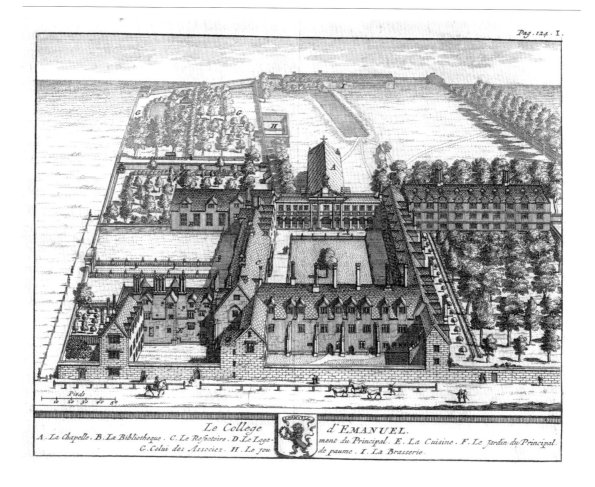

Pag.124.I.

Pieds
10 20 30 40 50

Le College d'EMANUEL.
A . La Chapelle . B . La Bibliotheque . C . Le Refectoire . D . Le Loge-
G . Celui des Associez . H . Le Jeu
ment du Principal . E . La Cuisine . F . Le Jardin du Principal .
de paume . I . La Brasserie .

35 Emmanuel College, Cambridge, by Pieter van der Aa after David Loggan, showing the College as it was in 1690

quer offices. This continued under the next Lord Treasurer, William Cecil, Baron Burghley, and Mildmay held his positions as Chancellor of the Exchequer and Under Treasurer until his death.[140]

Alongside his career in royal financial administration Mildmay had a long career in Parliament, sitting in the House of Commons twelve times, beginning in 1545. From 1558 he served in every Parliament until 1589, and from 1576 acted as one of the government spokesmen in the Commons.[141] The recurrent themes of his speeches in the Commons were the 'preservation of the cause of religion' and

the Queen's safety, and his Elizabethan career was devoted to strengthening these 'twin pillars' of state security.[142] Mildmay died at his house in Smithfield on 31 May 1589. His will requested that his burial avoid 'vaine funerall pompe' and asked for the superfluous cost to be given to 'pore preachers, pore schollers, and poore needye people'; but he also left rich gifts to his government colleagues and, to the queen herself, £100 for a jewel.[143]

The remaining buildings of the Dominican priory acquired in 1583 by Mildmay for his new college were largely complete, although some had been partly dismantled shortly after the priory was dissolved. In 1544 the buildings (with the usual reservation of lead) were granted to Edward Elrington. He must at once have begun pulling them down, as spoils of the Black Friars, including timber and stone, appear in the churchwardens' accounts of Great St Mary's for 1545.[144] The Guest House certainly appears to have been demolished, and the thoroughness with which materials were removed suggests deliberate clearance of at least this part of the site.[145] However, it seems clear that the main complex was still standing and was incorporated to some degree into the new college.

The Church, being large and in good repair, was converted into the college Hall (*34*), the eastern end being partitioned off to form a combination room below with master's rooms above. The new Hall was being plastered in 1586 so must have been largely complete by then.[146] David Loggan's 1690 view for *Cantabrigia Illustrata,* reproduced by Pieter van der Aa in 1707 (*35*), clearly shows the west end of the Church with its large window filled but still recognisable. Whilst extensively remodelled since, two buttresses are original, and so are parts of a window arch on first floor level.[147] The building to the north-east of the Church, possibly containing the Chapter House and Dorter if the priory had a northern Cloister, was extensively repaired and converted into a Chapel, with an antechapel having rooms over it at the south end.[148] The exposed masonry shows two techniques, a better earlier one in the lower courses with carefully dressed stones and a poor later one when the building was being repaired and adapted to college use.[149] Both the Chapel and the kitchen, with gallery above, in the west range are mentioned in the accounts in 1586 and 1587, by which time the Chapel conversion must have been nearing

completion.[150] When the new Chapel was built in 1679, this became the Library and is now a conference room known as the Old Library on New Court. Any buildings on the north side of the court, and possibly also at the north end of the west and east ranges, had already been removed and this was left open, apart from a wall and ornamental gateway inscribed *Sacrae Theologiae Studiosis posuit Gualterus Mild-maius a.d. 1584.*[151] From this gateway a path led to a passage between the Hall and antechapel and so on to the court beyond, forming the principal entrance to the original college.[152]

South of the Hall, the 1612 Speed map shows west and south ranges of buildings with the east side separated from the gardens by a wall. The buttressed west range may have been a converted claustral building if the priory had a southern Cloister. However, in 1587 Mildmay reserved rooms for the use of his family in a position which indicates the south range, known until rebuilt as the Founder's Range, and which he describes as 'recently constructed'.[153] This suggests it was not part of the monastic buildings, and the same may apply to the west range. By 1589, the year of Mildmay's death, the college as shown in Speed's map was probably complete. A 'dedication festival' took place late in 1587 and in the next year the first college order book and college accounts begin.[154] Much of the work was done by Ralph Symons, freemason, of Berkhamsted in Hertfordshire; stone from Cambridge Castle and the materials of St Nicholas' Hostel were reused in the buildings.[155] There was no further construction at the college until the building shown in the Loggan engraving extending southwards was built in 1631-2.

The King's Works

On his accession in 1509, Henry VIII (*36*) inherited around twenty royal houses and a small number of castles which were suitable for royal use, including the Tower of London, Dover and Windsor. By the time of his death in 1547 he owned perhaps seventy domestic residences.[1] The new properties were acquired by forfeiture, purchase, exchange and, after the Dissolution, by the conversion of monasteries to royal residences. To have such a large number of houses – more than any other monarch of England before or since – was in one sense a manifestation of Henry's acquisitive personality, but it was also a reflection of the peripatetic way of life of mediaeval and early-modern rulers, who were constantly on the move. This was partly to make the royal will effective by personal presence, partly for reasons of food supply and hygiene, and partly to enjoy the hunt in royal forests and parks.[2] Earlier kings, and indeed Henry himself in the first years of his reign, had relied heavily on the great monastic houses for hospitality on progresses, and in some, such as Rochester Priory, a suite of rooms had been made available for royal visits since the fourteenth century.[3] Sometimes improvements to monastic lodgings would even be funded by the Crown, as at St Augustine's, Canterbury, in 1520 for the visit of the Emperor Charles V.[4]

The suppression of the monasteries therefore posed a problem for the king in terms of accommodation, which was addressed by the Crown taking over certain monastic houses and converting them for use as royal residences.[5] These acquisitions were principally of monasteries that were convenient staging posts on regular journeys from the London palaces, to the south, west or north, and where Henry had stayed regularly and frequently in the past. For this purpose the king kept for himself eight suppressed houses: at Dartford, Rochester and Canterbury on the route to Dover and the south coast; at Syon, Guildford and Reading on the route to the west; and at St Albans and Dunstable on the route to the

36 Portrait of Henry VIII, Hans Holbein the Younger, 1537-47

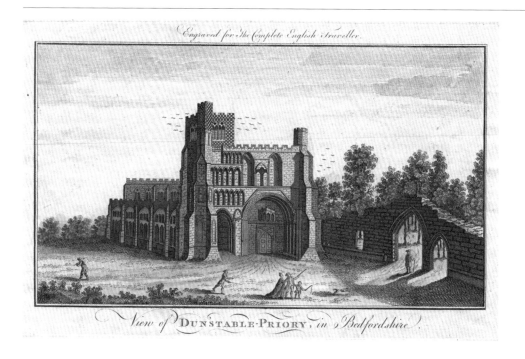

37 A 1771 engraving of Dunstable Priory, with the surviving Priory Church

north. Although Henry was familiar with all of these houses, such familiarity was not always a reason for acquisition. He had often stayed at Abingdon Abbey, which was well-placed on the route to Woodstock, but after careful consideration Reading Abbey was preferred for conversion into a residence.[6] However, little seems to have been done at Syon until its conversion into a munitions factory in 1545, so it was never really a royal residence.[7] In addition, monastic buildings were retained at Ashridge for the use of the royal children and at York and Newcastle to provide accommodation for the Council of the North, but other than in the Great Progress to York in 1541 Henry made no personal use of these.[8]

At several of these retained properties, comparatively little conversion work was necessary. At Guildford a royal lodging was erected in the early 1530s within the precinct of the Dominican friary, together with a garden: in 1536 the friars petitioned the king that he had built a 'place of honour' at their house but they did not have the funds to maintain it or the garden belonging to it.[9] So when the friary was suppressed in 1538, only repairs were necessary. Further repairs in 1543 reveal that the lodgings were on a considerable scale, with both king's and queen's sides, and rooms such as presence chambers, privy chambers, raying chambers (dressing rooms), bedchambers and at least one chapel.[10]

At Dunstable there is no record of what work was done, but in 1543-4 the master carpenter Lawrence Bradshaw was paid for 'drawing of platts for Dunstable', and both he and James Nedeham, the surveyor of the King's Works, were paid for visits to view work underway, so some modest improvements to the priory must have been made.[11] Only the Priory Church survives (37), evocatively illus-

38 *Ruins of the Cloister, Rochester Cathedral*, John Buckler, 1805

trated in Robert Sanders' *The Complete English Traveller*. Similarly, at St Albans little appears to have been done except for repairs at 'the king's mansion at the late monastery of St Albans' in 1544, so presumably the existing abbot's house was considered adequate.[12]

The works at Rochester were more extensive, although not all account books have survived. Those that have record that conversion works took place at least from early 1541, though probably from soon after the priory's suppression in April 1540, until late 1542. The recorded cost was over £1,300 and comprised the conversion of the east range of the Cloister, containing the Chapter House and Dorter, into royal lodgings, with suites of rooms for the king and queen. Only ruins remain of this range, picturesquely portrayed by John Buckler in 1805 (*38*). In the south range the Frater at first became a Hall, and later a Great Chamber. It may have been at this point that a 'great

halpas', or processional stair, was built to provide access to the royal lodgings, which would otherwise have been by way of the Hall. The lodgings seem to have occupied just these two ranges: the use of the west range of the Cloister, previously the Cellarer's Hall, is unclear; and on the north range Rochester Cathedral was transferred to the secular Dean and Chapter.[13]

Though Henry VIII visited and used most of these houses after he acquired and converted them – he went to Dunstable, Canterbury and Rochester four times each – some did not remain in Crown ownership for long after his death. Rochester, St Albans and Dunstable were soon granted or sold. Syon and Reading were granted to the Duke of Somerset, though they reverted to the Crown after his attainder. Dartford, Canterbury and Guildford survived in royal use until the seventeenth century.[14]

39 The surviving building at Dartford Priory, now a Registry Office;
originally a Gatehouse to Henry VIII's Dartford Manor House

Dartford Priory

By far the largest, most expensive and most magnificent monastic conversion undertaken by the king was at Dartford Priory. Dartford was the only house of Dominican nuns in England. Founded in 1349 by Edward III, the priory occupied a level but marshy site of around 10 acres on the western outskirts of the town. The new manor house was built on the site for Henry VIII between 1541 and 1544. Elizabeth I stayed there twice, and the building had already begun to be demolished during her time. Now only one gatehouse remains, used as a registry office (*39*).

The foundation of a monastery of nuns was first contemplated by Queen Eleanor of Castile, the wife of Edward I, and her son Edward II obtained a papal licence for a new foundation in 1321. However, it was more than twenty years before the priory was finally established. In 1345 Edward III sought the permission of the Bishop of Rochester to found a house of sisters of the Order of Preachers, as the Dominican Order is formally known, and the Archbishop of Canterbury supported the request. The bishop gave the king a favourable answer on 3 February 1346. The choice of Dartford was probably due to the generosity of William Clapitus, vintner and afterwards sheriff of London, who gave large sums towards the foundation. On 29 June 1349 the king granted Clapitus licence to assign two messuages and ten acres of land in Dartford to the sisters. In November of the same year the king applied to the pope for confirmation of the new foundation.[15]

The sisters were placed under the care of the Friars Preachers of King's Langley, Buckinghamshire, six of whom resided at Dartford. In 1352 Edward III paid £192 13s 4d towards building the friars a dwelling-house; Friar John Woderowe, the king's confessor, was appointed to superintend the works.[16] Then, in 1355, the king gave profits from certain Crown lands to be used for building the nuns' houses, and these were sufficiently far advanced in 1356 that a community of sisters were able to take possession and commence religious observance under the friars already there. On 19 November 1356 the king made the formal grant of the 'monastery of St. Mary and St. Margaret' for the weal of his soul, the souls of Queen Eleanor and Edward II, of all his ancestors and successors and all the faithful departed.[17] The house was granted to the sisters 'with its buildings, cloisters and enclosures dedicated to God, to the Virgin Mother of Our Lord and to the blessed Virgin Margaret'.[18]

A series of royal grants and orders shows the progress of the building. On 2 March 1358, the king empowered John Onle to take on as many workmen as were necessary for finishing the work, and also those needed for carrying timber and stone. On 24 September the same year, he gave 200 marks for the construction of the church, and 100 marks for lead to cover the church and other buildings.[19] In the spring of 1361, the masons' work seems to have been approaching completion. Simon Kegworth and others were appointed to gather as many carpenters, cementers and others as were necessary for the royal works at the priory, and also for carrying stone, timber and tiles, and a writ of 12 April required all sheriffs, mayors, bailiffs and others to assist.[20]

In 1535 the *Valor* gives the net annual revenues of the priory as just over £380, making it one of the larger monasteries and, therefore, not included in the first Dissolution of 1536.[21] The suppression of the priory took place at an unknown date, some time after 1 April 1539, when the Bishop of Dover begged Cromwell to let him 'have the receiving' of Dartford; pensions were granted to the nuns and the prioress had a pension of 100 marks.[22]

The creation of a large new royal house at Dartford Priory began in June 1541. It cost £6,600 in addition to the cost of demolition and removal of stone from Barking Abbey, and of timber taken from the king's woods.[23] The principal reason for this great expense was that, unlike at St Augustine's, Canterbury or Reading Abbey, very little of the monastic fabric was retained and adapted; instead, the house was newly built. Building materials

included nearly two million bricks, stone and lead from St Augustine's, and tiles taken from Rochester.[24]

The work was supervised, as at Rochester and at Canterbury, by James Nedeham, who at the height of the work in summer 1541 had over 500 men on site.[25] Surviving accounts show that the work commenced in June, with destruction of most of the priory buildings. Bricklayers were breaking down chimneys and walls and taking down tiles and slates of houses, and more 'breaking uppe of toumes and tome stones in the church'. There were under-miners employed 'castyng downe a towre' and carpenters taking away the ceiling of wainscot in the Dorter and taking down the ceiling under the roof of the church, as well as the roof itself, to be repaired and made to be set up again.[26] Later, labourers were engaged in carrying away the 'rubbisshe of the walls taken downe within the late cloister, chyrche and other places'.[27]

Work simultaneously began on the new house, the precise location of which is unclear, but which was probably built over the Cloister and part of the Church. The walls were a mixture of brick and stone, and the dressings included battlements.[28] The house comprised two suites of rooms, one for the king and one for the queen, which included for each a watching chamber, presence chamber, privy chamber, bedchamber, raying chamber (dressing room), wardrobe, closet, stool house and chapel; a withdrawing chamber is mentioned on the queen's side but not on the king's side.[29] There may also have been dining chambers, but these are not specifically mentioned. If the priory followed the common arrangement of the Church forming the north side of the Cloister, then the new house must have been, at least in part, on the site of the Church, since mention is made of the queen's privy chamber being 'the late steples'. This suggests that some of the Church was incorporated into the house.[30] The house did not have a hall, and so instead of the formal entry into the Lodgings being through the Hall, it was by way of a halpace, or processional stair, which was probably situated centrally in the south range. The halpace stair gave access to the king's and queen's watching chambers, and at its foot there was a carved stone dragon and a lion, both gilded and each holding a gilded vane. The stair was tiled with 9,000 paving tiles and painted.[31]

The Lodgings at Dartford would have been built around an Inner Court, to the north of the Great Court, an arrangement illustrated in a 1596 map.[32] From the entrance on the south side, the sequence of rooms would then run on each side and join again in the middle of the north range. This may explain the reference in the accounts to the building of a long wall of ragged stone with 'ij great gaybell endes and x buttryces in the same wall of the north side of the king's lodgens next the mote'.[33] The queen's lodgings must also have had a north side if the Church steeple was lowered and used as her privy chamber. As the steeple was usually at the east end of the nave above the crossing, it is likely that the queen's apartments were to the east and the king's to the west. The king's and queen's sides were not, however, identical in size and construction, since the accounts show that carpenters were making and framing five roofs: two long roofs (to be tiled) for the king's side (respectively 134 feet and 110 feet long) and two flat roofs (to be leaded) for the queen's side (110 feet and 92 feet respectively) and a third roof of 70 feet, each of them being 30 feet wide.[34] These dimensions suggest that the royal apartments were not entirely symmetrical. There was an entrance gate into the Inner Court at the lower level on its south-west corner, which survives. The Richard Godfrey engraving for Francis Grose's *The Antiquities of England and Wales* (**40**) shows it to have been of stone, and the building immediately to its south, and a short section of the south range, to have been constructed of brick. This may be the location of the 'great dower [door] for the entre entryng owt of the great cowrte into the new logyngs' for which 'inbowers' were paid in 1543.[35]

Archaeological investigations in 1976 also showed that the west range extended north from this gate and culminated in a kitchen on the ground floor. This may have been the king's or queen's privy kitchen, which the accounts show would have been connected with the royal apartments on the floor above by a brick vice, or spiral staircase.[36] Privy kitchens were often located below the most private royal lodgings, for both convenience and warmth.[37] There were other vices leading from the king's privy chamber to his garden, which was probably located to the west of the Lodgings; and similarly from the queen's privy chamber to her garden, probably to the east.[38] All the principal rooms, such as the watching chambers, presence chambers, privy chambers and bedchambers were lighted by bay windows, made of timber carried on brick arches supported on buttresses.[39] By spring 1542 the Lodgings were almost complete, and the king's glazier, Galyon Hone, was finishing glazing all the windows.[40] Internal fittings such as doors and panelling had to be made, and fireplaces and chimneys built; at least forty are mentioned in the accounts.[41]

The king made his first visit to the new house shortly afterwards. Records of Henry's almsgiving show that on Sunday 7 May 1542 he was at Westonhanger, on Sunday 14 May he was at Dartford, and by Sunday 21 May he

Dartford Priory, Kent.

was at Westminster.[42] He probably spent several days at his new house, since the accounts show archery butts were set up in the garden for 'the king's grace to shoote at' and a bridge was planked for him to ride over. [43]

Work on the house continued for almost the next two years. Gatehouses were built in the east and west of the Great Court, with new lodgings either side of them, while a range of lodgings was constructed on the south. These included lodgings for the Keeper, Sir Richard Long, with his own hall, kitchen, buttery and bedchamber.[44] A groom's chamber is also mentioned, which must have been for the Groom of the Stool, the principal Gentleman of the Privy Chamber. At this time Sir Thomas Heneage held the post. The Great Kitchen, the

location of which is unknown, was built in 1543, together with ancillary offices such as buttery, larder house, serving place, scullery and pastry house, reflecting the fact that a large number of people had to be fed and accommodated, not just the king and queen.[45]

The exterior was also completed, which must have presented an impressive and colourful sight. Some buildings in the Lodgings, as well as the Gatehouses, were battlemented and these, as well as many of the roofs, were decorated with pinnacles and gilded vanes. Most of the walls were plastered and then decorated by 'okeryng and penselyng' in red, black and white, whilst yellow ochre was used to pencil 'the gaytes and gayte houses rownde abowte the gret cowrte'.[46] Ochring and pencilling were

40 *Dartford Priory*, engraved by Richard Godfrey, 1784, showing the Gatehouse

techniques used to give a high quality and consistent finish to brickwork, since before the eighteenth century bricks were often uneven in both size and colour. After the bricks were laid, a thin coat of mortar or, at Dartford, plaster was applied around the edges of the bricks to smooth any irregularities. This was then scored horizontally and vertically to give the appearance of evenly sized bricks. The whole surface was then painted over with a mixture of red ochre and size, historically called ruddle. If the ruddle were applied to damp plaster, the colour would be absorbed in the same way as fresco and could last for a long time. Thin lines were then painted along the scored lines, to represent fine brickwork, and this was called pencilling. These lines were usually white, but might be black, and at Dartford the accounts record that both colours were used. Bricklayers usually carried out the work, but it was sometimes done by plasterers or tilers.[47]

However, despite the expenditure and all the work undertaken over a three-year period, Henry VIII only made one further visit to Dartford. He stayed from 21 to 26 June 1545, accompanied by the Privy Council, which met every day he was there, though the king himself was not present.[48] In 1548 King Edward VI granted the Priory and Manor of Dartford to Anne of Cleves. After her death in 1557, Queen Mary briefly restored the priory to the Dominican sisters. She died on 17 November 1558 and was succeeded by her sister Elizabeth. In 1559 three visitors chosen from the Privy Council came to Dartford and tendered the oaths of supremacy and uniformity first to the prior, and then to each of the nuns separately. They all refused to take it, whereupon the visitors sold the goods of the convent at a very low rate, paid the debts of the house, divided what little remained among the sisters, and ordered them to leave within twenty-four hours. The small remaining band of Dominican exiles, consisting of two priests, the prioress, four choir-nuns, four lay sisters and a young girl not yet professed, joined the nuns of Syon House, and crossed to the Netherlands.[49]

The priory site and royal manor house again reverted to the Crown, and Elizabeth kept them in her own hands. She stayed at Dartford on her return from her progresses into Kent in 1559 and 1573.[50] Some of the manor house buildings were demolished in 1598, and in 1606 James I granted the estate to

41 *Dartford Priory, Kent*, John Carter, 1783

Robert Cecil, Earl of Salisbury. He in turn conveyed it to Robert Darcy in 1612 and it remained in the Darcy family until the end of the seventeenth century. New owners from the early eighteenth century were not in residence, and most of the remaining buildings were demolished in the first half of the eighteenth century. Only part of one gatehouse survived, used as a farmhouse, illustrated by John Carter in 1783 (*41*).[51]

Reading Abbey

Reading Abbey, of which only the Inner Gatehouse survives intact (*42*), was selected as an essential royal residence and staging post on the route west, with the great advantage for the king in that it had its own hunting park. King Henry I, son of William the Conqueror, founded the abbey in 1121. A royal abbey from the outset, it remained under royal patronage until its suppression. It was granted enormous holdings of land and major religious relics to attract visitors and pilgrims, including the hand of St James the Greater.[52] No expense was spared in providing a church comparable in size and splendour with any other in England, and at the time of the Dissolution it was one of the ten wealthiest abbeys in the country.

When Henry I died in Normandy in 1135 his body was returned to Reading and buried in the front of the high altar of the then incomplete abbey. Over the burial vault a monument was subsequently erected, and in 1398 Richard II consented to confirm the abbey in all its rights and privileges, only on condition that the abbot would, within a year, honourably repair the tomb and effigy of King Henry their founder over his place of burial.[53]

As described by the great historian William of Malmesbury, writing around 1135, the abbey was built on a spur:

> between the rivers Kennet and Thames, on a spot calculated for the reception of almost all who might have occasion to travel to the more populous cities of England, where he placed monks of the Cluniac order, who are at this day a noble pattern of holiness, and an example of unwearied and delightful hospitality.[54]

Although the first monks at Reading were Cluniacs, the connection between Reading and Cluny appears not to have lasted beyond the thirteenth century, when it became attached to the general Benedictine Order.[55]

The abbey precinct occupied a substantial area of the mediaeval town of

42 The Inner Gatehouse of Reading Abbey

43 *Reading Abbey*, engraved by S Hooper, 1784, showing the Inner Gatehouse

Reading, and some thirty acres were enclosed within its walls.[56] Through the main gateway was the outer precinct, dominated by the great west front of the Abbey Church. Dedicated to the Virgin Mary and St John, the Church was built from 1121 in Romanesque style. The walls were faced with honey-coloured limestone from Taynton in Oxfordshire, though the finer and whiter Caen stone was used for the capitals and voussoirs in the Cloister.[57] The nave was longer than that of Westminster Abbey and the Church matched in scale and magnificence the great cathedrals of Gloucester, Canterbury, Peterborough and Ely that survive today.[58] In 1164 the Church was completed; it was consecrated by Archbishop Thomas Becket, in the presence of King Henry II.[59] The Lady Chapel at the east end was added in 1314.[60] Some of the bases of the piers remain, as do some decorative mediaeval floor tiles. Ruins survive of the Church's apsidal end, apsidal chapels and transept.

The abbey had five Gatehouses, the only one remaining being the Inner Gatehouse, shown in the engraving for Francis Grose's *Antiquities of England and Wales* (*43*). This gave access to the Cloister, south of the Church, and to the domestic buildings. Nothing now survives of the Cloister walk, although there are some ruins of some of the claustral buildings, and a modern garden has been created on the site of the cloister garth (*44*). Some of

44 The Cloister Garden at Reading Abbey, with Elisabeth Frink's sculpture 'Robed Figure'

the finely carved stone capitals are in Reading Museum.

The buildings around the Cloister were in their usual positions, with the Chapter House immediately to the south of the south transept of the Church. This had a high, vaulted roof, while its doorway, flanked by two large windows and three windows above, opened onto the Cloister. The walls are still standing, showing it to have been one of the largest chapter houses in England.[61] To the south of the Chapter House was a passage leading from the Cloister to the Infirmary, and beyond this on the east range of the Cloister was the Dorter, which was also very large, as it was built to accommodate as many as 200 monks. At the far end of the Dorter, beside the River Kennet, was the Reredorter.[62] On the south range of the Cloister was the Frater on the upper storey with cellars below. Again, it was built on a large scale and was over 164 feet long.[63] On the west range of the Cloister would have been the Great Hall and beyond that, to the west, the Abbot's Lodging.

The abbey came into the hands of the Crown because of the attainder of the last abbot, Hugh Faringdon, who was imprisoned in the Tower, probably early in the summer of 1539. Meanwhile it was assumed that the abbey was even then the king's, and on 8 September Thomas Moyle wrote to Cromwell from Reading that he, with Dr Layton and

'Master Vachell of Reading', had been through the inventory of the abbey plate 'at the residence', the Abbot's Lodgings.[64] There they found a room hung with 'metely good tapestry, which do well for hanging some mean little chamber in his majesty's house'.[65] There was another chamber 'hung with six pieces of verdure with fountains, but it is old and at the ends of some of them very foul and greasy'. They also noted several beds with silk hangings and in the church eight pieces of tapestry 'very goodly' but small.[66]

Soon after, Cromwell sent two of his most trusted servants, Richard Pollard and John Williams, to the abbey. On 17 September 1539, Pollard wrote to Cromwell:

> Pleasyth your Lordship to be advertysed that att my comyng to Readynge I did dyspatche Mr. Wrytheslys servant wyth every thyng accordyng to your comandment wyche amountythe to the some of cxxxili ixs viijd [£131 9s 8d] as apperythe by the partyculars herein inclosyd, and part of the stuffe receyvyd for the kings majesties use, wyth the schole house and church undefasyd. I and my followers have lefte hytt by Indenture in the custody of Mr. Penyson. And as for the Plate, vestements, copys and hangyngs wyche we have left hytt in the custody of Mr. Vachell by Indenture wych shalbe conveyed to London.[67]

The 'partyculars' show that the commissioners seized and dispatched to the king, as especially valuable, ten copes of green cloth of tissue, ten copes of white cloth of tissue, six rich copes of diverse sorts, four copes of baudekin, two altar cloths, a complete suit of vestments of crimson tissue, and a vestment of red tissue. At the same time they reserved for the king the valuable gold and silver including 41 oz of gold plate and 47 oz of broken gold plate; gilt plate,

378 oz; broken parcel gilt, 311 oz. The total of the plate that went straight to the king from this one wealthy abbey amounted to 2,645 oz.[68]

Two months later, on 15 November 1539, the Abbot of Reading, together with two priests, was executed as a traitor on a platform outside the gateway of his own abbey. With the execution of Abbot Hugh, the monastery passed absolutely into the hands of Henry VIII, together with its property, declared to be of the clear annual value of £1,908 14s.

Reading Abbey frequently provided accommodation for royal visitors during its 400-year history, being especially popular with Henry III during the thirteenth century; he visited no less than five times in the year 1246 alone. It continued to attract monarchs regularly during the fifteenth century, and parliaments and council meetings were held there. Henry VIII visited the abbey during his first progress in 1509 and stayed many times subsequently, including in August 1529 when he visited in the company of Anne Boleyn.[69] Part of the attraction was that Reading Abbey had its own fine hunting park, described in a grant in 1548 as 'The whole park and liberty of a park in Whitley, Berks, with all the game and deer, male and female, which belonged to Redyng monastery'.[70] Though there is no record of the royal apartments at Reading before its suppression, which were probably in the Abbot's Lodging, they must have been considered suitable for royal accommodation.

There is no book of accounts showing what works took place at Reading to convert the abbey buildings into a royal residence, and it is possible that these were not extensive.[71] Since the buildings still offered appropriate accommodation, and the abbey was conveniently placed and with its own deer park, the change of ownership need have had little practical consequence.[72] Whatever works were

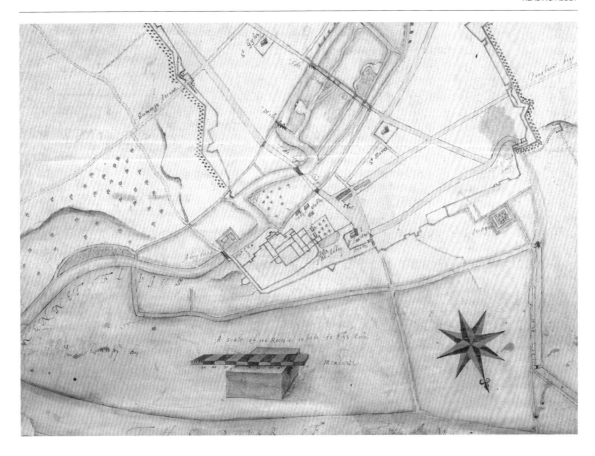

45 A detail of a plan of the Civil War fortifications of Reading, showing the Abbey buildings in *c*.1643

carried out must have been complete by August 1540, when the king stayed there with his Privy Council.[73] Edward VI, Mary and Elizabeth I all stayed at what was then called the King's Place, and repairs were regularly carried out. These cost the substantial sum of over £300 in 1568 and included repair of the windows by the Queen's Master Glazier, with the queen's arms and badges inserted in the Great and Privy Chambers.[74] They were noted by a Captain Symonds, who was at Reading in 1644 and described the dining room at what was by then called the Abbey House as having the arms and initials of Queen Elizabeth.[75] Otherwise there is no evidence that any major works were undertaken to the house itself.[76]

Therefore, the description given in the Parliamentary survey of 1650 probably represents the house as it was 100 years earlier:

All that capital messuage, mansion-house, at abbey-house, called Reading Abbey, consisting of two cellars, two butteries, a hall, a parlour, a dining room, ten chambers, a garret with a large gallery, and other small rooms, with two courtyards and a large gate-house with several rooms adjoining the said house and a small gardine . . . There is on the east side of the said mansion house, a great old hall, with a very large cellar under the said hall, arched, with some other decayed rooms between the sayd hall and the mansion-house,

46 John Speed's map of Reading, 1612, showing the abbey site marked as 'H' at the top right

with the ruins of an old large chappell, a kitchen, and several other rooms.[77]

This description can be taken with the plan of the Reading siege defences in 1643 (**45**), which illustrates the 'Abbey House'. The site is approximately rectangular, in a walled enclosure, with the main entrance from the north by way of the original Inner Gatehouse of the abbey. Beyond the entrance and at right angles to it lies the 'capital house', forming the west range of the Cloister. This appears from the map to have been a double range, with projecting wings towards the west, and probably combined the original Abbot's Lodging and the Great Hall. The Frater and Kitchen and the Dorter may have been converted to serve the house. The 'large chappell' may be the former Chapter House.[78] The 'small gardine', shown on the map planted with orderly rows of trees, lay on the other side of the entrance gate, to the west of the house.

The same arrangement is shown in John Speed's map from *The Theatre of the Empire of Greate Britaine* of 1612 (*46*).

The vast Church, where the remains of royalty had been interred, remained deserted but undisturbed so far as its fabric was concerned until 1548. The lead on the roof of the Abbey Church and buildings was then so considerable that the amount helps to form some idea of the extent of the premises. It was measured and estimated to weigh 417 fodders (a fodder was approximately one ton). Six great bells still swung in the church belfry.[79] Following Henry's death in 1547, the abbey passed to Edward VI, who granted it the following year to his uncle, the Duke of Somerset. He began demolishing the Church and the cloister walk, offering for sale the lead and bells melted down.[80] The stone from the Church was used for a variety of purposes, including the rebuilding of St Mary's Church in Reading, for works at the Tower of London and the Exchequer at Westminster, and for the Poor Knight's Lodgings at Windsor Castle.[81]

In the Civil War, during the siege of Reading, the royalist garrison built a fortification on the site of the Church to the north of the Cloister. This attracted return fire from the Parliamentarian besiegers, and may also have damaged other buildings.[82] Certainly the Parliamentary survey judged that by 1650 the buildings were only fit to be destroyed and the materials were valued at just £200.[83] The survey also refers to the stables and gardens:

> A large barn, formerly a stable, in length 135 ft., in breadth 30 ft., with a great yard and small garden, bounded by the hollow [or holy] brook, South, and the said great garden, North . . . All that garden or orchard called by the name of the great gardine, one acre . . . bounded by the said Forbury, North, and said great yard south.[84]

The stables were newly built in 1570, using timber from 100 oaks taken from 'Benname in the Countye of Barckshere for the Queen's Majesties howse and stables at Redddinge', at a cost of nearly £1,000.[85] The 'Queen's Stables' are also shown on the Speed map. Such a large expenditure on stabling suggests that the house may have been principally considered a place for hunting, rather than for longer residence. As well as the Great Garden, there was another to the east of the Cloister buildings:

> The Fermary garden, a messuage, tenement, malt-house, garden and orchard, so-called; bounded with the River Kennett South, and butting upon the way leading to Forbury from Orte Bridge.[86]

The name implies that the garden, orchard and buildings lay on the site of the former Infirmary.

St Augustine's Abbey Canterbury

St Augustine's Abbey, Canterbury, is the oldest Anglo-Saxon abbey in England. It is situated outside the eastern wall of the city, and at the time of its suppression in 1538 it had survived for almost a thousand years. Just a short distance from Canterbury Cathedral, now only ruins of the Abbey Church and Cloister remain (*47*). The fourteenth-century Great Gate, also called Fyndon's Gate, survives and later served as a gateway to the new house which Henry VIII created (*48*).

The monastery was founded in about 598 by St Augustine at the direction of King Aethelbert of Kent, who endowed it with gifts, and it was intended as a burial place for archbishops of Canterbury and kings. Aethelbert himself and several of his successors were buried in the church, as were also the first ten archbishops of Canterbury. The principal object of the foundation was to provide a residence for monks sent from Rome for the conversion of the English and it became a centre of great learning. St Augustine died in 604 or 605 and was buried in the cemetery. In 613 Archbishop Laurence consecrated the conventual church in the presence of Aethelbert and many others. The body of Augustine was removed from the cemetery and re-interred in the north porch, as was also the body of Queen Berta in the porch of St Martin. In 978 the church was re-dedicated by Archbishop Dunstan in honour of Saints Peter and Paul and St Augustine.[87]

After the Norman Conquest, Egelsin, the last abbot of Saxon times, fled to Denmark in 1070. King William I then appointed a Norman named Scotland as abbot. Scotland proved to be a capable head and began the complete rebuilding of the abbey, which was carried on by his successors.[88] By about 1100 a great Romanesque Church had been built, destroying the Anglo-Saxon Church, and the bodies of the early archbishops were moved from the north side of the old church to the eastern part of the new one. New monastic buildings were constructed around a

47 The surviving ruins of St Augustine's Abbey, with Canterbury Cathedral behind

Cloister to the north of the Church. On the east of the Cloister was the Chapter House, and beyond that the Dorter and Reredorter. The Frater was on the north side of the Cloister and a *Cellarium* on the west. Beyond the Cloister to the east, but linked to it by a passage, was the Infirmary Hall with its Chapel. To the south of the Church was the cemetery, with the sacrist's house beyond it, while outside the gate to the west an Almonry was built in 1154.[89]

A fire in 1168 resulted in the east end of the Church having to be rebuilt. After a pause in the late twelfth century, there was then a great period of reconstruction and expansion of the abbey from the mid-thirteenth century.[90] The rebuilding commenced in 1260 and continued for many years. Adam de Kyngesnoth, the chamberlain of Henry III, made large benefactions towards this in 1267.[91] The

Cloister, *Lavatorium*, Frater and Kitchen were totally rebuilt. In the west Cloister range, the *Cellarium* was replaced by a very grand new Abbot's Lodging. This range was then extended beyond the Cloister with the addition of a Great Hall.[92] A new crenellated Great Gate (or Fyndon Gate, later known as Palace Gate) was added to complete the Inner Great Court in 1309. To the north more land was enclosed, which provided space for a new Outer Court with a cellarer's range, brewhouse and bakehouse. In addition, a series of new lodgings was added to the east side of the Infirmary, a new cellarer's garden was enclosed, and in 1320 a new walled vineyard was created. Later additions included the surviving Cemetery Gate, built in 1390, and at the south-west end of the Church a large bell tower was added in the late fifteenth century. Finally, a new Lady Chapel was added at the east end of the Church.[93]

St Augustine's was sufficiently wealthy to escape the first dissolution of the smaller monasteries; in the *Valor* of 1535 the gross value of the possessions of the abbey is given as approximately £1,729, and the net value as just over £1,413.[94] But it was one of many monasteries that voluntarily surrendered, a mechanism which, by simple deed of gift, meant that all the house's property and possessions were transferred to the Crown, without any need for act of Parliament, inquisition or formal escheat. The first large monastery to surrender in this way was Furness in Lancashire in 1537, which formed a precedent for a process that was to become normal in the next phase of the Dissolution.[95] The first eight months of 1538 saw the voluntary surrender to the Crown of thirty-five monasteries, with all their property.[96] They included St Augustine's, where the abbot and his thirty brethren surrendered on 30 July.[97]

This simple legal process was clearly convenient to the Crown, and in many cases pressures were applied and inducements offered. At St Augustine's the scale of the inducement is revealed in a letter from the abbot to Cromwell:

> Desires Cromwell to be good to him, in that he may have his house at Sturrey to receive his friends in. Mr. Ant. Sentleger and Dr. Layton [the king's commissioners] said he would have 200 marks and the house of Sturrey. Perceives that, unless he dismisses his household, who would thus be forced to beg, he will have never a penny at the end of the year. Desires Cromwell to be a mean for him to the King, to whom he ha[...] freely surrendered his living, that he may have the lordship of Sturrey, with hunting and fishing, worth 52l. a year.[98]

This was a substantial pension and would have enabled the abbot to live in considerable style, equivalent to most gentry families. The other monks also received smaller pensions.

At first, there was no destruction on the abbey site except for the tomb of St Augustine and other shrines, destroyed in September 1538. This was when the shrine of St Thomas Becket in Canterbury Cathedral was removed.[99] A papal bull in December 1538 indicted Henry VIII that he had dug up the bones of St Thomas Becket and scattered his ashes, spoiled St Augustine's monastery, driven out the monks and put deer in their place.[100]

The use of St Augustine's as a royal residence may have been anticipated even before the surrender, since earlier in July 1538 Sir Richard Rich, Chancellor of the Court of Augmentations, wrote to Cromwell asking if he should send his own officers to survey the abbey rather than relying on the commissioners. Five months earlier Rich, unusually, had

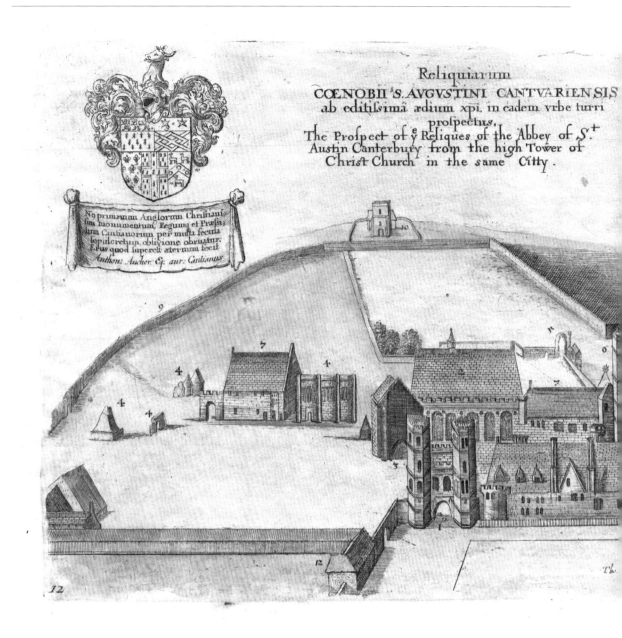

Reliquiarum
COENOBII S. AVGVSTINI CANTVARIENSIS
ab editissimâ ædium xpi. in eadem vrbe turri
prospectus.
The Prospect of ÿ Reliques of the Abbey of St
Austin Canterbury from the high Tower of
Christ Church in the same Citty.

Ne primorum Anglorum Christiani
sim monumentum, Regume et Præsu
lum Cantuorum per multa secula
sepulcretum, oblivione obruatur:
fidus quod superest æternum fecit
Anthon: Aucher: Eq: aur: Cantianus

49 St Augustine's Abbey, Canterbury, engraved by Daniel King, 1655, showing the king's house

personally surveyed Abingdon Abbey because it was intended to convert it into a royal house, though that plan was changed in favour of Reading Abbey.[101]

Certainly in 1539, the year after its suppression, the king ordered that part of the buildings of St Augustine's be converted into a royal residence. This was specifically stated to have been 'against the coming in of the Lady Anne of Cleves',[102] but it reflected a wider and continuing requirement. Henry himself had stayed at St Augustine's nine times before its suppression, lying as it did on a key route to Dover and the south coast.[103] Its conversion for future use would, therefore, have seemed a necessary undertaking, completing a chain of palaces at Westminster, Greenwich, Dartford, Rochester and then Canterbury, on the way to Dover.

The task of converting the monastery was given to James Nedeham, the surveyor of the King's Works, and lasted from 4 October to 21 December 1539, just a week before the new queen's arrival, increasing the time pressure for completion. Almost 350 craftsmen and labourers consequently worked day and night, using 31 dozen extra candles, in order for Anne to stay there just one night on 29 December, before moving on to meet the king at Rochester.[104]

The Abbot of St Augustine's was one of the twenty-four most senior abbots in England, 'mitred' or entitled to episcopal insignia. Hence the Abbot's Lodgings were already equipped to provide the essential accommodation required by the king.[105] These Lodgings formed the west range of the Cloister, immediately to the north of the Church, and included the Great Hall with separate porch and entrance staircase, a chapel, the abbot's parlour and a series of other chambers, all at first floor level.[106] The buildings, including the

high windows on the battlemented Hall, can be seen clearly in Daniel King's engraving of 1655 for *Monasticon Anglicanum* (**49**). The Great Hall, which was conveniently near the kitchen, became the King's Hall, and the adjacent abbot's parlour was converted into the watching, or guard chamber, which in all palaces and important houses was the outermost of the king's suite of rooms. The abbey kitchen remained in use and the chapel seems to have been retained. Though the internal arrangements are not clear, the completed building included a presence chamber, which was probably also used as a dining chamber, privy chamber, bedchamber, withdrawing chamber and closet.[107] The existing Great Gate, fine enough for any palace, and its adjoining buildings, which contained guest lodgings, were also retained, as shown in Turner's 1795 watercolour (**50**).[108]

The main challenge facing Nedeham was how to provide appropriate lodgings for the queen, which did not exist in the abbey. His solution was to demolish some old lodgings, 'which were ready to fall down', and build a suite to the west of the king's lodgings. This new building was a timber-framed structure, 13 feet 6 inches high, standing on brick basement walls and with a tiled roof, described in Nedeham's accounts as 'a great vawte roof'.[109] Internally it contained the usual sequence of rooms: a watching chamber, presence chamber, privy chamber, withdrawing chamber and closet, the chapel being shared with the king's side.[110] It connected in the west with the range south of the Great Gate 'alongst the highway',

50 *St Augustine's Gate, Canterbury*, JMW Turner, *c.*1793

which was converted into an 'outer great chamber' and 'inner great chamber'.[111] This substantial range is shown in King's engraving. In the east it connected with the King's Lodgings, with the king's bedchamber and queen's bedchamber separated only by a 'little chamber betwixt the two'.[112] Three new large bay windows were installed, one looking north and two south, over a new garden which was laid out and walled. Finally, both sets of lodgings were newly plastered and painted, the outside of the King's Lodgings being yellow ochred and his Privy Lodgings red ochred. The windows were glazed or re-glazed as necessary by Galyon Hone, the king's glazier, who added five 'arms of the king's and queen's and xi badges of theirs' to the glass.[113] The king's arms were also painted 'over the stairs entering into the hall within the court' and four representations of the queen's arms were painted, one in the watching chamber, two in the presence chamber and the fourth 'in oil of an ell square over the halfpace stair going into the queen's lodging'.[114] The total cost of the works was £650.[115]

The king subsequently visited St Augus-tine's four times.[116] However, there is no record of any further works on the Lodgings, though the Church was dismantled from 1541 and the roof of the kitchen, 'being old and worn and full of holes', was repaired in 1543.[117] The garden wall also had to be repaired after it was damaged during the demolition of the Church. When the king proposed a visit to Canterbury in the summer of 1542, Nedeham's men were set to work 'breaking of great rocks that were undermined of the ij great buttresses and the great steeple that fell over into the king's garden and upon the wall of the same garden'.[118] Much of the stone was shipped to Calais for fortifications, but some was sold by the cartload to local people for building.[119] The north-west tower of the Church, known as the Ethelbert Tower, was left standing, as was about half of the north wall of the nave. The northern half of the Ethelbert tower fell in the great storm of 1703, which finally destroyed the buildings.[120]

51 At Newstead Abbey, Nottinghamshire the retention of the west front provides a grand romantic feature

The Houses

Many monastic houses survived, at least in part, because their buildings were converted or adapted for use as domestic residences (*51*), either immediately after their dissolution or over the next century. The new owners came from a wide range of backgrounds, though most were necessarily wealthy, as comparatively few were granted the monastic properties as an outright gift.

Many noblemen benefited from grants of monastic land but, like the king himself, most of these had other principal houses and castles and saw no need to convert the monastic buildings, though the Duke of Norfolk adapted the Prior's Lodgings at Castle Acre, Norfolk, as a secondary residence, whilst the Earl of Shrewsbury converted part of Rufford Abbey, Nottinghamshire, for use as a hunting lodge.

At a lower level of society, many of these new owners were drawn from the ranks of royal servants. The Court was the centre of the political, social, intellectual and religious life of the nation. It was the focus of men's ambitions, the place where favour, rewards and fame could be won.[1] The king was personally involved in many aspects of government, including diplomacy, appointments, patronage, finance and occasionally military activities. His decisions had an impact both on politics and on patronage. Indeed, the key to patronage, especially the grant of lands, was the king's personal signature, so the location of the royal decision was necessarily where the king lived. In royal palaces and all larger houses, the king actually lived in the Privy Chamber, usually a suite of rooms to which entry was very limited. As a consequence, those men with the closest daily access to him were the gentlemen of the Chamber, who were especially well placed to talk up the merits or blight the hopes of would-be beneficiaries, as well as to benefit themselves.[2] They included men such as William Sandys, for many years Henry VIII's Lord Chamberlain, granted Mottisfont Priory in Hampshire; Sir Anthony Browne, the king's Master of the Horse, granted Battle Abbey, Sussex; and William Herbert, the king's brother-in-law and later Earl of Pembroke, granted Wilton Abbey, Wiltshire.

There was another important group of royal servants, overlapping

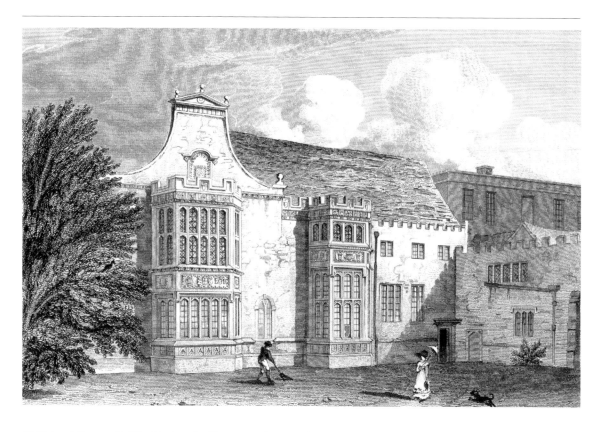

52 Richard Cromwell's Hinchingbrooke House, near Huntingdon

with this inner circle. Government had long since expanded beyond the possibility of detailed management by any one individual. Throughout his reign, Henry VIII had an institutional council to advise him and act in an executive capacity. He also depended heavily on individual ministers and servants, either directly or through a chief minister, initially Thomas Wolsey or, in the 1530s, Thomas Cromwell.[3] The men who filled these important roles in government and administration, including financial administration, during the period of the suppression of the monasteries were well placed to benefit from their royal service and relative proximity to the monarch. Cromwell himself received several grants of monastic property, including Lewes Priory in Sussex, which he converted into a house for his son, Gregory, while his nephew Richard Cromwell acquired and converted Hinchingbrooke Priory in Cambridgeshire (52). John Russell, later Earl of Bedford, acquired four former monasteries and turned one of these, Woburn Abbey, into his principal residence. At a lesser level, commissioners actively involved in the suppression of monasteries benefited too: men such as Dr Thomas Legh, who received Nostell Priory in Yorkshire, and John Tregonwell, who was granted Milton Abbey in Dorset. Others secured their rewards through their military service. Sir William Kingston, Constable of the Tower of London, received Flaxley Abbey in Gloucestershire, converted by his son into a house; Sir Thomas Dacre received Lanercost Priory, Cumbria, following his success at the battle of

53 Port Eliot House, Cornwall, built on the site of St Germans Priory

Solway Moss against the Scots.

Other beneficiaries of the Dissolution were gentry, often far distant from Court and government, who cemented their position in local society by acquiring monastic land and creating fine new houses. Whereas those men in government and the king's inner circle tended to prefer properties in the south-east of England, near to the royal palaces and at the centre of the monarchy, gentry owners often acquired their new houses in the Midlands, the north and the south west. They included men like Thomas Ridgeway at Vale Royal Abbey in Cheshire, John Eliot at St Germans Priory in Cornwall (*53*), and Thomas Hodgkins at Hailes Abbey in Gloucestershire. A few were merchants and

manufacturers. At Malmesbury Abbey, Wiltshire, the clothier William Stumpe was attracted by the combined opportunity to convert the house and use the claustral buildings for industrial purposes, while at Stoneleigh Abbey, Warwickshire, the wealthy London mercer Sir Thomas Leigh created an impressive country residence.

Not only did the background and purpose of the new owners vary widely, they also took a range of approaches to converting their acquisitions into new houses. By far the most common was the adaptation of the abbot's or prior's lodgings into a residence, reflecting the fact that by the late monastic period the superior often lived more like an aristocrat or knight than a monk, quite separate from the

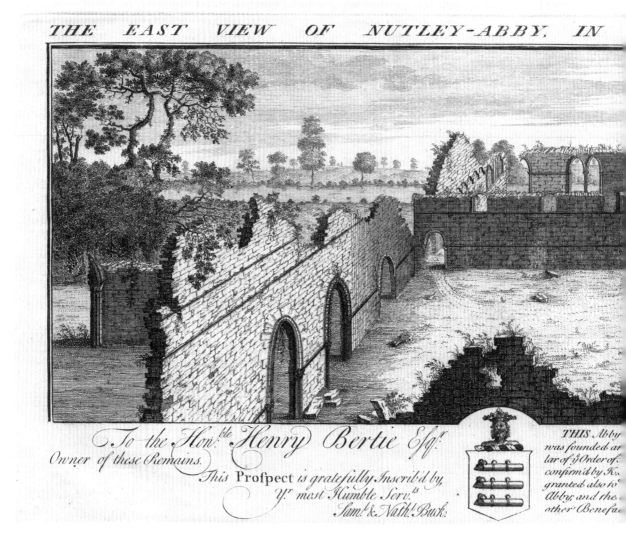

To the Hon.ble Henry Bertie Esq.r
Owner of these Remains.
This Prospect is gratefully Inscrib'd by,
Y.r most Humble Serv.ts
Sam.l & Nath.l Buck.

THIS Abby
was founded ar
lar of y Order of.
confirm'd by K.
granted also to
Abby, and the
other Benefa

communal life of the other monks. This meant, generally, that comparatively little work was required by the new owner, though there was also frequently additional new building. Sometimes the lodgings occupied a building set away from the cloister, as at St Osyth's Priory, Essex. More commonly, the abbot's or prior's lodgings occupied the upper floor of the west range of the cloister, as at Wenlock Priory, Shropshire, or Norton Priory, Cheshire. Often, though the lodgings formed the principal part of the house, elements of

the other claustral ranges were retained, as at Notley Abbey, Buckinghamshire, illustrated in 1737 by Samuel and Nathaniel Buck as 'Nutley-Abby' (**54**), and similarly at Torre Abbey, Devon.

In other houses, following demolition of the church, the whole or the greater part of the claustral buildings was used as the basis for the new house, and consequently parts of the cloister survive, as at Lacock Abbey in Wiltshire and Combe Abbey in Warwickshire. Although the usual approach of the Crown

COUNTY OF BUCKS.

...thervise called Sancta Maria de Parcho Crendon.
...Walter Giffard, second E. of Buckingham for Canons Regu-
...dicated to S.t Mary, Anno 1162, which Endowments were
...John; with additional Liberties and Imunities. He
...ab and his Heirs, the Gift of the Pastoral Staff of the s.t
...t Saints at Bradley, in the Diocese of Sarum, with divers
...Val. 457. 6. 8. Dugd. 495. 18. 5½ Speed.
S & N. Buck delin et Sculp.t 1730.

54 *The East View of Nutley-Abby in the County of Bucks*, engraved by Samuel and Nathaniel Buck, 1730

was first to demolish the monastic church, or to require that the new owner demolish it, in a number of cases the church survived and was incorporated into the fabric of the house, which may have been a great advantage at some sites. This expedient was applied not just to sites granted to favoured courtiers such as Sir William Paulet at Netley Abbey, Hampshire, and Sir Thomas Wriothesley at Titchfield Abbey, Hampshire, but also to minor gentry owners, as at Stavordale Priory, Somerset, and Buckland Abbey, Devon.

Another, and less common approach – perhaps because of the costs involved – was to demolish all or most of the monastic buildings and construct a completely new house. Edward Seymour, Duke of Somerset, took this approach at Syon Abbey, Middlesex, building an impressive new mansion of stone, but his steward Sir John Thynne did the same on no less a scale at Longleat Priory, Wiltshire. Others built a new principal house but retained some parts of the monastery as useful ancillary buildings or, as at the London Charterhouse, the church itself for use as a chapel.

There was, therefore, a very wide range of approaches and an equally wide range of owners, resulting in a variety of new houses, in terms of size, architecture and retained monastic features. Some of the new owners were closely involved in the conversion or construction of their house, others delegated; some spent substantial amounts of money to create an impressive residence, others economised and took over the monastic buildings intact. The following detailed studies explore many of these monastic conversions and the men responsible for the transformation.

HE LYVYNGE, WAS AIL AT ONE TYME, AND TO HYS
DEATHE: MASTER OF THE HORSE, TO KYNGE
HENRY THE EYGHT: & AFTER TO KYNGE ED
WARD Ŷ SYXTHE·CAPYTAYNE OF BOTHE THEYR
MAIESTES GENTLEMEN PENTIONERS·CHEFE
STANDARD·BEARER OF ENGLAND·IVSTICE IN OYER
OF AIL THEYRE FORRESTES,PARKES, & CHASES·BE
YOND THE RYVER OF TRENT·NORTHWARD·LEVTE·
NAVNT OF THE FORRESTES OF WYNDSOR,WOLMAI
AND ASHDOWNE·WYTH DYVERS PARKES&CHASES
SOWTWARD·ONE OF THE EXECVTORS, TO KYNGE
HENRY THE EYGHT·ONE OF THEYRE MAIESTES
HONORABLE PRIVE COVNCEIL:&KNYGHT AND
COMPANION, OF THE MOST NOBLE
ORDER, OF THE GARTER:·

HE ENDED HYS LYFE, THE SIXTHE OF MAYE, IN THE SECONDE YERE, OF KYNGE EDWARD THE SIXTHE, 1548.
AT BYFLET HOWSE IN SVRREY, BY HYM BVYLDED·AND LYETH BVRYED AT BATTEL IN SVSSEX, BY DAME ALICE
HYS FYRST WYFE·WHERE HE BE GAN A STATELY HOWSE, SENCE PROCEDED IN, BY HYS SONNE & HEYER
ANTHONY VICECOVNT MOWNTÆGVE·CHEFE STANDARD BEARER OF ENGLAND·LEVTENAVNT OF THE
FORREST OF WYNDSOR, WYTH OTHER PARKES·ONE OF QVENE MARYES HONORABLE PRIVEY COVNCEIL·AND
KNYGHT AND COMPANYON OF THE MOST NOBLE ORDER OF THE GARTER·HE HAD BY DAME ALYCE DAWHTER
TO SIR IOHN GAGE·KNYGHT OF THE MOST NOBLE ORDER OF Ŷ GARTER· CONTROWLER TO KYNGE HENRY Ŷ EYGHT·
& CHAVNCELER OF HYS DOWTCHY OF LANCASTER·& AFTER LORD CHAMBERLEYNE TO QVENE MARY·CONSTABLE OF Ŷ
TOWER OF LVNDON·AND ONE OF THEYRE HONORABLE PRIVEY COVNCEIL·SEAVEN SONNES·ANTHONYE, OF HIS PROPER NAME,
WILLYAM, HENRY, FRANCIS, THOMAS, GEORGE, & HENRY BROWNE·HE HAD AILSO BY HER, THREE DAWGHTERS,MARY,
MABEL, & LVCY·HYS SECOND & LAST WYFE, WAS THE LADY ELYZABETH GARRET·AFTER COVNTES OF LYN
COLNE·AND ONE OF DAWGHTERS, OF GERRALD·ERLE OF KYLDARE·BY WHOME HE HAD TOO SONNES·EDWARD,
AND THOMAS·WHYCH DYED BOTHE, IN THEYRE INFANCIE?

Battle Abbey

The monastic complex at Battle Abbey in East Sussex is unique in England in that it was built as the result of triumph in warfare, as close as possible to the site where William, Duke of Normandy, defeated the forces of King Harold on 14 October 1066. There is speculation as to exactly where the battle was fought, but most sources suggest that it was in the field by the river below the ridge on which the monastic buildings were eventually raised. What is certain, however, is that a majestic Norman Abbey Church was built on the spot where Harold was thought to have fallen, slain by an arrow piercing his eye, and a stone tablet records the commemoration today on the high altar of the vanished Church. William had ordered, as an act of atonement for the violence of his conquest, that a monastery be constructed on the site of the battle, but the valley was swampy and the slope presented construction difficulties, so the hilltop site was levelled instead and work was begun on the Abbey Church. Its choir was consecrated in 1076 and the entire Church was completed in 1094, after which work began on the Cloister and the build-ings of the outer court. The precinct of the Benedictine establishment was accessed from the town via an imposing Gatehouse, its offices set around the Cloister.

In 1529 John Hammond was elected Abbot of Battle and he was to be the last head of the community. Thomas Cromwell's notorious visitor, Dr Richard Layton, made a visit in the summer of 1535 and described Hammond as 'the veriest hayne, beetle and buserde and arentest chorle that ever I see' ('the meanest wretch, numb-skull and dim-wit, and the most out-and-out bumpkin I ever met').[1] The abbey's income at this time was £880 per annum, so it escaped the first round of the Dissolution under the *Valor*. However, in May 1538, Layton was at Battle again, taking an inventory of the contents; when that was completed, Hammond surrendered the abbey. Soon after, in August, King Henry gifted the

55 Sir Anthony Browne, a posthumous portrait of the late sixteenth century

56 The Gatehouse at Battle Abbey

abbey site to Sir Anthony Browne, a consummate courtier. The Letters Patent state that Browne received the 'grant in fee of the house and site of the late abbey of Battle, Sussex, now dissolved, the church, steeple, and churchyard thereof'.[2]

Browne was the son of Sir Anthony Browne senior, Standard Bearer of England, and had been in royal service since 1518, acting in several embassies and later as ambassador to the French Court. He was made a privy councillor and Master of the Horse in 1539, and served as an MP and JP. After receiving Battle from the king, who visited him there in 1539, Browne was subsequently made a Knight of the Garter, the insignia of which order he wears in a portrait (*55*) painted after his death in 1548. It is a strange image of an almost androgynous figure, with full red lips and a prominent nose, looking somewhat wistfully into the distance. He is dressed in an off-the-shoulder tunic, richly embroidered, while his head is covered with a bejewelled cap sporting, in royal allegiance, a red English rose. However, it is the inscription on the painting that warrants detailed scrutiny. It reports that he died at his house in Byfleet 'by hym buylded' and that he lies in Battle 'where he began a statly howse, sence proceded in, by hys sonne & heyer Anthony Vicecount Mowntaegue'. This confirms that Browne was a builder and that his son must have continued his father's works at Battle after 1548.

The monastic precinct set within the town of Battle, which grew up as a result of the complex, is guarded by the majestic amber-coloured stone Gatehouse (*56*), its south return wall revealing a blocked Norman arch of the original eleventh-century construction. It was extensively rebuilt and expanded in the mid-fourteenth century and extended again after the Dissolution. The Courthouse range

to the left on the approach up the slope from the main street is the first indication of the reconstruction that was carried out by Sir Anthony Browne's son, Viscount Montague. It is typical Tudor work with cross-mullioned windows and a battlemented parapet. Through the archway the Brownes' mansion, adapted from the former Abbot's Lodging, can be seen in the distance, subsumed within nineteenth and twentieth-century additions, now the home of Battle Abbey School. To view Browne and his son's original work it is necessary to follow the visitor route around the perimeter of the grounds and head for the two hexagonal towers of the Guest House on the terrace walk overlooking the battlefield. Here a great battery of off-set buttresses supports what is left of the apartments, a cavernous vaulted undercroft of the two-storey, eleven-bay range that the Brownes rebuilt after 1538. Although the Guest House has gone, it is depicted in the earliest of the known drawings of the abbey, which dates from about 1700, and again in a 1737 engraving (*57*) by Samuel and Nathaniel Buck.[3] The early drawing is a bird's-eye view taken from above the battlefield to the south of the precinct and corresponds closely with the Bucks' engraving. Like the Courthouse addition to the Gatehouse, the Guest House was lit by a grid of cross-mullioned windows and two oriels giving views across the battle site, all topped by a battlemented parapet. It was L-shaped in form and connected with the Abbot's Lodging, which is shown as two parallel structures aligned north-south: the Abbot's Hall to the west, lit by a tall traceried window in its south end wall, and a parallel section to the east that originally gave onto the Cloister; to the right on the same alignment is the Dorter where the monks slept (*58*). Although roofless and breached at the north end, the shell of this vast building survives today. Its

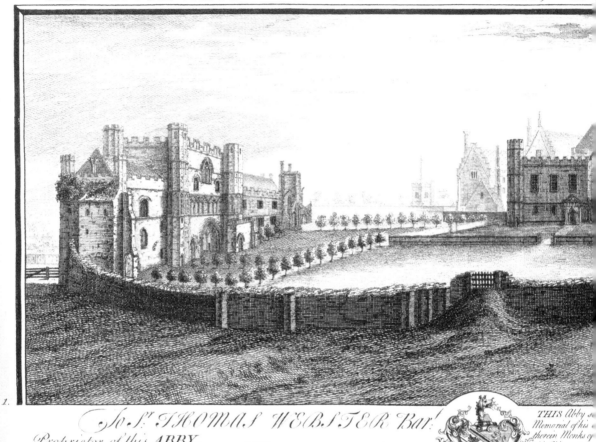

57 *The South-West View of Battel-Abby in the County of Sussex*, engraved by Samuel and Nathaniel Buck, 1737

Spot of Ground on which King Harold fell was founded by the Conqueror in...
...ts might be made for ye Souls of ye Slain. He dedicated it to St. Martin & placing...
...tow bestow'd upon it his Royal Manour of Wye, which according to ye Chronicles of...
...dreds, and granted it many ample Privileges, among ye rest Exemption from Episcopal...
...not taken away by Act of Parliament it still maintains. It was a large & Noble...
...ye Gateway (still entire) and ye other Remains. At ye Dissolution it was much...
...Browne & his Son Anthony Lord Visc.t Montacute built ye stately Pile on ye south...
...ued in that Noble Family till lately purchas'd by Sr. Thos. Webster Bar.t It had...
...ed at £80.0.0 75. Dn...

Novice's Chamber and Common Room on the lower floor, columned and rib-vaulted, are atmospherically numinous. Browne demolished all the other mediaeval buildings – Abbey Church, Chapter House, Frater and kitchen – but retained the Lodging for his mansion and the Guest House, which was remodelled, for additional accommodation.

At the northern end of the Dorter there is an open view to the left across what would have been the Cloister towards the rear east wall of the former Abbot's Lodging. Harold Brakspear's plan of the abbey complex, drawn up when he was called in after 1931 to restore the Abbot's Lodging, shows how the Dorter connected with other buildings now lost: the Parlour, Chapter House and the south transept of the Abbey Church (**59**). The rear wall of the Lodging provides a remarkable template of destruction and regeneration, not to mention an informative chronology of stylistic details from the thirteenth century to the fifteenth (**60**). At the southern end was the Frater that projected east towards the Dorter, with which it was connected by a stair, the stub of its south wall still surviving, sprouting the ribs of a lancet window. There are further thirteenth-century lancet windows with Y-tracery from the vanished Frater to the right, above which are traces of Romanesque arcading, and then comes the filigree tracery – thirteenth- and fifteenth-century – of the Cloister walk. Above this were the abbot's apartments and, set back to the west, the Abbot's Hall connected to a Great Chamber and private chapel. The fenestration on the upper floors of this façade has been altered and the top two storeys covered in unsympathetic render.

Tragically, there was a fire on the night of 31 January 1931, which gutted most of the Abbot's Lodging, but a watercolour of 1783 by

58 An aerial photograph of Battle Abbey, showing the layout of the site

Samuel Hieronymus Grimm shows what the interior of the Abbot's Hall looked like at the time.[4] Grimm's view is taken from the south, with the great window shown on the 1700 drawing of the building, the west wall lit by three more towering windows and the lower wall hung with portraits (*61*). Grimm also painted the external, west elevation of the Lodging, which comprised three separate elements.[5] There was a three-bay northern section with a pedimented classical doorway, the Abbot's Hall set back in the middle, and a further four-bay range to the south. This connected with the Guest House, its eastern end still intact, though the majority of the structure had been demolished. Interestingly, this south-east element of the Guest House

survived until at least 1784, when it is shown in a drawing by Francis Grose, later published in the *Beauties of England and Wales* (*62*).

Much of the former Abbot's Lodging was restored and altered after the 1931 fire by the architect Harold Brakspear.[6] His ground floor plan of the house identifies the monastic footprint of the former Abbot's Lodging, with its L-shaped section to the north, later infilled at the north-west corner, and the Abbot's, or Great, Hall to the south fronted on its east flank by the 'Abbot's Parlour' and a Dining Room. Another early view of the Great Hall, when the house was owned by Sir Augustus Webster, taken from the same vantage point as Grimm's watercolour, reveals that Gothick panelling had been installed by Sir Godfrey

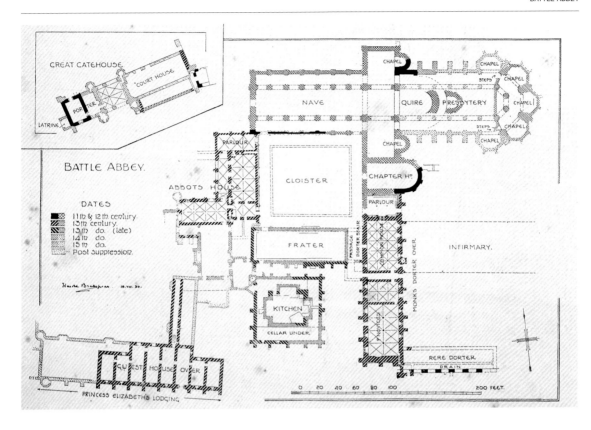

59 Harold Brakspear's plan of Battle Abbey

60 The Lodging at Battle Abbey

115

Great Hall at Battle Abbey.

Engraved by F.Hay, from a Drawing by F.Grose, Esq?.

for the Beauties of England & Wales.

62 Battle Abbey as it appeared in Francis Grose's late eighteenth-century drawing, engraved by F Hay in 1811

61 Samuel Hieronymus Grimm's view of the imposing Great Hall at Battle Abbey, 1783

Webster in a major restoration campaign he undertook at the Abbey after returning to Battle in 1812. Sir Godfrey also had the Abbey Church excavated and, in a true spirit of reverence and historicism, commissioned a huge canvas of the Battle of Hastings from Frank Wilkin, which still hangs in the Great Hall of the Abbey School.

63 Thomas Wriothesley, Hans Holbein the Younger, *c.*1536-43

Beaulieu Abbey

Beaulieu Abbey is situated on the south coast, at the edge of the New Forest, six miles from Southampton and overlooking the River Beaulieu. It was founded in 1205 on land gifted to the monks by King John and was the largest Cistercian house in England.[1] The site of the great Abbey Church is today marked in outline in the grass, in the heart of the precinct, enclosed by the ruined mediaeval walls. Some of the monastic buildings still remain, although most were demolished at the Dissolution and the stone used towards the building of a series of coastal defensive forts for Henry VIII in the 1540s. Following its suppression in 1538, the abbey was granted to Thomas Wriothesley (*63*), a few months after he had been granted nearby Titchfield Abbey.

Beaulieu is unique among Cistercian abbeys in having both gate-houses remaining.[2] The Outer Gatehouse survives as a garden feature, while the Great Gatehouse was converted after the Dissolution into a residence, now, after much expansion, Palace House (*64*). A second Tudor house was converted from the lay brothers' quarters in the west range of the Cloister, now called the *Domus*. The Frater became Beaulieu parish church, which can be seen in the aerial photograph (*65*).

Beaulieu Abbey had its origins in 1203, when King John granted to the Abbey of Cîteaux, as the head house of the Cistercian order, the manor of Faringdon in Berkshire, where some monks of the order had established themselves. This grant was on condition that a monastery should be built there.[3] Two years later, on 25 January 1205, John founded the monastery of St Mary of Beaulieu in the New Forest, with provision for thirty monks. On 16 August, 1205, the king sent letters to all the Cistercian abbots entreating their assistance in the building of the new abbey.[4] The Church seems to have been largely completed by 1227 when the Annals of Waverley describe the monks of Beaulieu as entering with great joy into their new Church on the Vigil of the Assumption.[5]

However, the Cloister and conventual buildings as a whole were not ready for occupation until 1246. On 17 June of that year the convent was dedicated by the Bishop of Winchester in the presence of King Henry III and Queen Eleanor of Provence, Prince Edward, the Earl of Cornwall,

64 Palace House, Beaulieu, converted from the Great Gatehouse

65 An aerial view of Beaulieu Abbey, with the site of the Abbey Church marked out and the parish church, converted from the Frater, south of the Cloister

and a great concourse of prelates and magnates. At the feast of the dedication the abbot made an offering of 500 marks and the king confirmed 239 acres of land in the New Forest.[6]

The monastery of Netley was colonised from Beaulieu in 1239 and in 1246 twenty monks and thirty lay brothers were sent from Beaulieu to establish the monastery of Hailes in Gloucestershire. About the same time another party of monks left Beaulieu to colonise the newly founded monastery of Newenham in Devon.[7] In common with other abbeys, Beaulieu was frequently visited by kings, and Henry III is recorded as visiting again in December 1268, while Edward I and Eleanor of Castile were also frequent visitors.

The precinct at Beaulieu was an area of around 58 acres enclosed by a wall about 12 feet high and a mile long, of which substantial sections survive. The Outer Gatehouse in the precinct wall gave onto a small lane, on the east side of which was the mill. At the end of the lane was the Great Gatehouse, beyond which was the Outer Court. The Cistercian statutes required that 'the stables of horses must be placed within the circuit of our abbeys and no house for habitation may be built without the gate, unless for animals, on account of avoiding the dangers of souls.'[9] In the Outer Court would be the guesthouses, stables, brewhouse, malthouse and workshops.

There are surviving monastic accounts, covering a single year from autumn 1269 to autumn 1270, which throw some light on life at the abbey in the mediaeval period. The accounts show expenditure for the various activities that combined to support the monastery as a self-contained institution, including a forester, shepherd, piggery, stables and forge. There were two infirmaries, one for monks and one for the lay brothers, a guest-house, a cellar and brewhouse, a granary, a

mill and a bakehouse.[10] There were also a parchment-maker, a shoe-maker and a skinner, as well as a carpenter, plumber and cooper, who would all have had workshops in the Outer Court.[11] Beaulieu aspired to be entirely self-supporting, as the Rule of St Benedict requires:

> The monastery should, if possible, be so arranged that all necessary things, such as water, mill, garden, and various crafts may be situated within the enclosure, so that the monks may not be compelled to wander outside, for that is not at all expedient for their souls.[12]

The Church and Cloister were in the middle of the precinct, with the monks' Infirmary to the east. Further eastward of these are two small fishponds, fed by a brook. The Church at Beaulieu covered a greater area than any other Cistercian church in this country.[13] It was 336 feet long and 186 feet wide and, as shown in the plan by Harold Brakspear (66), unlike any other English church but almost the same as the one at Cîteaux.[14] The master mason was a Frenchman, Durand, who had been responsible for building Rouen Cathedral.[15] The presbytery had an apse with an aisle, 12 feet wide, continued round it, and ten radiating chapels beyond. The nave and both transepts had aisles, and there was probably a low tower over the crossing.[16] Nothing of the Church remains standing except the south wall of the nave, next to the Cloister, but the foundations can still be seen.

The Cloister, 138 feet square, was to the south of the Church. On the east side were the Sacristy and Chapter House with the Dorter above and a projecting rere-dorter on the east. On the south side of the Cloister were the warming-house, kitchen and Frater, while in

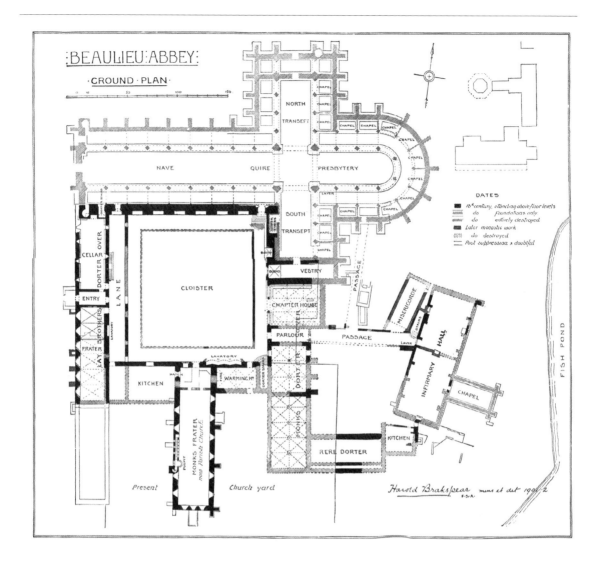

the west range was a long *Cellarium* containing lay brothers' buildings. To the east of these claustral buildings was the monks' Infirmary, consisting of a large hall, chapel, kitchen and the misericord.[17] The Frater, which projects from the south side of the Cloister, is 30 feet wide and 130 feet long. It has been preserved, as it was converted for use as a parish church soon after the Dissolution. In the west wall is the pulpit, reached by a narrow flight of steps in the wall, from which readings would be given at mealtimes when it was the monastic

Frater. At the back of the pulpit is an early example of a traceried window.[18]

In 1535 The *Valor* gave the gross annual value of Beaulieu as just over £428, and the net value of approximately £326.[19] This valuation made it one of the larger abbeys, and so not included in the first suppression. Under the Act of 1536, dissolving the lesser monasteries, more than two-thirds of the Cistercian abbeys were suppressed. Their inmates were, as a rule, transferred to the larger houses of the order. In March 1536, Abbot Browning of

72

Pl.1

BEAULIEU ABBEY, HAMPSHIRE.
Pub.d 7 Dec. 1783, by S. Hooper.

S. Sparrow

67 *Beaulieu Abbey, Hampshire*, engraved by S Sparrow, 1783

66 Harold Brakspear's plan of Beaulieu Abbey

Beaulieu died and Thomas Stevens, Abbot of Netley, was appointed his successor. In the following February Netley was suppressed, and all the monks went to their motherhouse at Beaulieu. Shortly after Stevens' appointment as abbot, he was eager to curry favour with Thomas Wriothesley. Hearing through a servant that he wanted a horse, 'My Lord of Beaulieu said he had nothing but should be at your commandment, and sent his men to take up for you his own riding horse, which you will receive herewith. His only fault is that he is too little for you, though the biggest in all his park.'[20]

On 2 April 1538 the abbot signed the surrender of Beaulieu to the commissioners Layton, Petre and Freeman, and induced twenty of the monks to do the same. The site was immediately granted to Thomas Wriothesley, on payment of £1,340 6s 8d.[21]

Crayford wrote to him on 17 April saying that Abbot Stevens, immediately before his

68 The *Domus*, converted from the lay brothers' range, seen from the Chapter House

surrender, let out the mill and parsonage of Beaulieu and the lodge at St Leonard's grange to his sister. On 26 April the ex-abbot wrote to Wriothesley, protesting against the detraction of his 'lewd monks, which now, I thank God, I am rid of'.[22] Abbot Stevens obtained a pension of 100 marks, and seventeen of the monks also received small pensions.[23]

The grant to Wriothesley was of 'the house and site of the late monastery of Beaulieu alias de Bello Loco Regis, Hants., the church, steeple, and churchyard of the same; the manor of Beaulieu, and the great close of Beaulieu'.[24] He converted the Great Gatehouse into a small residence, illustrated as it appeared in 1776, in *The Antiquities of England and Wales* (*67*). Wriothesley possibly intended it as a hunting lodge, at the heart of his newly acquired Beaulieu. He also extended the Gatehouse northward, with two projecting wings, whilst

the carriageway entrance was converted into a room, which had a Tudor fireplace until the 1880s.[25] These Tudor wings were demolished when the house was extended in the 1870s.[26] Additionally, a second house was constructed on the site, by adapting the *Cellarium,* including the lay brothers' quarters, which were in the west range of the Cloister. This monastic building was on two levels. On the upper level was the lay brothers' Dorter; on the lower level there was a four-bay cellar abutting the Church to the north, with a central passage through from the east into the Cloister, and the six-bay lay brothers' Frater to the south.

The original vault over the cellar was taken down and replaced by a single-span barrel vault, and the passage was also covered with a simple barrel vault. On the upper storey the side walls of the Dorter were retained to their full height.[27] To the south of the passage, in the former Frater, two bays were separated from the rest by a wall with a very large Tudor fireplace.[28] The room beyond this wall adjoined the monastic kitchen, which may have been retained, so its use as a hall is possible. The rest of the range to the south was originally single storey and probably served as the Lay Infirmary. It was covered after the Dissolution with a double-barrel vault carried on a dividing wall, and a storey added above.[29] Along with the former Dorter this would have provided extensive upper-level accommodation. The north wall of the building had to be newly built because of the demolition of the Church and contains Tudor two-light transomed windows. The whole building was covered in a tie-beam and purlin roof, of which the northern part was mediaeval, while the southern part, where the extra storey was added, was Tudor.[30]

The entire building was, therefore, of considerable size, around 290 feet by 35 feet and on two levels. The northern part, called the *Domus*, survives (**68**), but the southern part, the former lay brothers' Infirmary, was largely demolished, with only the lower section of the western wall remaining. Though these new houses were Wriothesley's secondary residences, on a far smaller scale than Titchfield, together they provided sufficient accommodation to entertain even royal visitors.

In common with the Tudor monarchs, James I adopted a pattern of summer progresses after he came to the throne in 1603, and Beaulieu was frequently on his itinerary for his visit to the south-west; he visited Beaulieu nine times during his reign, usually in August or September. James visited Beaulieu for the first time in 1606, perhaps as a mark of favour to the 3rd Earl of Southampton, but his love of hunting was probably a motive for his subsequent visits. In August

1613 the entertainment prepared for the king is detailed in the accounts of the Treasurer of the Chamber under 'Apparellings'. Richard Coningsby, Gentleman Usher, assisted by nine yeoman ushers and grooms of the Wardrobe or Chamber, spent four days in preparation for the King 'to see the play at football' and two days for him 'to see the Bull-baytinge'.[31] Although the royal entourage on progress was much smaller than at one of the main palaces in London, it still involved a large number of people. James I's frequent stays at Beaulieu suggest that the two houses must have been impressive and spacious.

Bindon Abbey

The oldest complete garden in Dorset surviving in its original form may have been begun soon after 1544, in the last years of Henry VIII, by Thomas Howard, second son of Thomas, the 3rd Duke of Norfolk, in what had been the grounds of the Cistercian Abbey of Bindon in the parish of Wool. Thomas was a cousin of Elizabeth Tudor who, when she became queen, made him 1st Viscount Bindon in 1559.[1] He died in 1582, by which time it is reasonable to suppose his ornamental gardens were in their prime. What makes Bindon so fascinating is not only its melancholy beauty, but the possibility that Lord Howard of Bindon was following a much earlier pattern of monastic hydraulics when he laid out his own watery grounds. The surviving Abbey House was built, originally as a garden building, for Thomas Weld at the end of the eighteenth century (**69**).

The Cistercians had settled at Great Bindon in 1172 for the potential of its water. Roger de Newburgh and his wife Matilda had built the abbey here after they had transferred the earlier monastic community from nearby Little Bindon. The Frome flows through a flat and, scenically speaking, rather dull area of the county, where it can be channelled, sluiced and controlled to water a wide fertile area. Their Abbey Church, a modest structure, lay within sound of the roar of two mill weirs. One mill, now lost, was for fulling cloth, the other was a grist mill, whose picturesque mill house, once smothered in old roses and deserted because of floods, like something painted by George Morland, has been carefully restored. Even in a dry summer the flow of the river over its weir is frighteningly strong and the abbey buildings actually lie well below the Frome's level above the weir. Bindon is a place where the river has to be handled firmly and skilfully, otherwise the fields would revert to marshland.

Thomas Howard was the river tamer the site needed, but he was not the man who first received the abbey property after the monks were expelled in 1539. In the *Valor* of 1535 its annual income was valued at

69 Bindon Abbey House

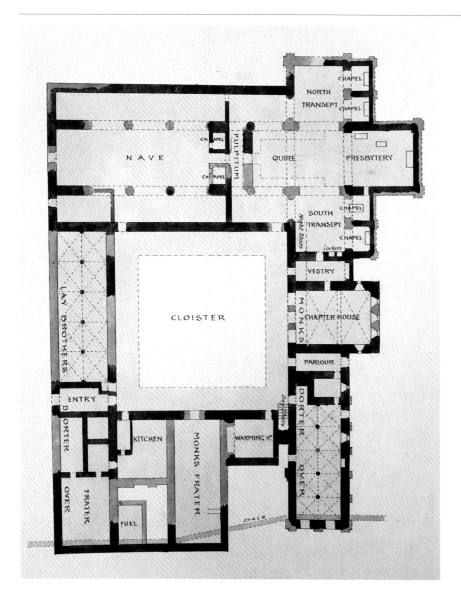

On the plan the following labels appear:

NAVE, CHAPEL, PULPITUM, QUIRE, PRESBYTERY, NORTH TRANSEPT, CHAPEL, CHAPEL, SOUTH TRANSEPT, CHAPEL, CHAPEL, Night Stairs, Lockers, VESTRY, CHAPTER HOUSE, MONKS, PARLOUR, CLOISTER, LAY BROTHERS, ENTRY, DORTER, DORTER OVER, Day Stairs, KITCHEN, MONKS FRATER, WARMING H., FRATER OVER, FUEL, Drain

£147 and it was scheduled for dissolution, but Abbot John Norman paid the Crown the vast sum of £300 to save it.[2] As a result, the abbey was re-founded in November of that year, the Letters Patent depicting two bishops and three monks making subservient obeisance to the king.[3] After its subsequent suppression in 1539, the abbey was granted in 1540 to Sir Thomas Poynings, who was to serve the king as Marshal of Calais and Keeper of the Castle at Guînes. Nervous, perhaps, of all the water at Bindon, Poynings shunned the complex site. Instead, he began its enduring relationship with Lulworth by using materials from the abbey to build a hunting lodge, Mount Poynings, a mile to the west of present day Lulworth Castle. Poynings died in Boulogne in 1545 and Howard, his brother-in-law, bought Bindon from Poynings' brother Edward and settled down there, turning the domestic

70 Brakspear's plan of Bindon Abbey

ranges of the abbey into a 'fair Mansion'.[4]

The buildings that Thomas Howard had bought lay in a rectangular complex (**70**) with the towered Abbey Church to the north and a Cloister to the south, around which were disposed the abbey apartments, all serviced by a hydraulic system of sluices and channels to the east.[5] A stream drawn off the Frome up-river entered this square of monastic structures at its south-western point, by the lay brothers' Dorter. It then ran along the south range, turned slightly to service the monks' Dorter on the east range, after which it was fed on the east to rejoin the river. Perhaps in 1544, only five years after the Dissolution, there would still have been some pensioned-off monks or skilled monastery servants in Wool village, who understood the system of sluices that kept these waters flowing. Using their labour and expertise Howard expanded the water-works boldly, digging out two large moated squares of garden, the lesser to the south-west of his courtyard house, the larger, with its big garden mount, immediately to the east. In both of these ambitious new gardens the flow of water along their canals was kept moving by an extension of the same system of sluices

that the monks had been using for the past three centuries.

That is a simplification of the garden canals at Bindon. In addition to these two broad, square moats of water and the Frome itself there is another fast-moving channel, cut in the nineteenth century, possibly as a trout stream for Cardinal Weld, who loved fishing. This flows over gravel between the river and the larger moated square of garden. A much older, slower channel runs between the two squares and the road. These two moated gardens with their canals make up a Tudor water garden on a grand scale, one befitting the house of a cousin of the queen.

To hydraulic engineering Lord Bindon added wit in the form of conceits, one to each garden within its moats. In the centre of the smaller garden is a little lozenge-shaped pond with a lozenge-shaped inner island. The larger garden has its inner horseshoe-shaped moat curled around a viewing mount.

The 3rd Viscount Bindon, the first viscount's second son, Thomas, who inherited the estates in 1600 after the death of his older brother Henry, was another builder. Previously, in 1586 at Waterston Manor, he had added a rich

71 The Lodge at Bindon Abbey

classical frontispiece to the vernacular fabric, and in 1608 he was adding a new gallery to the monastic buildings at Bindon. But it was this Lord Bindon, ultimately, who would be responsible for the decline and fall of the abbey. In 1605, using the abbey stones and materials from Mount Poynings, he began to build that quintessential Jacobean conceit, Lulworth Castle.[6] Perhaps he had tired of Bindon's damps and floods, but he was also intent on luring King James I to stay at an impressive hunting lodge out on Purbeck.

After his death in 1611 his cousin and successor, the extravagantly corrupt old seadog Thomas Howard, 1st Earl of Suffolk, succeeded in doing just that. Lulworth Castle was launched socially by the royal visit in

1615 and Bindon fell into neglect. When the 2nd Earl of Suffolk, Theophilus, ruined by his larger than life father, became strapped for cash in 1641 he sold both Bindon and Lulworth to a wealthy London merchant, Humphrey Weld. The epic Dorset story of its most remarkable county family, the staunchly Roman Catholic Welds, was thereby inaugurated at the worst possible time for such recusants, only a year before the Civil Wars broke out with the triumphs of militant Protestantism. During the course of the wars' marching and counter-marching Bindon Abbey's mansion was burnt down in 1644, but its gardens have lingered on, virtually unchanged in benign neglect, one of Dorset's rarest and least noted treasures.

Today, from the East Stoke to Wool road, nothing is visible except a low line of concealing woodland; though at the corner beyond Bindon Farm the road crosses one of the feeder channels that still keep the gardens alive, and all these water meadows are dotted with sluice gates. This is the land, 'a green trough of sappiness and humidity', which Thomas Hardy uses as the setting for some of the most nightmarish episodes in his *Tess of the d'Urbervilles*. It is his 'Vale of the Great Dairies' where the Frome runs clear and rapid, 'with pebbly shallows that prattled to the sky all day long'.

At a break in the woods where a drive comes out from Bindon a passing motorist can get a glimpse of the improbable fantasy world of the gardens. Two airily amateur buildings, the Lodge and the Retreat House stand one behind the other, styled in that appealing Gothick of the late eighteenth century which preceded AWN Pugin's scholarly muscularity. Nearest to the road is the Lodge (*71*), a turreted three-bay carriage shelter with cramped accommodation above. Now much decayed, it is still an engaging garden building in faded pastel colours, oxblood, grey-blue and dark ochre, embattled and pinnacled. Its wooden gates have cusped and interlaced tracery like a page from some contemporary antiquarian pattern book explaining the growth of Gothic architecture from the Romanesque. This and the Retreat House are Gothick intruders and belong to a later Weldian episode of the grounds, one more connected to the ruined abbey than to the Tudor gardens.

Immediately behind the Lodge lie the canals of the smaller garden, dredged but not disciplined, as a wild water garden of yellow water lilies, reeds and bullrushes. The moated island garden itself is quite flat and covered in rough grass and meadow flowers. At its centre is the lozenge-shaped pond with its small lozenge-shaped inner island, a retreat within a retreat, access to which is via a plank bridge over the slowly moving, lily-covered waters. While the water features at Bindon tend to be described as ornamental canals, this maze of rectangular pools is still trout filled and kept moving by at least eleven sluices linked to the water meadows. It is inconceivable that these pools would not have served as larders as well as for the fashionable gentry sport of fly fishing.

It is only possible to speculate as to the nature of the wooden pleasaunce or seat which must have occupied Bindon's island, but its planting may have been similar to that at William Cecil, Lord Burghley's Great Garden at Theobalds, which had nine frets: fences enclosing a square and twined about with fruit espaliers and rose bushes.[7] So the outer raised walk around Bindon's first square island, or the shore of its inner island, may have had similar screening frets. They would have given a purpose to the second and larger moated garden because its high mount would have overlooked the other's privacy. This second presents an entirely different experience to the first garden. A wide plank bridge, in its original Tudor position, leads into a solemn world of dark trees over wide, shadowed waters. Beeches, alders, sycamore and ash have taken over the whole square island, including the steep mount that rises by two stages in its centre. There are two raised walks: one around the island's shore and a parallel, longer walk around the outside of the moat (*72*). Either would have given the ladies of the house their exercise for the day. The atmosphere here is almost Arthurian, a quiet green gloom of short vistas, its silence broken only by the occasional splash of a brown trout rising in the moat. Everything is enclosed: a

72 A Canal Walk at Bindon Abbey

world of leaves and water with no sky.

This is the magical melancholy of the second garden today, but in its original concept it must have been very different. Pattern rather than flower colour was the essence of Tudor gardening. Low hedges or 'pallisadoes' of juniper, whitethorn, sweet briar and osier, set around with strawberries, primroses and violets, were staple features bordering turfed or gravel paths. The mount is partly surrounded by a horseshoe-shaped moat and it had a circling terrace half way up for viewing the patterns of these hedges. On the top would have been a wooden pavilion from which all the geometric knots and frets of the neighbouring island garden could have been enjoyed. Theobalds had a similar feature, which is described in 1613: 'There is also a little wood

nearby. At the end you come to a small round hill built of earth with a labyrinth around. [It] is called the Venusberg.'[8] This accords with the larger garden at Bindon, which may well have had a maze on the inner island, with the central mount as a tribute to Elizabeth as the Goddess of Love. The garden would have been sunny and extroverted where now it creates a mood of gloom and introversion.

Bindon Abbey haunted the consciences of the Welds in almost every generation. As ardent, persecuted yet still influential landed gentry they must always have dreamed of a Bindon restored to the monks. The brief reign of James II would have given them an equally brief charge of hope. Otherwise they lay low, paying their additional, punitive taxes, sending their sons to universities in Flanders for a

Catholic education and marrying their children off to the children of fellow recusant gentry. Half of a yellowing plan (*73*) of 'BINDON *ABBY* near WARE now in RUIN's' survives among the Weld papers.[9] The date is ripped off, but it was prepared for Edward Weld II, who died in 1775, and an inscription states that 'L' is 'intended for a Fish Pond in 1765'. Another of 1806, drawn on vellum and beautifully coloured for Thomas Weld, 'the Builder' as the family called him, shows the abbey complete with Thomas' arms in one corner.[10] This is the most detailed of all the Weld plans of the monastic establishment – there are five other reconstructions of the complex, nineteenth-century in style but undated and roughly drawn – and shows the configuration of the apartments around the monastic Cloister (*74*). So the site was something of an obsession for Thomas who 'was at the expense of clearing away the rubbish, in order to ascertain the disposition of the whole abbey'.[11] The parts of the ground plan coloured red are elements of the abbey that 'are not visible at present but remembered'. Weld also discovered the 1310 tomb slab of Richard de Manners, with the shadow of its lost brass image, which is still present in what was the south transept of the Abbey Church.

Thomas Weld's account books for the various years prove that in 1793 he was learning to think Gothic instead of the classical he had lately deployed in building his Catholic Chapel at Lulworth, paying for his agent John Hunt to make notes on Gothic churches during his several journeys about the country.[12] On 5 September 1793 money was given 'To Hunt to pay journeys spent in seeing Cathedrals £3.17.6 & £21'. On 18 October in York, Thomas seems to have studied that cathedral personally. The note for the day reads: 'Seeing the Cathedral 2.6'; and on the

next day: 'For cloaths at York making in all £4.10.6', which indicates that the visit was multi-purposed. Then, on 11 December, Thomas seems to have moved decisively with: 'to Cox [his contractor] for mending the road to Bindon 12.6', followed on 23 December by the mysterious: 'Paid ye two old men at Bindon up to this day inclusively £2.1.0'.[13]

The illustration of the site in John Hutchins' *The History and Antiquities of the County of Dorset* (*75*), taken in 1773, shows the mill house, accessed by a stone bridge across the river as it is today, behind a range of the ruined nave of the Abbey Church.[14] After 1793 the Bindon payments to carpenters and labourers multiply, culminating on 29 June 1794 in: 'To Cox for cleaning ponds at Bindon'. So the gardens were being restored while the new Gothick structures were going up. An entry of 6 July in 1796 of '£500 to Mr Tasker pd reemander of the principle' suggests, though does not prove, that John Tasker was the architect, moving from the classical dome of his 1780s Lulworth Chapel to an elegantly spiny, but quite unscholarly, essay in the Gothick style. The mason, Joseph Towsey of Blandford, was paid £55 11s on 11 August 1794, an advance on the £500 he would be owed. A final costing 'For ye Abby House & premises' of £1913 5s was made, presumably for both buildings, the Retreat House and the Lodge, on 27 July 1798.

It is not easy to describe the 'Abby House', for it is like no other garden building in England. In its original form it had four modest rooms on the ground floor with a much taller single room, the Chapel, on the first floor. As recorded in Pevsner's 1972 *The Buildings of England* volume for Dorset, when this was still consecrated, it had three large windows with simple Y-tracery and a plaster groin vault supported on groups of emaciated

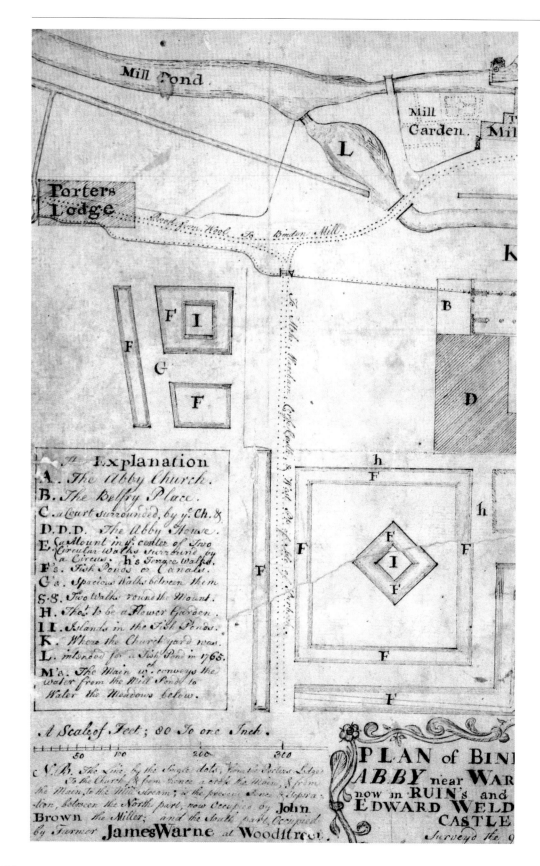

Mill Pond.

Mill
Garden.

Mill

L

Porters
Lodge

Road from Wool, To Bindon Mill.

F'
I

F

G

F

Explanation
A . The Abby Church.
B . The Belfry Place.
C . a Court surrounded, by ye Ch. &
D.D.D . The Abby House.
E . a Mount in ye center of Two
  Circular Walks surrounded by
  a Circus. h's Terrace Walks.
F's . Fish Ponds or Canals.
G's . Spacious Walks between them
S.S. Two Walks round the Mount.
H . That to be a Flower Garden.
I I . Islands in the Fish Ponds.
K . Where the Church yard was.
L . intended for a Fish Pond in 1765.
M's . The Main ye conveys the
  water from the Mill Pond to
  Water the Meadows below.

h
F

h

B

D

F'
I
F'

F

F

F

F

A Scale of Feet; 80 To one Inch.

50   100   200   300

N.B. The Line by the Single dots, from the Porters Lodge
to the Church & from thence across the Main, & from
the Main, to the Mill stream; is the present Line & Separa-
tion, between the North part, now Occupied by John
Brown the Miller; and the South part, Occupied
by Farmer James Warne at Woodstreet.

PLAN of BIN
ABBY near WAR
now in RUIN's and
EDWARD WELD
CASTLE
Surveyd the

134

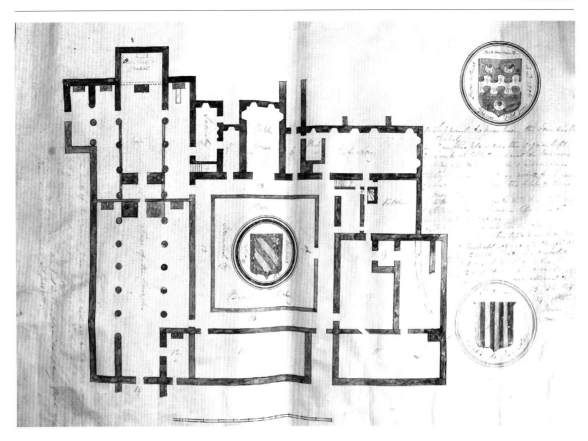

74 Plan of Bindon Abbey, 1806

73 The 1765 plan of Bindon Abbey showing the Water Gardens

Early English Gothic shafts with an altar on the blind east end.[15] Thomas Weld may have taken the lean Gothic shafts from the Chapter House at York Minster. It was a building of much charm and great significance for the Catholic community. While not registered as a place of worship until 1885, it clearly functioned as one from 1798 onwards.[16] At the same time that it was built, a grotto was hollowed out of the Tudor garden mount, so there was some concept in Thomas Weld's mind of devotion and pleasure being combined in one garden: a retreat house with humble accommodation below and a chapel above. The revived Tudor gardens and the ruins of the real Abbey would have acted as reminders of a lost age of faith.

It is impossible to leave this extraordinary site without mentioning the use which Hardy made of it in *Tess of the d'Urbervilles*. Woolbridge Manor, upstream from Bindon, was where Angel Clare and Tess came for their ill-fated honeymoon and he discovered with horror that she had lost her innocence some years earlier to the unscrupulous Alec. In an improbable piece of writing the distressed

75 John Hutchins' *South East View of Bindon Abbey*, engraved by James Basire, 1773

Angel sleep-walks out of the house with Tess in his arms, carries her across the Frome on a narrow plank bridge and, coming to the ruined choir of the Abbey Church, lays the frightened girl in 'the empty stone coffin of an abbot' against the north wall of the church. Still fast asleep, he kisses her twice on the lips, 'when he immediately fell into the deep dead slumber of exhaustion' beside her. Tess manages to raise him up, without waking him, and guides him back, still implausibly fast asleep, this time over the stone road bridge, to bed again. Hardy has brushed the Welds' Retreat House out of the chapter, but the empty stone coffin (*76*) still lies in the north transept of the Abbey Church, and all the other features of his melodrama survive in the grounds of Bindon Abbey, preserved by the traditional piety and historic awareness of the Weld family.

76 The empty stone coffin in the north transept of the Abbey Church, in which Hardy's Tess of the d'Urbervilles lay

Bisham Abbey

Bisham lies on the south bank of the River Thames in Berkshire, eight miles upstream from Windsor and thirty miles from London. A ridge of wooded hills rises steeply to the east, while the Church of All Saints stands on the riverbank about 218 yards north of the house. The house is in a formerly moated enclosure, around 328 yards square, and covering an area of about twenty-two acres. The moat has now been filled in, apart from a short northerly section. Bisham is highly unusual in that the site originally comprised both an Augustinian priory, largely demolished after the Dissolution, and a manor house that, even after the manor itself had been granted to the priory, was retained by the Earls of Salisbury. The house has survived intact, but of the priory only a part of the Cloister, a dovecote and barns remain. The rest of the site is today overlain with sports facilities at what is now the National Sports Centre. Bisham is also unusual in being one of the earliest examples of European and Renaissance architectural features in England, because its first two owners were Sir Philip Hoby (*77*) and his brother Sir Thomas Hoby. Both were well-travelled, cultured courtiers and ambassadors, and their experiences were reflected in the conversion of the house at Bisham.

Bisham was built on the site of a thirteenth-century preceptory of the Knights Templar, which remains the nucleus of the present house.[1] The order was suppressed in 1307 and the manor reverted to the Crown. It was then conferred on William, Lord Montagu, created Earl of Salisbury in 1337. In the same year a house of Austin Canons was founded by the earl, adjoining but independent of the Templar buildings, which continued to be used as a manor house.[2] Little is known about the priory buildings and their layout, but they were probably set within the moated site. The Church is illustrated in the fifteenth-century Salisbury Roll, and appears to be of substantial size and magnificence. It had twin towers at the west end, and a tower above the crossing, all topped with ogee spires.

77 Sir Philip Hoby, Hans Holbein the Younger, c.1532-43

There were north and south transepts with high-pitched roofs, and north and south aisles. If the 'quarante cloister' described in 1552 is also the priory Cloister, then the Church would probably have formed the north range. The 1552 grant of the site to Philip Hoby also describes the other buildings:

> The scite of the late Monastery there, whereof is standing the late prior's lodgings, buylded of tymber and brick and covered with tyles, sette between the Thamys and the Mancon howse of the late Countes of Sarum, wherein is a lytell halle, a parloure within the same, a small ketchyn and a pretty pantery with iiij chambers over the same, also the covent kitchyne with an entry leading from the seid priors lodginge to the same, also a garden plotte lyeng betwene the seyd kechyn, the late prior's lodgings, and the maltinge howse, also the churchyarde and soyle where the Abbey halle and churche late stode, being now altogether defaced, also certeyne lodgings, parcell of the scite of the seid late Monastery, standing on the north parte of the cowrte before the hall dore, together with one orcherde wherein standethe a dove house [...] and also a close called the covent garden, conteyning by estymacion viij acres.[3]

The Prior's Lodging and other buildings were probably to the south and south-east of the house. The 'dove house' survives and is further south, and the 'covent garden' was probably on the site of the orchard in the 1609 map.

The priory and manor house seem, therefore, to have been physically closely integrated, but the priory retained the interest and support of the Earls of Salisbury, both the Montagu family and their successors the Neville family, until the Dissolution. The priory received large sums of money and the Church was the burial place for several earls and many other family members. The support continued until the end but the prior, Richard Blackthorn, was eventually pressed into resigning in 1535, having hitherto resisted with the encouragement of the priory's patron, the Countess of Salisbury.[4] In this context, the physical proximity of house and priory is understandable: the Priory Church might almost be seen as a family chapel. With other enclosed orders, such proximity of the secular and religious would have been impossible, but Augustinian canons were required to work in the wider community, preaching, caring for the sick and administering the sacraments.

The *Valor* of 1535 gives the income of Bisham Priory as just over £185, which would have brought it within the suppression of the lesser houses. On 5 July 1536 it was surrendered to the king, but alone amongst all the monasteries of England was selected by Henry VIII to be re-established on a much grander scale, being converted into an abbey.[5] On 6 July 1537, John Cordrey, Abbot of Chertsey, Surrey, together with William the prior and thirteen monks, surrendered, on condition of being re-established as an abbey about to be founded by the king at the late Priory of Bisham. On 18 December the same year the king granted a charter to the new foundation of the order of St Benedict. It was to consist of an abbot and thirteen monks, and was founded by Henry to secure prayers for his good estate during life, and for the soul of Jane his late queen; also for the souls of his posterity and progenitors, and for the souls of all the faithful departed. This new Abbey of the Holy Trinity was endowed with the house and lands of Bisham Priory and also with the lands of Chertsey Abbey and of the priories of Cardigan, Beddgelert, Ankerwyke, Little Marlow and Medmenham, to the annual value of £661

14s 9d.[6] But the king's grief over the death of Jane Seymour soon passed, and with it his short-lived desire for prayers either for the living or for the dead. The Abbey of Bisham lasted for exactly six months, and then John the abbot, William the prior and the convent of monks were called upon to execute a second surrender of all their possessions, which they did on 19 June 1538.[7]

The manor house remained in the ownership of the Earls of Salisbury until the execution of Margaret, Countess of Salisbury, in May 1541.[8] On her attainder her lands passed to the Crown, and Bisham manor and its house were united with the priory land and conferred on Henry's divorced wife, Anne of Cleves.[9] Then, on 7 November 1552, Sir Philip Hoby was granted 'the mansion howse or capitall mese' and 'the scite of the late Monastery there [...] where the Abbey halle and churche late stode'.[10]

Sir Philip Hoby was a diplomat during the reign of Henry VIII. He travelled abroad with Hans Holbein the Younger in 1538 on Henry's commission to obtain portraits of possible royal brides, including Christina, Duchess of Milan.[11] In 1548 he was sent by Edward VI as ambassador to the Court of the Emperor Charles V.[12] Hoby travelled extensively in his role as ambassador, and was much exposed to Court life and culture. In 1552, he was admitted to the Privy Council, shortly before Bisham was granted to him.[13] In April 1553 he was sent again as ambassador to the Emperor.[14] However, after Edward's death on 6 July 1553 and the accession of Mary, with the return of England to Catholicism, he was recalled. Later in 1554 he was in Padua with his half-brother Thomas. They visited Mantua, then Caldiero and Venice in 1555. He then returned via Frankfurt and Brussels, and was back in England by 1556.[15] He had married Elizabeth

Stonor, but the couple had no children, so when Hoby died on 29 May 1558 at the age of fifty-three, he left Bisham to Thomas.[16]

Sir Thomas Hoby spent two years at St John's College, Cambridge, but in 1547 he left without graduating and moved to Strasbourg.[17] In 1548 he moved on to Italy, documenting his experiences in his diary. Thomas' first journey was explicitly for educational purposes.[18] His extended tour of Italy began in Venice, followed by visits to Padua, Mantua and Verona. He then crossed to Florence and Siena, writing: 'removed to the middles of Italy, to have a better knowledge of ye tongue and to see Tuscany'.[19] He travelled on to Rome, Naples, and as far south as Sicily, returning to England at Christmas 1550.[20] He moved to Padua again in 1554 as a Marian exile, returning to England in 1556.

Roger Ascham describes Hoby as 'many wayes well furnished with learning and very expert in divers tongues'.[21] Hoby's translation of Count Baldessar Castiglione's *Libro del Cortegiano* was published in 1561 and became one of the most influential books of the Elizabethan age, setting an agenda for the behaviour and attributes of courtiers and running through four editions.[22] In 1566, Hoby was knighted and appointed ambassador to France, but died in Paris three months later. The queen wrote to Lady Hoby assuring her that 'he dyed very commendably ... and so we would have you to rest yourself in quietness with a firm opinion of our especiall favour towards you,' signing off, 'your loving friend, Elizabeth R'.[23] Lady Hoby returned to live at Bisham with their four children. Both Hoby brothers, therefore, were well travelled and cultivated men with direct experience of European style and fashion, and this was to be demonstrated in their new house at Bisham.

78 Bisham Abbey viewed from across the River Thames

Parts of the original Templar preceptory buildings remain, forming the core of the Renaissance house (*78*). On the south front, the porch was built in the thirteenth century, and the door itself has thirteenth-century ironwork.[24] Through the porch, the screens passage has five arches, now blocked, which led to the thirteenth-century kitchens, while the Great Hall in the centre was the Templars' Hall.[25] The rooms to the north of the court-yard have some thirteenth-century walling and, as this is the only part of the original building correctly oriented, it may have been the Chapel.[26] The Cloister was to the east of the Hall, of which only the west range adjoining the house survives. It is low and irregular with six arches, four wide ones in the centre and a narrow one at either end.[27] It is probable that the Cloister dates to around 1370.[28]

At the time the mansion house was granted to Philip Hoby, on 7 November 1552, it was described as:

> Situate nere unto the Ryver of Thamys and adjoininge to the seite of the late monasterie there, being buylded partely of stone and partely of tymber and covered with tyles, wherein is conteyned a hall with a chembney, and at the lower end of the same is a pantery, a butery, a kechyne, a larder, and a lytell woodyarde. At the over end of the same assendinge by a fayre half pace is a greate chamber with an inner chamber and vj other chambers and logging uppon a quadrante, and underneath these chambers at the foote of the said hallf pace is a wyne seller [and] a quarante cloister with certeyne small loggings on every side of the same.[29]

The arrangement is shown in the 1609 map of

the Manor of Bisham surveyed by Elias Allen (*79*), which also shows the approach to the house by road: across the bridge from Marlow and past the Church. The cellar and western range of the Cloister, with the 'half pace' or staircase, are shown on the floor plan (*80*). The Great Chamber and other principal rooms were therefore on the first floor, above the cellar and cloister, and accessed by the same staircase. The Priory Hall and Church had been demolished before the site and manor were granted to Hoby and the place where they had stood, to the north-east of the house,[30] was just 'soyle'. The Church was amongst those that were systematically destroyed and the materials used for the king's new palaces; Bisham and Chertsey provided material for Oatlands Palace.[31] Hoby began further building works on the house in 1556 and on 2 January 1557 wrote to William Cecil:

> Your man has been here to view my work, but it is not sufficiently advanced; if he returns in three or four weeks he will be better able to serve your turn. Mr. Mason arrives with his wife to-morrow night, and the Lord Privy Seal on Monday. You would be welcome, but fear you can make no step without the licence of my Lady.[32]

The same year, 1557, Thomas Hoby returned to Bisham from his travels.[33] Philip then journeyed to Evesham and Bath, to take the waters for his health, while Thomas wrote in his diary that he 'remained at home to see his new building go forward'.[34] Thomas inherited Bisham in May 1558 on the death of his brother. He continued with the work begun by Philip, and 'There is no doubt that [he] was in some measure influenced by the buildings which he had seen in Italy and described in his journal'.[35] Part of Hoby's work was the

conversion of the Great Chamber to the principal room of the Renaissance house. This room was on the east of the house on the first floor, above the west range of the Cloister. In the mediaeval period it had an open timber roof, but Hoby inserted a plaster ceiling.[36] He also re-fenestrated it, inserting a semi-octagonal bay window, which remains in place today (*81*). At the northern end another large pedimented stone window was inserted with a transom and four mullions. Architecturally, elements were incorporated into the building which reflected the Hobys' travels. These include the chimneypiece in the Great Hall and the pedimented windows.[37]

The south front between the Great Chamber and the porch was added by the Hobys, with chalk below and stepped brick gables above.[38] The windows have cross-mullions and transoms with pediments, and those on the ground floor have brick voussoirs. When Thomas Hoby visited Munich in 1554 he noted that the town had 'not a house of tymber within it, but all of freestone and bricke in such cumlie order and due proportion that yt hath not his name all abrode for nothing'.[39] He used the idea of combining stone and brick at Bisham. The stepped gables are in the style of the Low Countries, prominently displayed on palaces of the Dukes of Burgundy in Bruges, Brussels and Ghent.[40] The fact that the palaces of the most fashionable court in Europe were mostly brick-built resulted in the aesthetic re-evaluation of what had previously been regarded as a cheap building material.[41] The large quantities of bricks needed to build a country house were almost invariably made on the site, or within a very short distance of it. The field immediately beyond the moat to the south of the house is named 'Bricke close' on Allen's map, which must have been where the brick

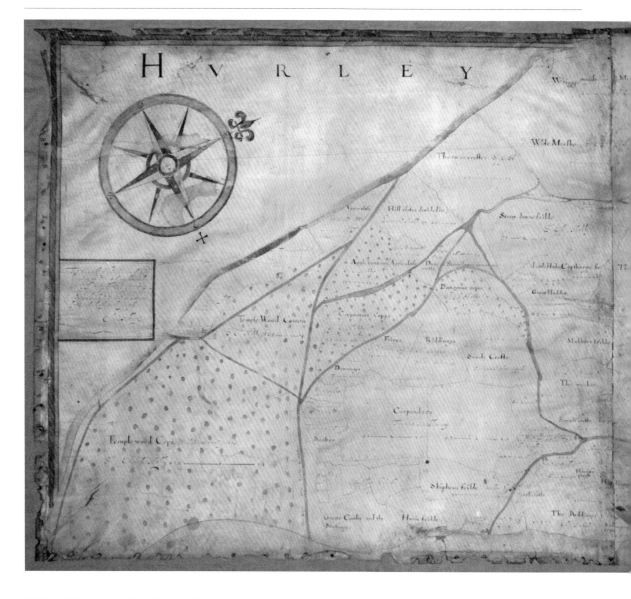

79 Elias Allen's map of the Manor of Bisham, surveyed in 1609

making took place. Bricks were probably used for the garden walls shown on the map, as well as for building the house, since the remaining sections of wall are brick. The pedimented windows inserted by the Hobys also suggest direct European influence. Philip Hoby was in Padua and Vicenza in 1555 and would probably have seen some of Palladio's earlier works there, with their pedimented windows.[42]

These windows at Bisham introduced a classical element to the buildings rarely used in England in this period.

The turret, built of brick, is recessed from the north. Hoby wrote in his diary in 1560 'This yeere was the turret built in Bissham.'[43] Constructed before the new lodgings were finished, and before the new garden and orchard were planted, the turret provides far-

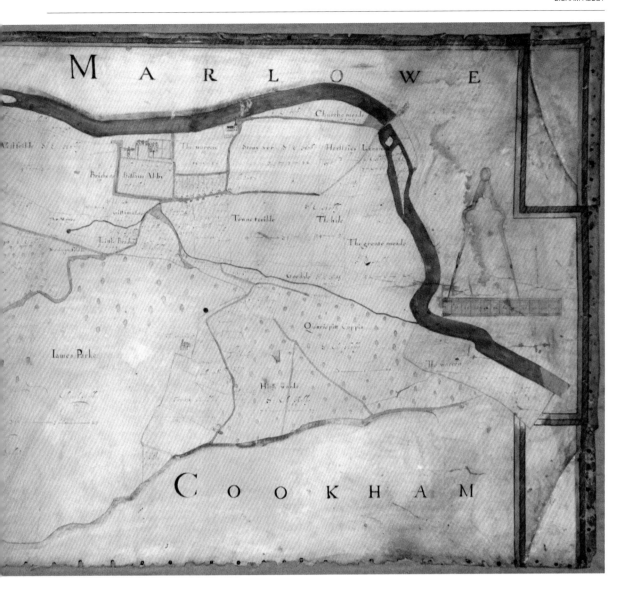

reaching views in all directions, both from the room on the upper floor and from the roof. Unusually, the turret was built at the centre of the house rather than at an outside corner and was probably used for banqueting.[44] Towers were also used for astronomical studies during the sixteenth century, as a place from which to view the night sky. To have a single turret was, by the Elizabethan period, a fashionable element of architecture, used for pleasure. That at Bisham had a flat roof onto which one could walk to admire the views from the top, out across the gardens and the river beyond. Flat roofs were the ultimate luxury if one could afford the leadwork.[45]

The tomb of the Hoby brothers in All Saints Church is of a refined continental style (*82*). The sarcophagus has a Doric order and

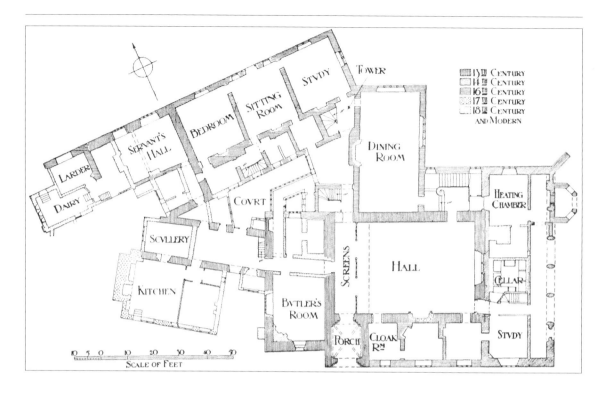

80 The ground floor plan of Bisham Abbey

81 The East Front of Bisham Abbey, with the semi-octagonal bay window above the west range of the Cloister

82 The tomb of Sir Philip and Sir Thomas Hoby in All Saints Church, Bisham

the panels on it are surrounded by an egg-
and-tongue moulding, but it is the poses of
the figures which are unique in England at
this date, and the fine cutting of the heads is
far in advance of English work.[46] Lady Hoby
wrote elegies for the tomb of over eighty lines
in English and Latin. The inscription describes
it as the tomb of 'Two worthye Knightes and
Hobies both by name', and after she had
brought Thomas' body back from Paris in
1566, 'this noble tomb she caused to make'.[47]

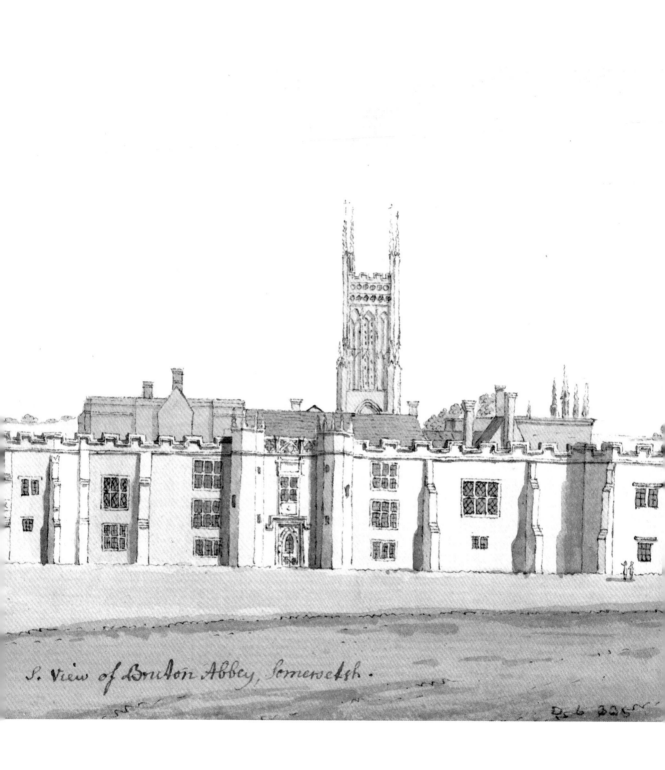

S. View of Bruton Abbey, Somersetsh .

83 *South View of Bruton Abbey House, Somerset*, Samuel Hieronymus Grimm, 1786

Bruton Abbey

The Dovecote overlooking Bruton, set high on a ridge to the south of St Mary's parish church, is the last survivor of a designed landscape that once centred on a Tudor mansion (*83*). This was created from the dissolved Bruton Abbey of Augustinian canons, founded as a priory by William de Mohun in 1142. The gaunt, roofless tower (*84*) has never been precisely dated, nor has its original purpose been determined. Its door and window frames appear to be recycled elements and its function has been obscured by later re-use as a dovecote, possibly after the Bruton Abbey estate was sold in 1776 by the Berkeley family to Sir Richard Hoare.[1] It may originally have been a prospect tower overlooking the park around the abbey, which had been created by the canons.

The building is first shown on an Ordnance Surveyor's drawing for a map of Somerset of 1808, but it appears in an earlier, though imprecisely dated, eighteenth-century engraving of Bruton Church taken from the north.[2] This shows the tower, its gabled roof intact and with a chimney rising from the south-west corner. An avenue of trees runs up the hillside to it, suggesting that it was functioning at this time as a focal point in the landscape. The watercolour depicts a building of two storeys only, and there is evidence of re-roofing, so it may well have been heightened in the later eighteenth century.

What becomes clear when walking the site is that the whole park, developed from the mediaeval landscape surrounding the lost abbey, was conceived as a pleasure ground for the Berkeleys, who lived in the mansion by the parish church. At this point the park was not a paled deer park like those at neighbouring Stourhead and Longleat; instead it was an ornamental landscape with some enclosed areas for deer, but threaded with tree-lined walks.[3] Some of these trees survived just above the railway line on the west side of the road to Wincanton until the later twentieth century.[4] It is also likely that there were designed water gardens adapted from the abbey fishponds, particularly at the north-east sector, parallel with the Bruton to Wincanton turnpike road, where there are the remains of a cascade and a sinuous watercourse. By 1539, when the abbey was dissolved, a park of some 30 acres had been created by the canons on

their demesne lands immediately south of the abbey,[5] but exactly when the land around the dissolved Bruton Abbey was turned into a designed landscape is not certain. However, the archival and building records provide pointers, and it seems that the most important eighteenth-century building activity was undertaken by Charles Berkeley, who was in charge of the estate from 1741 until 1765. It is known that he paid for the rebuilding of the chancel of St Mary's Church in 1743 and restored the Great Hall of the mansion after a disastrous fire in October 1763.[6]

There is little documentary evidence either of the character or extent of the mediaeval Augustinian priory, though it is believed that the Priory Church had been divided in two: the church of the canons and the church of the parishioners, the latter being the south aisle of the present building. It seems that bishops often sent men to Bruton who were to be trained for the priesthood, particularly in the fourteenth century, so the house was one of scholars. However, by the fifteenth century there was trouble in the house after John Schoyle was elected prior in 1419.[7] He was accused of serious offences in 1423 and was eventually deposed in 1429 and banished to

85 Bruton Church from the west

Berkshire. His successor, Richard of Glaston-bury, was no better, and after he died in 1448, to be succeeded by John Henton, Bishop Beckynton (Beckington) issued a series of injunctions for the canons to follow. The prior was ordered to appear before the bishop with all his canons in the Chapter House at Bruton to be told how they should conduct them-selves. Beckington decreed that the canons were not allowed to hunt, suggesting that the tower in the park was not intended as a stand from which to watch the chase, but for view-ing the landscape only. After compline everyone had to go to the dormitory without

further conversation. The bishop's strictures further mention the Infirmary, which was to be rebuilt, and the beer, which was to be improved.[8] Thereafter, order was restored and, following Henton's death in 1494, William Gilbert succeeded him as prior.

William Gilbert was related to the Fitz-james family, which had great influence in Bruton; their most important member being Richard Fitzjames, who served as Bishop of London between 1506 and 1522. Gilbert took his degree of Doctor of Divinity at Oxford on 8 February 1507, and three years later went to Rome to petition for Bruton to become an

86 *West View of Bruton Abbey House, Somerset*, Samuel Hieronymus Grimm, 1786

abbey. His entreaty was successful, and in 1511 he obtained a royal licence to assume the style of Abbot. Leland reports that Gilbert 'did great Cost in the Abbay of *Bruton* in Building, almoste re-edifying' the monastic complex.[9] It can be assumed that the newly styled abbey comprised the typical offices to be found in most mediaeval monastic establishments.

There are some clues at the parish church as to what Gilbert might have achieved architecturally at Bruton Abbey. His monogram is carved on the battlemented parapet of the north aisle, which is supported by buttresses with set-offs (**85**); both these architectural elements feature prominently on the Berkeley mansion in a series of eighteenth-century watercolours of the house by Samuel Hieronymus Grimm (**86**), which are included in an extra-illustrated copy of Dugdale's *Monasticon Anglicanum*.[10] The Church battlements also carry the shield of Bishop Fitzjames and the rebus of a beer barrel for Abbot Bere of Glastonbury (1493-1524), suggesting a clerical kinship at the time with Gilbert. It is likely, therefore, that the general architectural character of the later mansion owes much to Gilbert's campaign of rebuilding. Indeed, Berkeley might have retained some elements of the abbey façades, for there was a doorway on the north front of the mansion with what appears to be Gilbert's coat of arms carved above it. This is topped by an inscription taken from Virgil's *Georgics*: '*ignavum fucos pecus a praesepibus arcent*' (worker bees fend off the drones – an idle lot – from the hives), which suggests the influence of the scholar

87 *Architectural Drawings, Bruton*, Samuel Hieronymus Grimm, 1786

abbot.[11] Might this have been the entrance to the former Abbot's Lodgings? A further doorway on the west front (*87*), perhaps another part of the mediaeval building, has a quotation from Virgil's *Aeneid*: '*volvenda dies en attulit ultro*'. The full line translates: 'what no god dared to promise to your prayers, see the circling hour has brought unasked.' This is entirely appropriate for a scholarly monastic establishment.

John Ely was in charge of Bruton Abbey when Dr John Tregonwell received the surrender of the house on 1 April 1539. It comprised the abbot, prior and thirteen canons, of which five were graduates of the University of Oxford; it had been a veritable house of schol-

ars.[12] The abbey was granted to Maurice Berkeley on 22 March 1541 and there are two further Letters Patent of 1546 and 1550 conveying to 'Mauricio Barkeley' the estates and chapels of the dissolved abbey, the '*monasterio de Brewton*', and the Manor and Hundred of Bruton.[13] The later of these vellum documents has an initial letter enclosing a rather cherubic Henry VIII sitting below a canopy emblazoned with the words '*Vivat Rex*', while in the earlier he is depicted as the jowly-faced ruler he had become by 1546.

Maurice Berkeley came from the cadet branch of the family based at Stoke Gifford, just outside Bristol, rather than from the main family seat of Berkeley Castle. He rose to

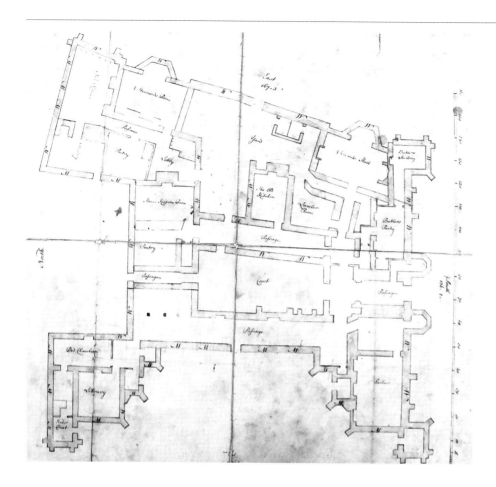

88 Eighteenth-century ground plan of the Bruton Abbey mansion

prominence in the Tudor court through Thomas Cromwell's household, where he was a servant in 1538, entering the royal household in 1539 as a Gentleman of the Privy Chamber; he then went into Queen Katherine Parr's employ in 1543. Berkeley achieved high status when, as a result of a successful military campaign in France, he was knighted on 30 September 1544. The following year he succeeded his elder brother as Chief Standard Bearer of England. He was, therefore, perfectly placed at Court to profit from the spoils of the Dissolution. It is not clear exactly what he inherited on the site, but a contemporary account, written just after the surrender of the

house, mentions the Frater and a first-floor room called the 'Doctor's Chamber'.[14] Whilst we have no precise idea of the character and extent of the abbey, a detailed eighteenth-century ground plan of the Tudor mansion that Maurice Berkeley built from the dissolved complex survives (**88**), along with the evocative Grimm watercolours of the house; Grimm visited Bruton in 1786 just before the mansion was demolished.[15]

Berkeley built his Tudor mansion parallel to the parish church on its south side, possibly retaining some of the abbey fabric within its oddly shaped east range and reusing architectural fragments in others. The east range was aligned at an oblique angle and may well have been a section of the abbey, possibly the Infirmary, or perhaps that section of the Abbey Church which originally connected with the parish church. The configuration of the rest of the house, particularly its south and west ranges, is generally symmetrical and ordered, with a towered entrance gatehouse to the south leading to an inner courtyard. Of Maurice Berkeley's mansion little more is known, but he lived in it until his death in 1581 and now lies armour-clad in the parish church alongside his two wives, both of whom pre-deceased him. Their tomb chest is decorated with strapwork panels set within a deeply shadowed niche fronted by Corinthian columns and round arches. However, in 1786 the west range of the mansion had a Parlour at the south-west corner and a Library on the opposite corner served by a bedchamber and water closet. Those were the only polite rooms on this floor; the rest of the ranges comprised servants' rooms and domestic offices. There was a further yard fronted by a screen wall in the east range over which, at first-floor level, was the Great Hall.

Grimm made his watercolour views from each point of the compass to give a detailed record of the architecture of Berkeley's stone façades. They were supported by blockish buttresses with set-offs, lit by rectangular bays and vast mullioned-and-transomed windows and topped by a battlemented parapet enlivened at points with crocketed pinnacles. The only anomalies were on the east front, where two canted bays lit by sash windows framed the Great Hall with its Gothick windows (*89*). It is likely that these features were part of a mid-eighteenth-century campaign to modernise the house undertaken by Charles Berkeley, perhaps after the disastrous fire of 1763. A separate Grimm

watercolour depicts the 'Ruin of the Barn door of Bruton Abbey'.

The only record we have of the interior of the Berkeley house comes from a series of answers to 'Querys of the Society of Antiquaries' after they had made a visit to Bruton in the mid-eighteenth century, certainly before the death of the 4th Lord Berkeley in 1773.[16] The local Bruton historian, Phyllis Couzens, has suggested a date of 1757 for the text. While it does not specifically describe the rooms of the mansion, there is an intriguing description of the paintings in the Hall, which included a 'half length Portrait of the first Lord Berkeley of Stratton in Armour very well painted, supposed to be by Vandyke'; another of Sir Henry Berkeley of Bruton, who was knighted by Queen Elizabeth in 1585; a half-length of Charles Lord Berkeley by Sir Peter Lely, and two self-portraits thought to be by Vandyke and Rembrandt.

The 4th Lord Berkeley left the abbey mansion to the Earl of Berkeley, his distant cousin, who sold it jointly to Henry Hoare of Stourhead and Sir Richard Hoare of Barn Elms. Sir Richard must have commissioned Grimm's carefully composed watercolours as a visual record of the mansion before he had it demolished.[17] This sad process is documented in some detail in Sir Richard's account books and tradesmen's vouchers for 1786-7.[18]

However, it seems that, initially, he was thinking of altering the house, for he paid Moulton & Atkinson of Old Sarum £43 11s between February and April 1786 for a survey plan and another 'for reducing the Abbey and for fitting up present house and Offices & disposing of the old materials'. This notion was short lived because the accounts record the pulling down of walls as early as 20 May 1786, when William Wallis was the mason in charge. Thereafter, between November 1786

E. View of Bruton Abbey. Somersetsh.

and May 1787, John Clarke's men were busy taking out all the internal joinery – partitions, floors, skirtings, architraves – and 'fitting up Packing Cases for Chimney Pieces'. On 24 March 1787, Clarke was paid for 'Two Men & Apprentice takeing down the Best Staircase', and on 30 June the same year 'The Executors of the late Sir Richard Hoare' paid Wallis 'for work at Bruton Abbey', by which time the mansion had almost disappeared.

After Sir Richard's death Bruton Abbey and its lands were settled on Sir Richard Colt Hoare of Stourhead, who in 1824 privately printed a book he had written on three former monastic establishments in his possession: Witham, Bruton and Stavordale. Colt Hoare introduced his topic of 'Monastic Remains' in true antiquarian spirit: 'Even the dilapidated ruins of a Monastic Establishment excite our attention and respect; and we become anxious to know its ancient state, and the many vicissitudes, which, during a long course of years, it

89 *East View of Bruton Abbey House, Somerset*, Samuel Hieronymus Grimm, 1786

may have experienced.' At Bruton Abbey, he wrote, 'not a single stone remains above ground to testify its former scite, which was to the east of the Parish Church,' but he was determined that its earlier presence should be marked for future generations. On the surviving section of the abbey park wall that runs parallel to The Plox he had a carved tablet set 'to commemorate the former existence of a Monastic Establishment at this place'. It reads, in Latin, of course, '*Haec Domus/ E Reliquiis/*

Abbatiae Olim De Bruton. Constructa/Et Ad Usum Ecclesiae/Nuper Conversa/Anno 1822/ R C Hoare Patrono'.

RICHARDVS GRENVILVS Mil. aur.

Neptuni proles, qui magni Martis alumnus
GRENVILIVS patrias sanguine tinxit aquas

Buckland Abbey

Hidden in a steep valley beside a tributary of the river Tavy, ten miles north of Plymouth Sound, Buckland Abbey was founded in the thirteenth century for a colony of Cistercian monks. Its secluded and sheltered position below the high ground of Dartmoor, where the bracken and heather gives way to rich arable land, meant that the monks would have been able to grow plentiful crops to sustain their community. After the Dissolution, the abbey became home in turn to the renowned Elizabethan seafarers Sir Richard Grenville (*90*) and Sir Francis Drake.

Buckland Abbey was the last Cistercian house to be established in Devon. It was founded in 1280 by Amicia de Redvers, the widowed countess of Baldwin de Redvers, 6th Earl of Devon and Lord of the Isle of Wight. Her supposed likeness is carved above a doorway at Buckland (*91*). Amicia's daughter Isabella de Fortibus, widow of William de Fortze, Earl of Albemarle, was a wealthy landowner in her own right and granted her mother land in Devon for the new monastery. It was dedicated in honour of God and the Blessed Virgin Mary and the Blessed Benedict. She gave the monks the manors of Buckland, Bickleigh and Walkhampton and the hundred of Roborough.[1] The abbey was established with an abbot and seven monks from Quarr Abbey on the Isle of Wight.

There are no extant building records for Buckland Abbey, but construction of the Church must have begun shortly after foundation, as it is all of one build of the late thirteenth century, with no later extension.[2] It is conventionally cruciform in shape, with originally four bays in the nave and two in the chancel. The stone used was a green and brown flecked slate, known locally as shillet, taken from quarries higher up the valley, with granite dressings from nearby Roborough Down for doorways, windows, pillars and arches.[3] The style is austere, with little ornament. Numerous internal details remain, including an original aumbry in the chancel.[4] The tower over the crossing was crenellated as a

90 Sir Richard Grenville, in an engraving from *Heroologia Anglica*, 1620

91 Carved head of Amicia de Redvers, founder of Buckland Abbey

result of Edward III's licence of 1337 during the Hundred Years War, when Plymouth and its surrounding areas were threatened by French invasion.[5] The Cloister was built of the same materials and, because of the contours of the site and drainage, was sited to the north of the Church, rather than to the south in the usual Cistercian arrangement. The eastern range would have contained the Sacristy, Chapter House, Parlour and Monks' Day Room, with the Dorter over; the north range the Frater and kitchen; the west range the accommodation for the lay brothers.[6] The Cloister must have been quite small, as the nave of the Church, which formed the south range, was just seventy-eight feet in length. Only a section of the north range wall now survives.[7]

Several other abbey buildings still exist. The Cider House, to the north of the Cloister, possibly housed the monastic Infirmary, whilst the adjacent Tower Cottage, with a battlemented tower, may have been the Abbot's Lodgings.[8] To the south-east, and remarkably close to the Church, is the early

fifteenth-century barn, which is some 164 feet long and illustrates the scale of building necessary to cater for the monastic establishment.[9] East of the barn is another mediaeval building, possibly the guest house. The abbey, as was usual, would have had a precinct wall and there was certainly a gatehouse with a room above it.[10]

The sixteenth and last abbot was John Toker or Tucker. He was blessed by the Bishop of Exeter as Abbot of Buckland on 7 June 1528, and ten years later surrendered the house to the king. At the Dissolution there were twelve monks, who were all granted pensions: Tucker had £60 per annum and the monks various sums beginning with Thomas Maynard, who was given £5 6s 8d, down to John Jordan who received £3 6s 8d.[11] The revenues of the abbey were just over £241, so it escaped the first phase of the dissolutions.[12] From the *Valor* it is clear that at the end of its existence the abbey possessed little more property than is mentioned in the original grants.[13]

Buckland Abbey was surrendered on 14 December 1539 and the lands, Church, conventual and domestic buildings, which were then intact, were granted to George Pollard of London for a term of twenty-one years. But Pollard must have disposed of his interest, as on 26 May 1541 the king granted the monastery, together with the Church, belfry and all houses, buildings, barns, orchards, gardens and pools 'in consideration of the good, true, and faithful service which his well-beloved servant, Richard Greynfeld (Grenville), knight, heretofore done to us'.[14]

Sir Richard Grenville, who thus acquired Buckland Abbey buildings and part of the estate, was Marshal of Calais until October 1541. The grant was for:

The former Monastery of Buckland in the

county of Devon. The site of the said former monastery with demesne land appertaining to the same.[15]

The grant lists: 'Farm of the site there, with apple orchards, gardens, lands, meadows, feedings and pastures' and details the acreage of these, together with other lands in Somerset, to an annual value of £35 3s 6d. After deducting a tenth retained by the Crown to preserve feudal tenure, and £20 as a gift, the remaining sum was £11 13s 2d, which at the standard twenty years' purchase meant Grenville paid £233 3s 4d.[16]

The Grenvilles were a substantial gentry family, with lands in both Devon and Cornwall. Sir Richard seems to have bought the estate as a home for his son Roger, who clearly resided briefly at Buckland, since in August 1544 he buried his son Charles at nearby Buckland Monachorum.[17] But there is no evidence of any early conversion works, and Roger drowned in July 1545 while commanding the *Mary Rose.* Sir Richard himself died in 1550, and Buckland, together with the other Grenville estates, passed to his grandson Richard, who was then just seven years old.[18] After living with his mother, who quickly remarried, the younger Richard was in London for three years from 1559 to 1562, but fled after killing a man in a brawl. Family influence meant that he was quickly pardoned for this offence, and in June 1563 he reached his majority and entered into his considerable estates. Late in 1564 or early in 1565 he married Mary, the daughter of Sir John St Leger of Annery. In 1568 he accompanied his kinsman Warham St Leger to Ireland, where he remained for eighteen months.[19]

Grenville first became involved in maritime adventures about 1569, probably as an investor rather than a seafarer himself.

Reflecting his local status and lands, he was a knight of the shire for Cornwall in 1571, and at some point between 1574 and 1576 he was knighted and served as sheriff of Cornwall in 1576-7. In 1578 Grenville became interested in Sir Humphrey Gilbert's plans for planting a colony in the New World and for seeking the north-west passage. Gilbert made two voyages, in 1578 and 1583, in which Grenville was probably an investor, although he does not seem to have sailed on either of them. Gilbert was lost at sea on the latter voyage, but his plans were immediately adopted by his cousin, Sir Walter Raleigh, and in these plans Grenville's involvement was practical and immediate.

In April 1585 Grenville departed to plant an English colony on the mainland of North America at Roanoke Island, within reach of the Spanish treasure route, and after leaving the colonists he embarked on a highly profitable privateering voyage. He returned to Roanoke the following year and was assembling ships and men for a further voyage in 1587, but with preparations being made for the Armada, there was a prohibition on any ships leaving England on private expeditions. Grenville was therefore instructed to hand all his ships over to Sir Francis Drake. Although he contributed three ships to the fleet that sailed against the Armada in 1588, Grenville seems not to have been at sea himself. This may have been because of his local status and responsibilities in Devon and Cornwall, including, as deputy lieutenant, for home defence.[20]

Grenville was at sea again in 1589, raiding in the Azores, and then returned there in 1591 as vice-admiral and in command of the queen's ship *Revenge,* to intercept the Spanish treasure fleet from America. When a superior number of Spanish ships approached, the admiral, Lord Thomas Howard, ordered retreat, but Grenville sailed alone into the

enemy force. He himself was mortally wounded, most of his crew killed, and his ship largely destroyed.[21] Sir Walter Raleigh wrote an account of Grenville's actions in his final battle:

> But Sir Richard utterly refused to turn from the enemy, alleging that he would rather choose to die, than to dishonour himself, his country, and her Majesty's ship … the comfort that remaineth to his friends is, that he hath ended his life honourably in respect of the reputation won to his nation and country, and of the same to his posterity, and that being dead, he hath not outlived his own honour.[22]

The work of converting Buckland from a monastery into a fine Tudor residence is ascribed to the younger Grenville. No work would have taken place until after he attained his majority in 1563, but probably the main construction only commenced in the early 1570s, after he returned from Ireland and settled in Devon.[23] The date in the plasterwork above the fireplace (**92**) in the Great Hall

is 1576, implying that most of the work was complete by then.

Unusually, the Abbey Church had not been demolished at the Dissolution, and Grenville chose to adapt it to use as the heart of his new country house. He incorporated a large part of the mediaeval fabric, adapting it for his own purposes. The transepts were demolished, but the rest of the Church was retained. The principal room of the new house was the Great Hall, created by dividing the nave of the Church, and here much of Grenville's work survives. The Hall occupies the ground floor of the crossing, and it had two floors of chambers above it in the tower. The walls of the room are oak panelled, and the central feature is the large granite fireplace with an ornate plaster frieze above. All around the room is a frieze of foliage and flowers divided up by carved animal masks and figures including musicians, while shield-bearing satyrs support the ceiling. The floor, decorated with red and white triangular tiles, was laid some eighteen inches above the original floor of the Cister-

93 *The East View of Buckland Priory in the County of Devon*, engraved by Samuel and Nathaniel Buck, 1734

cian Church, beneath which are the graves of monks buried in the nave.[24]

The Hall, because of the tower above, is not open to the roof – a very early instance in a major house in Devon – but it is, nonetheless, sufficiently high to allow for a mezzanine floor on either side.[25] The entrance to Grenville's new Hall was through a door in the north-west corner, which implies that the Cloister, of which the nave formed the south range, was wholly demolished, or at least opened up. The 1734 engraving by the Bucks (**93**) shows that there were buildings extending further to the north than they do now, on the site of the Cloister.

The chancel, to the east of the Hall, was converted into a service room, and this may also have been the use of the remaining west end of the nave, where the mediaeval west door survives. The south transept was demolished to create large windows to let more light into the Hall, except for its west wall, which

formed part of a grand staircase giving access to the upper floors. The roofline of the transept can still be seen on the south wall of the tower (**94**).[26] Grenville also built a new kitchen wing, with access through a screens passage to the east of the Hall. It is possible that stone from the demolished Cloister was used in its construction. The Elizabethan kitchen survives, with its enormous open hearth on the south wall, the chimney breast supported by a granite lintel under a brick archway and a second, smaller fireplace. A number of small rooms around the kitchen served as stores or for servants.[27]

New openings were made in the monastic guest house, and one window has dripstones with Grenville badges.[28] This strongly suggests that the building also formed part of Grenville's conversion works, perhaps to provide additional accommodation, though exactly how it was used is no longer clear.[29] It is likely that new walled gardens would have

94 The south wall of the crossing tower at Buckland Abbey, with the roofline of the transept visible

been laid out around the house, as shown in the Bucks' engraving. The Tudor gardens probably occupied the same site and there is still a garden there with a central fountain like that shown by the Bucks.

In spite of all his conversion works, Richard Grenville only enjoyed his new house at Buckland for a few years. In December 1580 he agreed to sell the buildings, land totalling some 500 acres and 'all the implements of household stuffe nowe being within the said house' to John Hele and Christopher Harris for the sum of £3,400.[30] Hele and Harris were merely the representatives of the real purchaser, Sir Francis Drake. He had returned earlier that year from his circumnavigation of the world and had been given £10,000 in bullion by Queen Elizabeth, wealth that Drake was anxious to convert into land, for the security and status it brought. Grenville, conversely, probably wanted ready cash to fund his own voyages, and had other estates in Devon and Cornwall. Considering what his grandfather had paid for Buckland in 1541, £3,400 was a very good price and more than the property was worth, so this must have persuaded him to

95 The traceried window above the chancel arch at the crossing

leave his newly converted house.[31]

In the event, Sir Francis took up residence in early 1581, but does not seem to have made many further alterations at Buckland.[32] The late sixteenth-century porch, which leads into the Great Hall, has a heavy moulded granite doorway with leaf carvings in the spandrels. Above the doorway are three plaques bearing Drake's heraldic symbols. The left one is a glove, the right one a knight's helmet and the central one the Drake arms. The porch may have been built by Drake, or he may have added the plaques when he bought the house.[33]

At the west end of the first floor what is now called Drake's Drawing Room has fine sixteenth-century panelling.[34] This suggests that it may have been Grenville's Great Chamber, or the panelling might have been added by Drake. The layout and use of the other rooms on the two upper floors are not known, but presumably included bedchambers, closets and other domestic offices. On the top floor the crossing of the Abbey Church can clearly be seen, as all four arches survive. The Chancel arch was lower and directly above it was a window with tracery, of which the head

survives, retained as a decorative feature in the Tudor house (95). In this top Tower Room is a granite framed fireplace attributable to Drake. It has a plaster overmantel bearing Drake's arms with the Latin inscription 'Sic Parvis Magna' (thus great things from small).

After Drake's death in 1596 the estate passed to his brother William and the Drake family remained for almost 400 years, other than a brief period during the Civil War. However, an inventory taken in the 1660s showed a much-diminished estate of 277 acres, a small mill, four orchards, woods, two gardens, hopyards and nurseries.[35] A major restoration scheme was begun in 1776, and it was at this time that the fine Georgian staircase and other panelled rooms in the east wing were completed.[36] In January 1938 a chimney flue caught fire and spread throughout the nave of the old Church. The roof collapsed and great damage was done to that part of the house, though structural repairs were completed within two years.[37] The estate was sold in 1946 and the house and gardens presented to the National Trust, though it is administered by Plymouth Museums.

96 The picturesque ruin of Buildwas Abbey Church by Michael 'Angelo' Rooker, 1772

Buildwas Abbey

When the topographical artist Thomas Robins came to Buildwas Abbey on 20 July 1759 to prepare sketches for an engraving of the monastic ruins there, just as he had done earlier at Hailes in Gloucestershire, he was confronted with the twelfth-century Abbey Church, surviving almost intact, but with its roofs stripped of lead and open to the elements. It was in the same state when Michael 'Angelo' Rooker produced his beautiful 1772 watercolour of the interior of the ruined nave (*96*), the roofless crossing being used at that time as a hay store. Robins was one of the first artists to venture into Shropshire to enjoy first-hand the bizarre juxtapositions of smoky industrial premises and scenic ancient ruins along the River Severn (*97*). Like Hailes, the Abbey House at Buildwas was occupied in the mid-eighteenth century as a tenanted farmstead and, along with the ruined Abbey Church and Cloister, became a perfect subject for later artists of the Picturesque, including Paul Sandby, John Sell Cotman and JMW Turner. Understandably, they set up their easels to the south of the Abbey Church and made the ruined Romanesque nave and crossing tower the principal focus of their compositions.

The configuration of original monastic buildings, raised at Buildwas under its second abbot, Ranulf, between the 1150s and his death in 1187, did not follow the usual Cistercian pattern with the church sited to the north and the claustral buildings and offices attached to it on the south. Due to the lie of the land and the need to drain the complex into the River Severn, which flowed to the north of the site, the cruciform Church was constructed on a terrace to the south. It was attached by its north transept to the range containing the Sacristy, Chapter House, Parlour and Day Room, with the monks' Dorter above, running northwards from it, the ruins still visible in an aerial photograph (*98*). The Infirmary extended out eastwards from the Cloister to connect with the Abbot's Lodgings, thereby creating a second court.

It is presumed that the charter, which was granted by Bishop Hugh de Nonant in November 1192, dated at Buildwas, marked the consecration of the completed Abbey Church. Thereafter, building work continued into the thirteenth century, with the monks expanding their agricultural

97 *Buildwas Abbey*, Thomas Robins the Elder, 1759, with the River Severn in the background

estate. The assessed income of the Shropshire and Staffordshire estates amounted to £114 in 1291 and the abbey continued to prosper into the fourteenth century. Then, however, the discipline in the house appears to have deteriorated, culminating in the mysterious murder of an abbot in 1342, which left the house in disarray. By 1344 Buildwas had a debt of £100 and in 1349 it was hit by the Black Death. Raids from over the Welsh border in Powys, when monks were taken prisoner and the abbey's treasures stolen; the need to lease out lands for much needed rental income; and a fall in the number of lay brothers all had disastrous effects on the community. By 1377 there were no more than six monks and by 1381 the number had fallen to four.

This sad decline continued throughout the fifteenth century, with successive abbots extending leases on property to raise money,

and a visitor appointed in 1521 to give an account of the community reported that the abbey was 'very far from virtue in every way'.[1] It is unsurprising that, when it was surveyed for the *Valor* in 1535, the net annual income of the abbey was only £111, way below the £200 benchmark needed for its continued survival. The abbey surrendered late in 1536 and in the following year the monastic complex was granted by Letters Patent to Edward Grey, Lord Powis.[2] Grey initially paid an annual rent of £55 for the property from July 1537, but he acquired the abbey and its properties outright on 31 March 1545.[3] The Letters Patent mention 'the site of the late monastery, church steeple and yard of the same'.[4]

Lord Powis died in July 1551, and it was perhaps in the knowledge of his impending death that a grant was drawn up on 9 May that year, between Grey, William Charleton and

98 An aerial photograph of Buildwas Abbey, showing the layout and the surviving ruins

Jasper Powate, which granted the 'site of the late abbey of St Mary Buylldewas, with belfry, cemetery, lands etc. and granges in cos [counties] Salop, Staff. and Derby, to the use of Cecilia, dter. [daughter] of 1. [Grey] by Jane Orewell, and heirs'.[5] A slightly later copy of the conveyance, dated 29 May, gives more detail of the grant and the heirs to which it related. The 'buildings and lands of Buildwas Abbey ... given to him [Lord Powis] by Henry VIII' were to be held in trust 'to the use of his legitimate issue, or, in default of such, to the use of

Edward Gray, his son by Jane Orwell, and his heirs, and in default, then to his daughters, Jane, Ann, Joyce and Cecilia'.[6] This suggests that Lord Powis might not have begun to convert the abbey ruins into a domestic dwelling at his death. It was perhaps left to his illegitimate son Edward, who came of age in 1568, to construct the dwelling house. If so, his ownership was short-lived.[7] He sold the property to his kinsman Sir Edward Herbert, the second son of William Herbert, 1st Earl of Pembroke, who received a 'grant of livery and

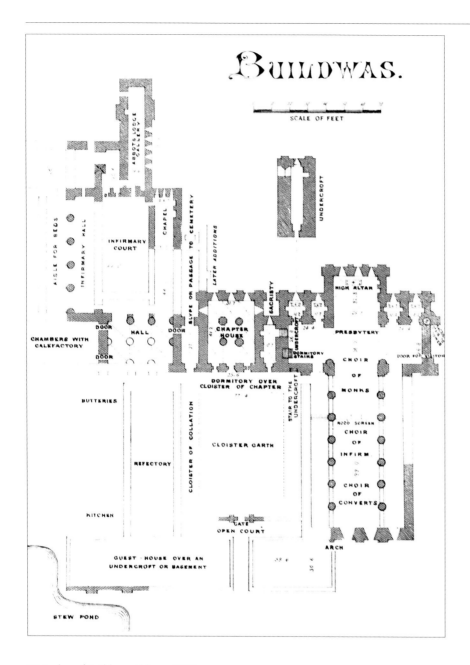

99 A plan of Buildwas Abbey, *c.*1900

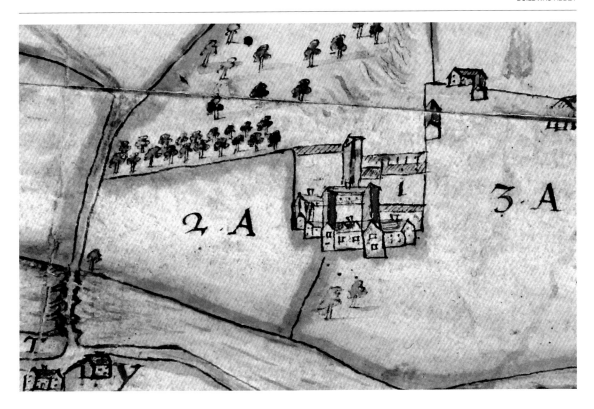

100 A detail of the map of Buildwas Abbey, surveyed by William Fowler, 1650

seisin [freehold]' on 12 July 1582 of the 'dwelling house called le Mannourhowse of Buyldowes alias Byldwas now or late in occupation of Edward Grey, esq.'[8] Grey was later to sell the lordship and castle of Powys, also to Sir Edward Herbert, in 1587.

Rather than create his dwelling around the Cloister, as William Sharington had done at Lacock, Edward Grey built an imposing house enclosing the Infirmary Court, incorporating the Abbot's Lodgings and the Infirmary, and extending it further westwards in a long range north of the Cloister parallel to the former Refectory, the site of which is shown on a plan (**99**) of about 1900.[9] Although much of Grey's Elizabethan house has disappeared, his grand mansion is shown on a map of 1650 (**100**), plotted and surveyed by William Fowler for

the then owner, Sir William Acton.[10] He had acquired the 'site of the abbey, manor of Byldwas, rectory and advowson of same' at some point between September 1648 and February 1649.[11] Prior to his purchase the property had been mortgaged and was described in a document of 20 March 1606 as the 'lordship or manor of Bildwas; cap. [capital] m. [messuage] or mansion house late site of monastery of Blessed Virgin Mary; demesne lands etc.'[12] Thomas, Lord Ellesmere, bought it in 1617 and his son John Egerton, 1st Earl of Bridgewater, sold it to Acton.[13]

Fowler's charmingly naive sketch of the abbey buildings on his map is the only record we have of the great mansion before its reduction in size during the later ownership of the Moseley family. They had inherited the prop-

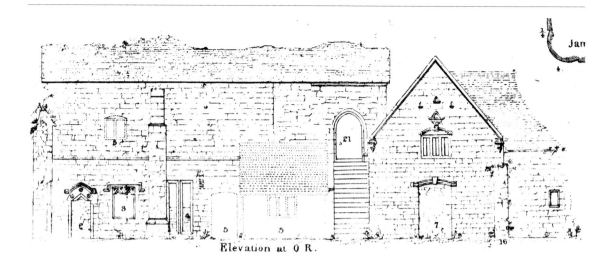

Jan

Elevation at O R.

101 Joseph Potter's drawing of the west elevation of the surviving dwelling at Buildwas Abbey

erty through a daughter of one of the Actons, who married Walter Moseley of Mere, near Enville in Staffordshire, 'in the reign of Charles II'.[14] The main north façade faced the river – 'Sabrina Flu' – and was lit by a battery of windows, with sharply-pointed gables above set along red clay-tiled roofs.[15] Unfortunately, the Elizabethan house is always out of view in later paintings of the complex, so it is difficult to determine from these exactly when it was partially demolished, but later maps give some indication of its gradual demise.

In 1837 Walter Moseley had a map drawn up of the properties he owned in the parishes of Buildwas and Sheinton, which includes an accurate ground plan of the abbey complex and the adjacent mansion. By this time the main dwelling had been reduced to the former Abbot's Lodgings. The courtyard ranges, particularly on the north side, had been breached, but the long west range survived. The aisle columns of the former Infirmary Hall are clearly marked, but now as isolated structures in the courtyard. This process of fragmentation is clearly illustrated by Joseph

Potter in *The Remains of Ancient Monastic Architecture in England* of 1844. This confirms the veracity of the 1837 ground plan on Walter Moseley's map, but records the demolition of the west range. The only room that is identified is the 'Abbot's private Chapel, or Dining-room' on the first floor of the main domestic block, which was lit by a large window facing south; this is not the lower-lying Chapel at the south-west corner marked on the 1900 plan.

Potter's west elevation of the surviving dwelling (*101*), which faced the internal courtyard, shows it to have been built of squared and coursed masonry, with offset buttresses and mullioned windows – some made of oak – with cusped heads; there were also some pointed-arched hoodmoulds with carved head stops and the head of a crowned woman above the three-light window in west wall of the former Chapel. All of this looks as if fragments of the abbatial buildings were recycled when the mansion was constructed, much as at Bruton in Somerset. Indeed, Potter's Plate 32 is a compendium of architectural details of the 'Abbot's Dwelling', ranging from the Romanesque period of the abbey's foundation through to fourteenth-century Gothic fragments. What survives on the site today, therefore, is essentially the former Abbot's Lodging and the lower-lying Abbot's Chapel at the south-west corner. The wills of both Edward Grey and Sir William Acton mention furniture and hangings, presumably tapestries, but give no indication as to the rooms within the house, where they were present, nor how the accommodation was arranged.

HONORATISS. D. IOANNES HARINGTON BARO DE EXTON. EC

Nodo Firmo.

Hollandus calamo generosi pectoris ignes
Expressit, faciem sculpta tabella refert.

Combe Abbey

Combe Abbey is situated four miles to the east of Coventry, in the heart of Coombe Abbey Country Park.[1] The abbey was founded in 1150 in the valley of the Smite Brook and colonised by Cistercian monks from Waverley Abbey in Surrey, the oldest of the English Cistercian houses.[2] By the late thirteenth century it was the richest monastic house in Warwickshire. Although the Abbey Church was demolished soon after the Dissolution, the claustral ranges largely survived and were transformed into a Tudor courtyard house by John Harington of Exton (*102*). Princess Elizabeth, daughter of James I, lived in the care of the Haringtons at Combe between 1603 and 1608, which indicates how grand a house it was. Despite subsequent remodelling, parts of the original buildings of the twelfth-century east range and the fifteenth-century Cloister walk have survived, as well as parts of the Tudor house. Combe is presently a country house hotel, the entrance to which is through the original Chapter House door. Despite many later changes to the abbey, the visitor is plunged directly into the historic mediaeval heart of Combe.

The Abbey of St Mary, Combe was founded on 10 July 1150 by Richard de Camvill.[3] Its original endowments consisted mainly of small parcels of land near Coventry. There are no surviving records of the construction of the abbey; however, works must have taken place over an extended period, as there are masonry remains from the twelfth century to the early sixteenth century. The Abbey Church had a nave of nine bays with aisles and the piers were circular with square bases. According to Warwick Rodwell's plan, based on the architect William Eden Nesfield's records made in the 1860s, the nave of the Church was around 121 feet long and 55 feet wide including the side aisles.[4] When Nesfield created a moat on the site of the Tudor entrance court in 1863, he dug away the foundations of the entire nave, crossing and presbytery, leaving only the transepts.[5] Now only a few floor tiles of the Church survive.

102 John Harington, Baron Harington of Exton, engraved by Crispin de Passe

The Cloister, 111 feet square, was to the north of the Church, probably to take advantage of the Smite Brook for water and drainage, and doors led from the north aisle into the east and west cloister walks. The presbytery was also aisled and was of four or five bays. The transepts were short and wide, probably with two chapels in each.[6] The cloister walks are likely to have been originally made of wood, but were reconstructed in stone in the fifteenth century retaining their original width. The east and west walks both had seven windows, but the north had only six with a small doorway at the west end. In the east range, beyond the north transept, were the Sacristy, Chapter House and Parlour. The Dorter would have been on the upper floor of this range, with stairs providing access to the Church. The Frater was in the north range of the Cloister, with the monastic kitchen at the west end. The west range would have contained the lay brothers' accommodation, with its own Dorter and Frater.

Despite later phases of rebuilding, a considerable amount of this mediaeval structure survives and can still be seen. The entrance of the Chapter House was retained by Nesfield and incorporated in his new east wing, and the major elements of this are original, not Victorian re-creations. The primary fabric dates from the late twelfth century and is constructed from the local red sandstone. At the centre is the ornate doorway, flanked by a pair of windows (**103**). The arch is of four orders with decorated capitals and shafts and the hood moulding is decorated with a broad chevron. Each of the windows has fourteen small columns and capitals carved with late Romanesque detail.[7] The arches inside the hotel reception, which occupies the area of the Chapter House, are Victorian, but incorporate some genuine mediaeval masonry in their plinths.

To the south of the Chapter House entrance is a smaller mediaeval doorway which opened into the monastic book-room and Sacristy. To the north of the Chapter House is another mediaeval doorway which gave access to the Parlour and sub-dorter. Nesfield moved this doorway southwards when he rebuilt the east range in 1864 but it is still close to its original position.[8] The arch is of three orders, each carried by a scalloped capital. In the north Cloister walk, part of the back wall survives with late twelfth-century arcading, probably part of the *Lavatorium*, which would have been close to the entrance to the Frater. In the west range a substantial section of the outer wall survives, incorporated in the later house.

The south walk of the Cloister was only built in 1509, when Sir Edward Raleigh of Farnborough bequeathed £30 to build the south side of the Cloister and to glaze the windows. He left 20s to the abbot, 6s 8d to every priest, and 3s 4d to every professed monk not in priest's orders. In return they were to keep the yearly obit of Sir Edward and his wife Margaret. This bequest enabled the Cloister to be completed.[9] However, this walk was demolished at the same time as the Church after the Dissolution.

The *Valor* of 1535 gave the clear annual value of the house as approximately £211, just above the limit for inclusion in the first Dissolution of 1536.[10] But in December 1538, when the commissioner John London was on his Warwickshire visit of suppression and about to visit the Carthusians of Coventry, he wrote to Cromwell reminding him that Combe was only two or three miles from Coventry, that the abbot and all his friends were at Cromwell's commands, and that he would be glad to 'go through' with that house also. He supposed that the abbot would leave his house and lands 'like an honest man' and it would be well to take the house while it was at its best. In another letter he stated that Cromwell could not have a more commodious house than Combe Abbey, and that the longer he waited in seizing it the worse it would be.[11]

As a result of this letter, the abbey was surrendered on 21 January 1539 by Abbot Robert Kynver (*alias* Bate), by Oliver Adams the former abbot, and by twelve other monks, to the commissioners John London and Edward Baskerfyld for the king's use, together with all its possessions in the counties of Warwick, York, Leicester, and Northampton.[12] The abbot had only held office for a year, having been merely placed there by Cromwell's influence in lieu of Abbot Adams 'to secure a voluntary surrender'. He was rewarded by obtaining the very considerable pension of £80, while the late abbot received nothing.[13]

London wrote on the day of the surrender to Sir Richard Rich, Chancellor of the Court of Augmentations, asking for the speedy ratification of the pensions he had assigned in order to encourage others.[14] Writing somewhat later to Cromwell, London described the suppression:

> I have, with much ado, dispatched the priory of Black Monks at Coventry, the Charterhouse, and Combe abbey. […] At Combe I left the house with the implements unspoiled. Harford, now sheriff of Coventry, informed me that the abbot of Combe had 500*l.* in a feather bed at his brother's house. I searched the bed and found but 25*l.*, which the abbot readily confessed was to pay certain debts at Candlemas, and was put there because he could ill trust any servant he had. He surrendered the house the same day twelve month he was made master and left it, everything considered, in a competent state. I found there 15 monks and 68 servants. To stay spoil and for the safeguard of evidences, let the surveyors come as speedily after me as may be. […] I have from these three houses over 800 oz. of plate which I will bring with me at my coming to London. My servant shall deliver you such ornaments as I have sent up.[15]

After its suppression the king granted Combe

104 *Princess Elizabeth, later Queen of Bohemia*, Robert Peake, 1603

Abbey for life to Mary, Duchess of Richmond and Somerset, widow of the king's illegitimate son.[16] Following her death in 1557, a forty-year lease was granted to Robert Keilway at £196 8s 1d per annum.[17] Keilway was a lawyer and adviser to Edward Seymour, Earl of Hertford and later Duke of Somerset, with whose support he was appointed to the important and lucrative position of Surveyor of the Court of Wards and Liveries in 1546. It is a testament to his ability and moderation that he retained his office under four sovereigns, through various changes in religion, and despite the fall of his patron Somerset in 1549. His daughter and sole heiress, Anne, married John Harington of Exton, Rutland, in around 1571.[18] It is not recorded when the Haringtons moved to Combe, but it is likely to have coincided with their marriage.[19]

Harington's family held the most extensive estates in Rutland during the late sixteenth century. Through his marriage to Anne, he also acquired Combe Abbey on her father's death in 1581. They had two sons and two daughters. Harington divided his time between Exton, which had been magnificently renovated by his father, and his new property at Combe. He served regularly as an MP, especially after his father's death in 1592 and, as a leading local landowner, as JP in Rutland and Warwickshire and as deputy lieutenant in both counties in the 1590s.[20] By the end of Queen Elizabeth's reign Harington was one of the leading knights in the country, whose wealth equalled that of many barons. On the accession of James I, Harington took care to consolidate his position, travelling to Yorkshire to meet the new king and subsequently entertaining him to dinner at Burley-on-the-Hill. In June 1603 Princess Elizabeth, who was later to become Queen of Bohemia, stayed at Combe Abbey on her journey south, where she was later painted by Robert Peake (**104**). In July Harington was raised to the peerage at James' coronation as first Baron Harington of Exton and in October he was appointed Elizabeth's guardian. Elizabeth and her entourage were then established at Combe.[21] An attempt was made in November 1605 by the Gunpowder plotters to kidnap her, but it was foiled by Harington.[22] Subsequently it was felt that Elizabeth's household should be moved to Kew and by 1608 she was introduced to Court in London, but Harington remained her guardian and head of her household until her marriage in 1613.[23]

Harington incurred substantial costs in maintaining Elizabeth's household and in 1612 he petitioned for the privilege of coining brass farthings for three years in recompense. These coins were known as Haringtons. This grant was agreed before his wife and he accompanied Elizabeth and her husband, Frederick V, the Elector Palatine, to Germany in April 1613. In Heidelberg Harington spent four months arranging the princess' financial and household affairs. During the return journey he died of fever at Worms on 23 August 1613, aged seventy-three.[24] He had probably lived at Combe for over thirty years and the major building of the late sixteenth century was his work.[25]

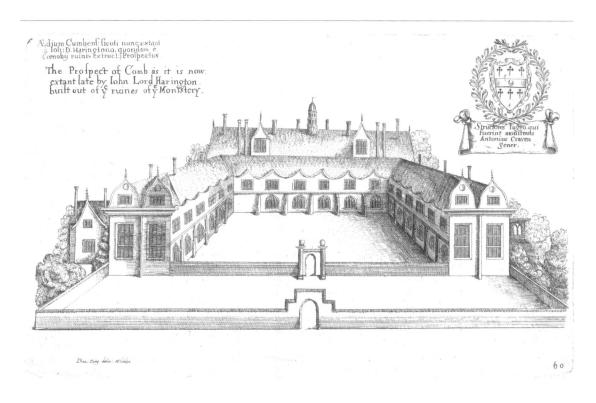

Ædium Cumbenf: ficuti nunc extant
à Ioh: D. Haringtono, quondam è
Cœnoby ruinis extruct.) Prospectus

The Prospect of Comb as it is now.
extant late by Iohn Lord Harington
built out of ý ruines of ý Monastery.

Structores Lugeo qui
fuerint monstrans
Antonius Craven
gener.

105 Daniel King's engraving of *The Prospect of Comb as it is now*, 1655

After the Dissolution, the abbey had been used as a residence between 1540 and 1580, but the major conversion was probably not carried out by tenants whose occupancy was short. It is likely that the initial conversion during this period was restricted to the west range.[26] The major task of converting the abbey into a fashionable Tudor courtyard house was carried out by John Harington, probably beginning around 1581, after his wife's inheritance of Combe. The earliest expressly dated feature was one of the first-floor chimneypieces in the south-west wing, which bore Harington's arms and the date 1590, although this was sold with other architectural fittings in 1925, when a large part of the house was demolished.[27] After the abbey's suppression, the Church was destroyed, together with the south cloister walk, leaving the remaining three ranges of the Cloister from which the new house was built. It is likely that the other claustral buildings remained substantially intact apart from the Church.[28] The site of the nave became the rectangular outer entrance court shown in Daniel King's perspective view in 1655 (*105*). This view shows the house as it was left by Harington, before subsequent remodelling. Where the south cloister walk joined the east and west walks, the entrances became door-ways to the new building, though unusually there was no central entrance. Harington integrated the remaining three fifteenth-century Cloister ranges into his new house. Where possible, existing masonry walls were used for the ground floor rooms, but much of the first floor was of new timber-framed construction.[29] The cloister walks were retained as a corridor

106 The west and north ranges of the Cloister at Combe Abbey

giving access to the ground floor rooms. Above the Cloister ranges Harington built a timber-framed upper storey with oriel windows, still there today (*106*). A stone façade was added later.[30]

The east and west sides of the Cloister, as built by Harington, were originally symmetrical. The remaining west side retains most of its sixteenth-century features, and is of two storeys and seven bays. The south end of these ranges ended in Dutch-style gables with scallop shell ornament that were fashionable at the end of the sixteenth century (*107*). These gables with their large mullioned-and-transomed windows introduce symmetry to the new house and create a grand impression for the approaching visitor. The interiors were equally impressive

and fashionable as can be seen in Jackson's drawing for Hall's *Baronial Halls and Picturesque Edifices of England,* with the very large window and ornate fireplace (*108*).

In the east range, the five oriel windows above the Cloister lit the long gallery, which overlooked the central courtyard. The rooms behind were lodgings, and there was a Great Chamber at the southern end with a very large window in the gable. This room, traditionally associated with Princess Elizabeth, had its own entrance up steps from the Great Garden on the east side of the house. At the top was a highly ornate porch with Renaissance decoration, above which were the arms of the princess.[31] This porch, which must have been built by Harington for the princess after 1603,

107 The south end of the west range, with its Dutch-style gables

is visible in King's engraving but was dismantled in 1863.

The monastic north range, which contained the Frater, was demolished and rebuilt with two large rooms parallel to the Cloister walk, which was retained. On the west was a new Great Hall, while the smaller eastern room is labelled 'Chapel' on a plan of 1678. At the northern end of the west range was the mediaeval kitchen, which is likely to have been retained by Harington since it remained on this site until the early twentieth century.[32] It would have adjoined or been in close proximity to the Great Hall.

In 1622 Combe was sold to Elizabeth, widow of Sir William Craven, former Lord Mayor of London and numerous changes were made during the subsequent centuries. In 1634 William, Baron Craven obtained a licence to enclose 650 acres, marking the beginning of Combe Park. In the 1660s Craven leased the property to his godson, Sir Isaac Gibson, who built a wing projecting westward from the southern end of the west wing. In 1680 Lord Craven's nephew Sir William Craven took up residence; he appointed William Winde, a Dutch architect, who worked on rebuilding the west range. Between 1771 and 1776 the park was remodelled by Lancelot 'Capability' Brown between 1771 and 1776, who removed the formal gardens and created a large lake by damming the Smite Brook. The lake, called the 'Great Pool', is shown on a 1778 map. It was dammed

108 *Combe Abbey, Warwickshire*, drawn by JG Jackson, showing an interior

near the remains of the monastic fishponds. In the 1860s the east wing of the house was demolished, and a new block built by William Eden Nesfield. Combe remained in the hands of the Cravens until after the Great War, when decline set in; the contents of the house were auctioned, and the estate was sold in numerous parcels. The abbey was bought in 1925 by JG Gray, a speculating builder, who demolished much of Nesfield's wing, remodelled the interior of the remaining part and lived there until his death in 1963. It was then bought by Coventry Corporation who created 'Coombe Abbey Country Park'. The present country house hotel was developed in the 1990s.[33]

Combermere Abbey

Combermere Abbey, near Whitchurch in Cheshire, sits low at the end of
a winding entrance drive which threads through a landscape of gently
unfolding pastureland dotted with oaks. The east front of the house,
gleaming in freshly painted render, bristles with pinnacles and pointed-
arched windows, while a battlemented and arrow-slitted curtain wall
extends to the left. At this point there is no sign of the eponymous mere,
though marshy bottoms along the drive suggest that this has always been
a watery place, perfect for the foundation of a monastic establishment.
It explains why, in 1133, on this wooded site close to the mere at the
boundaries of three counties – Cheshire, Shropshire and Staffordshire –
Hugh Malbank of Nantwich founded a Savignac abbey dedicated to St
Mary and St Michael. Nothing is known of the original monastic
complex, but it must have conformed closely to another Savignac house
at Buildwas in Shropshire, founded two years after Combermere. There,
unusually, the Cloister was sited to the north of the Abbey Church, and
therein lies a conundrum that must be faced in any reconstruction of the
monastic complex at Combermere. Even though it was later to become a
Cistercian house, Combermere was never visited by Harold Brakspear,
that indefatigable chronicler of such houses at the turn of the twentieth
century, and has never been subject to thorough archaeological investigation. As a result, any projected configuration must remain conjectural.

Apart from a series of disputes between the monks of Combermere and
other religious houses in the region, little is documented of the abbey
buildings until 1220, when Abbot Thomas de Gillyng was denounced to
the General Chapter for building against orders. There is also evidence of
the presence in the community, between 1266 and 1271, of Robert, a lay
brother who was keeper of the works for Henry III.[1] The abbey's reputation for indiscipline and involvement in local disorder continued until
the Dissolution, the low point being the murder of a monk by one of

109 Portrait of Sir Richard Cotton, 1579

110 The Gothick west front of Combermere Abbey

Abbot Christopher Walley's servants, which was hushed up for more than six months. The abbot's behaviour was reported to Thomas Cromwell, who was urged to put a more 'discreet head' in charge.[2] This was presumably John Massey, who was Abbot of Combermere when it was surrendered on 27 July 1538. Thereafter, in August 1539, Sir George Cotton and his wife Mary were granted 'the house and site of the later monastery of Combermere, Cheshire, the church, steeple, and churchyard thereof'.[3] Sir George died in 1545, and it was his son, Sir Richard (*109*), who converted the abbey into a new house.

In 1970, when the architectural historian Nikolaus Pevsner approached Combermere while researching for his *Buildings of England*

volume on Cheshire, he was, typically, less than enthusiastic about the late Regency Gothick house overlooking the mere (*110*). In fact, his entire entry on the house is rather dismissive, both of the original abbey itself, and the spiky Gothick house that replaced it. This must be due to his frustration in trying to disentangle the surviving monastic remains from the Gothick overlay, combined with his habitual antipathy towards country houses. He found the entrance side 'confusing', the porch 'recent and not in line with the front entrance' and the wings 'not regular either'.[4] As for survivals of the monastic complex, he reported: 'Little of it remains, and what does, though always called part of the refectory, is not convincing as such.'[5]

Fortunately, as a result of a remarkable

restoration of the north wing of the house commissioned by Sarah and Peter Callander Beckett and overseen by their architect Andrew Arrol, the surviving portions of the monastery have been discovered and the configuration of the claustral buildings can now be plotted with more certainty. However, this reconstruction depends upon the monastic use of what is now called the Library, but which occupies a great hall of the original abbey. Pevsner followed earlier authorities in stating that this room was 'supposed to be part of the monastic refectory', but was then puzzled by its siting on the first floor: 'the refectory surely was on the ground floor'.[6] There were many such first-floor refectories in English monasteries – those at Newstead Abbey and Forde Abbey to name just two – but the implication in Pevsner's account is that the surviving hall at Combermere was part of the Abbot's Lodgings and not the Refectory.

The original use of the space before it was adapted after the Dissolution is important to determine because refectories in monastic complexes, particularly Cistercian houses, are normally found within the cloister, whereas the Abbot's Lodgings, though sometimes located there, are often set apart, but attached to them. In their *Magna Britannica* of 1810, Daniel and Samuel Lysons remarked that 'the present library, which is forty feet by twenty-seven, is supposed to have been the refectory, but seems to have been altered soon after the dissolution; the ceiling and wainscot being much enriched with the ornaments then in use.'[7] JP Neale followed this interpretation in his 1829 *Views of the Seats*, as does Charles Hulbert, word for word, in his 1844 *Memorials of Departed Ages*, who found that 'the walls of the present Seat are chiefly those of the Old Abbey, recently coated and ornamented in the Gothic style.'[8] The *Victoria County History*

entry on Combermere, published in 1980, is more expansive:

> The abbey buildings lay on a level terrace on a south-facing hill-slope. The claustral buildings were south of the church and surviving portions, which are now incorporated in the house, are the south cloister and adjacent rooms, including those at the south corner which were probably kitchens, and a short length of the east range. The decoratively timberframed upper storey of the south range includes in its eastern part the late mediaeval refectory which has a hammer-beam roof with the arms of the abbey on each main spandrel. Abutting the east end of the south side of the refectory a smaller room may have been the misericord.[9]

This account has its compass bearings confused. What survives of the monastic complex is a range that faces west and a short section at the south-west corner that extends eastwards. Fortunately, when Peter de Figueiredo and Julian Treuherz came to Combermere for their *Cheshire Country Houses* book they got the orientation correct, stating that the present house was 'formed from the west range of the cloister', but they were more circumspect when it came to the original use of the Library.[10] They argued, plausibly, that the monks' Refectory would normally have been on the south range of the Cloister and that the high status of the surviving hammer beam roof suggested that 'the room was the Abbot's Hall, on the first floor of the west range of the cloister'.[11] Writing up the house for *Country Life* a little later in 1994, John Martin Robinson followed their lead, stating firmly that 'the church and most of the ranges about the cloisters were demolished, leaving only the west range. This contained

111 *Panorama of Combermere Abbey, c.1710-20*

the abbot's private accommodation, including a fine, late-mediaeval hall on the first floor which was retained as the nucleus of a new gabled and half-timbered house.'[12]

Later authorities have accepted this interpretation, most notably the three authors of an excellent 2003 archaeological report on tree ring analysis of the surviving mediaeval timbers at Combermere.[13] Their paper includes a plan of the 'possible arrangement of the Abbey buildings' drawn up on the assumption that the surviving Great Hall is of the Abbot's Lodgings rather than the monastic Refectory and, therefore, detached from the Cloister.[14] Their ring-dating analysis of the Great Hall roof proves that its timbers were felled in 1504, which must mean that Abbot John refurbished the roof before his death in 1516. There is no doubt that the monastic buildings were in a poor state of repair at this

time, because in 1496 the house was exempted from clerical taxation on the grounds of poverty.[15] Abbot John may well have spent money on refurbishing the Great Hall in his private apartments rather than upgrading the abbey complex and its important buildings. Abbot Chard embarked upon a major campaign of rebuilding at Forde Abbey at this time, which included a new Great Hall for his private lodgings, but his work also extended to a sumptuous new Perpendicular Gothic Cloister in the fan-vaulted style like that at Gloucester Abbey.

The authors' plan accompanying their timber dating analysis marks the present Library in the western range of a small courtyard to the north of the Abbey Church; they site the Cloister to the south of the nave in the usual arrangement. It is far more likely, however, that the present house forms the west arm of the Cloister and that the Abbey Church was sited further to the north, as at Buildwas. If the range at the south-west was where the monastic kitchen was sited then it would be at the farthest point from the Church where almost all mediaeval kitchens were located. What we do have, however, are two important early eighteenth-century archival images of Combermere, which offer some clues, and there are the recent discoveries made during the restoration of the north wing.

The first image is a spectacular painting of the house from the west set within its landscape (*111*), before the mere was extended across the west front of the house.[16] This shows a symmetrical timber-framed gabled structure, the end wings projecting slightly, commanding a formal walled courtyard; there is a further brick walled courtyard to the rear, possibly aligned on the foundations of the former Cloister. The roof of the Great Hall, with its cupola, is visible behind the three

112 *The West View of Combermere Abby, in the County of Chester*, engraved by Samuel and Nathaniel Buck, 1727

central gables, suggesting that the northern wing to the left was a Cotton addition to the original monastic range. The elaborate timber framing of the central section is supported on masonry, as at Vale Royal Abbey near Northwich. Set back at the south-west corner to the right is another timber-clad element, which is likely to have been the monastic kitchen. The painting is unsigned and undated, but John

Harris has given it a tentative date of circa 1710-1720 based on topographical style.[17] Judging by the architectural details of the pleasure pavilion across the water, the forecourt lodge and the stunning arcs of white ironwork gates it is unlikely to be later than 1725.[18]

The second visual record is an engraving of 1727 by Samuel and Nathaniel Buck of the

113 *Portrait of Henry VIII, c.1579*

east, or rear, façade of the Cotton house (*112*). The Great Hall with its cupola is visible again behind the three central gables, and from this vantage point it is much clearer that the northern wing was a Cotton addition to the original monastic range. The curious round-arched arcading which produces a covered loggia is suggestive of the remains of the Cloister, but is likely to be a Cotton embellish-ment, as there is similar round-arched arcading on the screen in the Library and on three sides of the cove of its ceiling. However, more telling is the presence on the southern projecting wing of two blocked pointed-arched openings; presumably these were once the part of the south Cloister walk.

The abbey was granted to Sir George Cotton, an Esquire of the Body and

114 The Library ceiling at Combermere

Comptroller of the Household to Henry VIII's illegitimate son, the Duke of Richmond. He followed legal precedent, set down by the Court of Augmentations, and demolished the Abbey Church and most of the monastic complex, but retained the west range of the Cloister with its newly refurbished Great Hall. He did not have long to live, dying in 1545, and it was left to his son, Sir Richard, to create a country house with timber-framed façades out of the ruined abbey. A tablet with the date 1563 discovered in the eighteenth century probably records the completion of the first phase of work: 'Master Richard Cotton and his sons three both for their pleasure and commoditie this building did edifie in fifteen hundred and sixty three.'[19] The woodwork screen in the Great Hall carries a later date of 1580, so the interior fitting up may have continued after that date.

Sir Richard's portrait is set within the woodwork overmantel of the chimneypiece in the Great Hall. Alongside him is the king that made it all possible, a bejewelled Henry (*113*), who looks down above the royal coat of arms, which features a Welsh dragon. Robinson suggests that these paintings were part of an 1820s remodelling by Lord Combermere with 'Wardour Street' woodwork and 'ancestral' portraits and heraldry to create the Library.[20] Recent restoration has uncovered a massive stone fireplace behind the later chimneypiece, so this may be the case, although the portraits might have been moved here from elsewhere in the house. Although some of the woodwork of the overmantel is made up of unrelated

115 A spandrel in the roof with the carved arms of Combermere Abbey

sections, it is clear that the basic structure of the screen is Elizabethan and dates from Sir Richard's time.

The Gothic ribbed ceiling and cove with its round-arched decoration (*114*) is also of Sir Richard's campaign, having been suspended beneath the Tudor hammer beam structure that survives in the roof above it. This last is a wonderfully numinous space, its north wall squared with interlocking framing, while above, moulded trusses arch up to meet in elaborately carved bosses at the ridge. In the spandrel braces of these great timbers, quatrefoils enclose the arms of the abbey, which feature a crozier (*115*). It is here in the shadows at the north end that Andrew Arrol has discovered the supporting braces of what he believes to be a dais canopy, proving that

Abbot John was refurbishing his private apartments in the early sixteenth century rather than re-roofing the monastic Refectory. In the Library below, this canopy is expressed in the squared ribbing at the north end, while the three other sides of the coving all have round-arched decoration. Ribs crash into each other at the junction of the mediaeval and the Elizabethan, suggestive of the charmingly gimcrack campaign of the Cotton adaptation and renewal.

Forde Abbey

On the approach to Forde Abbey from the north, through the extensive walled garden at the rear of the house, the visitor comes across a long battlemented range of jumbled projecting and recessed elements lit by mullioned-and-transomed windows, with the odd opening of hexagonal glazing. To the right of the Georgian glazing there is a row of four-centred, arched blind windows and above them a steeply gabled roof. These once lit the north wall of the Great Hall of the Abbot's Lodgings (*116*), raised between 1522 and 1528 by Abbot Thomas Chard, who was in charge of the monastery at the Dissolution.[1] On the left, set at right angles to the main block, is a gabled range lit on its first floor by thin lancets, while blocked arched openings on its north façade suggest entrances to further buildings now lost (*117*). This vast wing, with its stone-vaulted undercroft, was the monks' Dorter, connecting via a parlour with the Chapter House, whose roof can be seen with its jaunty open cupola. A door in the undercroft leads out to the grounds where, having skirted the rear of the Dorter range and noted the traceried late Perpendicular Gothic east window of the former Chapter House, now converted into a chapel – hence the cupola – the south front of the former abbey comes into focus (*118*).

If Iris Murdoch had invented Forde as a setting for one of her early novels, such as *The Bell*, critics would have said her imagination had run too far ahead of her. As the eye moves along this implausibly lengthy façade, exuberant late-Perpendicular Gothic lapses over into early sixteenth-century Renaissance, with the Commonwealth's club-footed classicism thrown in at the centre for good measure. These disparate styles should not go together in one house, but at Forde Abbey they do. The range begins on the right with the blockish former Chapter House; then, set back, comes the surviving rear wall of the former Cloister, with its panelled Perpendicular tracery. The centrepiece, with its diminutive

116 The interior of the Great Hall of Abbot Chard at Forde Abbey

117 The North Front of Forde Abbey

porte cochère struggling under the weight of the Serlian great window above, which lights the Saloon, was added by Edmund Prideaux, who bought the house in 1649. It dwarfs in bulk Abbot Chard's magnificent early sixteenth-century Gatehouse Tower, but at least this manages to rise above it. To the left of the Tower there are four surviving bays of Chard's Great Hall, emblazoned with Renaissance decoration, followed by the remainder of the former Abbot's Lodgings, expanded and re-fenestrated by Prideaux. An attempt has been made to pull the whole elevation together with a battlemented parapet.

Forde Abbey began as a Cistercian community, its priory having been established about 1133 by Richard Fitzbaldwin (de Brionne) on his land at Brightley, near Okehampton. However, the land there was found to be infertile and Fitzbaldwin's sister Adelicia offered the monks another site by the river Axe in Thorncombe where, between 1141 and 1148, they built a new priory dedicated to the Virgin Mary. This became known as 'Ford' after the river crossing nearby. John of Forde was the first prior; from 1186 he was abbot of the daughter house at Bindon and, between 1191 and 1214, Abbot of Forde. The abbey complex

took the typical form of a cruciform church attached to conventual buildings, but because it was sited on the south bank of the Axe the Abbey Church was built to the south of the Cloister in a reversal of the usual arrangement. The Abbot's Hall and Lodgings were in a separate block to the west, all of which can be seen in Harold Brakspear's redrawn plan (*119*).

Thomas Chard was a well-educated man from a family of clerics. Born in about 1470 at Tracey Hayes outside Honiton[2] he was educated at the Cistercian college of St Bernard's in Oxford, now St John's College, where he was described as *vir magna doctrina*

et virtute clarus (a shining example of virtue and learning).[3] He procured several livings in Devon and Cornwall and from 1513 to 1527 was an inspector of English Cistercian houses, appointed by the Abbot of Cîteaux in Burgundy. He was elected Abbot of Forde in 1521, having travelled extensively in England and perhaps also in France, which might explain the cultural sophistication of the additions he made to Forde after 1522.

Abbot Chard's rebuilding of the complex can be seen in his Tower and Great Hall, as well as in the surviving northern arm of the Cloister. Here the Purbeck marble shafts of

118 The South Front of Forde Abbey

the original arcading have been revealed behind the Perpendicular casing overlaid on it in the early sixteenth century (*120*). However, it is on the exterior that Abbot Chard's knowledge of European decoration is displayed, in a series of carved panels set just below the embattled parapet, in which soldiers thrust at each other and griffins and sphinx-like winged women sit back-to-back (*121*). Elsewhere, green men clutch branches, while a bearded man and helmeted woman converse through scrolling foliage from panel to panel. This Renaissance detail, beautifully carved from golden Ham Hill stone, sits within a mediaeval Gothic frame. Chard's Tower has a Perpendicular Gothic fan vault and the rooms above are lit by a battery of oriel windows. Here the decoration is typically late mediaeval, with heraldic devices set in lozenges, though just below the parapet there are two more Renaissance-style panels and an inscription in Latin

giving Chard as the builder – '*factum est Toma Chard, Abb*' – and the date, 1528.

The abbey was surrendered in 1539 and the complex and lands were leased to Richard Pollard of King's Nympton, Devon, who had been Justice of the Common Pleas. Pollard was a lawyer and engaged in the preparation of the *Valor,* later holding the post of General Surveyor in the Court of Augmentations. His most infamous act was to destroy the shrine of Thomas Becket at Canterbury and supervise the removal of two chests of treasure from the monastery. Together with his brother Hugh and William Petre, he was responsible for closing most of the monasteries in the southwest. Petre and Hugh Pollard arrived at Forde in March 1539 and Abbot Chard surrendered the abbey to them on 8 March.[4] Thereafter, Hugh Pollard and Petre went off to Montacute to close the Clunaic priory there. For his services to the king during the Dissolution,

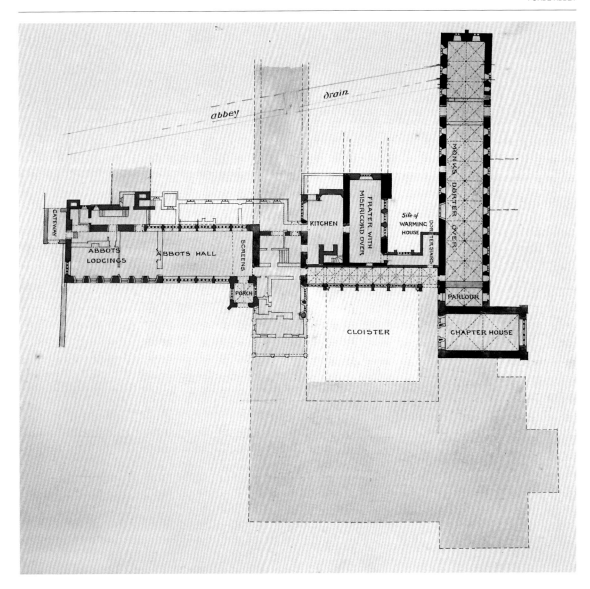

119 A plan of Forde Abbey, originally by Harold Brakspear

120 The north range of the Cloister at Forde Abbey

Richard Pollard was given Forde Abbey, though initially on a lease. He eventually bought the abbey and its properties for £417 in May 1540, the deed of sale being signed by Richard Rich, Chancellor of the Court of Augmentations.[5] Richard Pollard survived Cromwell's downfall and was knighted in 1542, though he died the same year. His eldest son John sold Forde Abbey in about 1558 to his cousin, Sir Amias Paulet of Hinton St George. William Rosewell purchased Forde Abbey in about 1581, and the Rosewell family owned the house until it was sold in the mid-seventeenth century to the lawyer and politician Edmund Prideaux.

It is likely that the Abbey Church and three arms of the Cloister, if it was ever completed by Abbot Chard, were demolished at the Dissolution and that the Pollards, Paulets and Rosewells made domestic use of the surviving monastic buildings rather than constructing anything new. Prideaux retained all of these and converted some of them into state rooms, adding a storey over the surviving north range of the Cloister and enlarging a gallery on the first floor that had been the Abbot's office, to create the Saloon, which projects from the main façade. This double cube was built specifically for Prideaux's stunning collection of Mortlake tapestries woven from the Raphael Cartoons. Sir Henry Rosewell, a staunch Puritan, was responsible for converting the former Chapter House into a chapel in the early seventeenth century.

121 Carved panels on the exterior of the Cloister at Forde Abbey

Abbot Chard's Great Hall is a majestic space. Its original six bays, which extended to eighty feet, were shortened by Prideaux to four bays by the insertion of a dividing wall to provide a private dining room where once Abbot Chard had enjoyed his meals at a high table raised on a dais. Windows in the north wall were blocked up, panelling was installed, and a fireplace introduced. Prideaux made a bedroom in the space above the new dining room and raised the former Abbot's Lodgings to three storeys. It would seem that money had run out in the 1530s, for where Chard had probably projected a stone vaulted roof a framed wooden covering was built; this is not of Prideaux's campaign and must be earlier. A big-eared face like a mediaeval court jester

pokes its tongue out cheekily on one of the bosses of its ribbing (*122*). John Leland visited Forde in the 1530s and recorded that Abbot John of Ford had been 'buried without great pomp in his monastery which the abbot [Chard] is now restoring most magnificently, at quite incredible expense'.[6] Perhaps this 'incredible expense' was insufficient to complete his major refurbishment and explains why the surviving Cloister (*123*) is covered with a simple, ribbed plaster vault rather than the stone-vaulted fan one would expect – a proto-Gothic Prideaux solution to vie with the sumptuous Inigo Jones-inspired ceilings of the state rooms on the floor above.[7]

122 A boss of the vaulted roof of Abbot Chard's Great Hall

123 The surviving cloister walk interior at Forde Abbey

Hailes Abbey

The demise of the Cistercian Hailes Abbey, founded by Richard, Earl of Cornwall, in 1246, began in 1538 with the destruction of the Shrine of the Holy Blood, which had made it celebrated as a place of pilgrimage since the late thirteenth century. In 1270 Edmund, Earl of Cornwall, second son of the founder, returned from Germany with 'the precious blood of Christ which had been sent as a great present to Charlemain from Greece'.[1] On 14 September that year, the Feast of the Holy Cross, attended by monks from the convents of Hailes and nearby Winchcombe, Edmund carried the vessel 'in solemn procession' to be laid in the Abbey Church at Hailes.[2] Thereafter, a magnificent stone Shrine, its foundations discovered in the 1899-1908 excavations, was built for the relic and sited behind the high altar in the sanctuary, which was transformed over the next seven years for its presentation with five pentagonal chapels radiating out from the ambulatory. It was said that 'a man being in mortal sin could not see the blood, but as soon as he was absolved he might quickly discern it'.[3] One side of the glass phial containing the Holy Blood was much thicker than the other, and it was only when the priest was satisfied that the penitent had paid for enough masses that the more transparent side was presented to him and he could discern the relic. In this devious way the monastery was enriched, its site the focus for pilgrims seeking absolution from sin. Unsurprisingly, given that pardoners were licensed to issue indulgences or pardons for sins, the Holy Blood is mentioned in Geoffrey Chaucer's Pardoner's Tale, written a hundred years after Edmund's gift:

> By God's Precious heart and by His nails
> And by the blood of Christ that's now at Hailes.

By 1538, however, Thomas Cromwell had appointed commissioners in every county to destroy all relics and their shrines, including the Holy

124 Stone fragments in St Michael's Church, Buckland, Gloucestershire, which may have come from the Shrine at Hailes Abbey

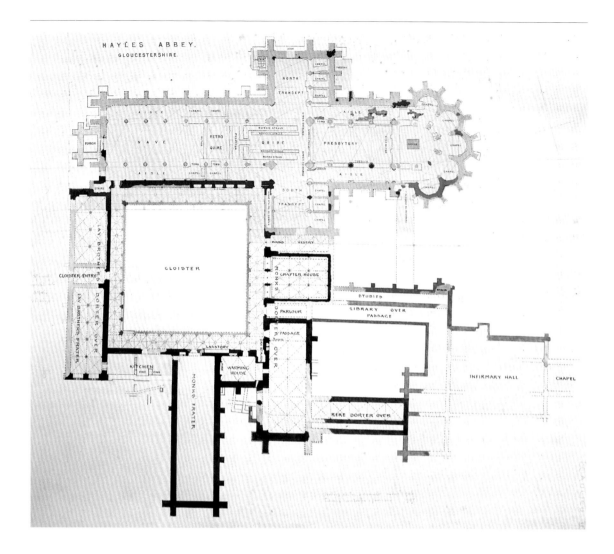

125 Plan of Hailes Abbey by Harold Brakspear

Blood of Hailes, but with the command that 'the garnishing of the Shrine' be salvaged and 'reserved for the King'.[4]

The Holy Blood was 'enclosed within a round Beryl, garnished and bound on every side with silver'.[5] When Hugh Latimer, Bishop of Worcester, took possession of the glass phial containing the Holy Blood he reported to Cromwell that the fluid within it, thought to be the blood of a duck, appeared to be 'an unctuous gum and a compound of many things', but it was not blood.[6] The phial was sent to London and examined there by the Bishop of Rochester who pronounced the contents to be 'honey clarified and coloured with saffron'.[7] Retiring Abbot Stephen Sagar seems to have been complicit in the despolia-tion at Hailes because he wrote to Cromwell asking that he might destroy the empty Shrine. During the excavations it was found to have measured 8 feet by 10 feet and was sited 42 feet from the rear wall of the central chapel.[8] If its design were similar to that of the contemporary shrine containing relics of St Edward the Confessor in Westminster Abbey, it would have been a rectangular stone plinth on which the relic was displayed in a 'cabinet of crystal'.[9] It may be that painted stone frag-ments from Hailes, now in St Michael's Church, Buckland are not the remains of an altarpiece, but perhaps part of the Shrine (*124*).

In December 1539 Abbot Sagar and twenty monks surrendered the monastery and, there-after, the commissioners of the Court of Augmentations ordered that the following houses and buildings should remain unde-faced: 'The late Abbot's lodynge extending from ye church to ye Frater Southwood with Payntre, butter, Kitchen, larder, sellers and ye lodynges over ye same'.[10] Robert Acton was put in charge of dismantling the rest of the abbey complex before Richard Andrews, who was making a profitable business dealing in monastic properties and stripping their assets, was granted the site in 1542 and given the title of Constable of Hailes. In 1543, on the marriage of Henry VIII to Katherine Parr, Hailes was given to her as part of her dowry; her brother, William Parr, Marquess of Northampton, subsequently leased Hailes in 1550 to Henry Hodgkins. He was a local landowner, had acquired other ex-monastic property in nearby Winchcombe and had acted as Keeper of Sudeley Castle between 1547 and 1549. Hodgkins bequeathed Hailes to his daughter Alice and her husband William Hoby of Marden in Hampshire; the Tracy family subsequently bought it in the early seventeenth century.[11]

We owe our understanding of the layout of the mediaeval abbey at Hailes to two amateur archaeologists, the Revd William Bazeley and Wellbore St Clair Baddeley, who excavated the site between 1899 and 1908. St Clair Baddeley followed up the investigation in 1908 with a history of Hailes entitled *A Cotteswolde Shrine*, which first brought the relic of the Holy Blood to the attention of a modern read-ership. The architect Harold Brakspear had drawn for them another of his meticulously detailed plans, which Sir James Fowler, later Custodian of Hailes Abbey and creator of the first museum on the site, illustrated in his history and guide to the abbey, published in 1928.[12] Brakspear's plan (*125*) reveals a typical monastic layout of a cruciform Abbey Church with a Cloister to the south. Around it were ranged the usual elements of the Chapter House with the monks' Dorter above it, the kitchen and warming house flanking the Frater, and the Abbot's Lodgings on the west range of the complex, originally the lay brother's quarters, but which had been

126 The site of Hailes Abbey showing the ruins of the Cloister and the layout of the abbey

upgraded in the fourteenth century after the Black Death.[13] It was within these Lodgings that part of the post-Dissolution house was created, overlooking on its east façade the surviving Cloister (*126*).

There is a rare and wonderfully detailed map of Hailes and the surrounding area drawn in 1587 by the Elizabethan map maker Ralph Treswell (*127*), which shows the monastic precinct with all its attendant buildings, including the parish church and, at its heart, the 'Manor Howse' that was created from the dissolved complex.[14] From Treswell's vignette it is clear that the surviving range of the monastery had been increased in size, with a parallel range to the west. The west façade has a crenellated entrance tower at the south-western corner and a lower section

extending north with a projecting wing. The roofs of the original monastic range can be seen to the rear, together with the north-eastern corner of the Cloister. A likely chronology for the house is, therefore, that the original west range was converted by Hodgkins and that this was subsequently doubled in size by his daughter and son-in-law, William Hoby, after 1570 and before 1587 when it was drawn by Treswell. Unfortunately, there is no sixteenth-century description of the dissolved complex to set against that shown on Treswell's map. The first topographical account was written over a hundred years later when that indefatigable traveller, Celia Fiennes, rode in 1697 from Moreton-in-the Marsh 'over steep stony hills' to 'Hales' where she found 'a good old house' with 'a pretty Chap-

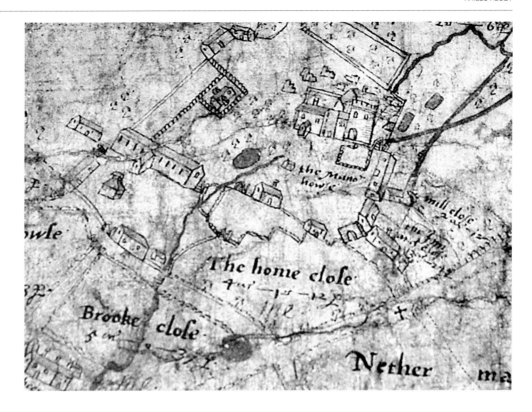

127 Detail of a map of Hailes Abbey by Ralph Treswell, 1587

pel with a gallery for people of quality to sitt in, which goes out of the hall, that is a lofty large roome'.[15] This is a vestigial account but gives some idea of the interiors of the house depicted by Treswell. The hall must have been accessed from the gatehouse and the projecting wing must be the chapel.

The 'Manor Howse', now styled 'Hales Abbey', is recorded in two early eighteenth-century engravings by Jan Kip and Leonard Knyff of 1712 and by Samuel and Nathaniel Buck of 1732. These show, respectively, west and east views of the house. The Kip-Knyff view (*128*) corresponds to the Treswell vignette but gives more detail of the fenestration of the hall, which is lit by large mullioned-and-transomed windows, and the projecting chapel, both seen by Fiennes in 1694. The only architectural feature of this front visible on the Bucks' view (*129*) is the cupola at the junction of the south and west ranges; otherwise this 1732 east view is a true record of the former Abbot's Lodgings and the surviving cloister garth. Significantly, the Kip-Knyff view omits the Cloister entirely, opting instead to display a vast formal garden, which may, or may not, have been laid out before 1712; the Cloister appears in two later eighteenth-century images of the complex and survives in ruins today.

The veracity of the Bucks' east view of the abbey is confirmed by Thomas Robins' delightful watercolour of the complex (*130*), painted in about 1748, with which it accords precisely.[16] At this point the Tracys had let out the house as two farmhouses, so instead of

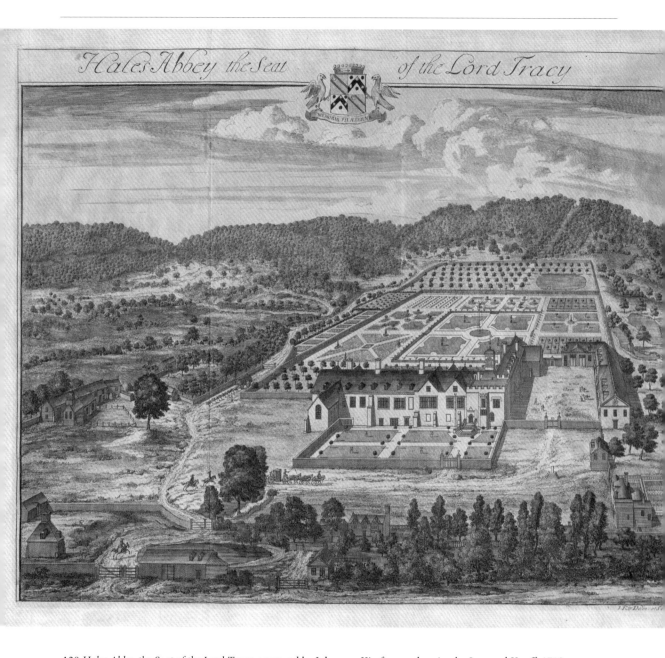

128 *Hales Abby, the Seat of the Lord Tracy*, engraved by Johannes Kip from a drawing by Leonard Knyff, 1712

129 *The East View of Hales Abby in the County of Gloucester*, engraved by Samuel and Nathaniel Buck, 1732

working to a specific commission, Robins may well have stopped off at Hailes to paint the complex for a proposed engraving, as he was to do at Buildwas Abbey and Wenlock Priory in Shropshire. His charming painting is so meticulously detailed that it is possible to examine the intricate mediaeval tracery of the east façade, some of which survives (**131**), and the seventeenth-century cross-mullioned fenestration of the south range with its row of dormer windows above; also the projecting gatehouse block at the south-western corner. Both images suggest that the formal gardens shown in the 1712 engraving were probably fictions; so too was the stable block on the south side: a projection of what might have been planned at that time, but never executed. As with so many of Robins' beautiful paintings of mid-century houses and gardens, we have a contemporary descriptive corroboration from another traveller. On 26 May 1757 Dr Richard Pococke set out from Evesham and came to 'Halls Abbey … at the rise of a small stream which falls into the Isbon'.[17] Always attuned to the ownership and antiquity of a place, he

reported that it 'is in Ld Tracey's family', of nearby Stanway and Toddington manors, 'and was one of their seats about sixty years ago'.[18] Taken together with Robins' watercolour, his description gives a fair account of what had survived of the abbey up to the middle of the eighteenth century:

> Very little remains of the old buildings, except a part in the front, with a handsom bow window call'd the Abbot's Chamber, some fine arches, which they say was the cellar, one entire side of the cloister, and the outer wall is all round, several large barns and a pidgeon house near 40 feet square with buttresses at each corner, and a chapel now in service all of hewn stone.

However, by the time the Revd Samuel Lysons drew it in 1794 for his *Antiquities* only one corner tower, a gable end and the partially submerged, ruined Cloister of the property were still standing.[19]

130 *View of Hailes Abbey, Gloucestershire*, Thomas Robins the Elder, *c.*1745

131 Hailes Abbey ruins, with the surviving mediaeval tracery

Lacock Abbey

In early evening, the sun slants from the west across the golden stone ranges of Lacock Abbey (*132*), low-lying in its meadows by the meandering Avon. When the National Trust visitors have all gone home, one can sense the peace and tranquillity that Ela, Countess of Salisbury, its first abbess, sought when she established a nunnery for Augustine canonesses here in 1232 and where she was buried when she died in 1261.[1] Sited close to the village, yet within its own sylvan landscape of oaks and elms, the flat riverine terrain rising up on the east to the wooded slopes of Bowden Hill, the place must have seemed an earthly paradise to William Sharington, who bought the abbey after its suppression in June 1540 and began to rebuild it as a family home.

Sharington was of Norfolk stock and little is known of his formative years in East Anglia, but by 1538 he was in the retinue of Sir Francis Bryan, Chief Gentleman of the Privy Chamber; had become Page of the Robes and Groom by 1540; and achieved elevation to the Privy Chamber in 1541. In Hans Holbein the Younger's chalk study he appears thoughtful and assured with a penetrating gaze under hooded eyelids, his delicate mouth shadowed by a thick moustache and full beard, red and bristly, accentuating the length of his long face. The sketch, on pink-primed paper, must date from Holbein's second visit to England of 1532 to 1543, when Sharington was at the height of his influence at Court.[2]

There are further Holbein connections at Lacock, particularly in the design of the Muniment Room table in Sharington's tower and in a portrait of Henry VIII, thought to be by the artist. When Charles Henry Talbot was researching at the house in the early twentieth century he noted:

> a portrait of Henry VIII – always reputed to be by Holbein – [which] was, no doubt, in the possession of Sir William Sharington. Ivory Talbot placed it in a fixed stucco frame, in the dining-room, from which I removed it. The picture,

132 Lacock Abbey, Wiltshire

when taken down, appeared to be in a very bad state. It was on the original panel, but Messrs. Dyer and Sons transferred it to canvas, considering that operation to be absolutely necessary. A great deal of detail came out, and there is no reason to doubt it is Holbein's work, as the picture is a very fine one.[3]

The painting was subsequently sold and a portrait of John Ivory Talbot was cut down from a larger canvas and fitted into the stucco frame. The Holbein of the king is thought to be in a collection in America.

There is a much later portrait at Lacock of the man who by 1548 owned no fewer than fourteen manors and estates in Wiltshire and the surrounding counties, was a successful merchant and moneylender and kept several ships at Bristol where he was Vice-Treasurer of the Mint in the castle.[4] He abused his position at the Mint shamelessly and together with Thomas Seymour of Sudeley Castle was arrested on charges of debasing the coinage by illegally clipping the coins it issued, and also for embezzlement. Whereas Seymour was beheaded for treason, Sharington confessed and was pardoned on forfeiture of his lands. These, however, were restored after a vast payment of £8,000 and he regained royal favour. In the three-quarter-length portrait (*133*) Sharington's red beard has grown to

biblical proportions and he stands proudly against a classically pure architectural backdrop, dressed in black robes with a fur collar, clutching his riding gloves and with a dagger thrust into his belt. Its gold hilt, elaborately chased, seems to be crafted into a sinuous creature with pronged claws and an upturned tail. Could this be the scorpion that Sharington took as his badge, with which he sealed his letters, after which he named one of his ships, that is emblazoned on the ceiling ribs and table of his Muniment Room, and that features within three strapwork cartouches on his tomb chest in Lacock parish church?

Sharington's exact birth date around 1495 is not recorded, but it may be that he was born under the star sign Scorpio in either October or November and that he adopted the scorpion for that reason. Certainly the sign reflects his fiercely independent character and his desire to control, while the scorpion itself acts as a venomous warning to those who might be inclined to cross him. His third wife, Grace Paget, whom he married in 1542, adopted the unicorn badge of her family (Farrington), which Sharington had carved alongside his scorpion on one of the ceiling bosses of the Muniment Room vault. It is likely that their conjoined ciphers and the initials W and G mark their marriage and suggest that the tower was built to celebrate

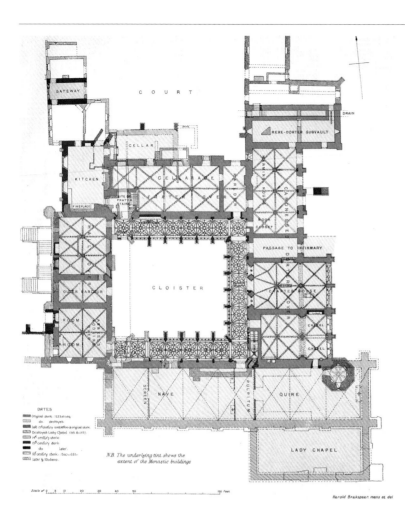

134 Plan of Lacock Abbey by
Harold Brakspear

Labels within the plan:

GATEWAY
COURT
DRAIN
CELLAR
RERE-DORTER SUBVAULT
KITCHEN
FIREPLACE
PASSAGE TO INFIRMARY
CLOISTER
OUTER PARLOUR
ROOM
ROOM
SCREEN
NAVE
PULPITUM
QUIRE
LADY CHAPEL

DATES
Original work. 1232 below...
do.   destroyed.
Late 13 century completion of original work.
Destroyed Lady Chapel 1315 & 1331.
14 century work.
15 century work.
do.   later.
16 century work. 1540–1550.
later & Modern.

N.B. The underlying tint shews the extent of the Monastic buildings

Scale of   0   5   10   20   30   40   50   100 Feet

Harold Brakspear mens et del

---

their union. The scorpion also featured with his and her initials on a pavement of tiles laid in the Stone Gallery, which were taken up in the nineteenth century.[5]

When the abbey was surrendered on 21 January 1539, it was described in the documentation as 'a hedde house of nunnes of S. Augsteynes rule, of great and large buildings, set in a towne'.[6] At the time of its suppression the abbey buildings comprised 'Church, mansion and all oder houses in very good astate'.[7] It had obviously been well administered, as there were no debts owing. On 26 July 1540 the abbey and its possessions were granted to Sir William Sharington and he began immediately to convert the claustral buildings into a manor house, making the fifteenth-century Cloister the heart of the new mansion and destroying those elements that were superfluous to his plan, including the Church and the Infirmary. Almost all trace of these has disappeared, even the foundations. The nave of the Church extended along the south wall of the Cloister and its choir projected out east, just beyond the Sharington tower. A Lady Chapel had been added to the south wall of the choir in 1315. The Infirmary was a separate building to the east of the Cloister, orientated north-south and accessed by a covered passage. To the north of the Cloister

Sharington built a completely new ancillary courtyard, which survives almost intact.

We owe our understanding of the original abbey buildings and their uses to archaeological work undertaken at the end of the nineteenth century and written up with detailed analysis in 1900 for the Society of Antiquaries' journal *Archaeologia* by the architect Harold Brakspear, who produced a reliable plan of the complex (*134*). In addition to this interpretative work there are two important visual sources for the former monastic establishment: a sketch of the west front made in 1684 and an engraving of the south-east view of the nunnery of 1732. These show the monastic buildings after they had been converted by Sharington and before the great remodelling of the 1750s carried out by John Ivory Talbot. Taken together with Brakspear's investigations, they convey the precise character and extent of the abbey that Sharington adapted to create his mansion.

The sketch of the west front was drawn by the seventeenth-century traveller and antiquary Thomas Dingley, who visited the abbey on 30 April 1684 and recorded his findings in a journal. Dingley's *History from Marble*, published from this journal by the Camden Society in 1867-8, was the result of several years spent travelling in England between 1680 and 1684.[8] From Lacock he went the following day to neighbouring Sir Walter Long's Spy Park and passed Sharington's water supply on his way there, for he noted that a coat of arms in the abbey was 'the very same as that are cutt in stone over the door of the Conduit upon a steep hill which through pipes of lead conveys water to this Abbey'.[9] Sharington's Conduit is an extraordinary survival where the decayed coats of arms can still be made out, set within roundels of foliage, on the gabled façades.

Dingley's sketch of the west front of Lacock is the earliest recorded image of the house that Sharington constructed from the dissolved nunnery. His bird's eye view shows the entire range of the façade, from the service courtyard on the left, north side, to the corner of the former Abbess' Lodgings at the south corner with its own doorway. Set back behind this to the east, Sharington's octagonal tower rises up to its heraldic crown and domed staircase turret. All these elements are present in a ground plan of the house (*135*) given on a map dating to 1714.[10] The main entrance to the house is to the left, in the two-bay, gabled section, which probably led to a screens passage with the Great Hall to the right and the kitchen to the left leading to the Frater. The huge mullioned and transomed windows and the gables are reminiscent of the ranges that Sharington had devised in 1540 for his friend John Dudley, Duke of Northumberland, at Dudley Castle.[11] Significantly, the Sharington Range at Dudley also has a tall, octagonal prospect tower. Dates vary for Sharington's work at Lacock, with some authorities suggesting that the octagonal tower (*136*) is as late as 1553, the year of Sharington's death. However, it is far more likely that it dates from the 1540s, when he first embarked upon his building works and may, indeed, be coeval with the tower he was devising at that time for Dudley.

Dingley's sketch is also a precious record of the entrance forecourt, enlivened with a sundial, which survives at the south-east corner below the tower, and the grounds to the south of the abbey, where there are compartmental formal gardens enclosed by walls and tree-lined hedges. Similar tree avenues are recorded to the west on Samuel and Nathaniel Buck's 1732 south-east view of Lacock (*137*), but the area to the south of the

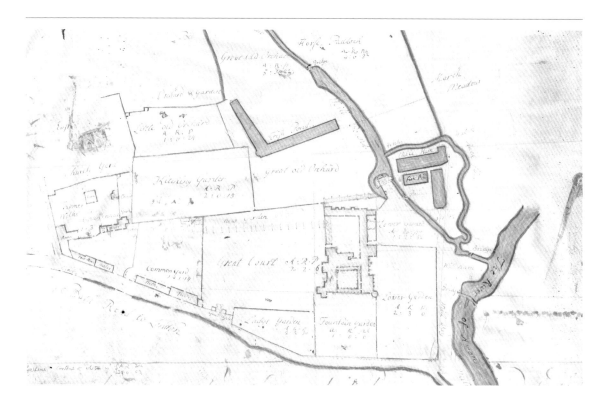

135 Detail from a map of Lacock Abbey, 1714

house is open fields beyond a bastioned walk-way, part of the great water garden laid out by John Talbot to the north-east of the house at some point after 1714 and before 1732.[12]

The Bucks' view shows the south and east façades of Sharington's house. The south front is dominated at its south-east corner by the tower and at the opposite end by the gabled former Abbess' Lodgings. In between, the north wall of the nave of the demolished Church can be clearly seen in the arcade of pointed arches inset with smaller blocked openings denoting the clerestory windows. Above this is Sharington's balustraded rooftop walk to the Prospect Room in his tower. The east range is the best-preserved elevation of the former nunnery. Although Sharington introduced several new mullioned and tran-

somed windows here – those that survive as fragments in the Reredorter have his mason's idiosyncratic shouldered consoles in the upper lights, with circles defining the junction of mullion and transom – the separate mediaeval elements of the abbey can be discerned.[13] They are miraculous survivals of the former nunnery; their interiors, columned and rib-vaulted, have that chalky, un-restored character rarely to be found in mediaeval buildings in England. To the left is the Sacristy (*138*) alongside the Chapter House; after that come the Warming House and the projecting Reredorter. On the floor above was the Dorter, or sleeping quarters for the canonesses, which Sharington transformed into the Stone Gallery. On his 1684 visit Dingley drew a stained glass window depicting a bishop 'in the Passage

136 Sir William Sharington's Tower at Lacock Abbey

leading out of the Great Dining Room towards the matted and Stone Galeries', both of which appear in a later inventory of the abbey.[14]

Due to John Talbot's Gothick rebuilding of the Great Hall in the 1750s, the original hall of both the nunnery and, subsequently, Sharington's house was lost. So too were Sharington's apartments on the south side of the complex, but the Stone Gallery on the east has a chimneypiece that must date from Sharington's period. It is elegantly austere, but its jambs are decorated with Renaissance military detail of shields, bows and arrows and drums delicately interlinked with ribbons. Above this gallery in the roof there is another miraculous survival of the mediaeval nunnery. Within the attic storey of what would have been the nuns' Dorter, its roof enlivened with cusped wind braces, Sharington inserted partition walls to

contrive another gallery, which leads at its south end via steps to his rooftop walk and Prospect Room. The coved cornice of this Long Gallery is studded with nails that must have been driven in to support tapestries. In the conversion of the abbey he also retained a further mediaeval roof, which survives, with three tiers of wind braces, over what had been the nuns' Frater.

An inventory of 1575 taken for Henry Sharington, who inherited the property on his brother's sudden death in August 1553, lists the rooms at that time and reveals the richness of the Sharington interiors.[15] Indeed, the inventory adds up to £1,047 12s 11d, which was a vast sum for the period. Many of the 'Turkey carpets', silk and velvet cushions, quilts, counterpanes, hangings and fine furnishings were kept in the 'greate

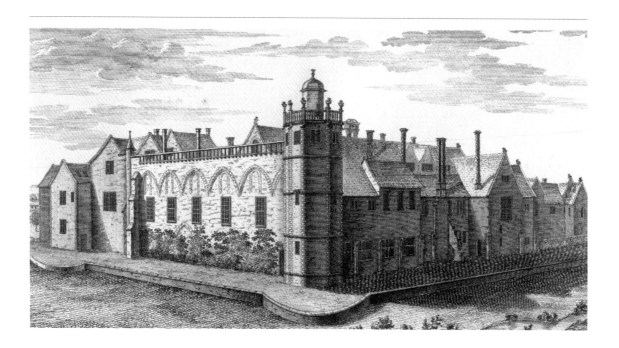

137 *Lacock Abbey in the County of Wiltshire*, engraved by Samuel and Nathaniel Buck, 1732

wordroppe', or Wardrobe Chamber, and brought out on formal occasions. The presence of the exotic carpets and 'Dannske' chests imported from Denmark reveal both Sharington's continental taste and that of his fellow Tudor courtiers. The 'hangings and other clothes of Arrys and Tapistrie', many made in Antwerp, comprised 'fyne vardor', or greenery, and 'peces of hanginge of Imagerie', or tapestries woven with figurative subjects, such as the biblical 'storie of Jepthae [Jephthah and his daughters from *Judges*, Chapter 11]' in the Great Chamber. The decoration of the Duke's Chamber seems to have had a watery, sylvan theme, with four hangings 'of fyne varder [verdure] of water flowers', a 'Carpet of Water flowers' and 'one little coverings of water flowers in the Inner Chamber'. The duke referred to may be either the Duke of Somerset, or Sharington's close friend John Dudley, Duke of Northumberland. 'Lady Thinnes Chamber'

had a 'Counterpointe [counterpane] of water flowers' and a 'coverled of Parke Worke' in her inner chamber. It would seem that Sharington kept a bedchamber for the wife of his confidant and architectural collaborator Sir John Thynne of Longleat. There were further hangings of water flowers in 'the long stone chamber'.

The first hints of contemporary Renaissance decoration come in the Long Stone Chamber where there were hangings bordered with 'Antyke', and in the 'Dark stone chamber', which had 'five hangings of flowers and byrds with antique borders', no doubt to complement the chimneypiece. 'Antique' or 'antik' work was a design signature of François Premier's court style and William Sharington's monument in Lacock parish church features pilasters of antique decoration similar, though more crudely modelled, to that on the chimneypiece jambs. The tapestry imagery

138 The Sacristy at Lacock Abbey

changed in the 'Parler', with '2 peeces of hang-ings of the storie of Sampson', and four others: one of 'Imagerie and three of byrds and beasts.' There were more tapestries in the 'Drawinge Chamber', the 'Quenes Chamber', Sir Henry's Chamber and in the Hall, and a 'coverled of vardor' in 'Mr. Mildemaies Chamber'.[16]

One of the most richly decorated of Shar-ington's original rooms was the 'Turret chamber' connecting with his muniment and prospect tower. This had several featherbeds, 'Downe pillowes' a 'Spanishe Rugge', a red damask canopy over the main bed, a 'Spanishe chayre', an iron cupboard and a sideboard. There was another Spanish carpet in the 'Grene chamber', which also had a compli-mentary canopy of green damask. In the Long Stone Chamber there was a 'sparver', a bed tester, of 'capline [a valance gathered up in swags] with curtines of taffata'. There were similar rich fittings and furnishings in 'Mr.

Talbots Chamber', Lady Thynne's Chamber and the Duke's Chamber. The 'Dyninge Chamber' was furnished with a long table and three 'tressels', a cupboard, a 'brusshinge boarde' and chairs and stools made of walnut. There were further tables, trestles and chairs in the Hall, and most rooms had 'Andirons' in the hearths.

The most valuable and richly decorated pieces in Sharington's house are listed under 'plate' and 'implements of householde'. These include 'a neste of gylte bowles', which were valued at a princely £22 18s 4d, 'three greate costed [ribbed] salts all gylte', valued at £19 17s 4d, 'one rounde standing sawlte with a cover garnished with cristall and agat', a 'standinge Cuppe with a cover all gilte' and a gilt tankard 'garnisshed with scorpions', as well as cups and bowls of parcel gilt. The rich table furnishings are entirely consistent with the sumptuous carved decoration of the two

tables in Sharington's tower, which, apart from the Stone Gallery chimneypiece, are the only survivors of his lavish interior decoration.

These tables are surely the most significant and sophisticated survivals of integral domestic furnishings of Henrician England, unparalleled anywhere in the country and rare examples of that obsession with Renaissance humanism and art. They are not merely pieces of furniture, such as portable examples like the Sea-dog Table at Hardwick Hall in Derbyshire, but are purpose-built fixtures, specifically designed for their octagonal spaces and set consciously within their stone pavements.[17] Supporting the table of the Muniment Room in the middle storey of Sharington's tower, bare-breasted, grinning satyrs leer out from beneath baskets heavily laden with luscious fruit, their modesty covered by acanthus-leaved loincloths (*139*). They are close in style to contemporary decorations by Rosso Fiorentino in the Château de Fontainebleau, which were known and readily available in England through etchings by Antonio Fantuzzi published by the School of Fontainebleau. However, they also betray the influence of goldsmith's work, especially in two designs by Hans Holbein, one for a table fountain, which Anne Boleyn had made for Henry VIII in 1533, and another for a clock-salt he devised around 1543 for Anthony Denny.[18] The lid of the Boleyn fountain is supported by cloven-hoofed satyrs, their arms aloft, which are remarkably similar to the Lacock beasts. Two meticulously drawn studies of the two tables (*140*), done by Harold Brakspear in 1892, are inscribed 'made 1550 but not later than 1553'.[19] It is likely that this

·Lacock·Abbey·Wiltshire· (6)

·Stone·Gable·from·Muniment·Room·in·Tower·
Made 1550 but not later than 1553·

Scale of _____ 2 Feet·

H Brakspear mens et delt 1892·

140 One of the drawings of the stone table in the Muniment Room at Lacock Abbey by Harold Brakspear

dating relates to two letters in the Thynne archives at Longleat that mention the carver, John Chapman, in Sharington's employ, who was about to be sent to Dudley Castle in June 1553.[20] Chapman had worked for Henry VIII, and it is known that he carved chimneypieces and 'beasts'.[21] Sharington's letter to Thynne of 25 June 1553, asking for his friend's patience in waiting for Chapman to return from Dudley, mentions 'the pedestal, whereon you will set your beast, [which] may be made and set up, well enough, before the beast be made'.[22] However, it is unlikely that Sharington would have waited for over ten years to furnish his tower, especially as the middle room appears to have been devised as a strong room in which to store precious valuables and important documents. As we have seen, the conjoined ciphers of Sharington and that of his third wife, Grace Paget, are carved on one of the ceiling bosses of the Muniment Room, and their initials are linked with love knots on the plinth of the table, suggesting that it was installed soon after their marriage in 1542.[23]

The table in the Prospect Room on the top floor (*141*) is much less aggressive in its styling and closer to classically inspired Renaissance decoration. In an informed and scholarly article on the two tables, David Adshead has suggested that the figures in the aedicules of the substructure represent the Seasons.[24] However, his decoding of the Latin

141 Stone table in the Prospect Room at Lacock Abbey

inscriptions on each of the four faces as relating to plenty, wine and food, one being *Apicius*, signifying the Roman cook and gourmet, is more plausible. The other carvings are of a pot-bellied Bacchus, with a wine flagon at his feet, Ceres, with a corn stook by her side, and another that is, as yet, unidentified. She appears to be a shepherdess with a lamb at her feet and a cornucopia of flowers in her hand. These figures are flanked by male and female terms supporting the tabletop above. Certainly, this iconography is entirely appropriate for a room in which favoured guests and the family would be served a banquet course after dinner as they enjoyed the prospect. While the lower table has motifs derived from northern European sources, particularly from France and Flanders, the upper table, as noted perceptively by Nikolaus

Pevsner, 'is reminiscent of Benvenuto Cellini, especially the base of his Perseus of 1545-54'.[25] It is known that in early life Sharington made a trip to Italy, where he may well have seen the Perseus in the Loggia dei Lanzi in Florence.

If the two tables in the tower are as early as 1542, then Sharington had over a decade to enjoy them, either in studious contemplation in his *studolio*, or Muniment Room, or in companionable feasting in his Prospect Room. He died suddenly, before 6 July 1553, the date of Edward VI's death, and was buried in St Cyriac's church in Lacock village. His beautifully ornate wall monument was erected much later in 1566, but he may well have had this designed before his death by his trusty craftsman John Chapman (*142*). It is a brilliant combination of mediaeval forms overlaid with Renaissance decoration, the tomb chest

226

142 Sir William Sharington's tomb
in St Cyriac Church, Lacock

canopied by a depressed Gothic arch whose spandrels have the letters W and S set within foliage, while the chest itself is enriched with strapwork panels enclosing his favourite scorpions. A Holbein design for a chimneypiece for King Henry, which can be dated to 1538-40, has very similar panels, which may also derive from Fontainebleau, possibly through etched designs by Jacques Androuet du Cerceau, while the framing pilasters, encrusted with 'antik' work, are identical to one used by Holbein as a backdrop for his 1523 portrait of the great humanist Erasmus.[26] Finally, above the arch, slender cherubs flank an armorial panel, while at the very top there is a shell-shaped lunette that recalls those on the so-called Holbein Porch at Wilton House. Sharington had sent Chapman to Longleat in order to devise a similar, two-storey porch that was built there in 1556-8, and it is believed that he went on to work on the Holbein Porch at Wilton around 1559-61.[27] Sharington's humanist interests and his extensive knowledge and command of contemporary Renaissance ornament are here displayed on a monument raised as a tribute to a highly cultured man, the epitome of the Henrician courtier.

Rich L^d: Chancelor

Leez Priory

The Priory of Little Leighs, now known as Leez Priory, lies on the south bank of the River Ter in Essex, sheltered by the gently rising banks of the river valley. Shortly after its suppression in 1536, the priory was acquired by Sir Richard Rich, Chancellor of the Court of Augmentations, who swiftly proceeded to build himself a magnificent new house on the site. Leez is exceptional in that Rich's building work involved the almost wholesale conversion of a religious house, including a large part of the Priory Church and Cloister, to post-Dissolution domestic use. Much of Rich's house was demolished in 1753, but enough survives to give an indication of the quality of his impressive buildings. The remaining buildings include the Inner and Outer Gatehouses and part of two sides of the outer courtyard, as well as Great Barns.

The Augustinian Priory of Little Leighs, dedicated to St Mary and St John the Evangelist, is believed to have been founded by Ralph Gernon and was probably in existence by the end of the twelfth century.[1] The priory acquired property rapidly, and its possessions mentioned in the Taxation of 1291 amounted to £121 7s 11½d yearly, which was actually more than its net value at the Dissolution. So it was never a wealthy monastery, but was nonetheless able to afford a full range of conventual buildings.

The building of the Church was begun at the east end, with the presbytery and crossing dating to the early thirteenth century and the west end completed towards the end of the thirteenth century.[2] In 1272 Hervey de Barham founded his chantry at the altar of St Thomas the Martyr in a chapel off the south transept.[3] The Church was not large; the nave was four bays and measured eighty feet in length and almost fifty feet in width, with two aisles. The large Lady Chapel was added to the north of the presbytery early in the fourteenth century and it is mentioned in the Dissolution inventory as possessing an alabaster table 'praised at 30

143 *Sir Richard Rich*, Hans Holbein the Younger, *c.*1532-43

shillings'.[4] The altar of Our Lady bore an image of the Virgin, her feet plated in silver.[5] At the crossing there was a steeple, which at the Dissolution contained a ring of five bells, valued at £33 6s 8d.[6]

The Cloister, around eighty feet square, was to the north of the Church. In the east range were the Sacristy and Chapter House, with the Dorter above. In the north range was the Frater, and in the west range the Cellarer's building with the monastic Great Hall above.[7] In 1381 the convent had licence to enclose 100 acres in Little Leighs to make this a park,[8] implying that there were stables of some size. A very extensive chain of fishponds extended beside the river from the west of the house, and two large ponds survive, one with a central island. These were probably monastic ponds, reused by Rich as a fashionable pond garden in the Tudor period. The Oath of Supremacy was signed on 6 July 1534, by Thomas Ellys, prior, John Andrew, sub-prior, John Darby, James Bartram, Thomas Russell, William Knyghtbredge, Thomas Eve, Richard Poowlly, John Homsted, Robert Hulle and Edmund Freke. The last three appear as the junior canons of Waltham in 1540, having probably been transferred there after the suppression of Leighs.[9] If these eleven were all the monks still in the priory, this emphasises just how small the house was by that time. The priory is returned in the *Valor* as being worth just over £114 yearly, with a gross value of approximately £141.[10] It fell, therefore, well below the £200 income limit for smaller monasteries. The date of surrender is not known, but it must have been between the end of February 1536, when the act suppressing small houses was passed, and the middle of May.

The site of the priory and various other possessions were granted on 27 May 1536 to Richard Rich (*143*), Chancellor of the Court of Augmentations.[11] Taking advantage of his position, he was one of the first to acquire monastic lands after the Dissolution.

Rich was born at Basingstoke, Hampshire, in 1496 or 1497 and may have studied at Cambridge University before entering the Middle Temple in February 1516 to become a lawyer. He served in a number of roles in Essex, securing the support of the leading local magnate, the Earl of Oxford, and Thomas Audley, then a senior knight of the shire for Essex, which resulted in his being returned to Parliament in 1529 as the member for Colchester. When Audley became Lord Chancellor in 1532, Rich finally enjoyed a powerful patron and was appointed Solicitor General in 1533 and knighted. It was as Solicitor General that he was notoriously responsible for the prosecution of opponents of the royal supremacy, including its two principal critics: John Fisher, Bishop of Rochester, and Sir Thomas More, the former Lord Chancellor. In both cases Rich's testimony contributed to their conviction for treason and execution. Rich married in about 1535, and certainly before May 1536, Elizabeth Jenks, the daughter and heir of a London grocer. The couple had at least three sons and nine or ten daughters. Elizabeth died in 1558.[12] Rich resigned as Solicitor General in early 1536, around the time of his marriage, and in April was appointed Chancellor of the newly established Court of Augmentations, charged with overseeing the financial aspects of the dissolution of the smaller monasteries, just before he acquired Leez. Further recognition of his rising status followed, with his selection as a knight of the shire for Essex in the Parliament of 1536, and his election as Speaker of the House of Commons. He was then appointed a privy councillor by August 1540.[13]

By the early 1540s Rich had achieved great

144 The tomb of Sir Richard Rich in Holy Cross Church, Felsted, Essex

success as Chancellor of the Court of Augmentations. The possibilities of such an office were considerable, and he managed to amass a large landed estate in Essex, centred on Leez Priory. The temptations it presented were equally great, however, and several times Rich was called to clear himself of accusations of corruption. He resigned the office in 1544 and for five months served as treasurer for the war in France. He resigned this post due to ill health, though there were again questions as to his probity. Thereafter, he held no major office but remained an active privy councillor during the mid-1540s, serving on various commissions.[14]

Soon after the accession of Edward VI, on 16 February 1547, Rich was created Baron Rich. A supporter of Edward Seymour, Duke of Somerset and Lord Protector, he backed the removal of Thomas Wriothesley from the chancellorship, and on 23 October was himself appointed Lord Chancellor as a reward for his loyalty. Despite his ties to Somerset, Rich was instrumental in ensuring the success of the coup of October 1549 and the removal of the Protector. However, by December 1551 he himself had fallen under suspicion and lost the chancellorship. Although he remained a privy councillor and was made lord lieutenant of Essex on 16 May 1552, he returned to live in Essex, where Leez Priory was his principal residence, and rarely attended the council.[15]

Although not active at Court, Rich was kept busy in Essex, where he was soon infa-

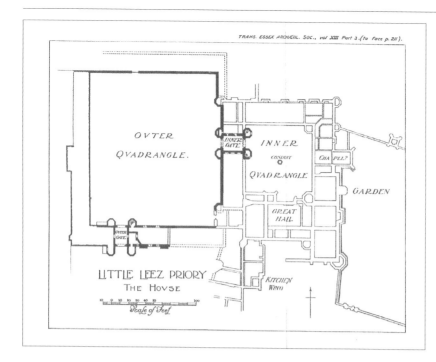

TRANS. ESSEX ARCHÆOL. SOC., vol XIII Part 3.(to face p. 211).

OVTER QVADRANGLE.

INNER QVADRANGLE

INNER GATE

CONDVIT

CHAPELL

GARDEN

GREAT HALL

OVTER GATE

LITTLE LEEZ PRIORY
THE HOVSE

KITCHEN WING

Scale of Feet

145 Plan of Leez Priory, showing the principal elements of Richard Rich's new house

mous for his energetic persecution of heretics. After Elizabeth I came to the throne in 1558, he ceased to be a councillor, though he occasionally offered advice to the queen and entertained her at Leez. Nonetheless, as a leading landowner and JP, Rich remained an influential figure in Essex during the early 1560s. He died on 12 June 1567 and is buried in a magnificent tomb (*144*) at nearby Felsted.[16] Rich acquired two monastic properties after the Dissolution, from which he constructed new houses for himself: a town house at St Bartholomew, Smithfield, and his country residence at Little Leez.[17] He built his new house at Leez of brick, around two courtyards (*145*). The outer courtyard was entered through a Gatehouse in the southern range, which survives (*146*). It is of two storeys, with an octagonal turret at each corner; one of the turrets contains a 'vice', or spiral staircase, which is carried up to give access to the leads. The outer parapet and the Gatehouse are

battlemented, and some ornate Tudor chimney stacks survive. The other ranges of the outer courtyard probably contained offices, service buildings and subsidiary accommodation.

Rich's inner courtyard was built on the Cloister of the Priory. It was entered through the Inner Gatehouse (*147*), which Rich inserted through the west range of the cloister. This survives and is one of the most impressive Tudor gatehouses in the country. Three storeys high, it is built of brick with stone dressings and has an octagonal battlemented turret at each corner. The gabled parapets are of brick and stone panels with a stone finial. The east face turrets are ornately decorated, being diapered and panelled in three stages, each with a band of trefoil-moulded bricks. The north-east turret contains an oak staircase rising to the first floor, while the staircase in the south-east turret rises to the upper floor. There is a moulded stone archway to the west face and a moulded brick archway to the

146 The Outer Gatehouse at Leez Priory

147 The Inner Gatehouse at Leez Priory

To Charles Sheffield Esq.r This Prospect is most humbly Inscrib'd by his Oblig'd Servants Sam.l & Nath.l Buck.

148 *The West View of Leez-Priory in the County of Essex*, engraved by Samuel and Nathaniel Buck, 1738

IN THE COUNTY OF ESSEX.

THIS Priory was founded by S.ʳ Ralph Gernon in the Reign of King Henry III. Ralph de Baldock Bishop of London visited this Priory in 1309, and made several Injunctions to be observed by the Prior and Convent. — The present Possessor is Charles Sheffield Esq.ʳ   An.Val. $\begin{smallmatrix}£4:1:4 \text{ Dug.}\\141:14:8 \text{ Sp.}\end{smallmatrix}$

Sam.ᵗ & Nath.ˡ Buck del et Sculp. Publish'd according to Act of Parliam.ᵗ March 25.ᵗʰ 1738

CONDUIT AT LEIGH'S PRIORY — ESSEX

149 The Conduit at Leez Priory, which includes monastic remains

east face. The spandrels of the stone arch are carved with fleur-de-lys and Tudor rose decoration, the brick with shields. The block between the turrets, above the archway, is of two storeys, each comprising a large room, with stone mullioned-and- transomed windows to the east and west faces. Both the rooms have original fireplaces, the lower being of stone and the upper of brick.[18] Although the gatehouse is all that remains of the buildings of the inner courtyard, Samuel and Nathaniel Buck's 1738 view, taken from the outer court, shows the whole of the west range of the inner court, which was originally the west range of the cloister, containing the cellarer's building with the monastic Hall above (*148*). It was two storeys high and had a range of small pinnacled gables; it may have been monastic work refaced.

In the centre of the inner courtyard is a hexagonal conduit, with an ogee cap, which survives (*149*). It is made of stone from the monastic buildings and probably reused a louvre of the monastic Great Hall.[19] On the south range of the inner courtyard Rich created a new Great Hall from the nave of the Priory Church, demolishing the eastern end of the Church containing the Presbytery and Lady Chapel.[20] The Bucks' view shows the west gable of the church with a large window and in the centre of the Great Hall is a large lantern with an ogee capping ball and pinnacle. The crossing and transepts of the Church were also included within Rich's plan and formed large principal private apartments in the new house. At first floor level they were probably the presence chamber and privy chamber. As several royal visitors stayed at Leez, including Edward VI, Mary, and Eliza-

beth I, the sequence of rooms would have been in the usual formal arrangement. Elizabeth stayed for four days in August 1561.[21] The Chapter House in the east range was also retained in the new house, and possibly used as a chapel.

To the south of the Outer Gatehouse are two large sixteenth-century barns, which were part of Rich's estate. The formal gardens were to the east of the inner courtyard and enclosed by brick walls. At each of the eastern corners was an octagonal summerhouse, which would have been Tudor banqueting houses. The principal private rooms of the house would have overlooked these gardens.[22] The eastern arm of the Church, with the Lady Chapel, presbytery and smaller chapels, was not included in Rich's new house, and was removed.[23] Leez continued in use by the Rich family, later Earls of Warwick, but most buildings were demolished in 1753.[24]

150 *Portrait of a Young Man*, possibly Gregory Cromwell, Hans Holbein the Younger, *c.*1535-40

Lewes Priory (Place House)

Willliam de Warenne and his wife Gundrada founded the Priory of St Pancras at Lewes around 1081. Warenne called the site chosen for his new foundation 'my island of Southover'.[1] It was situated on a chalk spur, commanding the wide tidal estuary of the River Ouse, which stretches seven miles south to the sea. Separated by the valley of the Winterbourne stream from the Saxon hill town of Lewes, the site was dominated by a newly constructed Norman castle half a mile to the north.

After its dissolution, Lewes Priory was granted on 16 February 1538 to Thomas Cromwell, who immediately set about converting part of the priory complex into a home for his son Gregory, who may be the young man in the contemporary portrait by Holbein (*150*). The house was ruinous by 1676 and later demolished. The site was bisected by the Lewes to Brighton railway in the mid-nineteenth century and only some standing chalk and flint rubble walls of the priory survive.

William de Warenne, from Varenne in Normandy, had supported William the Conqueror in his military activities from the 1050s. Warenne fought at the Battle of Hastings and, as one of the Conqueror's inner circle, benefited by the grant of large amounts of land following the conquest of England. By 1070 he had been given the 'rape' of Lewes and later acquired Acre in Norfolk through his marriage to Gundrada. Warenne built a castle at both locations and, seeking security in the afterlife, subsequently founded a monastery at Lewes. His son, William de Warenne II, later founded a monastery at Castle Acre, with monks from Lewes. Warenne was created Earl of Surrey in 1088.

The story of the foundation of Lewes Priory, outlined in the foundation narrative, describes how William de Warenne and Gundrada, whilst on pilgrimage in 1076, visited the Abbey of Cluny in Burgundy. Having in mind, 'by the advice of Sir Lanfranc the Archbishop to found a religious house for our sins and the welfare of our souls',[2] they chose to found it from the Cluniac Order. Around 1077 the Abbot of Cluny sent four monks to establish Warenne's new foundation at Lewes, including Lanzo, the first prior. Cluny was the largest abbey church in Europe by the mid-twelfth century, and remained so until the sixteenth century when St

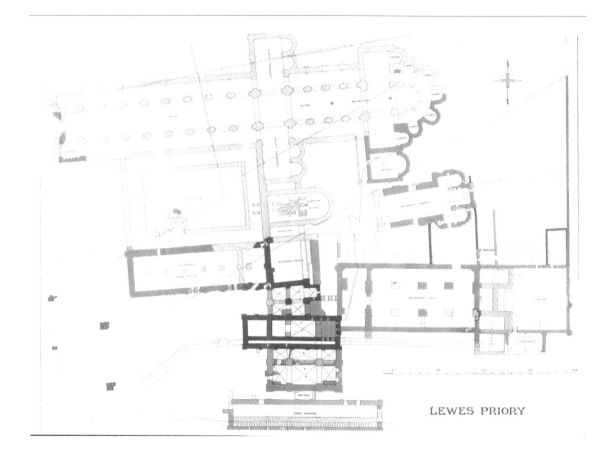

151 A plan of the monastic complex at Lewes Priory by Harold Brakspear

Peter's in Rome was deliberately built to be larger. Lewes Priory was the first and foremost Cluniac monastery in England.

Gundrada died in childbirth at Castle Acre in 1085 and William died in 1088 after being struck by an arrow while besieging Pevensey Castle. Both were buried at Lewes and their bones were discovered in lead cists during construction work for the railway in 1845. A chapel was built to house the remains at the church of St John the Baptist in Southover, within the former Lewes precinct, which was originally part of the *Hospitium* of the priory.[3] Gundrada's ornate marble tomb cover, rediscovered around 1770, is also displayed at Southover.

On Warenne's death his son, William II, arrived in England to take over his father's estates. He is credited as being the second founder of the Priory of St Pancras and he survived for a further fifty years, long enough to see most of the work complete. During the 1090s many donations were made which enabled the new earl to complete his parents' project. Powerful spiritual benefits, as well as the right of burial at the priory, were believed to accrue to those who donated property.

As a result, the first phase of building work was completed before 1100, at a time when Cluny was being rebuilt. This early work used grey Quarr limestone from the Isle of Wight, some of which survives in the Infirmary

152 The surviving ruins at Lewes Priory

Chapel, the Frater and the first Reredorter.[4] Work proceeded rapidly on the construction of the new monastic Great Church, built in Romanesque style, and the east end must have been complete at the time of its dedication, some time between 1091 and 1097.[5]

As the monastery grew, the increasing size of the community necessitated alterations to the accommodation and a major new building scheme was required, which began about 1145, funded by William de Warenne III.[6] This phase used Caen stone and Sussex marble, which would have created a magnificent impression. The church was complete by 1147, when Archbishop Theobald of Canterbury consecrated it.[7] In its heyday, Lewes was one of the wealthiest monasteries in England, with annual revenues in 1291 of £1,014, almost equal to that of Westminster.[8] This enabled the construction of one of the largest monastic churches in Western Europe.

The dimensions of the Priory Church are described in detail in Giovanni Portinari's account of 1538 and confirmed by later archaeological investigation.[9] Portinari made a schedule of the various dimensions of the Church before he began his demolition work after the priory's dissolution. He describes a very large church, 420 feet long and 69 feet wide, increasing to 150 feet wide across the transepts. The main body of the Church was 63 feet high. At the east end there was a 93 feet high vault 'in the manner of a steeple' above the high altar, and another above the crossing, 105 feet high 'where there are five bells'.[10] There was another 'steeple which is set upon a corner' of the west front, 90 feet high.[11] The scale of the columns supporting the roof was equally massive; the eight under the two vaults were 14 feet in diameter, while the twenty-four 'ordinary pillars' were 10 feet in diameter.

By the 1170s the monastery had increased in size to 100 monks and the buildings around the Cloister were expanded to accommodate the larger numbers. Later additions to the monastic complex included work on the Infirmary in 1218-19 and the completion of a Lady Chapel in 1229. In 1268 Prior William de Foville left £200 in his will for the completion of two western towers,[12] though in the event only one was raised.

Brakspear's plan of 1904 (*151*), based on archaeological excavations by St John Hope,

153 *Portrait of a Lady*, possibly Elizabeth Seymour, Hans Holbein the Younger, *c*.1535-40

shows the buildings to have been of a traditional layout with the Cloister to the south of the Church. The east range contained the Chapter House, while further to the east of this range were the large Infirmary and small Infirmary Chapel, accessed by a passage to the south of the Chapter House. A doorway to the south of this passageway led into the Calefactory. The Dorter was on the upper floor of the east range, accessed by night stairs next to the southern transept, and ruins of the Dorter and Reredorter survive (*152*). The Frater occupied the whole of the southern range, with the kitchen at its west end, which had a large oven, 17 feet in diameter.[13] A large circular *Lavatorium* was in the rectangular Cloister, near to the entrance to the Frater. The granary complex, comprising bakery and brewery, was to the south and west of the kitchen.[14]

The west range was not excavated by St John Hope, but would have contained the Cellarer's Hall and the Prior's Lodgings. The

Lodgings would have been built from the late twelfth century onwards, as before this the prior would have slept in the Dorter with the other monks.[15] The north walk of the Cloister was probably occupied by carrels, and the monastic library would have been close by in the south transept.[16]

The main gate of the priory was in the north wall of the precinct and part of it remains in Southover High Street, adjacent to St John's Church and former *Hospitium*. The walled precinct extended to almost forty acres and included many other buildings supporting the priory. These, mentioned in obedientiaries accounts of the 1520s and 1530s, included a fish house, a horse mill, stables, a forge and a glazier's workshop.[17] There was also a large pigeon house in the shape of a cross, which survived into the nineteenth century, and the fishponds remained until relatively recently, appearing on early Ordnance Survey maps.

At the time of its dissolution, Lewes Priory, together with its daughter house at Castle Acre, had revenues of over £1,315 a year according to the *Valor*. By the beginning of November 1537 Thomas Cromwell and the Duke of Norfolk had reached a financial arrangement, agreed by the king, who 'thought it well bestowed', to divide these monastic properties between them.[18]

On 16 November 1537 the priory was 'voluntarily' surrendered by Prior Robert Crowham and twenty-three monks. Lewes was the first monastery where all the religious, and not only the head of the house, were then granted pensions.[19] The priory and its extensive lands were granted on 16 February 1538 to 'Thos. lord Crumwell, Keeper of the Privy Seal. Grant, in fee, of the late monastery or priory of Lewes, Sussex, and the site, &c., of the same; the church, steeple, and church-

yard'.[20] After allowing for annual rent to the Crown of £77 14s 6d and pensions to the former monks, the grant netted Cromwell an additional income of £354 15s 2d, as well as the priory site as a new residence for his son Gregory.[21]

Gregory Cromwell was born by 1516, and was educated at Pembroke College, Cambridge. After Henry VIII's marriage to Jane Seymour in 1537 his father arranged a match between him and the queen's sister Elizabeth, the widow of Sir Anthony Oughtred. Elizabeth may be the lady in the portrait by Hans Holbein the Younger (*153)*. The couple were married on 3 August 1537 and their eldest child, Henry, was born the following February. In early March they travelled to Lewes, which seems to have been intended as a principal residence, as Gregory became a JP for Sussex, his first official position. However, after the appointment of his father as constable of Leeds Castle in January 1539, Gregory moved there. In April that year he was summoned to Parliament as a knight of the shire for Kent and appears never to have returned to Lewes.[22]

Even before the formal grant was made, no time was wasted in preparing the priory buildings for Cromwell's occupation. The first part of the work was the demolition of the Church, which was carried out by Giovanni Portinari and his Italian workforce. On the 13 January 1538 Cromwell's accounts show a payment of 40s 'for the coste of the saide Iatalyon to Lewes agayn'.[23] Gregory Cromwell was evidently sent by his father to take possession of the monastery and supervise the work, as on 11 March £20 was given to him 'by my Lorde commandment at his going to Lewes'.[24] On the same day £60 was paid 'to Portynary & other Italyons for their charge to Lewes & for suche necessaries as they must occupye there'.[25]

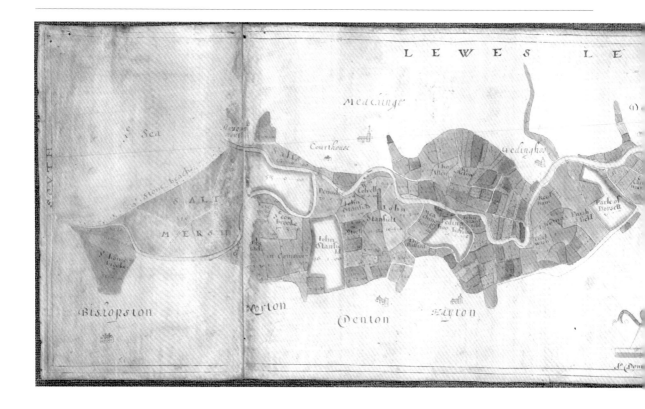

154 John De Ward's map of Lewes, 1620

Two letters survive, written by Portinari to Cromwell in March 1538, that describe in detail the process he used for the demolition work. In the first, dated 20 March, Portinari wrote:

This letter is to tell your Lordship how we have arrived here and have seen the church, which we have found different from what was thought of it, that is in size, length and bigness, in which there is much to do … On Friday morning we shall begin to cut the wall behind the high altar where are placed five chapels that go round about it, and so four columns which uphold a vault that is above the high altar, and all this we wish in the first place to level to the ground in such manner and form as your Lordship will understand.

First we shall cut away the bottom of the foundation and cut it away to the height of a yard and a quarter so that a man may get under to work and pass to the other side, which is about a yard and a half or two, and put beneath planks of a thickness of 3 inches from one side to the other and put on each side a prop a yard long or thereabouts; and so one goes on, following by degrees, cutting and propping, and similarly the four columns within so that each can stand upon two props. And when the said chapels and columns have been cut and propped on that side and you wish to bring them to the ground the props on that side only will be burnt either with fire or with powder, as we may judge best, and so we reckon to bring them to the ground.[26]

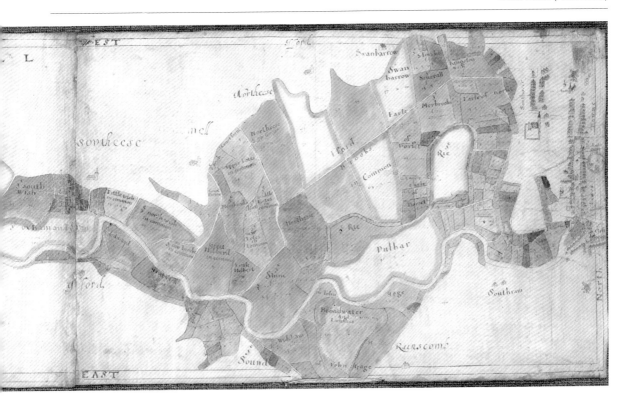

The second letter, dated 24 March, reports the progress made since the previous letter:

As by letter I told your Lordship of the side behind the high altar which stands beneath a vault [tribuna] upheld upon four round columns, and behind which are five chapels which surround the said vault. The which chapels and vault are surrounded on the outside by a wall of 70 yards, that is 210 feet. All this, in the name of God, and with a good beginning is plucked to the ground, and was thrown down in two turns which was on Thursday and Friday last, the 21st and 22nd instant. And presently we shall pull down a very high vault which is placed a little before the altar, the which is set upon four great pillars … And this shall be for the second turn

as may undoubtedly be hoped, and of what will follow in everything your Lordship will have notice … On Tuesday will be begun the casting of the lead, which for the best part is already down and will be cast with such diligence and saving as may be possible.[27]

Once Portinari's work was complete, the buildings were quickly ready for occupation. No new house was created, but rather the Prior's Lodging and certain other supporting buildings in the precinct were taken over in their entirety. This house later became known as Lords Place. That these existing buildings were eminently suitable is confirmed by a letter from Gregory Cromwell to his father, dated 11 April 1538, saying the house 'doth undoubtedly right much please and content

155 A detail from John de Ward's map of Lewes, showing Place House

me and my wife, and is unto her so commodious that she thinketh herself to be here right settled'.[28] The two had evidently already moved into occupation, together with their new baby son. Whilst there are no contemporary descriptions or surviving ruins, a good idea of the extent and layout of the house can be gathered from a lease granted to Nicholas Jenney on 27 November 1540, after Thomas Cromwell's execution and the transfer of the

property to the Crown.

The site granted to Jenney included all houses, buildings, gardens, crofts, meadows and marshes within the priory wall, by estimation twenty acres. But reserved to the king were the 'church, Cloister, house called Le Frater, and all other buildings which the king has ordered to be thrown down within the space of three years; together with all the lead, glass, iron, timber, stones and tiles accruing therefrom, with free ingress and egress at all times to fetch them away'.[29] This strongly suggests that Portinari had not completed the demolition work on the Church, or even begun demolishing the claustral buildings.

The grant goes on to reserve to the king 'le great Gatehouse and all the buildings in the same' together with the buildings which formed the Prior's Lodging and subsequently the new house:

> All upper buildings and rooms from the hall towards the west, viz. 'le hall place' and 'le pantry' with a little chamber opposite the pantry;
> the room called 'le Chapell' with 'le hall place' and the steps downwards through the west door of the church;
> Two buildings called 'Wynesellers';
> a lower room called 'le Chequer' and 'le old storehouse' under the steps, and also a building called 'le countynghouse' above 'le storehouse';
> also 'le utter chamber', another chamber called 'le Greate Chamber', le littell chamber with 'le entre' between the said utter chamber and 'le grate Chamber';
> le gallery with the new buildings above and below on the north end and west of the said great chamber, with the steps in the south end of the same room;
> also the priory kitchen and the bakehouse with free ingress and egress from the aforesaid new buildings through 'le greate Malthouse' to the said kitchen and bakehouse.[30]

The house clearly comprised both the formal, high status rooms required by the prior and the new owner – hall, outer chamber, great chamber, little chamber, gallery and chapel, mostly on the upper storey – and the service rooms – kitchen, bakehouse, malthouse, wine cellars, pantry, counting house and exchequer, and storehouse. The upper storey rooms could be accessed via two staircases, one from the west door of the Church, and the other at the south end of the Gallery, as well as via the hall. The house probably occupied a double range on the west of the Cloister, comprising the Cellarer's Hall and store and service rooms and, to the west of those, the Prior's Lodging, with the kitchen at the south end. The 'new building' referred to was the Prior's Long Gallery, constructed early in the sixteenth century.[31] This must have been sited at the north end and to the west of the Lodging. There was a 'garden adjoining the new said buildings and le Malthouse', also reserved to the king.[32]

The house was demolished in the late seventeenth century, but it is depicted on John De Ward's map of 1618 (*154*).[33] Viewed from the east, the house is shown (*155*) as L-shaped, surrounded by a stone wall and, intriguingly, as having a large tower topped with a spire at the north-west corner of the walled enclosure. This suggests that the south-west tower of the Church, referred to by Portinari as 'the steeple which is set upon a corner of the forefront'[34] was retained. This may explain why that is the only part of the Church still above ground; it was only demolished along with the house, over 130 years later than the rest of the Church. The tower probably contained the 'steps downward through the west door of the church' referred to in the grant. De Ward's map also shows a building at right-angles to the west range and Prior's Lodging which can only be the Frater. The ruins of the Frater are shown in the Bucks' engraving of 1737 (*156*), so it certainly was not 'thrown down within the space of three years' as specified in the grant, and presumably was adapted for use as part of the house. It must have been in good condition at

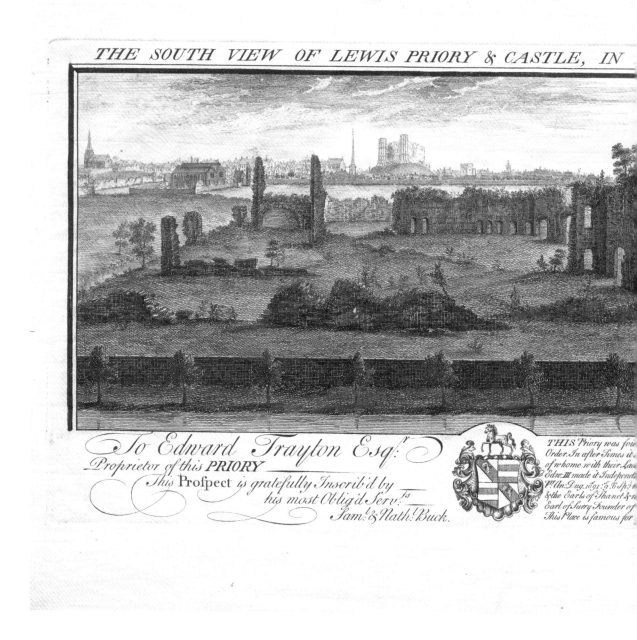

THE SOUTH VIEW OF LEWIS PRIORY & CASTLE, IN

To Edward Trayton Esqr
Proprietor of this PRIORY
This Prospect is gratefully Inscrib'd by
his most Oblig'd Serv.^{ts}
Saml & Nathl Buck.

THIS Priory was fou
Order. In after Times it...
of whome with their La...
Edw: III made it Independe...
y.^t An: Dug. 1691 ...
& the Earls of Thanet & ...
Earl of Surry Founder of
This Place is famous for

156 *The South View of Lewis Priory in the County of Sussex*, engraved by Samuel and Nathaniel Buck, 1737

OUNTY OF SUSSEX.

by Wm de Warren Earl of Surry for Monks of the Cluniac
Benefactors viz: ÿ succeeding Earls of Surry & others, several
ried. It continued a Cell to ÿ Abby of Cluny in Burgundy till K:
m it was granted with all its Appendages (valued at 920.4.6:
nce that ÿ Priory has been in ÿ Possession of ÿ Dukes of Dorset,
w: Frayton Esq.t. The Castle was built by ÿ same Wm de Warren
rs now are ÿ Noble Families of Norfolk, Dorset, & Abergavenny.
re fought between K: Hen.III & his Barons.
Sam.l & Nath.l Buck del: & Sculpt: Publisht according to Act of Parliament March 28 1737.

the Dissolution, as it had been newly re-roofed in Horsham stone in 1533-4.[35]

Henry VIII visited Lewes in August 1538, so the house must have been sufficient to accommodate him and his entourage. In June that year Gregory reported to his father that a yeoman of the guard had 'come this day to your Lordship's house at Lewes and viewed the lodgings, stating that the king would be here'.[36]

In 1559 the site of the priory and the house were acquired by Sir Richard Sackville following his appointment as Lord Lieutenant and senior knight of the shire for Sussex. He, or his son Thomas, may have remodelled the house, possibly in the early 1570s when a visit by Elizabeth I was anticipated. Certainly decorative plasterwork, fine floor tiles and Caen stone with Renaissance carving have been found, and Sackville had visited the Château d'Ecouen in 1571, which had majolica tiled chambers.[37] The house was extremely large and had thirty-seven hearths.[38] Sackville's son and grandson occasionally used the house into the early seventeenth century, but by 1676 it was described as ruinous and was later demolished.[39]

London Charterhouse

The London Charterhouse, which remains a secluded almshouse in the City of London, was converted from a Carthusian monastery to a magnificent Tudor courtyard house by Edward North (*157*). The origins of the London Charterhouse lay in the mid-fourteenth century. The Black Death reached England in the summer of 1348 and was at its height in London in the early months of the following year. When the capacity of the city graveyards became inadequate, Sir Walter Manny, as a work of charity, rented from the Master and Brethren of St Bartholomew's a close of some thirteen acres known as Spital Croft, to be used as an additional graveyard for victims of the plague. Ralph Stratford, Bishop of London, dedicated the graveyard on the Feast of the Annunciation 1349. On the same day the foundations were laid of a chapel wherein masses were to be celebrated. A hermitage for two inmates was erected, in which continual prayers were to be offered for the dead.[1]

The Grande Chartreuse, the motherhouse of the Carthusian Order, is situated in a remote mountain valley north of Grenoble. All early Charterhouses were founded in desert places, and the *conversi* – lay brethren – were accommodated in buildings at a considerable distance from those of the monks. The earlier English foundations at Witham and Hinton in Somerset and at Beauvale in Nottinghamshire had conformed to this pattern. More recently, however, continental houses were being founded on urban sites, as at Paris and Bruges, where the strict and secluded community served as a living contrast to the worldliness and vice of the city. The first suggestion of a London Charterhouse seems to have come from Bishop Northburgh, who had visited and admired the Charterhouse at Paris. He approached Manny with the suggestion that they should cooperate in the foundation of a monastery in Spital Croft.[2]

Manny's foundation charter was dated 28 March 1371, and John Luscote, Prior of Hinton, was appointed to administer the project. About

157 *Edward North, 1st Baron North*, in a later engraving of 1825

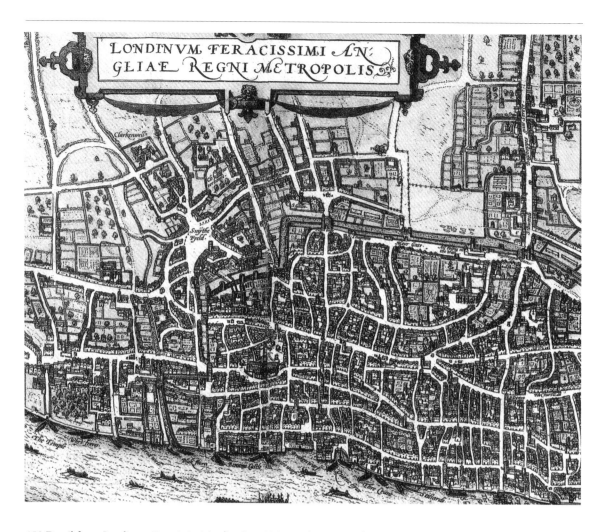

158 Detail from *Londinum Feracissimi Angliae Regni Metropolis*, a map of London in 1572, showing the location of the Charterhouse near Smithfield

the Feast of the Ascension (15 May) the founder and the prior made an agreement with Henry Yevele, the celebrated master mason, to build the first cell and begin the Great Cloister. Seven months later, on 15 January 1372, Manny died and was buried before the high altar in the chapel of the graveyard, now to be the monastic Church.[3] Meanwhile, Prior Luscote summoned monks from each of the existing Carthusian houses to become founding members of the new community: a monk and a lay brother from

Hinton, two priests from Witham in addition to deacon *clericus redditus* John Gryseley, and two from Beauvale. Luscote lived with them in makeshift buildings for many years, but he died in 1398 before the communal rooms and the great wall of the enclosure had been completed.

Carthusian monks lived as contemplatives and utter poverty was mandatory. They were not to associate with outsiders under any circumstances and their monastery, albeit in the city, was conceived of as a miniature wilderness, populated by hermit-monks. Apart from a communal mass each morning, most of the time the monks prayed in silence or sang the canonical hours in the privacy of their own cells, marked not with a name but a single letter of the alphabet. Except for a communal meal taken at noon on Sunday, meals were served through a hatch in each cell and the monks lived entirely solitary lives, copying religious books and tending their individual enclosed gardens.[4]

The Charterhouse, shown on a 1572 map (*158*), is now a quiet enclave between Barbican and Smithfield Market to the north of Charterhouse Square. It was planned with stone buildings of superior quality and the surviving parts of the Gatehouse, Church, cells and other buildings reflect this. The entrance is through the Gatehouse, which was built around 1405 of flint chequerwork faced with brick and ragstone dressings.[5] The Great Cloister was constructed on a grand scale of 300 by 340 feet. Two more grants of land, one by the Hospitallers of St John in 1384, the other by Westminster Abbey in 1391, gave the Charterhouse fields to the north of their existing property. These parcels of land combined to give the monks some thirty acres, providing space not only for an orchard surrounding three sides of the Cloister, but also for a vegetable garden, hayfield, and wilderness to the north, harbouring at least the smaller species of game. This area remained without addition or diminution until the suppression of the house.[6]

The Charterhouse was built over a long period as the monks relied on private benefactors to finance the building, with the Great Cloister being constructed cell by cell as funds permitted. It was intended to be a 'double' house, that is, one for twenty-four monks and a prior. Twenty-five cells were eventually built

round the Cloister in a clockwise direction beginning at the south-western angle, where the doorway led to the outer world. The chapel originally built for the graveyard was used as the conventual Church. The Carthusians, differing from every other order of monks and canons in this, gave no architectural prominence to their churches. The original building was a simple rectangle of 94 by 38 feet, divided internally into presbytery, choir, and a small 'body of the church' at the western end, separated from the choir by a wooden screen with two altars against its western face.[7] In a Charterhouse, in contrast to other monastic houses, the community rooms were very small and few in number. There was no Dorter, Warming-House or Abbot's Lodgings, and the Frater was used only on Sundays and feast days. At the London Charterhouse the Frater lay between cell A (the Prior's) and cell B, and was presumably built in conjunction with those cells in about 1371.[8]

Immediately to the west of the Church was the Little Cloister, now the Master's Court. It was constructed in 1436 and its western range of buildings held guest rooms for visiting monks. Beyond this to the west was the second court (now Wash-House Court), round the three outer sides of which were the quarters of the lay brothers, kitchens, brewhouse, and cellars. Finally, in the last decades of the house's existence, a new cell was built for the prior and three little cells to accommodate an influx of postulants. These were located at the south-east corner of the precinct, east of the Church. This group of buildings, outside the Cloister, has in great part survived to the present day in use as the domestic and administrative offices of the courtyard house built by Edward North and its successor, Sutton's Hospital. The Great Cloister, however, has disappeared save for portions of the external wall incorporating the entrance of cells A and B in the western alley, and T and V on the eastern.

By the time of its dissolution, the reputation of the Charterhouse had stood very high for at least fifty years. However, the Carthusians, along with all other subjects of the king, were required in the spring of 1534 to swear to the first Act of Succession. When the commissioners arrived on 4 May to tender the oath Prior Houghton replied in the name of all that Carthusians did not meddle with the king's affairs; they asked only to be left in peace. Houghton knew that further demands would come and urged his monks to spend their time in prayer and preparation for their trial, which quickly followed. Houghton, together with the Priors of Beauvale and Axholme, was tried on 28 and 29 April 1535 and condemned to death for refusal to accept the royal supremacy. They were executed at Tyburn on 4 May.[9] All three were canonised in 1970.

Once Houghton had been imprisoned, Humphrey Middlemore took charge of the Charterhouse, and had as his principal counsellors William Exmew, the procurator, and Sebastian Newdigate. When they resisted all persuasion to take the oath they were removed to Newgate, where they remained for a fortnight chained to posts. Finally, on 11 June, they were tried and condemned, and on 19 June executed. In all, eighteen Carthusians were executed, seventeen of them professed monks of the London Charterhouse.[10]

The *Valor* of 1535 returned the gross income of the Charterhouse as £736, with a net income of £642, well above the £200 limit for the first round of suppressions. Their properties included numerous tenements near the monastery and about the City, pastures in Marylebone and Holborn, a 'messuage' called 'Blumsburye', as well as manors across the

country including Ogbourne in Wiltshire and Cromer in Norfolk.[11] Notwithstanding this high level of income of the Charterhouse, within a few weeks of the removal of the recalcitrants in May 1536 the rump of the community was induced to surrender the house. However, it was not until 15 November 1538 that the Charterhouse was finally disbanded. Prior William Trafford and sixteen choir monks received pensions; the six surviving lay brothers received nothing.[12]

After the monks had left, the Church, Cloister, and other buildings were divided up into three portions, but by June 1542 the whole place was turned over to the king's servants and used as a storehouse for the king's tents and hunting nets. It was thus for some years virtually derelict, save for the occupation of some of the cells by a family of Italian court musicians of the name of Bassano. Finally, on 14 April 1545, the whole site was granted to Sir Edward North. He received 'the said house and site, the churchyard and chapel in the same, lead. &c, the gates called the West-gate in St Sepulchre's parish and the Estgate in St Botolph's parish'. He was required 'to permit Louis Gaspar. John, John Baptist and Anthony Bassani. Italians, the King's servants, to enjoy their houses, &c, as long as they remain in the King's service'.[13]

Edward North was born around 1504 in London, the sole son of Roger North, a merchant and haberdasher. After attending St Paul's School, he entered Lincoln's Inn in 1522 to train as a lawyer. He secured his financial and social status in 1528 by marrying Alice, the widow of two wealthy London merchants.[14] North's marriage permitted him the opportunity to speculate on the land market. On 1 January 1533 he bought the manor of Kirtling, Cambridgeshire, which was to become his principal seat and the nucleus

159 The Great Hall of the London Charterhouse

of his estates in East Anglia.[15] About that time he also came to the attention of Sir Brian Tuke, Treasurer of the Chamber, and in 1531 joined Sir Brian as joint Clerk of Parliaments. North also worked for Thomas Cromwell, and it was probably the minister's influence that enabled him in March 1539 to succeed Sir Thomas Pope as Treasurer of the Court of Augmentations. In January 1542 he was knighted, and by July 1544 had been appointed Chancellor of the Court of Augmentations.[16]

After the death of Henry VIII in 1547 North was made a privy councillor, but he soon fell out with Protector Somerset, who in August 1548 connived at his being eased out of the chancellorship. But in the *coup d'état* against Somerset a year later North was one of the first to join the dissident councillors in London and to sign the letter listing the Protector's offences.[17] He then became a strong supporter of the Earl of Warwick, later the Duke of Northumberland. After the death of Edward VI, North at first backed the attempt by Northumberland to place Lady Jane Grey on the throne but soon joined the defectors to Mary's cause. Despite his initial disloyalty Mary elevated him to the peerage in April 1554 as Baron North, and restored to him the Charterhouse, which had passed briefly to the Duke of Northumberland. He was not reappointed to the Privy Council, but as well as regularly attending the House of Lords, he continued to participate in Court life.[18] After the accession of Elizabeth I in 1558, however, he withdrew from Court and,

160 *Interior of the London Charterhouse Great Hall,* engraved by J Lewis, 1815

apart from regular visits to the Charterhouse (as when he entertained the queen for several days in July 1561), he lived his last years in retirement at Kirtling. He died on 31 December 1564 at the Charterhouse, but asked to be buried at Kirtling.[19]

Six months after North was granted the Charterhouse, in the autumn of 1545, he commenced an ambitious and extensive programme of conversion and rebuilding. First, his workmen demolished much of the Priory Church, the Little Cloister and most of the monks' cells around the Great Cloister, though the doorway of Cell B survives.[20] The Chapter House and a long section of the west Cloister Walk were retained, as was the Inner Gatehouse of about 1405.[21]

Probably in the following year, building work began on the new courtyard house. The principal court, now called Master's Court, lay on the site of the Little Cloister. The north range comprised a new Great Hall (*159*) constructed of rubble stone with brick used for the heads above the three main windows; stone from the demolished Priory Church was used for the walls and the single buttress. The Hall was originally open to the roof, though a ceiling was added in the late Elizabethan or early Jacobean period (*160*).[22] The roof was also topped with a lantern, a prominent feature in William Toms' view of the Charterhouse (*161*), but this was replaced by a simpler design in the early 1840s, which was then destroyed by fire in 1941.[23] On the upper floor to the north of the Hall lay North's Great Chamber, a very grand room which overlooked the Privy Garden. At the time of North's death in 1565 the Great Chamber was

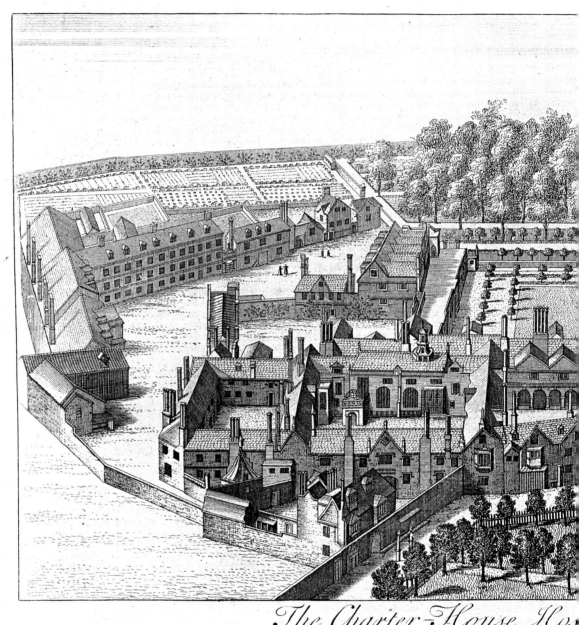

The Charter-House Ho[

161 *The Charter House Hospital*, engraved by William Toms, 1739

richly furnished with tapestries, carpets and chairs upholstered in cloth of gold and damask.[24] Today, the Great Chamber is larger than North's room because there was originally an ante-chamber to its east, the two being combined in the 1950s.

The east range of North's courtyard house on the upper floor contained a dining chamber and two other chambers for domestic use, and at the south end a bedchamber with an oriel window, visible in Toms' view, and designated the Gazing Chamber.[25] The south range on the upper level was a fashionable Long Gallery providing opportunities for exercise and recreation. The west range contained the kitchen and domestic offices on the ground floor and North's Privy Chamber on the upper floor, a large room with windows on both sides.[26] The staircase or 'halpas' in the courtyard giving access to the Privy Chamber was probably added after North's death.[27] This range was combined with the three elements of retained monastic buildings to the west which served as domestic offices and was later known as Wash House Court.

To the east of the new house the Bell Tower of the Priory Church survives (*162*). This had been built in the early fifteenth century at the east end of the Church, with another stage added in 1512, and was topped with a battlemented belfry and a spire, though the turret shown in Toms' view was added in 1614. At ground floor level the Bell Tower served as an anteroom to the Chapel, which was created by North from the Chapter House. In 1565 it was furnished with richly decorated altar cloths of velvet, damask, satin and cloth of gold.[28] The Chapel was originally separate from the house, the linking cloister to the north of Cloister Court being a Jacobean addition at the same time as the Chapel was increased in size. North also turned the Great Cloister

162 The Bell Tower at the London Charterhouse

garth into a large, formal garden. He demolished the monastic conduit at its centre and built a new conduit to supply water to the north of the formal garden, beyond the monastic Wilderness. Part of the west Cloister walk was retained, however, and turned into a bowling alley, and on the upper level into a gallery with views over the garden. In 1565 this contained a large hanging, so it must have been enclosed and glazed.[29] It would have been accessed from the antechamber of North's Great Chamber.

Following North's death the Charterhouse was sold to Thomas Howard, 4th Duke of Norfolk. In 1571 North's gallery was demolished by the Duke to create an open terrace above and a new cloister beneath, which became known as the Norfolk Cloister (*163*). It was an imposing structure, 263 feet long, almost the same length as the monastic Cloister Walk. Nearly half survives, the remainder having been demolished in 1872.[30] The west wall is the wall of the monastic Cloister and the vaulting and east wall of brick was built by Norfolk. It was originally plastered internally and glazed. Both the terrace and the Cloister

163 The Norfolk Cloister at the London Charterhouse, built by the Duke of Norfolk

offered views of the formal garden, while the terrace also overlooked the Privy Garden.[31] By the 1580s there was also a tennis court to the west of the north end of the Norfolk Cloister, but this is more likely to have been added by the Duke rather than by North.[32]

Following his involvement in the Ridolfi plot and his pursuit of a marriage with Mary, Queen of Scots, the Duke of Norfolk was arrested in September 1571, convicted of treason in January 1572, and executed on 2 June 1572. His estates, including the Charterhouse, should have passed to the Crown by attainder, but Queen Elizabeth waived the Crown's rights and the Charterhouse passed to his eldest son, Philip. He lived there in the late 1570s, but after he inherited Arundel House in the Strand from his grandfather in 1580, he

only occasionally stayed at the Charterhouse. Then, like his father, he was convicted of treason in 1589, imprisoned for life, and his estates forfeited to the Crown. The Charterhouse was granted in 1601 to Philip's half-brother Thomas, Lord Howard de Walden, who was created Earl of Suffolk.[33] But the Earl was spending heavily on Audley End House in Essex and Charlton Park in Wiltshire, and it is unclear whether he carried out any works there before he sold the Charterhouse for £13,000 to Thomas Sutton in 1611.[34] So for forty years few, if any, changes were made to Lord North's great house, other than the further improvements by the Duke of Norfolk. Only with Sutton's new almshouses and school was the Charterhouse further transformed, and today it survives as an almshouse.

Malmesbury Abbey

The great nave of the ruined Malmesbury Abbey rides along the crest of this Wiltshire hilltop town like some ancient trireme, its buttressed hulk lit by tall arched and traceried windows, while at the former crossing a huge Romanesque arch rears up to support the shattered wall (*164*) from which, until its fall in 1479, a soaring tower once rose to a spire which rivalled in height that at Salisbury Cathedral. At closer quarters, approaching the south doorway through the churchyard, bands of sinuous carvings gradually come into focus, their mandorla panels alive with draped biblical figures, a riotously figurative preparation for the majesty of Christ in his Glory, flanked by two angels, in the shadowy recesses of the porch beyond. These richly patterned carvings are a perfect counterpoint to the blank austerity of the interior, with its sturdy Norman columns, arcaded triforium and clerestory canopied by a lierne vault. This stony simplicity is reflected in the boxy Watching Loft, set high in the triforium, like an abbatial hide for the ghost of Aldhelm or William of Malmesbury, the abbey's two celebrated sons, to keep an eye on the townsfolk as they worship below.

The Abbey Church was the centrepiece of a vast complex of monastic buildings, which had superseded the early Saxon community established at Malmesbury in the middle of the seventh century. Its rising star had been Aldhelm, who was Saxon by birth and related to the Wessex kings. After a brief period of study in Canterbury, he returned to Malmesbury and was appointed abbot in 675. Aldhelm built a new church in honour of the Saviour, St Peter and St Paul, and further churches within the monastic precinct to St Michael and St Mary.[1] It was probably during his abbacy that the rule of St Benedict was introduced at the abbey. Aldhelm died in May 709 and his body was buried in St Michael's Church; there it lay until 955, when it was transferred to the Abbey Church and deposited in a shrine. King Athelstan was also buried in Malmesbury in 939 at St

164 The crossing tower at Malmesbury Abbey with the Romanesque arch beneath

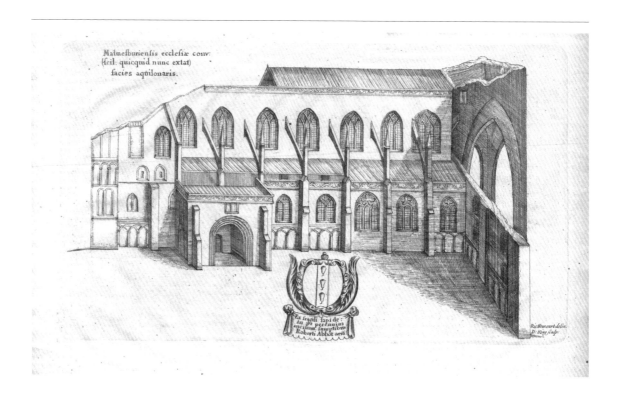

Mary's Church. William of Malmesbury writes that 'his noble remains were conveyed to Malmesbury [from Gloucester] and buried under the altar'.[2] Athelstan's monumental tomb in the north aisle of the present Abbey Church, with its crowned effigy lying under a vaulted and pinnacled canopy, dates from the fifteenth century; its tomb chest is empty.

The Saxon monastic complex was completely overhauled by Abbot Aelfric from about 974, who replaced the secular clergy with monks, made St Mary's Church on the site the chief church of the monastery and added various conventual buildings. After the Norman Conquest Warin, a French monk from Evreux with a great veneration for Aldhelm, was appointed abbot. In 1078 he removed Aldhelm's body from a vault where it had been hidden during the Danish raids and placed it in a magnificent shrine. Two years later, after the miraculous cure of a young

deformed boy, Warin ordered that Aldhelm should be venerated as a saint. It is this post-Conquest Abbey Church and monastic community that William of Malmesbury, the most gifted English historian of the twelfth century, who died in about 1142, would have known and about which he writes. Soon after his death, perhaps as early as 1145, St Mary's Church was replaced by the nave of what was to be the great Romanesque Abbey Church, its east end terminated by a round apse, at the apex of which was the shrine of St Aldhelm and three apsidal chapels forming a chevet. The new Abbey Church had advanced sufficiently for its dedication to be discussed and a service to be held there in 1177. Of this late twelfth-century date were also the Cloister walk, which was remodelled in the fifteenth century, the Chapter House, Frater and Dorter. The Infirmary was sited to the east of the Chapter House, while south-eastwards

165 *Malmesbury Abbey*, engraved by Daniel King, 1655

was the Abbot's Lodging with its garden and chapel. On the north side, sloping down steeply to the river, was the principal convent garden threaded by streams and planted with fruit trees.

When the king's visitors, Dr Petre and John Ap Rice, arrived at the abbey in August 1535 to assess the income of the monastery for the *Valor*, they gave a detailed description of the spiritualities and temporalities of the establishment. The abbot had control of the monastery buildings and environs, which covered about six acres; also the convent garden, streams, ponds, fishery and fruit trees, covering about forty-three acres, and kept for the abbot and convent to walk in. Nearby there was a water mill and a dovecote.[3] Ap Rice and other officers received the surrender of the house on 15 December 1539, when the buildings thought to be worthy of preservation were entrusted to Sir Edward Baynton, while William Stumpe, a Malmesbury clothier, occupied the less valuable monastic structures, possibly acting as Baynton's deputy. Thereafter, on 20 November 1544, Stumpe was granted by Letters Patent 'the site of the house of Malmesbury with all the buildings of the same with the church, frater, cloister, chapter house, garden, and orchard'.[4]

William Stumpe was the richest Wiltshire clothier of his generation, though he was of humble origins. His father was a weaver and his brother a husbandman, both of whom lived at North Nibley in Gloucestershire. Nibley is not far from Berkeley Castle and Stumpe's first step towards wealth and status was his marriage by 1519 to Joyce, a daughter of James Berkeley, who lived at nearby Bradley just outside Wotton-under-Edge. Stumpe is recorded as a resident of Malmesbury in 1524, when he was assessed as one of the town's four richest inhabitants. In the *Valor* of 1535 he is noted as paying rent to the abbey for his tenancy of a mill, and later that year he paid £200 for all Sir Roger Tocote's property in Malmesbury, as well as renting another of the abbey's mills.[5] His importance within the town was recognised in 1536 when he was appointed as one of the receivers of the newly established Court of Augmentations; he was one of seven receivers to retain his office after the Court's reorganisation in 1547.[6]

When John Leland reached Malmesbury in 1542 he made an understandable mistake, given Stumpe's prominence in the town, believing that the clothier had bought the entire site of the abbey: 'the hole logginges of thabbay be now longing to one *Stumpe*, an

265

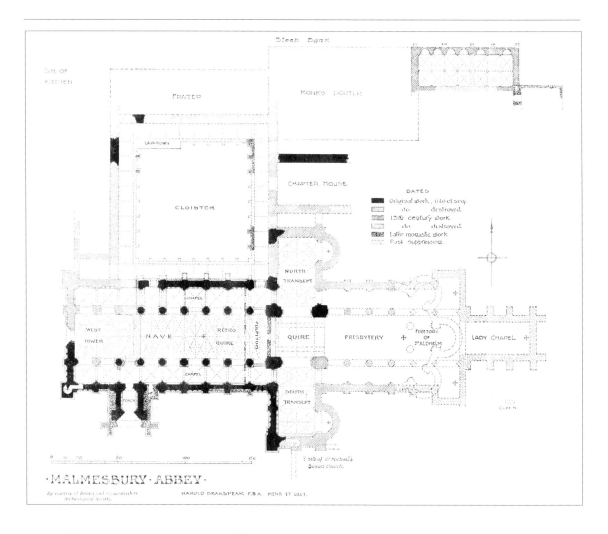

166 Harold Brakspear's plan of Malmesbury Abbey

exceeding rich Clothiar that boute them of the King'.[7] Leland further reported that 'at this present tyme every Corner of the vaste Houses of Office that belonged to thabbay be fulle of lumbes [looms] to weve Clooth yn', and that Stumpe had devised an ambitious plan to 'make a stret [street] or 2 for his Clothiers in the bak vacant Ground of the Abbay that is withyn the Toune Walles'.[8] These towered and bastioned walls are depicted in a remarkable bird's eye painting of Malmesbury, dated to April 1646.[9] However, this scheme was never carried out. Two years later Stumpe, having paid just over £1,517, took possession of the whole monastic site and its lands, but it is clear from Leland's account that he had already lobbied for the nave of the Abbey Church, shown in Daniel King's engraving of 1655 (*165*), to be preserved and presented to the town: 'This *Stumpe* was the chef Causer and Contributer to have thabbay Chirch made a Paroch Chirch.'[10]

After the surrender, most of the major elements of the abbey were demolished,

167 *Malmesbury Abbey, Wiltshire*, Peter de Wint, 1784-1849

including the presbytery and Lady Chapel at the east end of the Church, the Cloister, which was sited to the north, the Chapter House that connected with the north transept, the Frater beyond, and the Dorter to the north-east, all of which are marked on Harold Brakspear's plan (*166*). As far as the Abbot's Lodging was concerned, Stumpe retained the foundations of the thirteenth-century building, part of Abbot William of Colerne's building programme of 1260, including the striking undercroft, its columns still reaching upwards to rib vaults that have disappeared, its cusped lancets giving spectacular views of the valley below. At one corner a spiral staircase rises up which would once have connected with the Dorter. On this firm foundation, which teeters above the sharply sloping river valley, and which is still visible on the north façade with its battery of lancets, he built a new house in typical Cotswold vernacular style, with large chamfered cross-mullioned windows and a gabled roofline, shown in Peter de Wint's

watercolour (*167*). This house survives intact on the site today (*168*), though it has been extended to the east by a subsidiary block in matching style, which was designed most sympathetically by Brakspear in 1909 and built for Elliot Scott-Mackirdy.[11] Further minor alterations were made to the interior of the house in 1923.[12]

William Stumpe's house is U-shaped in plan with an entrance porch (*169*) in the south-east angle giving onto a central Hall, which was flanked by large chambers to the west and to the east. Another large chamber faced south in the western projecting wing and the kitchen occupied the eastern wing. These were the principal rooms on the ground floor. Today, the Hall survives intact, but the west range has been opened up to form a library which functions almost as a long gallery. The Tudor rose is prominent in a plasterwork frieze in the Library and on the spandrels of an original fireplace in the Hall. Unsurprisingly, there is a record that Henry

168 Malmesbury Abbey House as it is today

169 The Porch at Malmesbury Abbey House

VIII visited Stumpe when he was hunting nearby in Braydon Forest. Thomas Fuller describes this impromptu visit:

> King Henry the Eighth, hunting near Malmesbury in Bredon Forest, came with all his court train, unexpected, to dine with this clothier. But great housekeepers are as seldom surprised with guests as vigilant captains with enemies. Stumps commands his little army of workmen, which he fed daily in his house, to fast one meal until night (which they might easily do without endangering their health), and with the same provision gave the king and his court train (though not so delicious and various) most wholesome and plentiful entertainment.[13]

If the story is true, rather than apocryphal, it is doubtful whether Stumpe could have accommodated such a retinue in his modest dwelling, and it suggests that there were other substantial buildings at the property, which have since been demolished. Certainly, a range survives attached to the Tower in the grounds, which have been crafted into one of the most atmospheric and beautiful gardens in the country. These were created after 1994 by Ian and Barbara Pollard and make several references to the abbey,[14] the ruined crossing tower of which rears up above the abundant flowers and the sharply-edged topiary to remind visitors of the monks who once walked these grounds.[15]

170 The surviving part of the Church at Milton Abbey

Milton Abbey

King Athelstan founded the Benedictine Abbey of Milton or Middleton in 933 for the repose of the soul of his brother Edwin. He buried his mother there and bestowed upon the abbey numerous relics procured from Rome and Brittany. Little is known of the original monastic buildings, though the seal of the abbey shows a church with three spires, suggesting that there was a nave with western towers, but no traces of the nave were discovered during excavations in 1865.[1] Nothing remains of this early church at Milton; the present building dates from 1309 after a fire had destroyed its predecessor. The new Abbey Church was built in grey limestone in a restrained Early English style, but the tower and north transept in golden Ham Hill stone were added later in the fifteenth century in Perpendicular Gothic style (*170*). The nave and the Lady Chapel have gone and so too have all the domestic buildings of the monastic complex except the Great Hall of the former Abbot's Lodgings, though traces of the Cloister, or at least the slype between the Abbey Church and the Chapter House, are still visible on the north transept. The Cloister would have been sited to the north of the Church, and on the usual Benedictine arrangement the east range would have included the Chapter House and Parlour, with the Dorter on the upper floor. The north range would have contained the Frater and the west range the Cellarer's Hall. The nave of the Church would have formed the south range of the Cloister. These buildings have all disappeared and were probably demolished, along with the nave, at the time of the Dissolution.

The abbey avoided the first stage of suppression because its annual income of £665 in the *Valor* of 1535 was well above the £200 limit. However, Abbot John Bradley eventually surrendered the house and its twelve monks on 11 March 1539. On 23 February the following year the king granted the house and site of the abbey, together with the Church, steeple, churchyard and the Manor of Milton, to John Tregonwell, a lawyer and commissioner for the suppression of the monasteries in the West Country, who paid £1,000 for the property.[2] He gave the remaining east end of the Abbey Church to the local parishioners and was buried there in 1565. Taking appropriation to the limit, his brass kneeling figure

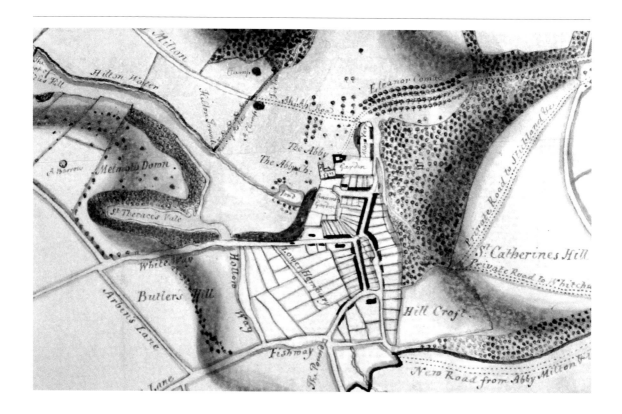

and heraldry were set within a recycled mural monument that had been constructed for someone else.[3] Tregonwell seems to have adapted the Abbot's Lodgings, to the east of the Cloister and north-east of the Church, to create his new house. A plan of 'the Abby' on a 1769-70 survey map drawn by William Woodward (*171*) shows a courtyard house in this location. The surviving Abbot's Hall was in the south range of the house and the west range may have contained the principal apartments. Later descriptions suggest that the north range, with its Gatehouse, and the east range provided lesser domestic offices including the kitchen. How much of this courtyard house, other than the south range, formed part of the Abbot's Lodging and how much was built by Tregonwell is unknown.

The late fifteenth-century Abbot's Hall built by Abbot Middleton in 1498 remained

the core of the Tudor courtyard house, though most of Tregonwell's additions to the former monastic complex were swept away in the mid-eighteenth-century remodelling carried out by Joseph Damer, Lord Milton. Not only did the Tudor house suffer in this drastic campaign of demolition, but also the market town of Middleton set around the skirts of the abbey, which was razed to the ground to provide the seclusion required for a Georgian country house set within a landscaped park by Lancelot 'Capability' Brown. Only one house remained of Middleton, its inhabitants having been re-housed in the model village of thatched cottages that climb the hillside well out of sight of the mansion and its grounds.

John Tregonwell was a lawyer of Cornish stock, who had been chosen as one of the King's Proctors in the divorce case between Henry VIII and Katherine of Aragon; he was

171 An estate map of Milton Abbey by William Woodward, 1769

subsequently knighted for his services to the king. He was also a senior judge, served on many commissions, and was later an MP. The property remained in the Tregonwell family until the eighteenth century, when it passed out of the family to Sir Jacob Bancks, son of the Swedish ambassador to the Court of Charles II. Bancks owned it when Samuel and Nathaniel Buck surveyed it for their 1733 engraving (*172*). Their view is taken from the north-west and shows the great fragment of the Abbey Church, alongside which is a range of domestic buildings. These form Tregon-well's Tudor mansion. Further buildings of the market town can be seen in the distance. Bancks did little to the complex and it was sold in 1752 to Joseph Damer of Winter-bourne Came, who had married a daughter of the Duke of Dorset and would become Baron Milton in 1753.

The Buck view features the west range of the Tregonwell house with its jumble of disparate elements and a central staircase tower. Above this range, to the rear, the gabled roof of the Abbot's Hall in the south arm of the courtyard is just visible. Writing about the 'Abbey House' much later, but with the benefit of personal knowledge of the site, the county historian John Hutchins gives an atmospheric account of what Tregonwell had retained at the Dissolution.[4] Apparently, there were 'more remains of this abbey than of any other in the county … owing to Sir John Tregonwell's having an early design of procuring the grant of it, which preserved both it and the church'. Sited on rising ground close to the Abbey Church 'its form was a long square. The north front was a very low ancient range of building, with small narrow windows, perhaps the dormitory or cells of the monks', while the

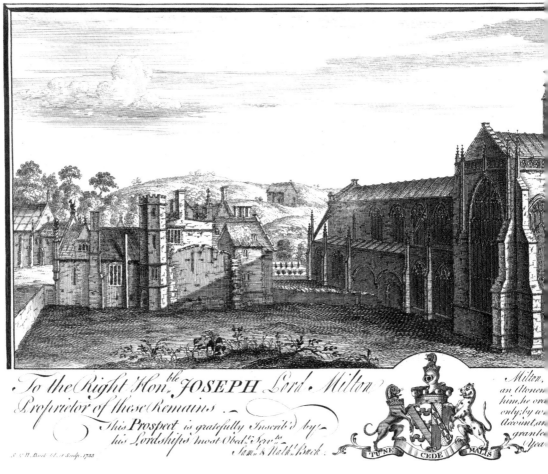

To the Right Hon.ble JOSEPH Lord Milton
Proprietor of these Remains

This Prospect is gratefully Inscrib'd by
his Lordships most Obed.t Serv.ts
Sam.l & Nath.l Buck.

TUNE CEDE MALIS

172 *The North West View of Milton-Abby in the County of Dorset*, engraved by Samuel and Nathaniel Buck, 1733

entrance was via a 'large gate into a small court, whose old buildings were very irregular in form and height, as indeed was the whole fabric'. Clearly Hutchins was incorrect in this respect – the Dorter would have been in the east range of the Cloister, which was demolished after the suppression, not in the courtyard house. This description accords perfectly with the west range as depicted by

the Bucks. Abbot Middleton must have done some updating in the courtyard, as Hutchins mentions under a window 'a W with a crown over it, and an M with a crosier through it, and between them 1529'. Across the courtyard there was a porch giving access to the 'hall … under which there was the servants' hall and kitchen, and over them two or three small apartments, all modern'; these were, no doubt,

OUNTY OF DORSET.

lleton or Melton-Abbas was built by K.Ethelstone to make
th of his younger Brothers:who being falsly Accused to
Sea in a Boat; without Oars or Sails,and with one Page
was drowned .He also built another Monastery on this
Seven Years Penance. At the Dissolution this Abby was
VIII. to the Family of Tregonwell who resided here 160
rchase came into that of the present possesor .

An.Val.Dugd. £.578.13.11.Speed.£720.4.1.

Lord Milton'. The 'great dining-room' at the north end of the western range was 'beautified by Sir John Tregonwell; for on the balustrade at the top are lions, &c holding shields, on which were the arms of Tregonwell and Kelway'. Near this was the 'Star-chamber', and further west was another court and 'an old ruinous room, all wainscoted, called the Bull Room, perhaps from evidences being kept there'. At the south end of this court, steps 'descended into the cloisters, and led to a door in the lower part of the north aisle: this was pulled down 1730'. Again, this cannot refer to the monastic Cloister, which had been demolished. Opposite the 'great north gate' was a building called the 'Still House', which Hutchins takes to have been the Infirmary. This is possible, as the monastic Infirmary would have been separate from the Cloister. There were further initials – the Middleton-Milton rebus (a mill over a tun) – and the date 1515 on its walls; it was pulled down in 1753. The 'ancient fabric' was 'entirely taken down except the hall, 1771, in order to rebuild it, as it now appears'.

Before this wholesale demolition in 1771, Lord Milton had initially made do with the domestic buildings of Tregonwell's Tudor house, merely re-facing and remodelling the existing courtyard ranges and fitting up some new apartments. Bishop Pococke visited Milton in 1754 and gave a useful description of the house. After noting Tregonwell's monument in the north aisle of the Church, Pococke goes on to describe the house that he had created:

> There are great remains of the Abbey, as a hall with a fine carved screen, a date on it of about 1428; a room called the Starchamber, from the wooden ceiling in compartments adorn'd with gilt stars; most of the other rooms are alter'd, but some of the old building which was very

alterations made either by Sir Jacob Bancks in the 1730s or by Lord Milton in the first phase of his work at the abbey. Bancks pulled down a kitchen at the east end of the courtyard in 1737, possibly opening up the east of the courtyard as depicted in the survey map. He also made alterations in the west range, particularly at its south end, 'but he lived only to finish the shell, and they were completed by

173 The Abbot's Hall, Milton Abbey

fine remains. Lord Milton is casing it all round in a beautiful modern taste. The town is a very poor small place.[5]

Abbot Middleton's Hall (*173*), in the south range of Tregonwell's courtyard house, is a dramatic space dominated by a massive hammer-beam roof. Its supporting brackets are carried down the wall in stone shafts, which terminate in carved angels holding shields; there are further heraldic shields beneath the windows, on the wall over the dais and in the bay window. Although Pococke ascribes a date of 'about 1428' to the tripartite

screen, it is obviously of a piece with the Hall, and he is likely to have misread 2 for 9, though its curvaceous, cusped Gothick cresting must be due to Lord Milton's 1754-5 campaign, which was carried out by John Vardy. Lord Milton commissioned from the architect alternative schemes in classical and Gothick for the external elevations, and Vardy produced a beautiful Rococo design for the proposed Great Room on the first floor in the centre of the long west front.[6] It is not clear just how much of Vardy's scheme was carried out, for Woodward's 1769-70 survey map recalls precisely Hutchins' description of the Tregon-

174 Milton Abbey, from John Hutchins' *History and Antiquities of the County of Dorset*, 1774

well house, while the staircase tower featured in the 1733 Buck view is shown projecting from the façade.[7] It seems that Vardy's schemes were never realised while he was in Lord Milton's employ, and that when Sir William Chambers was appointed in 1770 he was directed to demolish the unfinished fragment and begin again from scratch. However, having dispensed with Vardy, Lord Milton, in a contrary move, directed that Chambers, a notably classical architect, should adopt and adapt Vardy's original Gothick plans.[8]

Roger White has argued convincingly that the plate of Milton Abbey (*174*) published in the 1774 edition of Hutchins' *History and Antiquities of the County of Dorset* shows Vardy's original Gothick scheme before it was altered by Chambers. It is highly likely, therefore, that the form and several elements of

Vardy's work were retained in the rebuilding.[9] In 1775 James Wyatt followed Chambers, who had despaired of Lord Milton: 'Unfortunately for me, I have these three or four years past been building a Cursed Gothick house for this unmannerly Imperious Lord, who has treated me as he does everybody, ill.'[10] Wyatt fitted up most of the important rooms in the fashionable Adam style and he was later employed by Lord Milton in 1789 to restore the Abbey Church.

175 The South, or Georgian Front at Mottisfont Abbey

Mottisfont Priory

National Trust visitors to Mottisfont, having parked their cars in the fields to the north of the house, make a beeline either for the walled garden, with its stunning display of old-fashioned roses collected by the Trust's Garden Adviser, Graham Stuart Thomas, or head for the café in the stables before tackling the house to experience the deliciously epicene atmosphere of the exquisite Rococo-Gothick Saloon painted by Rex Whistler or to view canvases from the Derek Hill collection of twentieth-century art. Few go with the object of deciphering the character and extent of the original monastic complex – a priory rather than an abbey, being re-titled only in the eighteenth century – from which the present house was constructed. Yet vestiges of the Priory of Augustinian Canons of the Holy Trinity set within its idyllic valley by the River Test are still visible and the Tudor house that was adapted from it by William Sandys, Henry VIII's Lord Chamberlain, can still be discerned even though it has been encased in a Georgian skin (*175*).

Mottisfont Priory was founded in 1201 by William Briwere, or Brewer, but was not consecrated until 1224. A Rental Book kept about 1340 by the cellarer, Walter de Blount, gives a good description of the monastic establishment with its spring – the 'fons' – from which the name Mottisfont derives – which supplied two watermills.[1] There were two gardens – the '*Magnum Gardinum*' and '*Coumbesorchard*' – an apple yard, pasture, meadow, tannery, two dovecotes and 'a certain place within the infirmary close of fruits trees and meadow'.[2] It was, therefore, a fairly substantial feudal complex and important enough for John of Gaunt's daughter, Maud of Lancaster, to be buried there.[3] The priory flourished until the Black Death that decimated the community and from which it never recovered. In 1410 the canons complained that the priory buildings were in disrepair, their lands were being plundered and all their manors and granges were in ruins; and in 1457 the prior wrote to Pope Calixtus III that, owing to 'an earthquake and other disasters' his church and its buildings had been 'greatly crushed and loosened so as to need costly repairs'.[4]

In 1494 Henry VII obtained a papal bull for its suppression, which was never carried out, but the priory was eventually suppressed at the

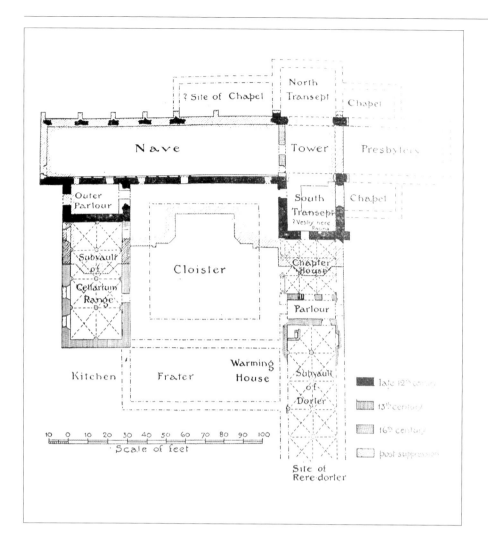

North Transept

? Site of Chapel

Chapel

Nave

Tower

Presbytery

Outer Parlour

South Transept

Chapel

?Vestry here Piscina

Subvault of Cellarium Range

Cloister

Chapter House

Parlour

Kitchen

Frater

Warming House

Subvault of Dorter

late 12ᵗʰ century

13ᵗʰ century

16ᵗʰ century

post suppression

10 0 10 20 30 40 50 60 70 80 90 100
Scale of feet

Site of Rere-dorter

Dissolution of the smaller monasteries in 1536. Henry Huttoft, head of the Customs at Southampton, who had been a benefactor and had carried out a number of improvements to the Church, begged Thomas Cromwell to grant him the building.[5] However, the priory and its lands were granted to the Lord Chamberlain, William Lord Sandys, who acquired them in exchange for the two villages of Chelsea and Paddington. The Letters Patent of July 1536 state that Sandys and his wife, Lady Margery, were granted 'the site &c. of the later priory of Holy Trinity, Motisfount, and the church,

churchyard, messuages, &c. of the said priory'.[6]

Sandys was the epitome of a Tudor court diplomat, being a close friend of the young King Henry and supporting his queen, Katherine of Aragon. He was made treasurer of Calais and became a Knight of the Garter in 1518. His diplomatic skills were later tested during the negotiations between Henry and François Premier at the Field of the Cloth of Gold. Sandys' standing within Henry's Court is demonstrated by a visit Queen Katherine made to The Vyne in 1510, and he retained his friendship with the king after the annul-

176 The floor plan of Mottisfont Abbey

ment of the royal marriage. Ever the diplomat, he received Henry's new queen, Anne Boleyn, at The Vyne in 1535. He was well placed, therefore, to secure the grant of Mottisfont Priory. Surprisingly, there appears to be no surviving portrait of Sandys, merely a view of his back in an eighteenth-century engraving of the State Opening of Parliament in Henry's reign.[7]

There is some debate as to how Sandys adapted the priory buildings after his acquisition, but it is clear that he intended to make Mottisfont his principal seat. In August 1538, two years before his death, according to a letter written by the parish priest John Atkinson to his Hampshire neighbour Lady Lisle, Sandys was 'keeping household in my house at Mottesfont ever since the beginning of May, and I think will continue till All Hallow-tide to oversee his works there. He makes a goodly place of the priory and intends to lie there most of his life.'[8] Sadly, Sandys was to die two years later, so the major works were continued and completed by his elder son and great-grandson, the second and third Lords Sandys.

The uncertainty over what was achieved at Mottisfont after 1536 concerns the true extent of the original monastic buildings and their

subsequent adaptation when the priory was transformed into a domestic dwelling. The *Victoria County History* is a good starting point, as its entry on Mottisfont is illustrated with a plan (*176*) of the priory.[9] The present house can be seen to have utilised the nave, tower and south transept of the Priory Church, together with the 'Outer Parlour' adjoining the subterranean *Cellarium* on the west range of the Cloister. The remaining buildings to the south and east of the Cloister – the Dorter, Frater, Warming House and Kitchen – would seem to have been demolished by Sir Richard Mill when he remodelled the house in the early eighteenth century. Certainly this is what H Avray Tipping thought when writing up the house for *Country Life* in 1921: 'Lord Sandys' transformation of the nave of the monastic church was retained … but, whereas his complete plan will have been that of a quad-rangle, Sir Richard Mill, while thickening the main or north range, entirely removed the southern range of buildings.'[10] When Christopher Hussey came to Mottisfont in 1954 he followed the same reasoning:

Sandys converted the nave of the church into

177 Mottisfont Abbey: the *Cellarium*

the middle block of his new house, with the cloister as its forecourt, flanked by lateral wings built on the chapter house and cellarium. All but the stumps of these wings were pulled down by Sir Richard Mill in forming the present south elevation.[11]

At this date the ruins of the Chapter House survived below the steps to the south-east wing. Hussey surmises that their preservation, as well as that of the *Cellarium* (*177*) to the west, 'is no doubt due to their having been incorporated into the wings of the Sandys house'.[12] Then he made an odd leap of reasoning: 'the disappearance without trace of the cloister's south range containing the frater and warming-room, and of the dormitory range that adjoined the chapter house, is presumptive evidence that Sandys pulled them down because he was planning an open quadrangle'.[13] The rather skewed logic is that, although such domestic ranges 'were those found most convenient for the Tudor adapters', they were 'already dilapidated and the church itself in better repair'.[14] It should be noted that Hussey made no mention of the Prior's Lodging, which was often the central core of these converted houses.

This narrative was taken up by Gervase Jackson-Stops in his 1978 guidebook to Mott-

178 The North Front of Mottisfont Abbey, built on the nave and tower of the Priory Church

isfont, which quotes John Leland's remark, made soon after 1540, that Sandys 'began to translate the old building of the priory, and to make a fair maner place' out of the complex, but that 'the worke is left onperfecte'.[15] In doing so, Sandys adapted the nave 'as his principal range of apartments', dividing it into two floors, chopped off the tower at roof level and demolished the north transept and the eastern end of the Church with its two side chapels forming the present north front (*178*).[16] However, to aid his analysis, Jackson-Stops had sight of a 1724 map made for Sir Richard Mill by the surveyor Christopher Mason (*179*), which shows the exact form of the sixteenth-century house.[17] This clearly depicts a large quadrangular building of gabled ranges with two courtyards and a projecting L-shaped

extension to the south façade. Jackson-Stops believed that these courtyards represented the surviving priory buildings, which were merely adapted by the Sandys family for domestic use, thereby producing a 'residence both palatial in size and up-to-date in plan, without the enormous expense and time of building entirely afresh'.[18]

The vignette on this 1724 survey map is the only record we have of the Tudor house before it was partially demolished by Sir Richard Mill at some point in the early eighteenth century, but before 1743. A survey of this period dated 1726 mentions 'the Great house, Gardens, Stables, Coach houses, Fish ponds', all of which are indicated on the map.[19] In an archaeological report on the Mottisfont estate, Christopher Currie speculates that the

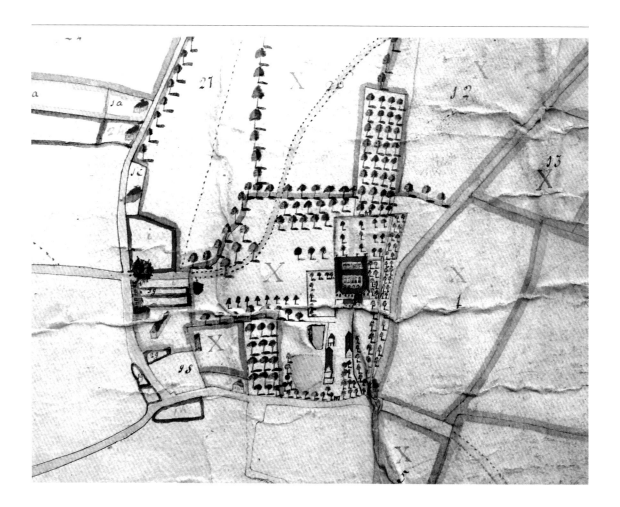

priory buildings might have 'represented a double cloister plan' and that the Infirmary Court mentioned in Blount's Rental Book was south of the main Cloister.[20] Apparently, parch marks in the ground in dry summers only show the main Cloister as complete, although 'a court of sorts is shown to the south'.[21] Currie surmises that the indistinct nature of these ghostly outlines suggests that some of the buildings of the second courtyard were of timber, rather than of stone, as in the Cloister.

Reflecting the antiquarian interest of the period, Mill changed the property's name to Mottisfont Abbey and had an engraving made in 1743 of the house as newly 'repaired & beautified'.[22] While he may have demolished

much of the Tudor house, itself built within the priory ranges, several elements were retained and survive today, including a pointed arch, with its transitional trumpet capitals bursting into foliate forms (*180*), which gave access from the lost south-east chancel chapel into the south transept; two shafts of the Chapter House relocated to the porch; the rib-vaulted *Cellarium* on the west side; the arched soffit of the *Pulpitum*, originally linking the nave and the choir; and the arch between the lost north transept and the tower, which was uncovered by the removal of stucco by Mrs Marianne Vaudrey-Barker-Mill in renovations that were completed in 1908. There are further glimpses of foliate capitals

179 Map of Mottisfont Abbey by Christopher Mason, 1724

and arch segments in the Georgian house remodelled within the nave.

As regards the precise configuration and the interiors of the Tudor house there is an inventory of 1540, made at Lord Sandys' death, that has been used by James Rothwell to devise a conjectural ground plan and elevations, which are now shown in video form and on presentation boards at Mottisfont.[23] However, it is clear from the inventory that Lord Sandys had achieved very little at his death and, as Leland attests, his 'worke [was] left onperfecte'. The current guidebook suggests that 'structurally at least, the house was complete or nearly complete'[24] by then, but the inventory mentions few rooms compared to the detailed and extensive inventory taken of Lord Sandys' 'Goods at the Vyne on his death'.[25] This suggests that he had merely begun to convert the Priory Church and that it was left to his descendants to develop the Cloister and the southern court beyond.

The most important room in the early house was the Great Chamber, decorated with rich tapestry hangings, one of which depicted the history of King David; there were several turkey carpets, 'Four Flanders chairs covered with leather', cushions of needlework and a very expensive clock that was valued at the princely sum of 26s 8d. Rothwell's conjectural ground plan places this room at the west end of the former nave, with its adjacent 'Chamber next to the Great Chamber' and an 'Inner Chamber' probably in the same location. These also featured tapestry hangings with the biblical subjects of King David and Solomon, 'Job, Abraham & Isaac & others', Solomon and Sadoch and the Judgement of Solomon.

An intriguing item in the Inner Chamber, which suggests that building works were still in progress in December 1540, is 'a chimney piece of imagery not hanged of the history of Minos'. The other major room mentioned is the Parlour, which may have been converted from the monastic Parlour which adjoined the Chapter House in the east range or perhaps the 'Outer Parlour' at the north-west corner; this also had an attendant chamber next to it and a further inner chamber. The rich furnishings continued in these rooms, with turkey carpets, cushions and curtains; the Parlour also had chairs, tables, forms and trestles, indicating that this is where meals were taken. The chamber next to it was used as a bedroom and

decorated with sumptuous furnishings including red and gold hangings, a four-poster bed
with a tester 'of russet satin cloth of silver and
tinsell striped' with a fringed valance and 'five
curtains of blue and yellow sarcenet and a
quilt of blue and yellow'. The 'old chamber
next the parlour' was another bedroom with
similar furnishings of damask.

As well as the domestic apartments, Sandys
had contrived a chapel within the former
nave. Rothwell places this plausibly at the east
end of the nave close to what is now called
Chapel Porch. Here there were vestments,
altar cloths and cushions of 'bruges satin', two
pairs of 'grete candlesticks', a 'crosse of copper'
and a silver chalice. The offices comprised a

kitchen and buttery, perhaps in the west
range, where the priory kitchen had been
located at the south-west corner of the Cloister next to the Frater. Finally, a 'chamber over
the gate' is mentioned, which had hangings
and a feather bed. It is not clear where this
might have been, though Rothwell's reconstruction provides for an Inner Gatehouse
within what would have been the Frater and
also an Outer Gatehouse giving access to the
south courtyard.

Rothwell has based these gatehouses, the
siting of a Great Hall within the western range
and the provision of king's and queen's chambers elsewhere on 'archaeology and on a study
of comparable houses including Newstead

180 A Transitional trumpet capital at Mottisfont Abbey

Abbey'.[26] The Vyne inventory of the same date has almost identical rooms, including chambers in gatehouses, to those marked on the Mottisfont ground plan, and so must also have informed this reconstruction. The present guidebook states that 'there is no listing in the inventory of a Great Hall, a standard feature for the times'.[27] We must presume, therefore, that if such an apartment was constructed, as Rothwell suggests, it was added to the former monastic complex after Lord Sandys' death. What is striking about the video reconstruction of the conjectural elevations of Tudor Mottisfont is that its gatehouses feature tall angle turrets in Hampton Court style, while the 1724 vignette of the house clearly shows simple unadorned ranges with gabled roofs. It is, of course, merely a vignette rather than a detailed architectural drawing, though it does mark an L-shaped range to the south façade, breaking the symmetry, which does not feature in the reconstructions.

Engraved by T. A. Dean

Netley Abbey

Today the extensive ruins of Netley Abbey, managed by English Heritage, preserve a sense of the quiet seclusion sought by the Cistercian monks who built the complex in the thirteenth century. Dedicated to a monastic life of strictness and simplicity, they wanted to recreate the peaceful isolation of early desert hermits and rediscover the purity of early monasticism in a self-supporting community. In common with other Cistercian abbeys, Netley was built in a remote location, cut off from the world by woodland and heathland on the landward side and by the sea to the west. It is sited on the east bank of Southampton Water, some three miles south-east of the modern city of Southampton, sheltered by high ground to the north and east. It is almost exactly halfway between the mouths of the Itchen and Hamble rivers, while sixteenth-century Netley Castle is positioned between the abbey and the shore. Unusually, Netley has significant remains of large parts of the buildings and is the most complete Cistercian monastery in southern England.

After the Dissolution, Netley was developed into a Tudor house by William Paulet, Marquess of Winchester (*181*) and remained occupied until 1676. It was subsequently sold for building materials and after the buildings were demolished in the early eighteenth century, the romantic ruins became an attractive destination for tourists and artists, as captured in John Constable's 1816 drawing (*182*). Another visitor was Horace Walpole, who described them in 1755:

> The ruins are vast, and retain fragments of beautiful fretted roof pendent in the air, with all variety of Gothic patterns of windows wrapped round and round with ivy … they are not the ruins of Netley, but of Paradise. – oh! the purple abbots, what a spot they had chosen to slumber in![1]

So, although most of the Tudor building has been demolished, almost all

181 *William Paulet, Marquess of Winchester*, engraved by TA Dean, 1828

the walls of the thirteenth-century Church remain.

The Abbey of Netley, dedicated to the honour of the Blessed Virgin and St Edward the Confessor, called the Abbey of St Mary of Edwardstow, was founded for Cistercian monks in 1239. It was also known as Letley or *L[a]eto Loco* (Happy Place). Peter des Roches, Bishop of Winchester, had planned to found the monastery but died in 1238 before the completion of his project, and the actual foundation was carried out by Henry III. In 1244 he granted £100 'for the foundation of the church whereof the king wishes to lay the first stone as founder'.[2] His name can be seen carved into one of the foundation stones for the crossing of the Church. As soon as the monastery was founded it was colonised by monks from the Cistercian Abbey of Beaulieu, known as *Bello Loco,* or Beautiful Place, on the opposite side of Southampton Water. They

would probably have occupied temporary wooden accommodation initially, but by 1245 the community was clearly well enough established for its abbot to be appointed.[3] In 1251 Henry claimed sole responsibility for the foundation, and ordered substantial quantities of lead, also granting thirty oaks for the Church. In 1252-3 he gave the abbey 300 acres of uncultivated land at Roydon in the New Forest. He also gave a silver gilt processional cross, which suggests that by 1253 the abbey was operational.[4]

The Cistercian order took its name from the Abbey of Cîteaux in Burgundy, which was founded in 1098. The monks aimed at literal observance of the rule of St Benedict along the most austere lines. Meat was banned from their diet, and their buildings were simple and free from ornament, the windows filled with plain glass and all paintings prohibited. The presence of women within the precinct was

182 *Netley Abbey,* with Southampton Water in the background, John Constable, 1816

forbidden.[5] Their first English house was Waverley Abbey, founded in 1128, while Tintern followed in 1131 and Fountains and Rievaulx in 1132.[6] When the numbers in any house grew too large, it could send out at least twelve brethren, with a thirteenth as abbot, to found a new monastery.[7] Netley was one of the last Cistercian houses to be founded in England and at the time of the Dissolution there were seventy-seven Cistercian abbeys in England and Wales.

Monasteries thus founded were to be in places remote from the conversations of men. Their communities were self-contained, with division into *monachi*, the monks, and *conversi*, the lay brothers. The *conversi* were precluded from learning to read and write, and provided manual labour in the abbey's workshops, fields and granges. The monks' white frocks and cowls gave the Cistercians the name of white monks, as opposed to Benedictines or black monks.[8]

The plan of the Abbey Church transepts and choir at Netley, with a square- ended, aisled eastern arm, as illustrated by Harold Brakspear (*183*), was the standard design of an English Cistercian church from the early

thirteenth century. But the tracery of the large east window (*184*) reveals the influence of Henry III's architectural patronage at Westminster Abbey, which he had begun to build in 1246, the same time that Netley was being built.[9] On the south side of the Church was the Cloister, a square of 115 feet with walled alleys covered with wooden pent roofs enclosed by ranges of buildings.[10] The Chapter House was in the east range, with the Dorter on the upper floor of that range. Accommodation for the lay brothers was in the west claustral range.[11] A separate building to the east may have been the Abbot's Lodgings, or a building for special guests.[12] The Frater extended southwards at right-angles to the Cloister walk, whereas in other monastic orders the Frater was usually parallel to the Cloister.

The *Valor* of 1535 estimated the gross revenue of Netley Abbey at just over £160, whilst the clear income was only £100.[13] This valuation placed it among the poorest of the Cistercian houses in England.[14] On 30 May 1536 Sir James Worsley and the other commissioners, John Paulet, George Paulet and William Berners, presented their report on the religious houses of Hampshire. Netley

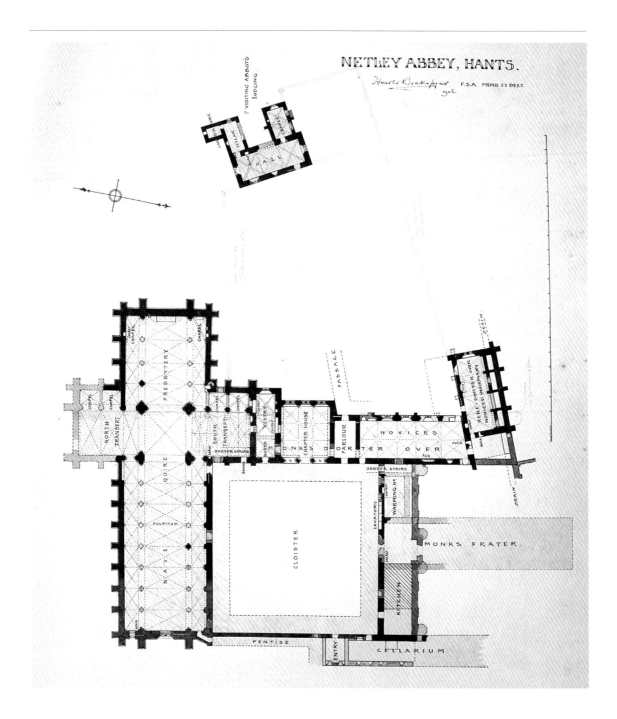

183 Plan of Netley Abbey by Harold Brakspear

184 Netley Abbey, the ruins of the east end of the Church

is described in this as: 'A hedde house of Monkes of thordre of Cisteaux, beinge of large buyldinge and situate upon the Ryvage of the Sees. To the Kinge's Subjects and Strangers travelinge the same Sees great Relief and Comforte.'[15] On its suppression in 1536, there were only seven monks remaining at Netley.[16] They were described as 'all being priests, by report of good religious conversation' and all but one wished to remain as monks.[17] They migrated to the larger Cistercian Abbey of Beaulieu, from which their predecessors had originally come three centuries earlier.[18] Netley's buildings were described as 'large' and 'great' and as 'in a good state of repair'.[19]

Following its dissolution, the lands belonging to Netley Abbey were divided between several new owners. On 3 August 1536, the king granted to William Paulet (two of whose brothers, somewhat suspiciously, had been the commissioners who reported favourably of this house in the previous May) the site and buildings of the suppressed abbey.[20]

William Paulet, 1st Marquess of Winchester, was born at Fisherton-Delamere in Wiltshire. He was the eldest of four sons of Sir John Paulet of Basing in Hampshire and Nunney in Somerset, whose main residence was Basing House. He was, therefore, very much of gentry stock, rather than the old aristocracy. Taking up the legal profession, Paulet possibly went to Thavies Inn and then to the Inner Temple, where he became a barrister and was marshal between 1505 and 1507. Initially, his career

293

185 Aerial photograph of Netley Abbey showing the layout of the house

was local, being sheriff in Hampshire in 1511, 1518 and 1522, and JP for the first time in 1514. He was knighted between 1523 and 1525 – the exact date is uncertain – and in 1525 he inherited Basing on the death of his father.[21]

Paulet was a protégé of Richard Fox, Bishop of Winchester, and was steward of the diocese of Winchester. His Court career began when he was appointed to the lucrative post of joint Master of the King's Wards in 1526, and in 1531 he alone was made Surveyor of Wards' and Widows' Lands. This was formalised in 1540 by the creation of the Court of Wards, with Paulet as Master, and when it was expanded to the Court of Wards and Liveries in 1542, he was appointed Master for life.

From the mid-1520s Paulet spent much of his life at Court and was included in the intimate counsels of the King. Henry must have trusted him because in May 1532 he was made Comptroller of the Household, and by the following year he assumed joint control of the King's Woods with Thomas Cromwell. In 1536 he was among those first selected by Henry as part of his 'pryvey counsel', the emergency

186 The ruins of William Paulet's new house at Netley Abbey, showing its brick construction faced with stone

council named during the crisis of the Pilgrimage of Grace. The Privy Council was formalised in 1540 and in 1542 Paulet was named a privy councillor. In 1545 he was made Lord President of the Council, a position he retained under Edward VI. He was present at many important ceremonial events including the baptism of the future Elizabeth I in 1533 and that of Edward, Prince of Wales in 1537. He bore the second sword at Edward's coronation in 1547 and was chief mourner at his funeral in 1553. He then carried the orb in the coronation ceremony of Queen Mary. It is clear that he had become an important courtier at the centre of political events.

In 1537 Paulet was appointed Treasurer of the Household and in 1539 he was created Baron St John. On 6 May 1543 he was installed in the Order of the Garter and later that month he was promoted to Lord Great Chamberlain. Around 1545 he became Great Master of the Household, but he relinquished this and the Lord Presidency in 1550 when he became Lord Treasurer, a post he held until his death.

For a few months in 1547 Paulet was Keeper of the Great Seal after the dismissal of Thomas Wriothesley. In January 1550, as a leading member of Edward VI's council, he was raised to the Earldom of Wiltshire and finally, on 11 October 1551, created Marquess of Winchester at a grand ceremony in the presence of the king. As the great political survivor of the age, something of his charm as well as his abilities can be appreciated from

NETLEY call'd otherwise *Lettley-Abby* was founded by *K.H.III. A*
which last it was call'd *S.t Edwards Place*. He endow'd it with *Lands* in *y.*
part of which, was desecrated (as *Tradition* says) by converting *y.* West end o*
Chappel. In which State it continued a long time —— When *y.* then *Proprieto*
down, & the principal *Undertaker* endeavouring to throw down the West Wall,
1. The Sea near Southampton.   *An: Val:* { 100 : 12 : 8.° *Dug.* 160 : 2 : 9. *Speed.*}

187 *The North View of Netley Abbey in the County of Hampshire*, engraved by Samuel and Nathaniel Buck, 1733

EY ABBY, IN HAMPSHIRE.

...r Cistercian Monks, & dedicated to S.t Mary & S.t Edward; from
... of his Reign. It was a large Building built in form of a Cross, some
...rch into a Kitchen & other Offices; but the East end was kept for a
...'d this stately Fabrick, the Roof & a great part of the Walls were pull'd
...h'd to death in his Enterprize. The present Proprietor is — Cliff Esq.r

S. & N. Buck. delin. et sculp. 1733.

108

188 *Netley Abbey, The South Transept*, engraved by Richard Godfrey, 1776

Queen Elizabeth I's jest, when she visited him at Basing in 1560, that 'if my Lord Treasurer was a young man I coulde fynde in my harte to have him to my husbande before any man in Englande'.[22]

After his acquisition of Netley in 1536, Paulet wasted no time in converting the abbey buildings into a great courtyard house reflecting his political position and aspirations. Its scale is evident in an aerial photograph (*185*). Hearth tax returns for 1665 show that by that time it had fifty hearths, making it one of the largest houses in Hampshire.[23] Paulet had considerable recent experience of building, as he had completed a large amount of work at

Basing the previous year, where in 1535 he spent two weeks overseeing the construction work. It must have been completed to a royal standard because in October of that year the king visited him at Basing.[24] Similarly, Netley must have been converted to an equally high standard as Queen Elizabeth visited for two days in August 1560.[25]

The new building work at Netley was largely carried out in brick, as at Basing, although some stone was used for facing, the combination of materials still visible in the ruins (*186*). Much of the brickwork has now gone due to a deliberate attempt in the nineteenth century to clear the ruins of what was perceived to be later clutter.[26] In converting the buildings Paulet retained most of the Abbey Church, the remains illustrated in the engraving by Samuel and Nathaniel Buck in 1733 (**187**). He only demolished the north transept, as at Mottisfont, parts of which are now set up as a landscape gardener's ruin in adjoining Cranbury Park.[27] The nave was converted into a large, eight-bay Hall with the lord's dining area at the crossing, while at the west end of the nave a new kitchen was made and brick ovens and hearths were installed. A new doorway was cut into the south side of the centre of the nave so that the Hall could be entered from the courtyard. A wall was built across the Church to divide the Hall from the presbytery at the east end, and that in turn became Paulet's Chapel.[28]

In the south transept Paulet created a new private wing, with joists inserted to create an upper floor which can be seen in the 1776 engraving by Richard Godfrey (**188**). This was the Great Chamber, the finest room in the house, and it had windows overlooking the Fountain Court to the west and new gardens to the east. In the east range of the Cloister had been the Vestry, Chapter House, Inner Parlour, and novices' room; these were retained for use in the Tudor house.[29] Since the rooms could no longer be accessed from a covered cloister walk, doorways were inserted to allow movement between the rooms internally. On the upper floor of this east range the Dorter was converted into a fashionable Long Gallery which had at least two staircase entrances and, like the Great Chamber, windows on two sides.

The Cloister garth became the Inner Court, the principal court of the Tudor house, and a fountain was added. The Court is now a lawn, and at its centre is a mound which marks the position of the fountain, which would have

been an important feature, a symbol of Paulet's prestige and power.

In the southern range of the Cloister, Paulet demolished the Frater and inserted a new central entrance doorway, flanked by two polygonal turrets. The south wall of this range of buildings is of sixteenth-century brickwork. Similar turrets were added at each end of the range, and this would have given the entrance to the house an impressive appearance from the Outer Court. In this range the Warming House and Kitchen were also pulled down except for their north walls.[30] A visitor would thus pass through the grand entrance into the Inner Court with its impressive fountain and the Hall opposite. This courtyard plan was the same as at Titchfield and Mottisfont, both converted from abbeys, and at secular buildings such as the contemporary Cowdray in Sussex. The west claustral range, which had housed the lay brothers, seems to have been retained unchanged and may have been domestic offices, communicating with the kitchen.

By the standards of the day, Paulet lived to a great age. He had served four Tudor monarchs and held a succession of major offices. He continued as a Privy Councillor and Lord Treasurer under Mary. He took the place of Speaker of the House of Lords as late as 1566 when 'the decay of his memory and hearing, griefs accompanying hoary hairs and old age' at last led to his retirement.[31] Naunton writes of how, when questioned 'he had stood up for thirty years together, amidst the change and ruins of so many Chancellors and great Personages. "Why", quoth the marquis, "*Ortus sum e salice, non ex quercu*" i.e. "I am made of pliable willow, not the stubborne oak".'[32]

189 *Newstead Abbey, Nottinghamshire, West Aspect*, Peter Tillemans, *c*.1730

Newstead Priory

Newstead Priory, now known as Newstead Abbey, is situated on the bank of the River Leen, twelve miles to the north of Nottingham. At the Dissolution the priory was surrendered in 1539 and acquired by Sir John Byron in 1540. The grand house he converted from the priory is shown in an early eighteenth-century painting by Peter Tillemans (*189*). At the beginning of the nineteenth century it was home to the poet George Gordon Byron, who became the sixth Lord Byron. The mediaeval priory was never completely rebuilt and substantial remains from the monastic period form part of the present house. Although the Priory Church was largely demolished, the three claustral ranges survived and were transformed into a new Tudor courtyard house. The west front of the Church survives, as well as the Cloister and imposing Conduit (*190*). There are also two undercrofts, most of the Warming Room and the complete Chapter House. Newstead Abbey is set in a landscape of gardens and parkland covering more than 300 acres.

The Priory of St Mary of Newstead (*De Novo Loco*) in Sherwood, a house of Augustinian Canons, was founded about the year 1163 by Henry II in memory of the soul of his grandfather, Fulk V, King of Jerusalem.[1] Sherwood Forest was made a royal forest by the Norman kings and was popular with various monarchs as a destination for hunting. The first witness to the foundation charter was Geoffrey, Archdeacon of Canterbury. This charter, executed at Clarendon, conferred on the prior and canons a site near the centre of the forest: Papplewick, with its church and mill and all things pertaining to the town in wood and plain, together with the meadow of Bestwood by the side of the water; and 100s of rent in Shapwick and Walkeringham. At the same time the king confirmed to them lands in Nottinghamshire, the gift of Robert de Caus and John the cook. The great forest lands around the monastery granted to the canons by their founder were known in the old charter as 'Kygell' and 'Ravenshede'.[2]

The number of canons at Newstead was never great and despite gifts of land during the thirteenth century, the priory was seriously in debt in 1274.[3] It is possible that this can be attributed to a building programme as this is approximately the date of the west front of the Church.[4] There was

considerable work involved in rebuilding the nave of the Church around 1270, including the demolition of the entire north and west elevations and partial demolition of the south wall.[5] A few years later, in 1279, the prior and convent obtained leave to fell and sell the timber of the wood of 40 acres which had been given to them in 1245; such a step would bring them considerable financial relief.[6] However, the house was again in financial difficulties in 1295, when at their own request Hugh de Vienna was appointed by the Crown to take charge of their revenues. On 25 July 1300 another custodian, Peter de Leicester, a king's clerk, was similarly appointed and the house taken into protection by the Crown.[7] This coincides with a time when the west range of the Cloister was being re-fronted or even largely rebuilt.[8]

Much of the architectural history of the priory can be deduced by dating the remaining buildings. Most of the Church was demolished after the Dissolution, leaving only the west front, the south wall of the nave and part of the south transept. The Cloister was to the south of the Church and the earliest dateable feature is the buttress to the south-west quoin of the south transept, now in the east Cloister of the present house, which has early Romanesque masonry with fine diagonal tool-

191 The East Range of Newstead Abbey, converted from the east range of the Cloister

ing to a point west of the east processional doorway. There are twelfth-century round-headed doorways in the south-east and north-west angles of the Cloister, which had, therefore, reached its present size by 1200.[9]

In the east range of the Cloister, now forming the east front of the house, were the Chapter House and Warming Room (191). Over them was the Dorter with night stairs to the south transept and day stairs to the south cloister walk. In the south range was an undercroft with the Frater on the upper floor. The west range also had a vaulted undercroft beneath the Prior's Hall and the Prior's Lodging. The Chapter House dates to the early thirteenth century; it has a grand portal and rich masonry detail inside, with trefoil-headed arcading supporting a vault with ribs framed in dogtooth.

In the south cloister walk is the *Lavatorium*. A 1726 drawing of this by Samuel Buck shows it complete with an ornate lead cistern, carrying the arms of Prior Sandall, who held office from 1504 to 1526. It was sold by the fifth Lord Byron in the late eighteenth century.[10] To the east of the *Lavatorium* are the remains of the day stair which rises to the Dorter above. The ground floor of the present two-storey Cloister dates to the mid-fifteenth century, when the Cloister was rebuilt, reusing the twelfth-century footings. This was probably done to take advantage of the falling cost of glazing, which allowed the canons to read and study in more comfort.[11]

The prior's accommodation in the west range of the Cloister, adjoining the west front

192 The West Front of Newstead Abbey, with the Church façade and the oriel window in the former Abbot's Lodging

of the church, was updated impressively in the late fifteenth or early sixteenth century. At the north end of the range a new oriel window (*192*) was built which lights the Prior's Parlour on the first floor, and what is now known as Byron's Bedroom on the second floor.[12] In the Hall, the northernmost of the large square bay windows was inserted. The roof on this range was also replaced, which would have originally been covered in lead.[13] The painting by Tillemans shows this range, with a staircase leading up to the Hall. It also shows a square building with a pyramidal roof and a wind vane at the west end of the south range. This

was the mediaeval kitchen, which was demolished in 1765.[14] The *Valor* of 1535 gave the clear annual value of Newstead Priory as just over £167. However, although this was below the £200 assigned as the limit for the suppression of the lesser monasteries, this priory obtained the doubtful privilege of exemption, on payment to the Crown of the heavy fine of £233 6s 8d, and a patent to this effect was issued on 16 December 1537.[15] This exemption did not last long and the priory was surrendered on 21 July 1539. On 24 July Dr London, to whom the surrender was made, forwarded to Sir Richard Rich the pension list he had drawn up and asked for its ratification.

Immediately the surrender was accomplished, the custody of the site and buildings was granted to Sir John Byron of Colwick. Then, in May 1540, the 'house, site, church, steeple, churchyard, and of all the lands, mills, advowsons, rectories, &c. of the late priory' were sold to Sir John Byron for £810.[16] Byron was born in 1487 or 1488, the eldest son of Sir Nicholas Byron of Colwick in Nottinghamshire. The Byron family had extensive estates in Lancashire as well as in Nottinghamshire and Lincolnshire, which Byron inherited on his father's death in 1504; these gave him an extremely prominent position in local administration. He was also a soldier, serving in the royal army in France in 1513. By 1519, when he received the first of several offices in Nottinghamshire and in the administration of the royal forest of Sherwood, he was at Court and an esquire of the body to Henry VIII, retaining his place at Court throughout the reign. Byron was knighted by November 1522, shortly before he was appointed sheriff of Nottinghamshire and Derbyshire for 1523-4. He served three more times as sheriff – in 1527-8, 1542-3 and 1551-2 – evidence of his local status in Nottinghamshire, which he maintained for the rest of his life. He was also a knight of the shire for Nottinghamshire in the Parliament of 1529, and again in 1536.[17]

Byron's activities outside Court and Parliament were by no means confined to local affairs. During the Pilgrimage of Grace of 1536, he rallied to the 4th Earl of Shrewsbury, accompanying the Earl into Yorkshire and later acting as juror for the trial of several of the rebels at Westminster. He saw further military service against the Scots in 1542 when he equipped himself with twenty servants 'to serve the King's grace horsed and harnessed', and was responsible for levying a considerable body of men from Nottinghamshire.[18] He subsequently fought under the king in France in 1544. Byron was also active in the king's service as a commissioner for the dissolution of the monasteries in the north, after which he benefitted from the grant of Newstead Abbey in 1540. But he did not neglect his other estates, augmenting them by various grants and leases throughout his life. In Nottinghamshire he acquired further lands and leased various mills and coal-pits in the shire, as well as the manor of Bolsover in Derbyshire with its eight pits and coal mines. He does not appear to have served under Mary but was appointed *custos rotulorum* for Nottinghamshire by Elizabeth in 1562. He died on 5 May 1567.[19]

Although there are no archival sources for building work in the immediate post-Dissolution period, archaeological discoveries during an extensive survey in 1998 have shown how the priory buildings were adapted to domestic use.[20] Byron demolished the Priory Church, apart from its west front and part of the south nave wall. The south transept was also retained and incorporated into the house. The retention of the west front gives Newstead a grand romantic feature, captured in Joseph Skelton's 1823 engraving (*193*), but it also has the practical benefit of buttressing the west range of the house. The stone and lead from the demolished buildings were reused as materials for the adaptation to Byron's new building.[21]

The remaining three ranges around the Cloister were retained in their entirety, and an additional range was made to the north side, set against the south wall of the Church. These four ranges formed the core of Byron's new house, the layout clearly shown in a modern aerial photograph (*194*). The Chapter House was converted into a domestic chapel, while the surviving undercrofts beneath the Hall

193 *Newstead Abbey, Nottinghamshire*, engraved by Joseph Skelton, 1823

and Frater appear to have been unaltered. The
Dorter on the upper floor of the east range
was partitioned into chambers. The Prior's
Hall and private quarters on the first floor of
the west range were adapted to form the Hall
and principal rooms of the new house.[22]

One of the major changes made to the
house was to create a grand new entrance at
first-floor level, reached by a stairway on the
west front, shown in the Tillemans view. In
the monastic period, entrance to the claustral
buildings would only have been from the
Cloister or the Church. This new entrance,
made on the outside of the Hall, reflected the
change in the Tudor period to more outward-
facing houses and the improved circulation
that was required in the house at first-floor

level. To achieve this, new galleries were built
over the four cloister walks. These galleries
could be accessed from the Hall, but also from
the Cloister where the old day stair to the
Dorter was diverted into the South Gallery.[23]
Each gallery has three four-light mullioned-
and-transomed windows looking into the
cloister garth. New wings were added to the
house to the south-east and south-west,
producing two sides of a forecourt.

The Skelton engraving and the Tillemans
painting both show a large sixteenth-century
window inserted into the south bay of the
thirteenth-century west front of the Priory
Church. This odd-looking solution was
carried out because this part of the Church
façade had never screened a south aisle, as

194 Aerial photograph of Newstead Abbey, showing the layout of the house around the monastic Cloister

might be expected. In fact, behind this section of the elevation there were a series of rooms. On the ground floor was a parlour and the entrance to the north and the west cloister walks. Above these were apartments of the Prior's Lodging, and it is these upper rooms which were lit by the new window. This remained in place until the early nineteenth century when the original Gothic tracery was restored.[24]

Internally, some of the Tudor decoration survives. There are four sixteenth-century carved and painted overmantels in various rooms. The one in the room north of the Hall, now known once again as the Prior's Parlour, bears the date 1556, and is therefore attributable to Sir John Byron. It has a central coat of arms flanked by eight pike-men, with three busts above and five portrait medallions below. The overmantel in the Edward III room has seven portrait medallions and two diamond panel portraits. The largest overmantel is in the Duke of Sussex room and has eight portrait medallions in the centre flanked by bearded terms with their feet projecting below the pedestals. These colourful decorative overmantels deploy highly fashionable motifs and indicate the quality of the interiors commissioned by Sir John, who both attended the Field of the Cloth of Gold and visited the new royal palaces of Henry VIII.

15 54

S^R THOMAS,
DARCY OF CHICH
K^t. OF THE GARTER
IN THE TIME OF
HEN^Y. Y: 8TH Æ. Sue 4.9

St Osyth's Priory

St Osyth's Priory, a house of Augustinian Canons, was founded in the early twelfth century in the manor of Chich in Essex. The priory is contained within a triangle of land near the sea, ten miles south-east of Colchester, with Brightlingsea Creek to the west and St Osyth Creek to the south. Marshes and mudflats lie between Brightlingsea Creek and St Osyth's parkland.

Following its dissolution, the priory buildings were converted after 1553 into a mansion by Thomas Darcy, 1st Baron Darcy of Chiche (*195*). The priory is noted for the exceptional survival of the plan of claustral and service ranges, as well as the mediaeval fabric incorporated into Darcy's mansion. The buildings that remain include the largely intact late fifteenth-century Gatehouse and the Abbot's Lodging, the latter built in 1527 by the penultimate abbot, John Vintoner. The Gatehouse is amongst the finest examples in the country. There are also significant surviving and ruinous structures of the Tudor mansion including, most notably, the Darcy Tower.

Chich has been the site of two monasteries, one legendary and the other real. Legend claims that, born in the late seventh century, St Osyth was the daughter of an English king called Frithwald and his wife Wilburga, whose father was Penda, king of Mercia. Osyth was betrothed to Sighere, king of the East Saxons, but during his absence on a hunting expedition she persuaded two bishops to receive her vows as a nun. Sighere consented to this and made a grant to her of Chich, where she founded a nunnery and became abbess. A party of Danes invaded and beheaded Osyth, but she arose and walked, carrying her head in her hands, to the church of Chich, where her remains ultimately rested. Osyth was later canonised, but the legend is unreliable and it is extremely doubtful whether the nunnery ever existed.[1] Although the story of St Osyth may simply be a myth, it was clearly a powerful one, as an Augus-

195 *Portrait of Thomas Darcy, 1st Baron Darcy of Chiche*, unknown artist, *c.*1554

196 *St Osyth's Priory, Essex*, engraved by J Rogers, 1832

tinian priory was subsequently founded here in her honour. Dedicated to Saints Peter and Paul and St Osyth, the priory was founded around 1120, by Richard de Belmeis, bishop of London. By 1161, the priory at St Osyth's had been raised to the rank of abbey, though in modern times it continues to be known as St Osyth's Priory.[2]

The monastic buildings were laid out with the Abbey Church to the south and the Cloister to its north. The Church was destroyed after the abbey's dissolution, but the inventory taken at that time states that it consisted of a nave with a south aisle, a choir, two transepts, a steeple, a chapel on the south side, a chapel and vestry on the north side, and another chapel at the north-west. There were five bells, valued at £40.[3] The Cloister was about 98 feet square and the east range included the Chap-

ter House, with the Dorter at the upper level. The remains of the sub-vault of the Dorter are substantially of early twelfth-century work so it must have been amongst the first buildings constructed.[4] In the north range was the Frater, and its remains have been dated to *c.*1230-40.[5] Just to the north of the Frater was the kitchen, also of an early thirteenth-century date.[6] The west, or cellarer's, range contains two surviving late thirteenth-century cellars on the ground floor, so it appears that all the principal monastic buildings were complete by the end of the thirteenth century. To these the Great Gatehouse and its flanking ranges were added late in the fifteenth century, replacing an early thirteenth-century gate-house.[7] In about 1527, Abbot Vintoner built himself new Lodgings with Renaissance elements, including a large stone oriel window, to the north-west of the Cloister, and a wing linking the Lodgings to the west range of the Cloister. The new Abbot's Lodgings were of fashionable brick with diapering and stone or brick dressings. The linking wing and the south front of the Lodgings survive and these buildings, together with part of the Cloister, were to provide the core of the Tudor mansion house shown, together with the Bell Tower and Darcy Tower in Rogers' 1834 engraving (*196*).

Other buildings mentioned in the post-Dissolution valuation and inventory include the Old Hall, the New Hall, a Great Chamber over the Hall, the prior's, sub-prior's, sacristan's and bailiff's chambers, and several other chambers and offices.[8] The location of these is more uncertain, but it is likely, in common with other monastic arrangements, that the Old Hall was in the cellarer's range and would have been used for guests. The New Hall and Great Chamber above it would almost certainly have been part of the new Abbot's Lodgings. In 1538 an attempt was made through the Lord Chancellor, Sir Thomas Audley, to secure the continuance of Colchester and St Osyth's as secular colleges, but this failed and on 6 November Cromwell gave orders for their dissolution. However, the abbey did not actually fall until 28 July 1539, when it was formally surrendered by the abbot, John Whederykke, *alias* Colchester, John Russell, the prior, and fourteen others.[9]

The valuation of the possessions of St Osyth's at the time of its dissolution gives its gross income as just over £758 per annum, making it extremely wealthy. An inventory of the jewels, plate, lead, furniture and other goods of the monastery was made by the royal commissioners at the time of the surrender. Among the treasures listed were 'the skull of Seynt Osithes closyd in sylver parcel gylte'

and 'a croune of sylver gylte too sett apon the sayd skull garnysshyd with counterfett stones'.[10] The inventory gives a good idea of the value of items removed from monasteries at the Dissolution. St Osyth's shrine was garnished with 82oz of gilt plate, 82oz of white plate and an old coffin probably containing the so-called bones of the saint.[11] The plate was valued at £185 8s 6d, the ornaments of the church at £40 6s 10d, and the lead on the roofs at £1,044; but the jewels were not valued.[12] The monastery and a great part of its possessions, including all in the immediate neighbourhood, were granted to Thomas Cromwell on 10 April 1540, but on Cromwell's attainder on 29 June 1540 the monastery reverted to the Crown. On 1 June 1553, it was sold to Thomas, Lord Darcy, who paid the substantial sum of just over £3,974.[13]

Thomas Darcy was born on 4 December 1506, the only son of Roger Darcy of Danbury, Essex. Roger Darcy was a Gentleman of the Chamber to Henry VII and a considerable landowner in Essex and Suffolk. When his father died, the two-year-old Thomas Darcy's wardship was granted to one of Henry VII's favourite courtiers, Sir John Raynsford, who brought him up to be a soldier, made him a son-in-law by marriage to his daughter Audrey, and provided generously for him in his will.[14] Throughout his adult life, therefore, Darcy enjoyed considerable wealth and Court connections. Audrey Raynsford died soon after Darcy achieved his majority in 1527, and by 1532 he had married Elizabeth, the daughter of John de Vere, Earl of Oxford; and it was probably de Vere patronage that enabled his career to take off at that point. Darcy was knighted on 1 November 1532 and made a Knight of the Household either then or shortly after. He served on a number of commissions, sat as a member of Parliament,

and served in the war in France in 1543-4. In 1544 he became a Gentleman of the Privy Chamber and Master of the Tower armouries.[15] As a cousin of Edward Seymour, Duke of Somerset, Darcy prospered after the accession of Edward VI in 1547, and the following year was appointed one of four principal gentlemen of the Privy Chamber, especially responsible for the king's safety. He survived the fall of Somerset, forging close ties to John Dudley, Earl of Warwick, and in early 1549 was appointed a privy councillor, Vice-Chamberlain of the Household and Captain of the Guard. Then in April 1551 he was raised to the peerage as Baron Darcy in order to become Lord Chamberlain of the Household,

the pinnacle of his Court career. Darcy's principal political importance at this period was as a vital link between Dudley and the Court, controlling the flow of information to Edward and influencing the young king.[16] However, following the accession of Mary he was dismissed from his offices and briefly placed under house arrest. Though later pardoned, he did not resume his place at Court and occupied himself in Essex by helping to check the spread of Wyatt's rebellion and afterwards by supporting the restoration of Catholicism in the county. He died at Wivenhoe on 28 June 1558 and was buried in the parish church at St Osyth, where a monument was later erected to his memory.[17]

197 Aerial photograph of St Osyth's Priory, showing the layout of the house

It was only a short time after his acquisition of the site that Lord Darcy lost his Court position and offices, but following his pardon he was permitted by Queen Mary to reside at St Osyth's.[18] He then transformed the monastic buildings into a large new house, suitable to his status in Essex, the scale visible in a modern aerial view (*197*). The new house continued to be approached through the monastic Great Gatehouse, which is built of perpendicular bands of flint and ashlar stone (*198*). The Great Gatehouse and its flanking wings were retained as an impressive entrance to Darcy's new house, as well as to provide further accommodation, though in some places new doors, windows and chimneystacks were installed. The Gatehouse is of two storeys with an embattled parapet of chequerwork. In the main outer archway, the spandrels have finely carved figures of St Michael and the Dragon. A pair of niches flank the main arch; the moulded brackets have angels holding scrolls. Above the arch is a similar but taller niche, with an angel on the bracket holding a shield. On the north of the Gatehouse are the two semi-octagonal stair-turrets. The Gate Hall has a ribbed vault and the intersections of the ribs have richly carved bosses, the three central ones being the Annunciation, a crowned and veiled head of St Osyth, and a couched hart in a park paling.[19]

In order to create Darcy's new house, the

198 The Great Gatehouse at St Osyth's Priory

199 St Osyth's Priory: the south view of the house, originally the Abbot's Lodging, showing the archway and the oriel window above, with the Clock Tower

monastic Church, sited to the south of the Cloister, was destroyed, together with the cloister walk and the major part of the east and west ranges of the Cloister.[20] The Abbot's Lodgings (*199*) dated 1527, with its new Hall and Great Chamber, were less than thirty years old and probably provided the principal private accommodation for the new house without much modification. However, since the Lodgings were almost entirely rebuilt in 1866, except for the south front, the internal arrangements are unclear. Certainly, the external appearance in red brick with black brick diapering, as in the surviving front, was retained.

In the middle of the ground floor, shown in the early twentieth century photograph, is a wide stone archway flanked by doorways. Above the main archway is a large oriel window, modern externally, except for the moulded and carved head and the panelled and carved base and corbelling. The head moulding has a band of early Renaissance ornament with foliage and small nude figures.[21] The base moulding has shields and Tudor roses; the shields include the crossed keys and sword of Saints Peter and Paul, three crowns and a sword for St Osyth, and a rebus of Abbot John Vintoner. The moulded corbelling has two bands of carved foliage each with shields; the upper band contains six shields while the lower band has running vine ornament with remains of lettering intertwined, apparently the name Johannes Vintoner. There are five shields including Saints Peter and Paul, a rebus of a vine and tun, for Vintoner, and three combs, for

200 The Darcy Tower at St Osyth's Priory from the south

Tunstall, Bishop of London. A series of four shields on each side give the date 1527, one in Roman and one in Arabic numerals. The red brick wing of the same date as the Abbot's Lodgings, connecting to the Cloister must have been converted to some degree, because the original window openings were partly blocked and replaced with smaller square-headed stone windows.

Darcy's conversion of the Cloister buildings was more extensive. The Frater seems to have been adapted to use as the Great Hall, and there is a now blocked doorway at the west end installed by Darcy, perhaps to give access to the connecting wing and the Lodgings. It has now largely been destroyed except for the east and west ends. In the north wall was a connecting doorway to the kitchen wing. The monastic kitchen, conveniently placed to service both the private apartments and the Great Hall, may have been retained, though a modern wing now occupies the site. At the west end of his Great Hall, Darcy built his new Clock Tower faced, as with other parts of the new house, with ashlar and septaria chequer work. The southern part of the west range was demolished and a new gable end wall built with, again, chequer work, while a narrow extension was added on the west side, of red brick with octagonal projections at the angles. It is of two storeys with gables to the attics on the west side. This range contains thirteenth-century cellars on the ground floor, roofed with barrel vaults. The east range was most extensively modified. The southern part was demolished, the northern part extended further north, with new windows and doors installed. In the early-twelfth-century sub-vault, Darcy fitted new doors and windows, but some of the mediaeval floor tiling was retained.[22] The upper storey was entirely replaced with a new storey having external chequer work, while a surviving chimneypiece and three fireplaces below show that the range provided domestic accommodation.

Darcy also built the very substantial new Darcy Tower adjoining the east range (**200**). It is of three stages with turrets at three angles, square at the base and octagonal above; the parapets have a low gable on each face. The walls are of ashlar and septaria chequer work. Internally, a great staircase rises to the first floor, and a circular staircase in the turret gives access to the second floor and roof. The Tower would have offered views over the gardens and, as at contemporary towers at Bisham and Lacock, would have been used for banqueting. Darcy also built a large new barn, mostly timber-framed, adjoining the range west of the Gatehouse. Estates such as St Osyth's were, of course, expected to be productive and not only residences. The Abbey's precinct walls were also retained, though new cross-walls were added in the gardens. The walls of the kitchen garden and yards are partly of brick and probably all of mid sixteenth-century date, implying that Darcy created new formal gardens. Darcy's house must have been very impressive, as Queen Elizabeth I stayed on two occasions, visiting John, the second Lord Darcy. She stayed for three days in July 1561, and again for three days in August 1579.[23]

SEYMOUR

EDWARD

DUKE OF

SOMERSET

Syon Abbey

Syon Abbey, situated on the bank of the Thames at Isleworth, was acquired by Edward Seymour (*201*) in 1547. He came from an old-established family of landowners whose principal residence was Wolf Hall in Wiltshire. Seymour had been at Court as a page, then Esquire and Knight of the Body to Henry VIII, but it was the king's marriage to his sister Jane in 1536 that gave him new power and influence.[1] He was created Earl of Hertford in 1537 and proved to be a capable general at the centre of Henry's campaigns in France and Scotland. As a consequence he was closely involved with the masons and engineers who built twenty-four new fortifications against an anticipated French invasion between 1538 and 1540.[2] He was appointed head of a royal commission to inspect these, bearing responsibility for the design of much that was built, and was directly involved in their construction.[3] Later, Seymour maintained this interest and involvement in the architecture of his own houses.

At Henry's death on 28 January 1547, when Edward VI became king at the age of nine, Seymour, as his uncle and nearest relative, took the opportunity to seize power. He was appointed Protector of the Realm and Governor of the King's Person as well as Lord Treasurer, and was created Duke of Somerset.[4] This position effectively enabled him to exercise the authority of the king, and he required magnificent residences, appropriate to this new status, which would be public displays of his wealth and power. Since Edward VI's principal country base was Hampton Court, with its satellite palaces at Nonsuch and Oatlands, the Lord Protector needed to have a house nearby, and Syon was the perfect choice. He acquired it from the Crown on 23 July 1547 by Letters Patent granting him, as well as houses, castles, parks, forests and lands across many counties, 'the house, site, church etc. of Syon Monastery' and 'the manors of Syon and Isleworth'.[5] Only eight miles to the west of the city, Syon was easily accessible by river and convenient for communication with the

201 *Edward Seymour, Duke of Somerset*, engraved by Jacobus Houbraken, after Hans Holbein the Younger, 1738

202 Syon House, Middlesex

capital, the heart of Court life, culture and trade. The surrounding landscape belonged mostly to the Crown. As well as Syon on the Middlesex bank, Twickenham was on the south, while on the Surrey bank, opposite Syon, there was Richmond Palace.

Somerset would have already been familiar with Syon Abbey, since after the Dissolution it had been used as an armaments factory for the wars in Scotland and France.[6] Somerset Place, which he selected as his London house, was similarly conveniently placed between Whitehall in the west and the Tower in the east, and it was on the royal processional route through the City, past St Paul's. In his short period of power Somerset built these two impressive houses on the Thames and began work on a third, The Brails at Great Bedwyn in Wiltshire. This was close to his family house at

Wolf Hall, but was not large enough to be a suitable residence for the Lord Protector.[7]

Syon Abbey of St Saviour and St Brigit was the only Brigittine House in England. St Brigit of Sweden had founded the order at Vadstena in 1346, and her 'revelations', thought to be direct conversations with Christ, formed the basis for the nuns' way of life. The order attracted royal patronage and was founded in Twickenham by Henry V in 1415. When Henry came to the throne in 1413 he rebuilt the royal palace at Sheen, on the Surrey bank of the Thames opposite Syon, and proposed to found three monastic houses nearby to provide constant prayer around his residence. The orders chosen were the Carthusians, Celestines and Brigittines, and the houses were to be named Bethlehem, Jerusalem and Syon respectively. Work on Syon Abbey began in 1426 and the community was given permission to move to the new site in 1431.[8] The large Brigittine community comprised an abbess and fifty-nine nuns, with twenty-five men including thirteen priests, four deacons and eight laymen. The watery location was an essential part of the Brigittine vision; the motherhouse at Vadstena is sited beside a large lake. Water was interpreted allegorically as a fertile life-giving source, providing fish and bearing fruit by the riverbank, in turn becoming a physical and spiritual blessing.[9]

At Syon, as at all monastic establishments, the buildings were centred on the Church. Construction may have begun as early as 1426, but accounts show that the substantial sum of £5,629 was spent on the building between 1461 and 1479.[10] It was built of stone, mainly from Yorkshire or from Caen in Normandy.[11] The building work was slow and painstaking and the Church was not finally consecrated until 20 October 1488.[12] The mason in charge was Robert Westerley, the king's master mason, who was paid for drawing designs to be followed by the craftsmen at Syon, thereby demonstrating royal approval and an indication of the quality of the work.[13] The Church measured at least 100 feet in width and almost 200 feet in length and stood to the east of the present house, between the house and the river.[14] Unusually for England, but emulating the mother church at Vadstena, the high altar was at the west end of the Church, with a two-storey choir, for brethren below and nuns above.[15]

Because it was a double house with a shared church, many of the abbey buildings were duplicated. There were separate Cloisters for the brethren and the nuns, with separate Dorters and Fraters. There were also, possibly with shared access, a Sacristy, a Chapter House and a Library.[16] Accounts suggest that

these buildings, like most of those within the abbey other than the Church, were built of brick with stone used only as dressings for doors and windows.[17] The Swedish mother church still exists, and if the same arrangements were adopted as at Vadstena, the Nuns' Cloister at Syon would have been to the north of the Church and the Monks' Cloister to the south. There were many other domestic buildings within the abbey precinct, making it entirely self sufficient. These included a kitchen, a brewhouse, a malthouse, a bakehouse, a dairy, a cistern for fish with a fish house, a smithy, a horse-mill, a hoghouse and a washing house, emphasising the size of the community.[18] Work on the complex continued into the sixteenth century and the brewhouse was completed with a weathercock in 1507-8, while the roof of the Nuns' Cloister was repaired as late as 1528-9.[19] By the time of its suppression Syon was the tenth wealthiest monastery in England and the richest of all the non-Benedictine houses.[20]

Syon Abbey's suppression in 1539 was described by the chronicler Charles Wriothesley, who wrote that on 'the 25th daie of November the howse of Sion was suppressed into the Kinges handes, and the ladies and brethren putt out, which was the vertues [most virtuous] howse of religion that was in England, the landes and goodes to the Kinges use'.[21] The Crown initially retained the property, but the buildings were allowed to fall into some decay, though they were used as a place of confinement before her execution for Queen Katherine Howard in the winter of 1541-2. When the body of Henry VIII rested a night in the Church at Syon on its way from Westminster to Windsor on 14 February 1547, special renovation was necessary because of the deterioration of the buildings.[22] On Somerset's acquisition of the site, therefore,

203 *A View of Syon House from the Thames*, attributed to Robert Griffier, early eighteenth century

the Church and monastic buildings were still standing, as the king's corpse had lain there only six months earlier.

The present Syon House is the Tudor mansion that Somerset built adjoining the site of the Abbey Church (*202*). Although the interior has undergone several transformations, most notably by Robert and James Adam in the 1760s when the principal rooms were remodelled, its general external form of a three-storey quadrangle with a battlemented roof and corner turrets built around an inner courtyard remains unchanged; though the exterior was re-cased in the early nineteenth century.[23] Somerset began building his new house on a royal scale and at speed. Syon was constructed of stone, which was an expensive

and extravagant building material valued for its durability. The royal palaces of Whitehall and Hampton Court were built of brick, while Nonsuch was constructed of timber, slate and plaster.[24] However, demolishing the Abbey Church meant there was a ready supply of stone available on site. It was not unusual to plunder monastic buildings for the construction of new houses.[25] It is possible that the western end of the Church was incorporated into the fabric of the new house, but other than this, it is likely that Somerset's house was entirely new.[26] Its imposing appearance, set amongst gardens and close to the River Thames is captured in Robert Griffier's early eighteenth-century painting (*203*).

To manage the construction of Syon, as

204 A detail from a map of Isleworth by Ralph Treswell, 1587 showing the house with its wings in the top left quadrant

well as his other building projects, Somerset needed a professional office of works and he put his steward, Sir John Thynne, in charge of the office. Thynne, who later built Longleat House, had joined Somerset's staff in 1536 and remained with him for the rest of his life.[27] Somerset's commanding position at Court enabled him to set up an organisation similar to that of the Royal Works, and there were few private builders who could carry out construction work in so many places simultaneously.[28] The clerk of works at The Brails, Brian Teshe, wrote to Thynne in 1549 saying that he would go to London 'with a plat of all the levels of the courts and gardens' to obtain decisions for the marking of the ground and laying of foundations.[29] This implies that

Somerset had a direct and detailed involvement with the design of his houses and gardens and that he maintained a close interest in the architecture.

The layout of Tudor Syon can be deduced from a ground plan of about 1604, which shows the square plan of the house as it is today, but with two wings extending from the west front, which no longer exist. They are also shown on Ralph Treswell's 1607 map (*204*). An inventory taken in 1593 describes these wings as the 'brick lodgings', while the main house was called the 'white house'.[30] Possibly the 'brick lodgings' were abbey buildings which had been retained.

Built of stone, the house was very pale in colour, making it appear striking in the river

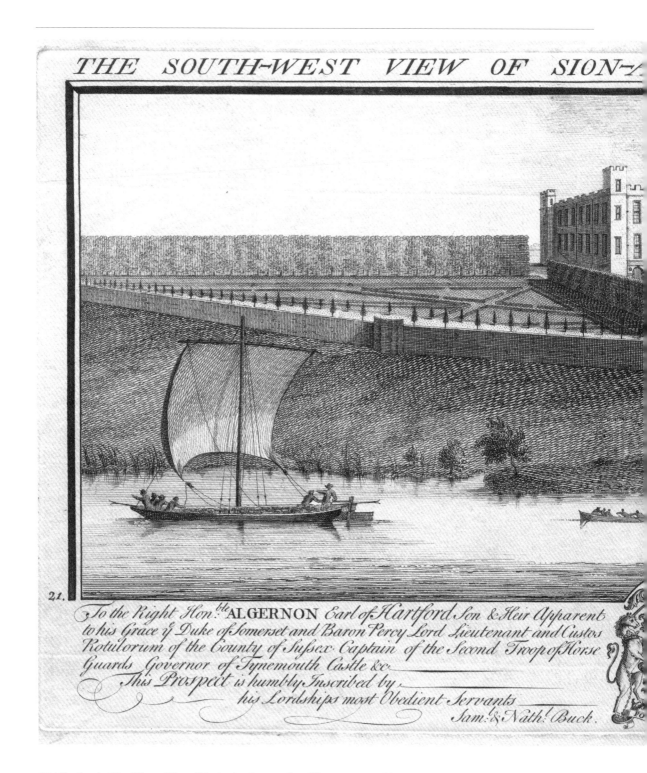

21.

To the Right Hon.ble **ALGERNON** Earl of Hartford Son & Heir Apparent to his Grace ỹ Duke of Somerset and Baron Percy Lord Lieutenant and Custos Rotulorum of the County of Sussex Captain of the Second Troop of Horse Guards Governor of Tynemouth Castle &c————— This Prospect is humbly Inscribed by————— his Lordships most Obedient Servants————— Sam.l & Nath.l Buck.

205 *The South-West View of Sion-Abby in the County of Middlesex,* engraved by Samuel and Nathaniel Buck, 1737

324

IN THE COUNTY OF MIDDLESEX.

THIS Abby was founded by K: Hen: V. A: D: 1414, to ye Honour of ye holy Trinity, the glorious Virgin Mary, ye Apostles & Disciples of God, & all Saints, especially St Bridget, for 60 Nuns under ye Government of an Abbess, & for 13 Priests, 4 Deacons, & 8 Lay-Bretheren, under ye Government of a Confessor, each Sex to live in a seperate Cloyster, & follow ye Rule of St Austin. That Prince endow'd it with 1000 Marks yearly out of his Exchequer. K: Hen: VIII dissolv'd it, & K: Edw: VI A: D: 1546 granted it to Edwd Duke of Somerset, but it being forfeited by Attainder that King granted it A: D: 1558 to John Duke of Northumberland. Q: Mary refounded it, and Queen Elizabeth again dissolv'd it. Tis now a Seat of his Grace ye Duke of Somerset. An: Val: 1581: 8: 4 Dug:

S. & N. Buck del: & sculp. Publisht according to Act of Parliament March 4ʰ 1737.

landscape. There were originally twin entrances, with the left-hand entrance leading into the Great Hall, from which stairs went up into the Great Chamber. The surviving accounts describe this as having lead on its roof, placing it on the top floor.[31] Beyond this was the usual sequence in Tudor palaces of Presence Chamber, Privy Chamber and Withdrawing Chamber. All these rooms had windows on two sides, looking over both the central courtyard and out across the gardens to the south. The east range was divided centrally, as it is today. The inner rooms, including the Bedchamber and Coffer Chamber, overlooked the central courtyard, but the Bedchamber, being on the corner, also had windows commanding the garden. The Long Gallery ran the entire length of the east range, with windows facing over the formal enclosed gardens to the east of the house, which were laid out on the site of the former Church. The window at the north end of the Long Gallery gave onto the Privy Garden which would have been on the site of the north Cloister, suggesting that both it, and probably the south Cloister, had been demolished when the house was built.

The house had a central courtyard described in the 1593 inventory as the 'Green Court'.[32] The entrance to the courtyard from the west is today central with a curved staircase, but the 1604 plan shows that there were originally twin entrances between the end two bays, in line with those on the west front. The level of the Tudor courtyard was lower than the present level, and a floor with yellow and green tiles was discovered during excavations, suggesting that there was a well or water feature in the centre, where the pond is today.[33]

Both Somerset Place and Syon had flat leaded roofs, like many other buildings of the period. There is no figure recorded for the cost of lead in the accounts for Somerset Place, although there was a glut of lead after the Dissolution, and in the case of Syon this was probably recovered from the abbey.[34] Access to the roof would have been by the staircases shown on the plan in each corner turret. Roof terraces were used for walking, and sometimes for entertaining, and provided views of the gardens below.

The abbey had thirty acres of gardens and orchards within its walls.[35] These, established over a century, would have been retained by Somerset. As well as its walled gardens, Syon Abbey also had two parks, Syon Park and Isleworth Park, later called Twickenham Park. The park at Twickenham was given to Henry VII by the abbey in 1506 in exchange for lands elsewhere, so Somerset received only Syon Park when he acquired the property. As with other houses and palaces situated beside the Thames, Syon would have been approached as often by water as by road, the view shown in the 1737 engraving by Samuel and Nathaniel Buck (*205*). In the angle between the square formal garden to the south of the house and that to the east was a triangular walled garden overlooking the river. Here Somerset built a high terrace, an elevated belvedere, which would have been a vantage point from which to view the river as well as the gardens.

By October 1549 Somerset was removed from power. Amongst the charges laid against him was that he had 'made Sale and Exchanges of the King's Lands … and wasted vast Sums in erecting Sumptuous Buildings'.[36] He was briefly imprisoned in the Tower, but released in February 1550 and all his property restored to him in April 1550.[37] In July 1550 he entertained Edward VI at Syon, suggesting that the new house was at least substantially complete by then.[38] However, in October 1551 Somerset was arrested again, put on trial, and executed on 22 January 1552.[39] In April 1552, Parliament declared his lands forfeit and all his property passed through attainder to the Crown, which retained Syon for the next fifty-two years, apart from a brief attempt by Queen Mary to restore the abbey in 1557-8. At the time of Somerset's death Somerset Place was still unfinished, whereas the majority of his correspondence is signed at Syon, revealing that he spent a considerable amount of time there.[40] There is no evidence of any major alterations to Syon between 1552 and 1558, so it is likely that it was complete by 1551, a very short timescale for such an ambitious project. The expenditure on Syon between 1 April 1548 and 7 October 1551 was £5,546 18s 10d; just over half the amount spent in the same period on Somerset Place, but still a considerable sum by the standards of the day.[41]

Titchfield Abbey (Place House)

The ruins of Titchfield Abbey, nine miles south-east of Southampton, are owned by English Heritage. The River Meon flows past the site and, although it is now a small stream, in the sixteenth century it was a tidal harbour and Titchfield was a port.[1] The imposing stone Gatehouse with its four-storey castellated octagonal turrets, still largely intact, was newly built across the nave of the mediaeval Abbey Church, whilst remarkably the original wooden gates remain. The high walls that still surround parts of the site were built in the sixteenth century. Through the Gatehouse is the site of the Great Court, which was created from the Cloister of the abbey, where a fine collection of mediaeval tiles survives.

The Abbey of St Mary and St John the Evangelist was founded on 15 August 1231, the Feast of the Assumption, by Peter des Roches, Bishop of Winchester, for Premonstratensian Canons. It was known as the Monastery of the Blessed Virgin Mary. The order, an offshoot from the Augustinian or Black Canons, was founded at Prémontré in France and they were known also as the 'White Canons' because their dress was entirely white. The Titchfield canons were a colony from the Shropshire Abbey of Halesowen and they lived a communal life under monastic vows, following the Rule of St Augustine, but were also involved in the wider community, preaching and teaching the Gospel. Under the rule their abbeys were designed to be houses of learning and seminaries for training missionaries and parish priests. Thirty-five houses of the order were established in England, of which Titchfield was the last.[2]

Premonstratensian churches are characteristically cruciform in plan, without aisles, and Titchfield follows this arrangement. The Church was 200 feet long, but only 25 feet wide, while the transepts extended 115 feet from north to south, the same as the length of the nave. Unusually, the Cloister is on the north side of the Church, probably because of the convenience of the water supply, and is about 95 feet square, enclosed by

206 *Thomas Wriothesley, Earl of Southampton*, attributed to Hans Holbein the Younger, c.1535

buildings.[3] In the east range were the Sacristy, Chapter House and Warming House, with the Dorter extending above them and Reredorter behind. In the north range were the Frater and Buttery and in the west range the Cellarer's Hall and guesthouse. The Chapter House had three arches at its entrance, the central one forming the doorway, and the room was vaulted.[4] The abbey also had its own farm buildings and a series of fishponds.

The surrender of the abbey took place before the king's commissioners John Crayford and Roland Lathom and was signed on 28 December 1537.[5] Crayford and Lathom described the Abbey Church as 'most naked and barren' and the lands 'very ruinous', estimating the cost of altering the buildings as at least 300 marks.[6] Evidently, the canons had already stripped the church of its valuables. At its suppression the abbey had an abbot and twelve canons and income of just over £249, so it was not one of the larger and wealthier monasteries.[7] On 30 December 1537, only two days after its surrender, the king granted Titchfield Abbey and its estates to Thomas Wriothesley (*206*). The estates included 300 houses and cottages, as well as six dovecotes, six watermills, four windmills and over 10,000 acres of land. These were granted with the 'site, circuit and precinct' of Titchfield Abbey to 'our trusty servant Thomas Wriothesley', in consideration of his 'good, true and faithful service'.[8] Wriothesley chose to make Titchfield the centre of his domain. In 1537 he was also granted Quarr Abbey on the Isle of Wight, whilst Beaulieu Abbey followed in 1538.

Thomas Wriothesley was born on 21 December 1505, the eldest son of William Wriothesley, York Herald. Educated at St Paul's School, London and Trinity Hall, Cambridge, his contemporaries included the antiquary John Leland and William Paget, later a fellow privy councillor; while his tutor in civil law was Stephen Gardiner, later Bishop of Winchester. He did not, however, proceed to a degree but instead pursued a career at Court. In 1524, aged eighteen, he became a client of Thomas Cromwell and by 1530 he was a King's Messenger and joint Clerk of the Signet under Stephen Gardiner, at that time the King's Secretary. During the 1530s he was also Cromwell's private secretary and his representative at the Privy Seal.[9] He was, therefore, at the centre of government from a young age.

In 1534 Wriothesley was admitted to Gray's Inn and in 1536 he was appointed engraver of the Tower mint. In 1537 he attended Prince Edward's baptism, indicating that he had risen from a bureaucrat to become a courtier. He was swift to take advantage of the material rewards that arose from such royal favour and the lands and property which became available after the Dissolution. Between 1537 and the king's death in 1547 he acquired, chiefly through royal grant, former monastic manors, abbeys and priories in eight counties, as well as three houses and a manor in London. Between 1544 and 1546 he was granted thirty-five ex-monastic manors.[10] Wriothesley's career continued to rise and in the 1539 Parliament he was a knight of the shire for Hampshire. The following year he and Ralph Sadler were appointed joint principal secretaries to the king, and both were knighted. Wriothesley was also appointed to the Privy Council. On 29 January 1543 he became joint chamberlain of the exchequer and on 3 May 1544, after the death of Thomas Audley, he became Lord Chancellor. On 1 January 1544 he was elevated to the peerage as Baron Wriothesley of Titchfield and on 23 April 1545 he was elected a Knight of the Garter. On the following day his son was baptised Henry

207 *Titchfield House, Hampshire*, engraved by Richard Godfrey, 1784

and the king stood as godfather.[11]

When Wriothesley acquired the abbey, he began immediately to convert it into a grand courtyard house, utilising many of the monastic buildings. The result is shown in Richard Godfrey's 1776 engraving (*207*). He re-named it 'Place House' – a corruption of Palace House – a name given to other such new houses in the Tudor period. When not re-using old materials, the house was built of Caen stone and brick. The mason responsible was Thomas Berty from Winchester, who was also engaged at Winchester Cathedral and in the royal programme of coastal fortifications at the castles of Calshot, Southsea, Haselworth and Hurst.[12]

Certain letters concerning the new Tudor building have been preserved.[13] On 2 January 1538, immediately after Wriothesley acquired Titchfield, Crayford and Lathom wrote jointly to him suggesting alterations to be made to the buildings and grounds. The letter makes it clear that Wriothesley had already provided the commissioners with a plan of his proposed works, and this implies that he must have been working on this even before the suppression of the abbey. Crayford and Lathom wrote: 'For lak of tyme & opportunite to mak a new plat I have sent your owne agayne corrected as we think meate: yf it like you no wors than us/ all shalbe well.'[14]

The letter describes how the cloister garth

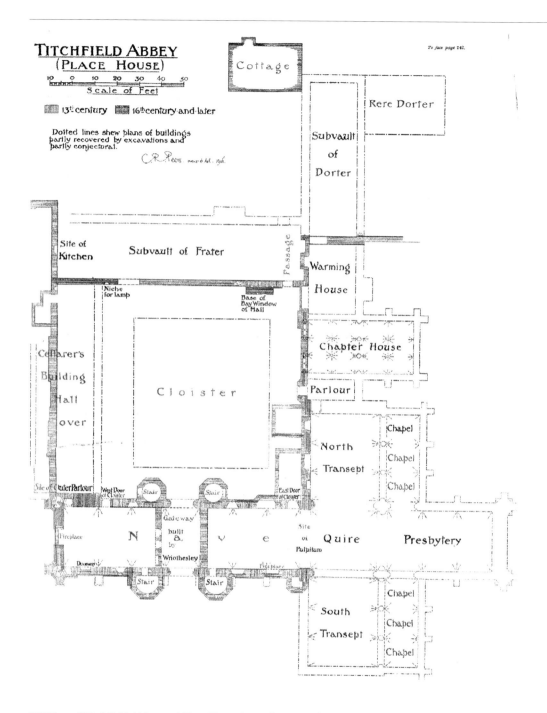

TITCHFIELD ABBEY
(PLACE HOUSE)

Scale of Feet

■ 13th century ■ 16th century and later

Dotted lines shew plans of buildings partly recovered by excavations and partly conjectural.

C R Peers, meas. & del. 1906.

To face page 242.

Cottage

Rere Dorter

Subvault of Dorter

Site of Kitchen

Subvault of Frater

Passage

Warming House

Niche for lamp

Base of Bay Window of Hall

Chapter House

Cellarer's Building

Cloister

Parlour

Hall over

North Transept

Chapel

Chapel

Chapel

Site of Outer Parlour

West Door of Cloister

Stair

Stair

East Door of Cloister

Fireplace

N

Gateway built & by Wriothesley

v e

Site of Pulpitum

Quire

Presbytery

Doorway

Stair

Stair

Fireplace

South Transept

Chapel

Chapel

Chapel

208 Plan of Titchfield Abbey and Place House by William St John Hope, 1906

332

was to be re-named the 'Greate Court' and the cloister walk to be retained as a 'Gallery' if Wriothesley so chose. The Cellarer's Hall in the west range was to be retained but to have new windows for light and a new entrance from the Great Court:

> The hall ys divised to stonde in plan coven-able for the p'mysses & the dore to appere in the greate court/ which wolbe Sqware every way an hundreth ffoote/ a gallery of xiiij foote brode & the same Leynth wt the corte if you list … you shall ascende in to yor hall wherof the Rowff ys made right ffayer the walles stondying & substanciall … ther must be lighte for the side of the hall.[15]

In the event, however, the west range seems to have been converted into servants' offices.[16] These works are shown in the 1906 plan drawn by Sir William St John Hope (**208**). The pantry, buttery, cellar and larder together formed the sub-vault of the Frater in the northern range of the Cloister, with the 'old kitchen' to the west of that range. The writers suggested that the sub-vault rooms be retained with the upper floor of the range to be used as lodgings:

> As for pantre buttre seller & lardor/ no man in Hampsher hath … better and more hansom cowched together/ the Kechyn ys large & old & may wt litle charge be maide new in the same place … The frater may be lodginge as you write & the side of the court all above/ undre that allmost the holle leyingh is there a buttre vaulted right well for lx tonn of bere or wyne/ next unto that estward the pantre/ wtin that the Sellor for wyne both vaulted awnswering to both.[17]

The commissioners initially advised taking down the steeple and all the Church except for the part joined to the Dorter, which is the north transept. This could be converted to a dining parlour and chapel on the ground floor, with chambers on the upper floor. There would be access to the leaded and battlemented roof, from which there would be views over the orchard:

> All the church must downe with the steple (onely that porcon which is north from the steple & knytt with the dorter to stonde) for yor dynyng plor [parlour] & chaple beneth/& for lodgynge above of two stories if you list/ leaded and battled above/ wt fayer Creste & prospecte west and south upon your gardyng orchard (?) & Court/ it was long to write all /to be breve/ you may have wt reasonable charge an house for the Kinge grace to bate & for any baron to kepe his hospitalite in … As for pluking downe of the church is but a small matter mynding (as we doubt not but you woll) to buyld a Chaple.[18]

In the event, Wriothesley's new chapel (**209**) was not made in the north transept but was converted from the Chapter House in the east range, the ruins surviving in 1783.

South-east of the Frater Crayford proposed a new Hall, 50 feet or more long. Its south wall would abut the north transept, and its dais or 'high desk' was to be at the Church end. This would have occupied the old Dorter, which was above the Warming House and Chapter House:

> Southward & next unto this [the Frater] the hall fightie ffoote or more in leyingh as you woll/ the hiegh desk to Joyne wt that porcon of the church that shall stond/ in the which as is said/ beneth next to the hiegh desk of the hall yor dynyng plor &c.[19]

209 *Titchfield House, Chapel*, engraved by J Bonner, 1783

This did not proceed, and instead the former Dorter was converted into a Great Chamber and Dining Parlour. Three weeks later a letter from Anthony Roke informed Wriothesley that 'Mr Mylle opinion ys nowe to have the hall of the ffrater',[20] a change from the original plan. Wriothesley must have agreed as the proposed Hall in the Dorter was abandoned for a new one in the Frater.[21]

The building progressed at speed and Roke's letter records: 'the pavemente of the body of the Church ys taken up *alredy* where ys scantly saved the xth tyle/ they be so rotten & worne thyn'.[22] However, such projects did not always run smoothly and to plan. On 25

March, Richard Lee wrote to Wriothesley:

> I have bene at Tychefeld, where as your werke procedeth well, but not so well as I wold they did they intende to make the rouf of yor hall shorter then I purposed hit/ by reason they will have the Scene covered, which verely shalbe a disvigueryng of it/ and lytell money saved thereby, but ye may remedy it if ye list and no money lost.[23]

The shortening of the hall roof seems to have been done by carrying up the front of the screens to the roof, rather than making a gallery above as usual.

Progress continued and on 12 April John Whyte wrote to Wriothesley: 'Your people at Titchfield are well, and all labouring to set forth your buildings.'[24] A letter from Crayford on the same day describes the state of Wriothesley's buildings in considerable detail. He had spent:

This day coferryng & divising … wyndowes & chymneys in the said north yle beneath/ & other places/ & also goying to Hampton [Southampton] to speke wt m. hutofft what shallbe payed for stone and freight which now ys comed from Cane … the halle rowffe wolbe redy soon after easter/ the walls afor easter will ryse on both sides to the hedes & volsaurs (voussoirs) of them/the porch ys tenn footes hiegh/ on the foremost part or front the lightes of the bay widow begynns.[25]

The house was being built to the highest standards of modern living with chimneys for new fireplaces where there were none before, and a fashionable bay window. Some of the elaborate brick chimneys survive. A new porch was built in the courtyard with steps to give access to the hall. The postscript to Crayford's letter gives further details of the conversion of the Church:

Wher yo wold part of the chauncell to be taken downe, for my sake, & part to stand for yor owne/ I will gyve place to you & let all stond, divided in three lodgynges/ halfe of the towre to be pcel of thone gallery/ thither half something abated to be yor study & for sweate waters/ the second galery towarde the Court.[26]

In the event, Wriothesley won the day and the greater part of the Church was retained. The nave, choir and presbytery formed the southern range of the new buildings, with only the south transept demolished. The south side of the Church became the main front of the house. The apartments on the upper floor at the eastern end of this range became the principal chambers, with new large windows. The new Gallery, with windows overlooking the courtyard and the garden, extended along the upper floor of the eastern range and provided access to the Great Chamber and Dining Parlour. The large new Gatehouse (*210*) was built across the nave of the Church. Adjacent to it, at the west end of the nave, was the porter's lodge, with a principal apartment above, which was subsequently used as a small theatre.[27]

The unwanted materials from the Church were to be sold and Crayford and Lathom's letter describes the process of selling the marble altar and paintings: 'Mr. Sherlond was here on Sonday … to visite yor manor & view or hospitalite wher as they hadd meate drink & lodging and have promysed to retorne and bye marble stones aulters ymages tables &c.'[28] Leland wrote in his *Itinerary* that: 'Mr. Wriothesley hath buildid a right stately House embatelid, and having a goodely Gate, and a Conducte castelid in the Midle of the Court of it, yn the very same Place wher the late Monasterie of Premonstratenses stoode caullyd Tichefelde.'[29] Licences were required for crenellation and Wriothesley's alterations were probably completed by 1542, in which year he received pardon for having fortified his manor house of Titchfield without licence.[30] To have a 'castled conduit', implying a mediaeval-style fountain, in the central courtyard indicates a house of some pretension, although nothing remains of the fountain today.

To the north of the abbey is a chain of large fishponds illustrated clearly on an early map (*211*). A letter from Crayford and Lathom

210 The Gatehouse at Titchfield Abbey

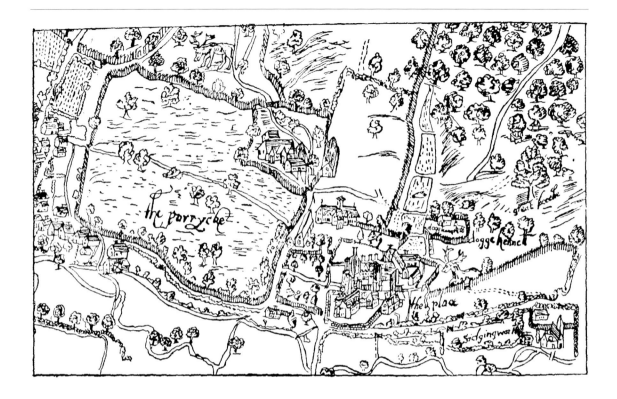

211 A detail from a map showing Place House, Titchfield, in 1610

describes how they went to view the four ponds, which were 'a mile in length to ford and harbour' and estimated to contain 100,000 'carpes, tenches, breams and pike'.[31] . The lower pond also acted as the main water supply to the abbey.[32] They have now been converted into a modern fishery called Carron Row Farm Lakes. The map also illustrates the hunting park and pale with deer, as well as kennels for the hounds. These would not have formed part of the abbey site and must have been established by Wriothesley. To the south a mediaeval tithe barn survives, probably built in the fifteenth century, which would have continued in use throughout the Tudor period.[33]

On 31 January 1547, as Lord Chancellor, Wriothesley announced the king's death to Parliament and then on 16 February he was created Earl of Southampton. On 20 February he bore the sword of state at the coronation of Edward VI.[34] But having attained the pinnacle of his career in the latter years of Henry VIII's reign, Wriothesley's fall from power was swift. By 6 March he lost his position as Lord Chancellor and was briefly imprisoned. The principal reason for this was his longstanding enmity and rivalry with Edward Seymour, the newly created Lord Protector and Duke of Somerset, together with the fact that the ascendancy of the reformist group on the Privy Council left him isolated. It took Wriothesley until January 1549 to recover his position at the council table, and a degree of leadership of the religiously conservative group. As a result, he was actively involved in

Somerset's removal from power in October 1549, acting in temporary alliance with the reform group led by the Earl of Warwick. However, this rapprochement did not last long, and by January 1550 he was placed under house arrest and removed from government. Seriously ill, he was authorised in June to retire to his house at Titchfield, but the journey proved beyond him and he died in London on 30 July 1550. Titchfield long survived him. The house stood until 1781, when it was partially dismantled for building stone and has since decayed.[35]

Torre Abbey

Torre Abbey was the wealthiest Premonstratensian abbey in England.[1] The order established all its monasteries in isolated, rural locations and Torre is situated in a wide valley at the northern end of Tor Bay on land sloping gently down to the sea. The abbey was founded in 1196, colonised by canons from the English mother house of Welbeck in Nottinghamshire and dedicated to St Saviour and the Holy Trinity. After its dissolution in 1539, the Abbey Church was demolished, and the south and west ranges were converted to a new Tudor house by Thomas Ridgeway. Substantial remains from the monastic period form part of the present house. There are vaulted undercrofts, a tower, an Inner Gatehouse and a large barn. The ruins of the Church and Cloister remain, including the entrance to the Chapter House.

Torre Abbey was founded by William Brewer, an influential figure in the Plantagenet Court, on land granted from his manor of Torre.[2] By the end of the thirteenth century, the abbey had been granted land throughout Devon and it benefited from the growth of Newton Abbot following the establishment of a weekly market. At this time there were twenty-six canons in residence, and the acquired lands made Torre wealthy. A licence to crenellate was granted by Edward III in 1348, and in 1370 the abbey acquired the manor of Torre.[3]

The ruins of the Church remain, aligned east-west and 180 feet long, of a cruciform plan. It consists of a nave and northern aisle with an arcade of six columns and a presbytery at the eastern end. The transepts each contained two chapels and a tower originally stood over the crossing, its fallen remains now in the centre of the Church. The Cloister, laid out to the south of the Church, was around 91 feet square and consisted of three ranges of two-storeyed buildings. There were roofed walks on all sides, which were originally wide, but were replaced with narrower walks with steeper roofs in 1370.[4] The abbey walls were built mostly of Devo-

212 The Abbot's Tower at Torre Abbey

nian limestone from local quarries, although around 1293 Roger de Cockington granted the canons the use of red 'breccia' from a nearby headland, which they used to build the barn.[5] The first floor of the west range consisted of the Abbot's Hall and apartments. Abutting the west face of this range is a square four-storeyed mediaeval tower, known as the Abbot's Tower (*212*). At ground level this gives access to a passage through the undercroft, and stone benches suggest that this was an extension of the canons' Parlour. The first-floor room in the Tower opens into the Abbot's Hall. In the south range, the undercroft is divided into two rooms; the eastern one has a fireplace in its east wall, showing it to have been a Warming Room. The first floor of this range originally consisted of a large Frater. The south-west corner of the Cloister contains a recessed *Lavatorium* and in the angle between the south and west ranges are the remains of the mediaeval kitchens, altered by the Tudor work. The kitchens were connected to the abbot's apartments by a spiral stair.[6] The

east range of the Cloister was not incorporated into the Tudor mansion and is now ruins. It includes the Sacristy, with a spiral stair to the first floor, and the Chapter House, which has a fine twelfth-century Norman doorway flanked by two windows (*213*). The first floor of this range would have been the Dorter. A short distance to the east of this range are the ruins of the Infirmary.

Adjoining the mediaeval kitchens in the south-west corner is the early fourteenth-century Inner Gatehouse, now called the Mohun Gate, which gave access to the inner court of the abbey (*214*). This is a three-storey battlemented structure with two passageways: a wide passage for mounted travellers and carts, and a small passage for pedestrians. The ground floor has a room for a gatekeeper with a fireplace and a door opening onto the cobbled pedestrian passage. There is a spiral stair within the south-east turret which gave access to rooms on the first and second floors, both with fireplaces. A stable block abutted

214 The Inner Gatehouse at Torre Abbey

the south wall of the Inner Gatehouse, which is illustrated in the 1661 view by Wenceslaus Hollar (215) but has since been demolished. This engraving also illustrates the ruins of a substantial building to the east which was probably the guest house, and a further gatehouse to the west of the abbey.[7] The antiquary Leland, visiting just before its dissolution, reported that the abbey had 'three fair gatehouses'.[8] To the south-west of the Inner Gatehouse is the large monastic barn, called the Spanish Barn because an Armada crew was imprisoned here. It is a complete thirteenth-century barn, 124 feet long.

In 1535, the income of Torre Abbey was just over £396, a considerable sum which meant that it fell into the later stage of the Dissolution.[9] The Deed of Surrender 'of the monastery and all its possessions in cos. Devon, Cornw., Soms., and elsewhere in England, Wales, and the Marches thereof' was dated 23 February 1539. It was signed by Simon Rede the abbot, Richard Mylton the prior and fourteen others. The Deed was enrolled as acknowledged, on the same day, before William Petre, the king's commissioner.[10]

Following its dissolution the abbey buildings and adjacent lands were initially retained by the king. Only in 1543 were they granted to Sir Hugh Pollard of King's Nympton. However, Pollard was a wealthy north Devon landowner who never lived at the abbey, but simply employed a steward who occupied the buildings and farmed the lands.[11] The site remained in the Pollard family until 1580 when it was sold by Sir Hugh's grandson to Lord Edward Seymour of Berry Pomeroy, the eldest son of the Duke of Somerset by his first marriage. When Seymour died in 1593 Torre was inherited by his son, also Edward Seymour. The Seymours, too, were major landowners, with over 16,000 acres in Devon and Wiltshire, and never resided at Torre.[12]

The man responsible for the conversion of Torre into a new house was Thomas Ridgeway. He was born in about 1566, the eldest

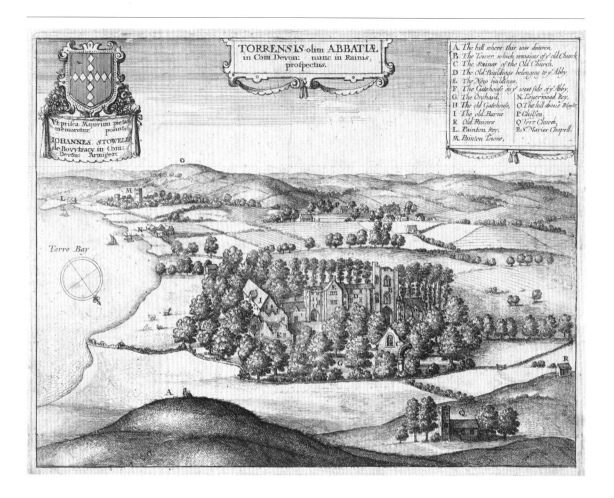

215 *Torre Abbey, Devon*, engraved by Wenceslaus Hollar, 1661

son of Thomas Ridgeway of Tor Mohun, Devon. This comfortable gentry background allowed Ridgeway's education at Exeter College, Oxford and the Inner Temple in London, which he completed only after 1587. He subsequently became a Devon customs official, and on his father's death in 1598 he inherited a patrimony consisting of at least four Devon manors.

In 1599 Ridgeway purchased Torre Abbey from Edward Seymour.[13] and for the next few years made Torre his principal residence. His rising local profile was confirmed by his appointment as sheriff of Devon in 1599, and

he was knighted in August 1600. He also had Court connections; his wife Cecily was a maid of honour to Elizabeth I, and his brother-in-law Sir John Stanhope became vice-chamberlain of the Household in 1601. It was probably through the latter's influence that Ridgeway was selected to help carry the canopy over the royal effigy at the queen's funeral in 1603. Ridgeway consolidated his Court ties early in the new reign of James I when he was appointed a member of Anne of Denmark's Council, with particular oversight of the queen's Devon estates. Shortly afterwards he was returned to the 1604 Parliament as his county's senior knight.[14] However, in this period he may also have taken part in the wars in Ireland under Lord Mountjoy. Certainly in 1603 he was appointed vice-treasurer and treasurer-at-wars in Ireland under Sir George Cary, whom he eventually succeeded as treasurer in April 1606. Later that year his Commons seat was declared vacant because of his Irish appointment and he seems thereafter to have resided in Ireland. There, he was very much involved in the Ulster plantations – moving Protestants from England, including from Devon, onto Irish lands. In this way he accumulated extensive estates in Ulster.[15]

Ridgeway lost his treasurer post in 1616 and was created Lord Ridgeway, baron of Gallen-Ridgeway. Subsequently he divided his time between Ireland and Devon. In 1622 he effectively purchased the earldom of Londonderry, in the gift of Sir James Erskine, and in return Ridgeway disposed of all his Ulster estates. He died in London on 24 January 1632 and was buried in the south aisle of the parish church of Tor Mohun.[16]

On taking possession of Torre Abbey in 1599, Ridgeway began a major building project, with the intention of converting the abbey into a grand home for himself and his family. In building his new house, Ridgeway retained the south and west sides of the Cloister, where the monastic buildings remain to roof height. Both ranges have undercrofts with vaults supported on central piers and windows in their outer walls. The west range containing the Abbot's Hall and apartments was converted into the principal rooms of the new house. Radical internal changes were required to convert the monastic buildings to Tudor domestic use. In the mediaeval period the south and west ranges were not connected above ground level and their floors were at different levels. In order to link the ranges, Ridgeway built a new stair turret over the south-west corner of the Cloister. The roof of this turret reused mediaeval timbers, which came possibly from the demolished east range.[17] In the south range a new floor was inserted halfway up the walls of the double-storey canons' Frater. This was accessed from the new stair turret at first-floor level and contained a new suite of living rooms with views over Tor Bay. These rooms were decorated with moulded plaster friezes. The floor above was used as bedrooms and both floors were heated by the installation of a large new chimneystack.[18]

In the west range, Ridgeway converted the former Abbot's Hall into a Great Hall with a screen passage at the south end. An alarm bell was hung in the Abbot's Tower to be rung in the event of a second attempted Spanish invasion. At the back of the Great Hall a new stone passage was made to the kitchens and a new staircase, reusing old flagstones.[19] The east wall of the Cloister, containing the Chapter House entrance, was retained in the Tudor house and it is likely that the Cloister remained an enclosed garden. The tower of the Church was also retained and can be seen on Hollar's 1661 view; it was demolished for safety reasons around 1770.[20]

216 A modern aerial photograph showing Vale Royal House

Vale Royal Abbey

Edward I founded Vale Royal Abbey at Darnhall, near Winsford in Cheshire as a Cistercian house in 1270, with the first community coming from the motherhouse at Abbey Dore in Herefordshire. However, due to the king's grandiose plans for a large monastery, a more extensive site was found four miles away at Whitegate near Northwich, where in 1277 Edward and his queen, Eleanor, laid a foundation stone on the proposed site of the high altar, decreeing that 'there shall be no monastery more royal than this one, in liberties, wealth and honour, throughout the whole world.'[1] Edward appointed Walter of Hereford, one of the most important royal master masons of his day, to supervise the building of a vast, cathedral-like church 421 feet in length, the longest Cistercian church in Britain.[2] The Cloister, sited to the south of the Abbey Church, was to be 138 feet square, surrounded by domestic buildings. The Abbey Church was eventually consecrated in 1283, after which work began on the Cloister. This was to be decorated with Purbeck marble columns, but due to revolts in Wales Edward redirected his funds to build castles such as Harlech and by 1290 he had lost interest in Vale Royal; from this the monastic establishment never recovered. The monks finally moved from their temporary dwellings into their main quarters in 1330, and in that year the east end of the Church was completed, but the rest was still a shell. In 1336 Abbot Peter complained that the vaulting and roof of the Church, together with the Cloister, Chapter House and Frater, were yet to be built. The complex, much reduced in scale, was not completed until the end of the fourteenth century, after injections of funds by Edward the Black Prince and later by Richard II. All that remains above ground of the great Abbey Church is a collection of pier bases called the Nun's Grave, which marks the approximate position of the high altar.

Vale Royal escaped dissolution under the 1536 Act, as it possessed an annual income of £540, but was eventually forfeited to the Crown in a special court held at the abbey in March 1539, with Thomas Cromwell sitting as judge. After a protracted negotiation, Thomas Holcroft, head of the king's commission of enquiry, was granted the lease of Vale Royal from the Crown. He was one of the Holcrofts of Holcroft Hall, near

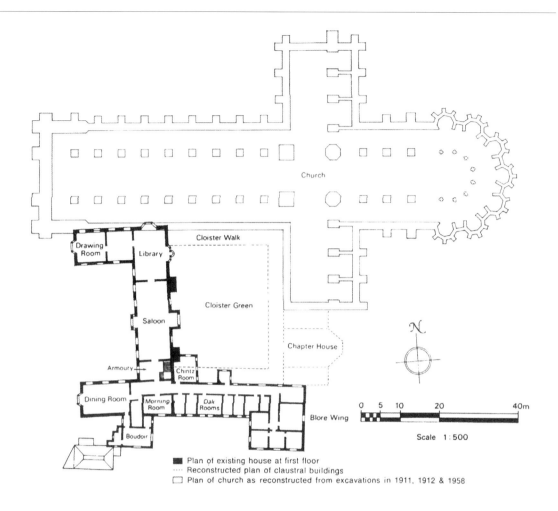

Culcheth in Lancashire, had been a member of the 3rd Earl of Derby's council and had been appointed to assist the commissioners for the Dissolution in Lancashire. He was already a lessee of Cartmel Priory where, after open opposition to Holcroft, four canons and eight husbandmen had been executed. Thereafter, as opportunities arose, Holcroft became one of the most ruthless and successful 'traffickers in monastic property'.[3] As one of the king's most trusted men in the region, he was rewarded for his loyalty by the grant of Vale

Royal Abbey by Letters Patent on 7 March 1544.[4] He paid £450,[5] and in subsequent purchases of monastic lands and properties in both Lancashire and Cheshire he was to spend the princely sum of £3,798.[6]

Demolition of the monastic buildings was very thorough, with the suppression commissioners giving their usual orders that the workmen should 'pull down to the ground all the walls of the churches, steeples, cloisters, fraters, chapter houses with all other houses, saving them that be necessary for a farmer'.[7]

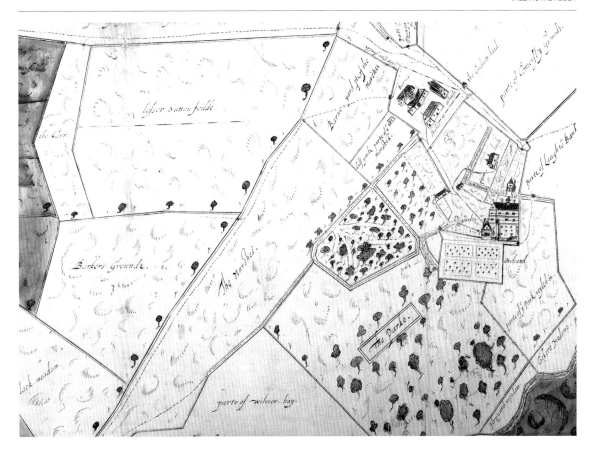

218 Map of Vale Royal Abbey, from the 'Survey of Vale Royal Manor House and Estate', 1616

Holcroft followed these strictures, leaving only the west and south ranges of the Cloister to be converted into a house, visible in the modern aerial photograph (*216*), while other ancillary buildings were retained for agricultural purposes. Holcroft wrote to the king in 1539 assuring him that he had 'plucked down' the Church as ordered.[8] The lead was taken to London, but Holcroft kept stonework and timber for the construction of his new house. The great Abbey Church stood to the north of the present house (*217*), its west end extending 85 feet beyond the main façade.[9]

Unfortunately there are no contemporary accounts or images of the Tudor house, but after its purchase by Mary, Lady Cholmondeley, in 1615 a survey of the Manor House and estate was taken.[10] This comprises a bound volume of fifteen folio sheets with coloured plans of the landholdings and is a rare and important record of the dissolved abbey site and the house, gardens and parkland that Holcroft had created from it. Folio 6 is a detailed, if naively drawn, plan of the Manor House, with its walled garden and orchard, gatehouse, pigeon house, stable, oxhouse, barns and a 'Conduit head'. The landscape beyond the walled enclosures comprises 'The Parke', which is railed off from surrounding meadows and several marshy areas (*218*). The

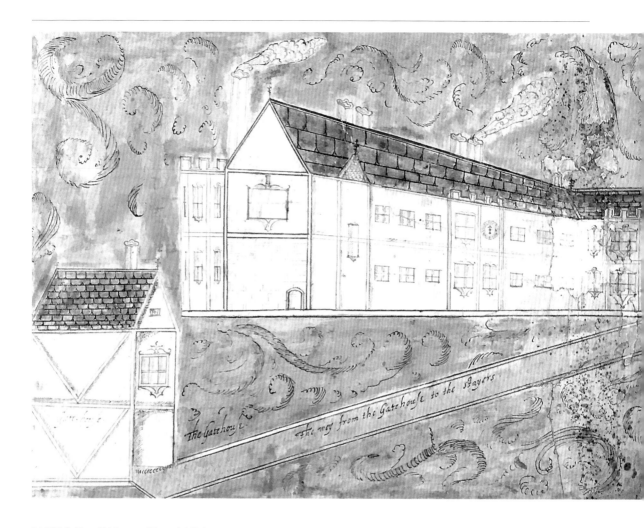

The Gatehouse

The way from the Gatehouse to the Players

219 'Vale Royall Mannor House', 1616

Vale-Royall-Mannor-House.

detail given of the house itself is rudimentary, though a lantern is shown on the gabled roofline. Fortunately, the volume begins with a beautiful colour-washed drawing of the whole extent of the west front of 'Vale-Royall-Mannor-House' (*219*) including the 'Gatehouse' and a detached building to the south, which is marked 'Goodwyf Hamlets House'. It is an extruded view of the U-shaped front, its lantern visible above the central range, while smoke issues from chimneystacks on the adjoining wings. A path – 'the way from the Gatehouse to the stayers' – leads up to the main central block, which has a halpace giving access to a castellated porch at first-floor level and then to a screens passage, with a Great Hall to its left and a Great Chamber to the right. There is a double-height bay to the left of the doorway lighting the dais end of the

Great Hall, and there are further canted bays with clocks, one to the right, which must denote a staircase, and others on the north wing and at the far north corner. The majority of the fenestration comprises cross-mullions, but the central section is lit entirely by decorative oriel windows.

From this it can be deduced that Holcroft contrived his house around the surviving west and south ranges of the former Cloister, to which he added two projecting wings on the west side. This remains visible in the modern aerial photograph *(220)*. He also re-clad the first floor of the south range with timber framing of chevron decoration, much as Sir George Cotton had done at nearby Combermere; this is shown in a 1774 view of Vale Royal taken from the north-east.[11] The monks' Frater was situated in this range and connected with the abbey kitchen at the angle between the south and west arms of the former Cloister. Holcroft divided the first-floor Frater, which still retains its elaborate roof, dated by dendrochronology to 1470-5, into apartments; a felling date of 1548, which indicates a Holcroft remodelling, has been established for one of the roof timbers above this range.[12] The former abbey kitchen, originally open through two storeys, was also sub-divided and remodelled, but an original stone doorway giving access to it from the west Cloister walk survives.[13] There are further arched openings of the original Cloister on the east wall of the west range that light the entrance passage.

Holcroft retained the Great Hall of the former Abbot's Lodgings in the west range of the Cloister and made it the core of his new house. Fortunately, King James I made a progress to Vale Royal in 1617 and John Nichols describes the drawing and the house it depicted in his *Progresses*:

> A drawing of Vale Royal, taken in the year previous to this visit represents the 'Manor House' as it had been new-modelled by its grantees, the Holcrofts. A gateway would admit the Royal party to a spacious court, round three sides of which the mansion displayed its bay windows and oriels, with a broad flight of twenty steps in the centre heading to the ancient refectory of the Abbey, seventy feet in length, still preserved entire, and containing among numerous portraits, those of the "bold Ladie" and her marital husband.[14]

As with the confusion over the original use of the surviving mediaeval Hall at Combermere Abbey, Nichols was wrong about that at Vale Royal, which was part of the Abbot's Lodgings rather than the Frater sited in the south range. Unlike the Hall at Combermere, which survives almost intact as a space, that at Vale Royal has been extensively remodelled. In the 1790s the Great Hall, screens passage and Great Chamber were opened up into one long room, the Saloon. The first campaign retained the external steps, but these were removed and replaced by an internal staircase in 1811. There was a further rebuilding by Edward Blore in the 1830s, when the coats of arms of the Saloon ceiling, which had been painted in 1824 in 'neutral tints', was emblazoned with heraldic colours, and the roof timbers were given cusped wind braces to enhance the Gothick effect.[15] Later work carried out by the Chester architect John Douglas continued Blore's Tudor style.

Walden Abbey (Audley End)

Visitors to English Heritage's Essex flagship, the prodigy house of Audley End at Saffron Walden, would be forgiven for thinking that it had nothing to do with the Dissolution. It is an early-seventeenth-century Jacobean house set in a landscape contrived in the eighteenth century by Lancelot 'Capability' Brown and it has Georgian interiors by Robert Adam. However, as the earliest guidebook declares, 'This house is not as old as the name it bears.'[1] That name commemorates Sir Thomas Audley (*221*), Lord Chancellor at the time of the suppression of the monasteries, who built a house on the site of the dissolved abbey of Walden.

The de Mandeville family held the manor of Walden after the Norman Conquest and established a castle and the later town of Walden there. Between 1139 and 1143 Geoffrey de Mandeville, Earl of Essex, founded a Benedictine priory at Brookwalden, beside the River Cam and the London to Cambridge Road. Earl Geoffrey's son frequented Walden and advised the prior to 'be content with a small church and little buildings', but the prior moved the conventual buildings on the south side of the Church to higher ground and made a new Cloister and Chapter House.[2] Earl Geoffrey the second was buried at Walden in 1167 and his brother William further endowed the establishment, which was elevated to the status of an abbey by Richard I in 1190. The Abbey Church appears to have been built in the mid-thirteenth century when in 1237 Edmund, Archbishop of Canterbury, 'granted indulgences in aid of the fabric'.[3] The Church was dedicated in 1258, when Bishop Hugh dc Balsham, Bishop of Ely, consecrated the Chapel in the Infirmary. Humphrey de Bohun, Earl of Hereford and Essex, rebuilt the Cloister before his death in 1361, after which the monastic complex was complete.

Abbot Robert Baryngton and his prior and monks took the Oath of Supremacy on 1 July 1534 and in the *Valor* of 1535 the abbey's net value was given as just over £372, thereby exempting it from suppression.[4] It

221 *Portrait of Sir Thomas Audley, 1st Baron Audley*, Biagio Rebecca, *c.*1769

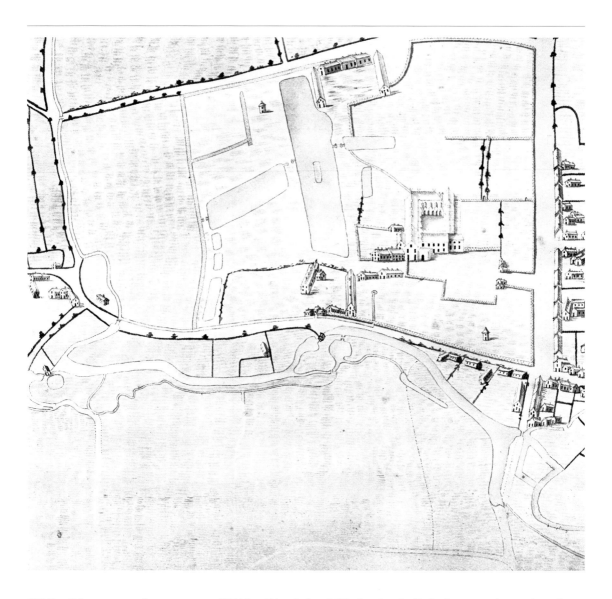

222 Detail from a copy of an estate map of Walden Abbey before 1600, showing the Tudor house, gardens and ponds

eventually surrendered on 22 March 1538; the whole site, buildings and other possessions being granted on 27 March to Sir Thomas Audley. It is presumed that the monastic complex followed the pattern of a cruciform Abbey Church with the Cloister lying to its south. However, as Richard, Lord Braybrooke, writing of his family home Audley End in 1836 stated: 'of the abbey of Walden all traces have long since been obliterated: nor can the site of the buildings be pointed out with any confidence.'[5] The official guidebook to Audley End, published by the Department of the Environment in 1958, argued more confidently that, although 'there are no upstanding parts of the Benedictine abbey of Walden, remains of the monastic buildings still surviving beneath the floor of the house suggest that the

223 Audley End House, Essex

inner court lying behind the hall marks the site of the cloister'.[6] This accords with early sheets of the Ordnance Survey, which mark the site of the abbey in the lawns to the east of the present house.

Thomas Audley was born at Hay House, Earls Colne, Essex. He was the son of Geoffrey Audley, a yeoman of moderate means, of Berechurch, Essex. A lawyer by profession, in 1510 he was admitted to the Inner Temple and as late as 1530 still had chambers there. Very much an Essex man, Audley served as an Essex JP continuously from 1520 to his death, as town clerk of Colchester from 1514 to 1532, and as an Essex MP from 1523. His rise at Court began when he joined the household of Cardinal Wolsey in 1527. In 1529 he was elected a knight of the shire for Essex and made Speaker of the House, a position he held until 1532. A close associate of Thomas Cromwell, he was knighted and made Keeper of the Great Seal on 20 May 1532, four days after Sir Thomas More resigned as Lord Chancellor. However, he had to wait until 26 January 1533 before being named Lord Chancellor himself, a position he held until his death. For the next seven years he worked in close partnership with Cromwell, but after Cromwell's fall Audley became the prime instigator and manager of parliamentary legislation. As such he was the mainstay of the Privy Council in London, where he remained whilst the rest of the Council moved with the king. Though he was not, perhaps, among the

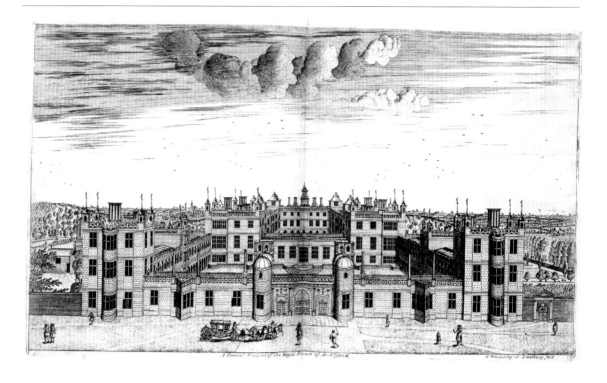

224 *The Royail Palace of Audley End*, engraved by Henry Winstanley, 1688

leading politicians of the reign, Audley was certainly highly valued as an adviser and administrator, particularly for his legal expertise.[7] He was well rewarded for such loyal service, being created Baron Audley of Walden on 29 November 1538, shortly after he was granted Walden, and being installed on 23 April 1540 as a Knight of the Garter.

Audley had already obtained Holy Trinity Priory, Aldgate, in 1534 in 'the first cut in the feast of abbey lands' and thereafter he received in 1536 St Botolph's Priory, Colchester and the Priory of Prittlewell, followed by Walden in 1538.[8] Unfortunately, there are no records of the construction of the great Jacobean house of Audley End and therefore no written account of the Tudor house that Audley created from the dissolved Walden Abbey, which was demolished to make way for it.

However, there are two documents that give some clues as to the form and extent of Audley's new house. The first is his will, which states that he had converted the abbey into his 'chiefe and capital mansion at Walden'; the second is an eighteenth-century copy of a lost estate plan (*222*), dating to before 1600, which records this courtyard house.[9] From this latter source and the results of excavations, PJ Drury and S Welch have produced an informed analysis of how the surviving monastic buildings were first converted into the Tudor mansion (Audley I) and how that building subsequently influenced the planning of the present Audley End House (*223*) (Audley II), built after 1603 and before 1614 by Thomas Howard, Ist Earl of Suffolk, which superseded it.[10]

Lord Audley's 'chiefe and capital mansion' shown on the pre-1600 plan was a courtyard house created out of the nave of the Abbey Church to the north and the surviving Cloister to the south. The crossing tower and east end of the Church were demolished, leaving the long nave for conversion, while the east arm of the former Cloister, which is clearly marked by an arcade, was given a first-floor gallery with pointed-arched windows to give access to the first-floor apartments. It is thought that Audley made a Great Hall in the west range.[11] Elsewhere the fenestration is notional, though all buildings had gabled roofs, while several monastic outliers were retained for ancillary use. The area around the house was subdivided into walled enclosures, one of which had a dovecote; further out there were two canalised pieces of water, no doubt developed from the mediaeval fishponds.

It is presumed that, when Thomas Howard began his great rebuilding of Audley End House, he demolished Audley's mansion entirely, but Drury and Welch have confirmed that Howard used the foundations of the Tudor house for the inner courtyard of his great house. The truncation of the palatial Audley End in 1721, which originally had an inner court and a vast entrance courtyard with a great gatehouse shown in Henry Winstanley's 1688 view (*224*), has made locating the Tudor house complicated.[12] However, Drury and Welch, having superimposed the pre-1600 plan onto a modern Ordnance Survey map, have concluded that 'the plan of the cloister/courtyard [of Lord Audley's post-Dissolution mansion] was followed exactly by the inner court of Audley End II, and although externally there is no sign of earlier work above ground level, the extent to which the lower parts of some standing walls of Audley End II are refaced earlier work must remain a matter of conjecture.'[13]

Although we have no record of the interi-ors of Audley's Tudor house and no inventory of its fixtures and fittings to give a sense of its opulence, his tomb in St Mary the Virgin, Saffron Walden, gives some pointers, particularly as it is thought to have been prepared for him before his death in April 1544. It is a striking and curious tomb chest in inky black marble which, to echo Thomas Fuller, 'is not blacker than the soul, nor harder than the heart, of him whose bones are laid beneath it'.[14] The inscription on the tomb reads:

> The stroke of death's inevitable dart;
> Hath now, alas, of life bereft the hart,
> of Sir THOMAS AUDLEY of the Garter Knight;
> late Chancellor of England under our Prince of might
> Henry the Eight, worthie of high renowne and made by him LORD
> AUDLEY of this towne.
> Obiit ultimo die Aprilis, Ann Dom 1544 regni regis Henrici 36
> cancelleriatus sui 13, aetatis 56.

The tomb is decorated with wreaths, roundels and classical pilasters in the style of Pietro Torrigiano's tomb for Henry VII in Westminster Abbey. The chest has a heraldic back-plate derived from his Garter stall plate in St George's Chapel, Windsor, framed with pilasters of 'antik' work. The pilaster detail recalls Renaissance-style decoration used by Sir William Sharington at Lacock and which features on his monument in the parish church there. At Saffron Walden, Nikolaus Pevsner ascribes the Audley tomb design to Cornelius Harman, to whom he also attributes the monument to John, 15th Earl of Oxford, at nearby Castle Hedingham.[15]

Wenlock Priory

The artist Thomas Robins had been busily sketching the ruins of the Priory Church (*225*) at Much Wenlock on 17 July 1759, three days before he reached Buildwas Abbey. It is assumed that, at the time, he was engaged upon a sketching tour of the Shropshire Severn, because there are several views of the river and its industrial landmarks, including the Inclined Plane at Coalbrookdale, in his sketchbook held at the Victoria & Albert Museum.[1] At Much Wenlock he found that there was much less left of the Priory Church than had survived at Buildwas Abbey, but it was far more romantically scenic, with heaps of earth in the south transept and vegetation sprouting from the walls (*226)*. Although Priory House at Much Wenlock is sited to the north-east of the location of the Church, having been adapted from the Prior's Lodgings and the adjacent Infirmary, Robins gives us a glimpse, through a jagged breach in the arcaded wall at the crossing, of the conical-roofed staircase turret set at the angle between the two domestic ranges. Apart from that, nothing else is visible of the dwelling that the wool merchants Thomas and Richard Lawley contrived out of the ruined monastic complex once they had bought the property on 20 September 1544 from the king's physician, Augustin de Augustini.[2]

Much Wenlock was originally founded in the Saxon period when Merewalh, King of Mercia, built a monastery for men and women at the site in 680. Merewalh's daughter Milburge was its second abbess and after her death was recognised as a saint.[3] The monastery was replaced by a college of priests in about 1040 and became a priory at the Norman Conquest when Roger of Montgomery, who owned the site, requested monks to be sent from Cluny to form a community at Wenlock. Soon after 1100 Milburge's bones were discovered at the priory, after which it became a place of pilgrimage. The main focus of the priory was its magnificent Church, built in sharply pointed Early English style by Prior

225 Wenlock Priory, Shropshire

226 *Wenlock Priory*, Thomas Robins, 1759

Humbert between 1200 and 1240. Of this only the south transept and St Michael's Chapel attached to the south-west corner of the nave survived the Dissolution, though its vast extent can be seen in the foundations.[4]

In line with most monastic establishments, particularly those of the Clunaic Order, the Church was sited to the north of the Cloister, shown in the plan of the priory site (*227*) dated *c*.1900. Intriguingly, at Wenlock the Infirmary, usually built outside the main circuit of offices, here connected with the Chapter House and was attached to the Prior's Lodgings. These two ranges survive today (*228*) and comprise the dwelling that the Lawleys formed after they acquired the priory. The ranges originally connected with the Warming Room, Dorter and Reredorter and were set around a quadrangle. The Infirmary

was one of the earliest buildings to be constructed in the eleventh century, with round-arched windows on the south façade and a main doorway decorated with Romanesque carving. The adjacent Prior's Lodgings is altogether different, with a lattice-work of Perpendicular-style windows over two floors set within a grid of buttresses, all oversailed by a vast, stone-tiled roof. At the angle of these two ranges rises the staircase turret with its conical roof, which was glimpsed by Robins when sketching, and made more prominent by Paul Sandby, who painted the ruins as seen from the north in 1779.[5] Later the subject of an engraving, his evocative, yet homely, view shows cattle grazing in the transept and a maid hanging out washing on a line (*229*).

The Lawleys did not therefore carry out a

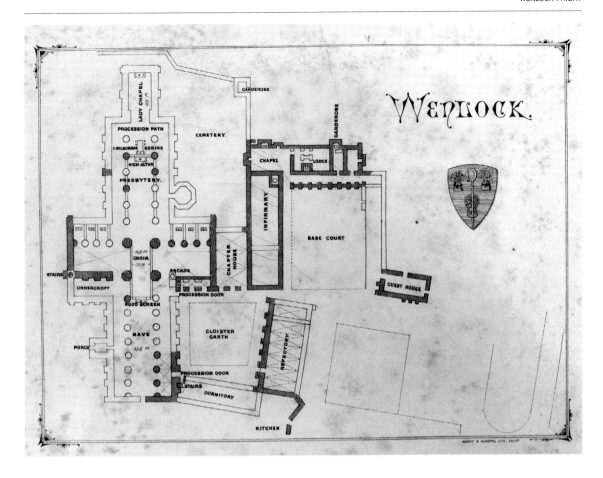

227 Plan of Wenlock Priory, *c*.1900

significant building campaign after 1544; they merely retained the Infirmary and the Prior's Lodgings and adapted them for their domestic use. Later architectural writers have recognised the importance of the Lodgings as one of the most significant surviving domestic buildings of the fifteenth century. Prior John Stafford built them in about 1430 when double internal corridors, later described as a gallery (*230*) were replacing external steps in elite domestic buildings; the Lodgings at Wenlock Priory are the earliest example of this development to survive.[6] That indefatigable antiquary John Britton included a

thorough account of it, written by a learned cleric, in his 1814 *Architectural Antiquities of Great Britain*. The Revd Hugh Owen visited the site on 23 January 1813 and describes the domestic ranges in helpful detail:

> A few paces south-eastward of the Chapter-house, are the remains of a second quadrangle, the buildings of which on two sides, are nearly entire. Those on the eastern side, it is presumed, belonged to the Lodge of the Prior, and, at the dissolution, were preserved for a mansion-house, by the first lay possessors of the monastery. This consists of a

228 Aerial photograph of Wenlock Priory showing the surviving ranges and the ruins of the Priory Church

long range of two stories, not very lofty, with a highly pitched, and tiled roof. Along the whole front runs an elegant Cloister, 100 feet in extent, composed of a series of narrow arches, in couplets, with trefoil heads, and strengthened, at frequent intervals, with slender, shelving buttresses. The cloister has an upper and a low ambulatory, communicating with the apartments of the ground and second floors.[7]

Owen gives a particularly informative account of the interior of the former Prior's Lodgings, mentioning both surviving mediaeval fragments and also contemporary alterations:

The only place that retains any trace of its original destination, is a small room with three narrow, lancet windows; in it is a huge slab of red stone, raised as an altar, which perhaps marks it to have been the private Oratory of the Prior: it is now used as a dairy. The upper ambulatory of the cloister opens to two spacious apartments in the second story, that have still traces of paintings, and till of late the figure of St. George might have been discerned. A clumsy Grecian chimney-piece appears to have been added by the Lawleys, who, in every other instance, were, probably, the destroyers of this stately monastery.[8]

Unfortunately, little survived of the original interior of the adjacent Infirmary block. In Owen's view, 'within, it has nothing remarkable'.[9]

229 *Wenlock Abbey, Shropshire, the South Transept and Converted Prior's Lodge.* An engraving after Paul Sandby, 1779

John Henry Parker followed Owen's informed account in his *Domestic Architecture in England*, which was published in 1859, but was at pains to identify any surviving mediaeval detail. He illustrated his text with a ground plan and a section through what he called the 'Abbot's House'.[10] On the ground floor were the usual domestic offices, but he believed that the room marked 'K' at the south end had been used by the prior as a private oratory; the altar within the bay window survives today. On the floor above, accessed via a spiral back staircase extending upwards from the kitchen to the prior's apartments, or by the larger stair in the angle of the two domestic ranges, there

was a great chamber – the Prior's Hall – heated by a large fireplace and lit from the east by four panelled and traceried paired windows, while a smaller room at the north end served as a parlour. Screens in this room, perhaps of later date, partitioned off a staircase leading to the garrets.

In his desire to convey the original mediaeval appearance of these rooms, Parker omits almost all later alterations, so it is unclear what might have been done by successive owners after the Dissolution. However, he noted that rooms on the ground and first floors had been 'modernized and converted into a dwelling-house', and a 'new staircase has

Gallery,
Prior's House,
Much Wenlock

230 The Gallery in the Prior's Lodgings at Wenlock

been added, and new partitions inserted'; he also spotted a 'cumbrous fireplace of late date' in the Prior's Hall.[11] Of more interest was the 'curious garderobe, the stone ceiling of which is carved with tracery in low relief' at the north-east angle of the former kitchen, and the Oratory recess with its stone altar: 'it is quite perfect, and is open underneath for the reception of relics. On the altar is placed a small and very curious stone reading-desk, richly carved with late Norman foliage.'[12] In the absence of inventories or a list of furniture in wills there is no record of how the rooms were furnished or decorated, but Parker speculates that a row of hooks on 'the wall-plate over the upper windows of the gallery' were 'probably used for occasionally hanging drapery to exclude the cold'.[13] Successive generations of owners, especially the Wynns, in the nineteenth century, have done much to stabilise the ruins and preserve the domestic ranges, but none more so than the current owner, who has added beautifully designed and stylistically appropriate carved woodwork in many of the rooms.[14]

GVLIELMVS HERBERTVS PEMBROCHIÆ COMES

Ang fe Semeray

PEMBROCHIÆ Comitis virtus tot Regibus vna
Duxit inoffenso tandem ipsum tramite ad astera

Wilton Abbey

Wilton Abbey lies in a chalk land valley in South Wiltshire, between Salisbury Plain to the north and Cranbourne Chase to the west, within the angle where the River Wylye and River Nadder meet, about two miles to the west of Salisbury. Downland rises from either side of the valley to wooded chalk ridges. During the ninth century Wilton was the royal seat of the kingdom of Wessex, where the king had a palace.[1] Destroyed by the Vikings in 871, it was rebuilt by Alfred, who, when he moved his capital to Winchester, gave the site of his palace for an abbey.[2] This abbey survived for almost 650 years and was recorded as the richest in England at the time of Domesday. Following the abbey's dissolution in 1539, it was granted to William Herbert in 1542 (*231*). A wealthy and powerful courtier, Herbert was created Earl of Pembroke in 1551. Over a period of twenty years he rebuilt the monastery to create a house that reflected his wealth and status, which remains in the ownership of the Herbert family.

A chronicle probably written at Wilton in the first half of the fifteenth century places the establishment of a nunnery in 830. The same source relates that in 890 Alfred laid the foundation stone of another house for women at Wilton. This took two years to build and its Church was dedicated to St Mary and St Bartholomew. Thirteen nuns are said to have taken the veil in the new house and to have been joined there by the nuns of the earlier foundation.[3] This account has been assumed to be a spurious late source, but more recently it has been suggested that it embodies a genuine narrative about the origins of Wilton Abbey. However, it seems likely that the abbey represents a more long-lived religious tradition, and that the foundation in 830 served as the enlargement of a much earlier minster establishment, possibly dating from the seventh century.[4]

Over its first two hundred years, the abbey was endowed with extensive properties and by the time of Domesday Book in 1086 the abbess controlled over 29,000 acres. From it, the abbey received an income of

231 *William Herbert, Earl of Pembroke*, in an engraving from *Heroologia Anglica*, 1620

£246 15s a year, the highest of any nunnery in England.[5] With this wealth, the abbey's buildings may have been impressive in scale, though there is no record of them except from the fifteenth-century antiquary, William of Worcester. He recorded after a visit that the Church contained '90 of my steppys' while the width of the nave with the two aisles was '46 of my steppys'. Harold Brakspear estimated that the ninety paces represented the nave only, giving dimensions of the nave as 146 feet by 72 feet.[6] The abbey seems to have been built on the conventional Benedictine plan with the Church forming the north range of the Cloister. The only independent building still standing, which must have formed part of the abbey and is known as the Almonry, lies slightly to the north-west of Wilton House. This, it has been suggested, was the abbess' Court of the Bellhouse, since it has on its roof a small stone erection to hold a bell.[7]

The income of Wilton included in the *Valor* of 1535 was just over £674 – the fourth highest of any nunnery in England. This made it one of the later monasteries to be dissolved and only on 25 March 1539 was the abbey surrendered. The abbess was allotted a pension of £100, a house at Fovant with its orchards, gardens, and meadows, and a cart-load of wood every week from Fovant wood; the prioress received a pension of £10, and thirty-one other nuns gained pensions ranging from £2 to £7 6s 8d.[8]

Following its dissolution Wilton Abbey was leased to William Herbert in 1540. Two years later, in April 1542, Herbert was granted for life 'the Manor of Wassherne, Wiltshire, certain woods specified in the manor of Brodechalke, [and the] house and site of Wilton monastery and certain meadows adjoining, and manors of Chalke and Brodechalke'.[9] This was extended to a grant in January 1544 'in tail male'.[10] The abbey and all of its considerable lands including 'messuages houses edifices dove houses stables mills barns orchards gardens waters ponds parks lands soil and hereditaments whatsoever' were transferred to Herbert.[11]

William Herbert was brought up in the household of the Earl of Worcester, his relation by marriage, after the death of his father when he was just three years old. In the summer of 1520, when Herbert was thirteen, he went to France with Worcester, who presided as one of the judges at the Field of the Cloth of Gold, at which 300 knights took part in a tournament to celebrate the meeting of Henry VIII and François I.[12] By 1526, Herbert was a gentleman pensioner to Henry VIII, and in 1535 he became an esquire of the body, making his way in the world of the Court and in close proximity to the King.[13] In 1537 he married Anne Parr, younger sister of Katherine Parr, who had come to Court to serve together with her sister as a maid to Katherine of Aragon, in the household of her daughter, Princess Mary.[14] When Katherine Parr then married Henry VIII in 1543 and Herbert consequently became brother-in-law to the king, his fortune was sealed.

Following the death of Henry VIII in 1547, Herbert was appointed as a guardian to Edward VI.[15] He was installed as a Knight of the Garter, made Master of the Horse in 1549 and created Baron Herbert of Cardiff and Earl of Pembroke in 1551.[16] In 1556 he was described in dispatches to the Doge of Venice as 'the most powerful personage in England'.[17] Between Herbert's acquisition of Wilton and his death in 1570, almost thirty years later, he had the opportunity and resources to develop the mediaeval abbey into a large house with gardens and park.

When Herbert acquired the abbey, the

232 A drawing of the East Front of Wilton House, from the 1566 *Survey of Lands of William, First Earl of Pembroke*

mediaeval ranges around the monastic Cloister were not completely replaced, but were instead adapted to domestic use and much of the fabric was retained.[18] Work on the rebuilding as a residence suitable to Herbert's position was in progress by 1543.[19] It was the practice of landed proprietors to have an accurate survey of their estates prepared, and Herbert commissioned such a survey in 1566, when his work on the rebuilding and gardens at Wilton was largely complete.[20] This surviving document, written in Latin, is the most important primary source of information about Tudor Wilton. It describes how the earl had built a 'capital Mansion' with its walled gardens, orchards and enclosures, circuits and surroundings, covering an estimated four acres.[21] The cost of rebuilding was more than £10,000, a very large amount that indicates how extensive the adaptation works were.[22]

When work was carried out on the restoration of the south front of the house between 1988 and 1991, mediaeval stonework was discovered *in situ*, confirming that the walls supporting what is now the Single Cube Room are on mediaeval alignments and incorporate mediaeval fabric. Archaeological investigation concluded that the sixteenth-century house was built over the Cloister and that there is a strong possibility that monastic period walling survives extensively up to at least first floor level.[23] Monastic carved doorways were uncovered which further confirmed that the house was built over the Cloister.[24] The cloister walk was about 3 feet below the present floor level and the mediaeval range was the same width as the present range.[25] The entrance to the house was from the east, through a Gate Lodge into a walled outer courtyard and thence under an archway in the

233 The East Front of Wilton House

centre of the east front, to the inner courtyard where the so-called 'Holbein Porch' on the north range led to the Great Hall. The survey includes a sketch of the house (*232*), which gives some indication of the appearance of the entrance courtyard and the east façade, of which much of the central portion survives (*233*).

Early elements of classical architectural forms clearly began to appear at Wilton, as evidenced by the Holbein Porch (*234*). The traditional attribution of the Porch to Holbein appears to have begun with the unreliable John Aubrey, but it can be discounted because Holbein died in 1543, some years before it was built.[26] The Porch was considered by Inigo Jones of sufficient architectural merit to leave it *in situ* when he carried out his remodelling

of the house from 1636.[27] It remained in the courtyard until it was removed in order to make way for James Wyatt's Gothick cloisters between 1803 and 1806. It was then dismantled and re-erected in the garden to the west of the house in 1826.[28]

Shell lunettes such as those on the parapet of the Porch first appeared in England in the 1550s, and remained in fashion until the 1570s.[29] Mark Girouard's dating of the Porch to 1559-61 places it in the middle of the period, and the height of the fashion, but it may be as early as 1551 and is remarkably sophisticated for its date.[30] It is likely that the Porch was carved by the sought-after mason John Chapman, who had worked earlier for William Sharington at Lacock and Sir John Thynne at Longleat.[31] As well as these classical

234 The 'Holbein' Porch at Wilton House

elements it has, much more traditionally, the Pembroke coat of arms flanked by bas-relief portrait roundels of the earl and his wife, placed above the lintel. Other roundels portray Herbert ancestors, real and mythical.

Lieutenant Hammond, visiting the house in 1635 before work on rebuilding the south range started, described it as a 'stately, and Princelike house', and continued:

> The Gallery, richly hung, and adorn'd with stately and faire Pictures; next through a neat withdrawing Roome into the Earles Bed-Chamber, which was most richly hang'd. The Chamber next the Garden, call'd the King's Chamber, the Hangings therein being Cloth of Gold, and on over the Chimney Peece is the statue of King Henry 8th richly cut, and

gilded over. Next I was shew'd the King's with-drawing Roome, and the Billiard table Chamber, next the Chappell, both richly hung. The great Dyning Chamber, very richly hang'd; in it is a most curious Chimney Peece, of Alabaster, Touch-Stone and Marble, cut with severall statues, the Kings, and his Lord-ships owne Armes richly sett out…Then I march'd downe through the fayre Great Hall, and stately 4. Square built Court, beautify'd about, with the Kings, and his [Lordship's] owne Armes, by the archt Cellers into the Garden.[32]

This description explains the layout of the principal rooms, which can be related to Colen Campbell's plan of 1717 (**235**). It implies that on approaching through the

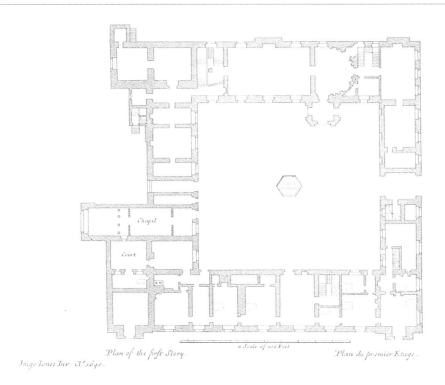

Plan of the first Story. a Scale of 100 Feet Plan du premier Etage.

235 Plan of the first storey at Wilton House, from Colen Campbell, *Vitruvius Britannicus*, 1715

Gatehouse, instead of crossing the courtyard to the Porch and entering via the Hall, Hammond was shown round the house in reverse order. He began by climbing the stair by the Gatehouse and first visited the Gallery. This suggests the Gallery may have been in the east range, at first floor level. The east range of the monastic Cloister would have contained the Chapter House on the ground floor, with the Dorter above. This means that the new entrance Gateway was made through the centre of this range, and the Gallery would have linked the rooms at the northern end of the east range with those at the southern end.

In the abbey, the south range would have contained the Frater. The new rooms in the south range were the withdrawing chambers,

the Earl's Bedchamber and the King's Chamber. The courtyard side of the south range had nine bays and was three storeys high, almost the height of the present building. Gadrooning carved in the centre bay between the first- and second-floor windows matches that on the east Gatehouse, indicating a unified design.[33] At least part of the ground floor of this range was a vaulted undercroft dating to the mediaeval period, which survived until the seventeenth century.[34] In the west range was the Chapel, and this range also contained Herbert's Great Dining Chamber, and as this would have been the cellaress' range in the abbey it may have originally been the Cellaress' Hall.

In the north range, Herbert's new Great

Hall would have been created from the nave of the Church. This provided the formal entrance into the house. The east end of the Church was demolished and a resistivity survey of the east and south lawns shows the outline of extensive buildings at the north-east corner of the house, presumed to be the footings of the east end. This was built over by Herbert, who created a detached kitchen in this position, reached through a back door of the screens passage of the Hall.[35] If the house followed the usual internal arrangement, there would have been a parlour on the ground floor to the west of the Great Hall, and access via a staircase to the major apartments on the first floor of the west range.[36] There would also have been a staircase at the east end of the Hall to give access to the apartments on the first floor of the east range.

To the east of the house was the entrance courtyard as depicted in the survey drawing, with a central gate lodge in the outer wall opposite the entrance to the house. This was a newly created entrance, as the mediaeval abbey would have been approached from the west.[37] The outer courtyard was 167 feet wide and extended 390 feet from the east front, while the Gate Lodge was 49 feet wide.[38] The drawing shows the Lodge to have been of a traditional Tudor design, and unlike the Porch no classical features are evident. It is accessed by raised ramps from the courtyard to a room above the arch, with windows to the front.

The earl also created large stables at the foot of Rowlington Copse, on the opposite side of the river from his new house.[39] This unusual siting of a stable block at a distance from the house was because the earl utilised Washern Barn for the purpose. The barn was built in the fourteenth century and forms the east range of the stables; parts of the original barn remain incorporated into the structure today.[40] This positioning of the stables, though less convenient for the house, gave direct access to the walks, or rides, through Rowlington. The survey of 1566 describes the ten-bay stables with their tiled roof, in which it was possible for eighty horses to stand.[41] It also describes gardens created by Herbert for his new house, including a large Pond Garden. The survey describes this as having 'quinque stagna', five pools, covering four acres, which had been created the previous year (1565) at a cost of £80.[42] The Pond Garden had walks and 'multe arbores fructu',[43] many fruit trees, suggesting that entertainment, appearance, sensual pleasure and exercise were at least as important as fish production.

The Home Park at Wilton, which lies to the south of the house and gardens, on the opposite side of the River Nadder, was enclosed with a park pale and was 600 acres, plus a further 300 acres for the Hare Warren, which was fenced off from the rest of the downland to preserve it for hare coursing.[44] Rowlington Copse is situated within the park. Herbert planted the copse, and the survey describes various enclosures as partly wooded, 'plantatur cum minimis fraxinis', planted with small ash trees, and shrubs of diverse species.[45] On the summit he built a 'Standinge' with 'diverse et pulchre perambulaciones', various and beautiful walks, around it.[46] It was described in the survey as the place 'in quo dominus stare potest ad supervidendum diversa loca pro placito suo', in which the Lord is able to stand to look out over different places for his pleasure.[47] Such a Standing, occupying a prominent position, would be a pavilion or tower from which the hunt was watched, and would usually have a banqueting room.[48] Possibly the Standing at Wilton had banqueting arrangements, as the earl both loved hunting and entertained extensively.

Wilton was a very grand house, suitable for entertaining royalty, and was visited by many monarchs. In 1552, the 1st Earl and fifty horsemen accompanied Edward VI in his progress through the West, and in August entertained the king for a night at Wilton.[49] Queen Elizabeth visited Wilton in September 1574.[50] An account of her visit, written in 1578, describes her being received by the 2nd Earl 'accompanyed with many of his honourable and worshipfull friends, on a fayre, large and playne hill […] about five miles from Wilton'.[51] The Queen proceeded to the house, where:

> her Majesty entered in att the outer gate of Wilton House, a peale of ordnance was discharged on Roulingtoun; and without the inner gate the Countesse, with divers Ladyes and Gentlewomen, meekly received her Highnesse. This utter court was beset on bothe sides the way with the Earles men as thicke as could be standing one by another, through which lane her Grace passed in her chariott, and lighted at the inner gate.[52]

Notes

INTRODUCTION

1 Joyce Youings, *The Dissolution of the Monasteries* (London, 1971), 13.

2 Simon Thurley, *The Building of England* (London, 2013), 15.

3 Ibid., 208.

4 Roger Lockyer and Peter Gaunt, *Tudor and Stuart Britain, 1485-1714*, 4th edn (London, 2019), 13.

5 GW Bernard, *The King's Reformation: Henry VIII and the Remaking of the English Church* (New Haven and London, 2005), 68.

6 David Knowles, *Bare Ruined Choirs: The Dissolution of the English Monasteries* (Cambridge, 1976), 121.

7 Ibid., 122.

8 Ibid., 122-3.

9 Bernard, 245.

10 Ibid.

11 Youings, 38.

12 Ibid.

13 Knowles, 162.

14 Ibid., 163.

15 Ibid., 155.

16 Youings, 38.

17 Knowles, 155.

18 Ibid., 157.

19 'Henry VIII: October 1535, 1-5', in *Letters and Papers, Foreign and Domestic, Henry VIII, Volume 9, August-December 1535*, ed. James Gairdner (London, 1886), 165-181.

20 'Henry VIII: August 1535, 21-25', in *Letters and Papers, Volume 9*, ed. Gairdner, 40-57.

21 Youings, 37-8.

22 Knowles, 158-9.

23 Bernard, 264-5.

24 27 Hen. VIII. cap. 28.

25 Ibid.

26 Ibid.

27 Knowles, 192.

28 *The Statutes of the Realm,* Vol. III (London, 1817), 569-74.

29 Youings, 91.

30 Ibid., 101, 115.

31 Ibid., 55.

32 Ibid., 118-21.

33 Knowles, 234.

34 Youings, 72.

35 Knowles, 241.

36 Ibid.

37 Ibid., 242.

38 Ibid., 238.

39 Bernard, 456.

40 31 Henry VIII, c.13.

41 Ibid.

42 Youings, 87.

43 Bernard, 473.

44 Youings, 88.

45 Knowles, 266.

46 Ibid., 267.

47 Ibid.

48 Ibid.

49 Ibid., 268.

ST PETER'S ABBEY (GLOUCESTER CATHEDRAL)

1 JJ Scarisbrick, *Henry VIII* (London, 1968; new ed. London, 1997), 513.

2 Ibid.

3 Ibid., 514.

4 GW Bernard, *The King's Reformation: Henry VIII and the Remaking of The English Church* (New Haven and London, 2005), 458.

5 'Gloucester: The cathedral and close', in *A History of the County of Gloucester: Volume 4, the City of Gloucester*, ed. NM Herbert (London, 1988), 275-88.

6 Lucy Toulmin Smith, ed., *The Itinerary of John Leland in or about the years 1535-1543 Parts IV and V* (London, 1908), 61.

7 'Houses of Benedictine monks: The abbey of St Peter at Gloucester', in *A History of the County of Gloucester: Volume 2*, ed. William Page (London, 1907), 53-61.

8 David Verey and David Welander, *Gloucester Cathedral* (Gloucester, 1979), 13. 'Houses of Benedictine monks: The abbey of St Peter at Gloucester', in *A History of the County of Gloucester: Volume 2*, ed. Page, 53-61.

9 Simon Jenkins, *England's Cathedrals* (London, 2016), 109.

10 'Houses of Benedictine monks: The abbey of St Peter at Gloucester', in *A History of the County of Gloucester: Volume 2*, ed. Page, 53-61.

11 'Henry VIII: September 1541, 26-30', in *Letters and Papers, Foreign and Domestic, Henry VIII, Volume 16, 1540-1541*, ed. James Gairdner and R H Brodie (London, 1898), 560-77.

12 'Gloucester: Introduction', in *Fasti Ecclesiae Anglicanae 1541-1857: Volume 8, Bristol, Gloucester, Oxford and Peterborough Dioceses*, ed. Joyce M Horn (London, 1996), 35-7.

13 'Gloucester: The cathedral and close', in *A History of the County of Gloucester: Volume 4,* ed. Herbert, 275-88.

14 Simon Thurley, *The Building of England* (London, 2013), 158.

15 Verey and Welander, 115-7.

16 Ibid., 83, 89.

17 Ibid., 89, 93.

18 Historic England List Entry Number 1271714.

19 Historic England List Entry Number 1245957.

20 'Gloucester: The cathedral and close', in *A History of the County of Gloucester: Volume 4,* ed. Herbert, 275-88.

21 Verey and Welander, 98.

22 Ibid., 102.

23 Ibid., 98.

24 'Gloucester: The cathedral and close', in *A History of the County of Gloucester: Volume 4,* ed. Herbert, 275-88.

25 Ibid.

26 Verey and Welander, 104.

27 Historic England List Entry Number 1245896.

28 Historic England List Entry Number 1271599.

29 'Gloucester: The cathedral and close', in *A History of the County of Gloucester: Volume 4,* ed. Herbert, 275-88.

THE COLLEGES

1 Joan Simon, *Education and Society in Tudor England* (Cambridge, 1966), 81-2.

2 GW Bernard, *The King's Reformation: Henry VIII and the Remaking of The English Church* (New Haven and London, 2005), 230.

3 'The colleges and halls: Jesus', in *A History of the County of*

Cambridge and the Isle of Ely: Volume 3, the City and University of Cambridge, ed. JPC Roach (London, 1959), 421-8.

4 Ibid., 421.

5 WG Searle, *The History of the Queens' College of St Margaret and St Bernard in the University of Cambridge, 1446-1560* (London, 1867), 230.

6 Ibid., 231.

7 Ibid., 232.

8 https://www.queens.cam.ac.uk/life-at-queens/about-the-college/college-facts/the-buildings/four-door-hut

9 'Houses of Benedictine monks: Durham College, Oxford', in *A History of the County of Oxford: Volume 2*, ed. William Page (London, 1907), 68-70.

10 'Trinity College', in *A History of the County of Oxford: Volume 3, the University of Oxford*, ed. HE Salter and Mary D Lobel (London, 1954), 238-51.

11 Ibid.

12 'Houses of Benedictine monks: Gloucester College, Oxford', in *A History of the County of Oxford: Volume 2*, ed. Page (London, 1907), 70-1.

13 'Gloucester Hall and Worcester College', in *A History of the County of Oxford: Volume 3*, ed. Salter and Lobel, 298-309.

14 Jennifer Sherwood and Nikolaus Pevsner, *The Buildings of England: Oxfordshire* (Harmondsworth, 1974), 218-21.

15 'Colleges: Buckingham College', in *A History of the County of Cambridge and the Isle of Ely: Volume 2*, ed. LF Salzman (London, 1948), 312.

16 'The colleges and halls: Magdalene', in *A History of the County of Cambridge and the Isle of Ely: Volume 3*, ed. Roach, 450-6.

17 'Houses of Benedictine monks: The abbey of Crowland', in *A History of the County of Lincoln: Volume 2*, ed. William Page (London, 1906), 105-18.

18 Ibid.

19 'Colleges: Buckingham College', in *A History of the County of Cambridge and the Isle of Ely: Volume 2*, ed. Salzman (London, 1948), 312.

20 'Houses of Benedictine monks: The abbey of Crowland', in *A History of the County of Lincoln: Volume 2*, ed. Page, 105-18.

21 'The colleges and halls: Magdalene', in *A History of the County of Cambridge and the Isle of Ely: Volume 3*, ed. Roach, 450-6.

22 Ibid.

23 Damien Riehl Leader, *A History of the University of Cambridge: Volume 1, The University to 1546* (Cambridge, 1988, repr. 1994), 49.

24 RW McDowell, 'Buckingham College', *Proceedings of the Cambridge Antiquarian Society*, 44 (1951), 1-12.

25 'The colleges and halls: Magdalene', in *A History of the County of Cambridge and the Isle of Ely: Volume 3*, ed. Roach, 450-6.

26 'Houses of Benedictine monks: The abbey of Crowland', in *A History of the County of Lincoln: Volume 2*, ed. Page (London, 1906), 105-18.

27 'Henry VIII: April 1542, 26-30', in *Letters and Papers, Foreign and Domestic, Henry VIII, Volume 17, 1542*, ed. James Gairdner and R H Brodie (London, 1900), 153-68.

28 *Oxford Dictionary of National Biography*, https://doi.org/10.1093/ref:odnb/896

29 'The colleges and halls: Magdalene', in *A History of the County of Cambridge and the Isle of Ely: Volume 3*, ed. Roach, 450-6.

30 Historic England List Entry Number: 1125500.

31 Historic England List Entry Number: 1046647.

32 'Houses of Cistercian monks: The college of St Bernard, Oxford', in *A History of the County of Oxford: Volume 2*, ed. Page, 86.

33 Ibid.

34 HM Colvin, 'The Building of St. Bernard's College', in *Oxoniensia: Vol. XXIV* (Oxford, 1959), 37-48, 39.

35 Ibid.

36 'Houses of Cistercian monks: The college of St Bernard, Oxford', in *A History of the County of Oxford: Volume 2*, ed. Page, 86.

37 Colvin, 39.

38 Ibid., 40, 43.

39 Ibid., 43.

40 Ibid.

41 Ibid., 40.

42 'Houses of Cistercian monks: The college of St Bernard, Oxford', in *A History of the County of Oxford: Volume 2*, ed. Page, 86.

43 Colvin, 40.

44 Ibid.

45 Ibid., 41.

46 https://www.sjc.ox.ac.uk/discover/about-college/college-buildings/15th-17th-centuries/

47 Colvin, 41.

48 'Houses of Cistercian monks: The college of St Bernard, Oxford', in *A History of the County of Oxford: Volume 2*, ed. Page, 86.

49 https://www.sjc.ox.ac.uk/discover/about-college/college-buildings/15th-17th-centuries/

50 Sherwood and Pevsner, 196.

51 Ibid.

52 Ibid.

53 https://www.sjc.ox.ac.uk/discover/about-college/college-buildings/15th-17th-centuries/

54 Sherwood and Pevsner, 194, 196.

55 https://www.sjc.ox.ac.uk/discover/about-college/college-buildings/15th-17th-centuries/

56 'St John's College', in *A History of the County of Oxford: Volume 3*, ed. Salter and Lobel, 251-64.

57 National Archives SC11/548 quoted in Colvin, 37.

58 Colvin, 37.

59 Ibid.

60 Ibid.

61 Ibid.

62 Ibid.

63 'St John's College', in *A History of the County of Oxford: Volume 3*, ed. Salter and Lobel, 251-64.

64 *Oxford Dictionary of National Biography*, https://doi.org/10.1093/ref:odnb/29272

65 Ibid.

66 Ibid.

67 'St John's College', in *A History of the County of Oxford: Volume 3*, ed. Salter and Lobel, 251-64.

68 Roger Lockyer and Peter Gaunt, *Tudor and Stuart Britain: 1485-1714*, 4th edn (London, 2019), 157.

69 'St John's College', in *A History of the County of Oxford: Volume 3*, ed. Salter and Lobel, 251-64.

70 Ibid.

71 Ibid.

72 Sherwood and Pevsner, 196.

73 'St John's College', in *A History of the County of Oxford: Volume 3*, ed. Salter and Lobel, 251-64.

74 Colvin, 37.

75 'St John's College', in *A History of the County of Oxford: Volume 3*, ed. Salter and Lobel, 251-64.

76 https://www.sjc.ox.ac.uk/discover/about-college/college-buildings/15th-17th-centuries/

77 'St John's College', in *A History of the County of Oxford:

Volume 3, ed. Salter and Lobel, 251-64.

78 Ibid.

79 Ibid.

80 https://www.sjc.ox.ac.uk/discover/about-college/gardens/

81 William Shakespeare, *Henry VIII,* IV. II.

82 Judith Curthoys, *The Cardinal's College: Christ Church, Chapter and Verse* (London, 2012), 2.

83 'Houses of Augustinian canons: The priory of St Frideswide, Oxford', in *A History of the County of Oxford: Volume 2,* ed. Page, 97-101.

84 Eleanor Chance, Christina Colvin, Janet Cooper, CJ Day, TG Hassall, Mary Jessup and Nesta Selwyn, 'Sites and Remains of Religious Houses', in *A History of the County of Oxford: Volume 4, the City of Oxford,* ed. Alan Crossley and CR Elrington (London, 1979), 364-8.

85 Sherwood and Pevsner, 118.

86 Ibid., 114.

87 Ibid., 118.

88 Ibid., 119-20.

89 Ibid., 123.

90 Chance et al., 364-8.

91 Sherwood and Pevsner, 123-4.

92 'Houses of Augustinian canons: The priory of St Frideswide, Oxford', in *A History of the County of Oxford: Volume 2,* ed. Page, 97-101.

93 Bernard, 228.

94 Ibid., 232.

95 Ibid., 231.

96 *Calendar of State Papers, Domestic Series,* Vol.4, Pt II, ed. JS Brewer (London, 1872), 1594.

97 David Knowles, *Bare Ruined Choirs: The Dissolution of the English Monasteries* (Cambridge, 1976), 59.

98 *Calendar of State Papers, Domestic Series,* Vol.4, PtII, ed. Brewer, 1594.

99 'Henry VIII: April 1524, 11-20', in *Letters and Papers, Foreign and Domestic, Henry VIII, Volume 4, 1524-1530,* ed. JS Brewer (London, 1875), 94-105.

100 'Henry VIII: July 1525, 1-13', in *Letters and Papers, Foreign and Domestic, Henry VIII, Volume 4, 1524-1530,* ed. Brewer, 655-73.

101 Ibid.

102 Chance et al., 364-8.

103 Curthoys, 6.

104 JG Milne and John H Harvey 'The Building of Cardinal College, Oxford' in *Oxoniensa, VIII and IX* (1943-4), 137-53, 138.

105 Ibid., 142-3.

106 Ibid., 142.

107 Ibid., 140.

108 'Henry VIII: July 1525, 1-13', in *Letters and Papers, Foreign and Domestic, Henry VIII, Volume 4, 1524-1530,* ed. Brewer, 655-73.

109 Curthoys, 11.

110 Ibid.

111 'Henry VIII: July 1530, 18-31', in *Letters and Papers, Foreign and Domestic, Henry VIII, Volume 4, 1524-1530,* ed. Brewer, 2934-45.

112 Ibid.

113 Curthoys, 16.

114 Ibid., 18-19.

115 Ibid., 19.

116 Ibid., 2.

117 Ibid., 40.

118 Ibid.,41-42.

119 Ibid., 47.

120 Christ Church', in *A History of the County of Oxford: Volume 3, the University of Oxford,* ed. Salter and Lobel, 228-38.

121 Curthoys, 49, 52.

122 Ibid., 79.

123 John Nichols, *The Progresses and Public Processions of Queen Elizabeth,* 3 vols (London, 1823), I, 208.

124 Ibid.

125 Ibid., 209.

126 Ibid., 210.

127 Ibid., 216.

128 'Friaries: Dominicans, Cambridge', in *A History of the County of Cambridge and the Isle of Ely: Volume 2,* ed. Salzman, 269-76.

129 Alison Dickens, 'A New Building at the Dominican Priory, Emmanuel College, Cambridge, and associated Fourteenth Century Bewsey Floor Tiles' in *Proceedings of the Cambridge Antiquarian Society,* Vol. 87 (1998), 71-80, 75.

130 'Friaries: Dominicans, Cambridge', in *A History of the County of Cambridge and the Isle of Ely: Volume 2,* ed. Salzman, 269-76.

131 William A. Hinnebusch, *The Early English Friars Preachers* (Rome, 1951), 133.

132 Dickens, 75.

133 'Friaries: Dominicans, Cambridge', in *A History of the County of Cambridge and the Isle of Ely: Volume 2,* ed. Salzman, 269-76.

134 Dickens, 74.

135 Mavis Batey, *The Historic Gardens of Oxford and Cambridge* (London, 1989), 15.

136 'Friaries: Dominicans, Cambridge', in *A History of the County of Cambridge and the Isle of Ely: Volume 2,* ed. Salzman, 269-76.

137 'The colleges and halls: Emmanuel', in *A History of the County of Cambridge and the Isle of Ely: Volume 3,* ed. Roach, 474-80.

138 Ibid.

139 *Oxford Dictionary of National Biography,* https://doi.org/10.1093/ref:odnb/18696

140 Ibid.

141 https://www.historyofparliamentonline.org/volume/1558-1603/member/mildmay-sir-walter-1523-89

142 Ibid.

143 *Oxford Dictionary of National Biography,* https://doi.org/10.1093/ref:odnb/18696

144 'Friaries: Dominicans, Cambridge', in *A History of the County of Cambridge and the Isle of Ely: Volume 2,* ed. Salzman, 269-76.

145 Dickens, 75.

146 'Emmanuel College', in *An Inventory of the Historical Monuments in the City of Cambridge* (London, 1959), 61-71.

147 Nikolaus Pevsner, *The Buildings of England: Cambridgeshire* 2nd edn (London, 1970), 69.

148 Ibid.

149 Ibid.

150 'Emmanuel College', in *An Inventory of the Historical Monuments in the City of Cambridge,* 61-71.

151 'The colleges and halls: Emmanuel', in *A History of the County of Cambridge and the Isle of Ely: Volume 3,* ed. Roach, 474-80.

152 Ibid.

153 'Emmanuel College', in *An Inventory of the Historical Monuments in the City of Cambridge,* 61-71.

154 'The colleges and halls: Emmanuel', in *A History of the County of Cambridge and the Isle of Ely: Volume 3,* ed. Roach, 474-80.

155 'Emmanuel College', in *An Inventory of the Historical Monuments in the City of Cambridge,* 61-71.

THE KING'S WORKS

1 Simon Thurley, *Houses of Power* (London, 2017), 181-2.

2 Howard Colvin, ed., *The History of The King's Works, Volume*

IV 1485-1660 (London, 1982), 2, 3.

3 Thurley, *Houses of Power,* 183.

4 Simon Thurley, *The Royal Palaces of Tudor England* (New Haven and London, 1993), 57.

5 Ibid., 56.

6 Thurley, *Houses of Power,* 183.

7 Colvin, 272.

8 Ibid., 3.

9 Ibid., 123-4.

10 Ibid., 124.

11 Ibid., 75.

12 Ibid., 240.

13 Ibid., 234-6.

14 Ibid., 7.

15 'Friaries: The Dominican nuns of Dartford', in *A History of the County of Kent: Volume 2,* ed. William Page (London, 1926), 181-190.

16 Ibid.

17 Ibid.

18 AW Clapham, 'The Priory of Dartford and the Manor House of Henry VIII', in *Archaeological Journal: Volume 83, Issue 1,* 67-85, 68.

19 'Friaries: The Dominican nuns of Dartford', in *A History of the County of Kent: Volume 2,* ed. Page, 181-190.

20 Ibid.

21 Ibid.

22 Ibid.

23 Colvin, 73.

24 Ibid., 68.

25 Ibid.

26 Clapham, 70.

27 Colvin, 70.

28 Ibid., 71.

29 Ibid., 70.

30 Clapham, 71.

31 Thurley, *The Royal Palaces of Tudor England,* 119.

32 Symondson's Estate Map of Dartford, 1596, Rochester Bridge Warden's Trust.

33 Colvin, 70.

34 Clapham, 71.

35 Colvin, 71.

36 Ibid., 70.

37 Thurley, *The Royal Palaces of Tudor England,* 161.

38 Colvin, 70.

39 Ibid., 71.

40 Ibid.

41 PW Borcham, *Dartford's Royal Manor House* (Dartford,1991), 15.

42 'Henry VIII: September 1542, 26-30', in *Letters and Papers, Foreign and Domestic, Henry VIII, Volume 17, 1542,* ed. James Gairdner and R H Brodie (London, 1900), 463-511.

43 Colvin, 71.

44 Ibid.

45 Boreham, 19.

46 Colvin, 72.

47 Timothy Easton, 'The Painting of Historic Brick', *Weald and Downland Open Air Museum Magazine* (Spring 2001), 26-8.

48 'Henry VIII: June 1545, 21-25', in *Letters and Papers, Foreign and Domestic, Henry VIII, Volume 20 Part 1, January-July 1545,* ed. James Gairdner and RH Brodie (London, 1905), 484-99.

49 'Friaries: The Dominican nuns of Dartford', in *A History of the County of Kent: Volume 2,* ed. Page, 181-190.

50 Ibid.

51 Boreham, 55.

52 Peter Durrant and John Painter, *Reading and the Abbey Quarter* (Reading, 2018), 16.

53 'Houses of Benedictine monks: The abbey of Reading', in *A History of the County of Berkshire: Volume 2,* ed. PH Ditchfield and William Page (London, 1907), 62-73.

54 William of Malmesbury *The History of the Kings of England,* trans. Rev John Sharpe (London, 1815), 509.

55 'Houses of Benedictine monks: The abbey of Reading', in *A History of the County of Berkshire: Volume 2,* ed. Ditchfield and Page, 62-73.

56 Durrant and Painter, 56.

57 Ibid., 42.

58 Ibid., 35.

59 'Houses of Benedictine monks: The abbey of Reading', in *A History of the County of Berkshire: Volume 2,* ed. Ditchfield and Page, 62-73.

60 Ibid.

61 Durrant and Painter, 40.

62 Ibid., 44.

63 Ibid., 47.

64 'Houses of Benedictine monks: The abbey of Reading', in *A History of the County of Berkshire: Volume 2,* ed. Ditchfield and Page, 62-73.

65 Ibid.

66 Ibid.

67 Ibid.

68 Ibid.

69 Ron Baxter, *The Royal Abbey of Reading* (Woodbridge, 2016), 128.

70 Ibid., 127.

71 Colvin, 220.

72 Baxter,138.

73 Colvin, 220.

74 Ibid., 221.

75 http://www.berkshirehistory.com/castles/abbey_house.html

76 Colvin, 221.

77 Baxter, 144.

78 http://www.berkshirehistory.com/castles/abbey_house.html

79 'Houses of Benedictine monks: The abbey of Reading', in *A History of the County of Berkshire: Volume 2,* ed. Ditchfield and Page, 62-73.

80 Durrant and Painter, 60.

81 Colvin, 36, 221.

82Ibid., 36, 222.

83 http://www.berkshirehistory.com/castles/abbey_house.html

84 Ibid.

85 Colvin, 36, 221.

86 http://www.berkshirehistory.com/castles/abbey_house.html

87 'Houses of Benedictine monks: The abbey of St Augustine, Canterbury', in *A History of the County of Kent: Volume 2,* ed. Page, 126-133.

88 Ibid.

89 Tim Tatton-Brown and Margaret Sparks, *St Augustine's Abbey and the Royal Palace* (Canterbury, 1984), 1.

90 Ibid., 3.

91 'Houses of Benedictine monks: The abbey of St Augustine, Canterbury', in *A History of the County of Kent: Volume 2,* ed. Page, 126-133.

92 Tatton-Brown and Sparks, 3.

93 Ibid.

94 'Houses of Benedictine monks: The abbey of St Augustine, Canterbury', in *A History of the County of Kent: Volume 2,* ed. Page 126-133.

95 Joyce Youings, *The Dissolution of the Monasteries* (London,

1971), 63, 64.

96 Ibid., 67.

97 Edward Hasted, 'The abbey of St Augustine: Abbots', in *The History and Topographical Survey of the County of Kent: Volume 12* (Canterbury, 1801), 177-225.

98 'Henry VIII: August 1538 26-31', in *Letters and Papers, Foreign and Domestic, Henry VIII, Volume 13 Part 2, August-December 1538*, ed. James Gairdner (London, 1893), 75-101.

99 Richard Gem, ed., *St Augustine's Abbey, Canterbury* (London, 1997), 143.

100 Ibid.

101 Youings, 67-71.

102 Colvin, 59.

103 Thurley, *Houses of Power*, 183, 184.

104 Tatton-Brown and Sparks, 3.

105 Colvin, 60.

106 H. U. Potts, 'The Plan of St Austin's Abbey, Canterbury', *Archaeologia Cantiana*, Vol.46 (1934), 179-94.

107 Colvin, 60.

108 Potts, 179-94.

109 Colvin, 60.

110 Ibid.

111 Ibid.

112 Ibid.

113 Ibid., 61.

114 Ibid.

115 Ibid., 60.

116 Thurley, *Houses of Power*, 183.

117 Colvin, 61, 62.

118 Ibid., 61.

119 Gem, 144.

120 Tatton-Brown and Sparks, 3.

INTRODUCTION TO THE HOUSES

1 Penry Williams, *The Later Tudors: England 1547-1603* (Oxford, 1995), 124.

2 Eric Ives, 'Henry VIII: The Political Perspective', in Diarmaid MacCullough, ed., *The Reign of Henry VIII: Politics, Policy and Piety* (London, 1995), 18.

3 Ibid., 13.

BATTLE ABBEY

1 Jonathan Coad, *Battle Abbey and Battlefield, English Heritage Guidebook* (Swindon, 2017), 41.

2 https://www.british-history.ac.uk/letters-papers-hen8/vol13/no2/75-101

3 Sir Whistler Webster demolished it before his death in 1779. The 6th Viscount Montague had sold the Battle Abbey estate to Sir Thomas Webster in 1721. The drawing is reproduced in Coad, 7.

4 The Grimm view is illustrated in Coad, 16.

5 The Grimm west view is reproduced in Coad, 43.

6 Brakspear's architectural drawings for the restoration are in the Wiltshire & Swindon History Centre, 2512/310/99PC: 'Battle Abbey, Sussex. Excavations, alterations and repairs 1924-1934'.

BEAULIEU ABBEY

1 David A. Hinton 'Excavation at Beaulieu Abbey, 1977' in *Proceedings of the Hampshire Field Club and Archaeological Society,* Vol. 34 for 1977 (July 1978), 49-52, 50.

2 WH St John Hope and H Brakspear, 'The Cistercian Abbey of Beaulieu in the County of Southampton', in *The Archaeological Journal, Vol.63* (1906), 129-186, 142.

3 'Houses of Cistercian monks: Abbey of Beaulieu', in *A History of the County of Hampshire: Volume 2,* ed. H Arthur Doubleday and William Page (London, 1903), 140-6.

4 Ibid.

5 Ibid.

6 Ibid.

7 Ibid.

8 *The Account-Book of Beaulieu Abbey,* ed. by S.F. Hockey (London, 1975), 10.

9 St John Hope and Brakspear, 140.

10 *The Account-Book of Beaulieu Abbey,* 44-5.

11 Ibid., 45, 204, 205.

12 Quoted in Paul Meyvaert, 'The Medieval Monastic Garden', in Elizabeth McDougall, ed., *Medieval Gardens* (Dumbarton Oaks, 1986), 28.

13 St John Hope and Brakspear, 148.

14 Ibid.

15 *The Account-Book of Beaulieu Abbey,* 3.

16 St John Hope and Brakspear, 148.

17 Ibid., 147.

18 Ibid., 162.

19 'Houses of Cistercian monks: Abbey of Beaulieu', in *A History of the County of Hampshire: Volume 2*, ed. Doubleday and Page, 140-6.

20 Ibid.

21 Lord Montagu of Beaulieu, *Beaulieu: Palace House and Abbey* (1978), 27.

22 'Houses of Cistercian monks: Abbey of Beaulieu', in *A History of the County of Hampshire: Volume 2*, ed. Doubleday and Page, 140-6.

23 Ibid.

24 'Henry VIII: Grants in July', in *Letters and Papers, Foreign and Domestic, Henry VIII, Volume 13 Part 1, January-July 1538*, ed. James Gairdner (London, 1892), 561-89.

25 Ralph Montagu and Mary Montagu-Scott, 'From Gate House to Palace House', *Beaulieu History Society Newsletter*, No.55, February 2015, 4.

26 Ibid., 5.

27 St John Hope and Brakspear, 166-7.

28 Ibid., 167.

29 Ibid.

30 Ibid., 168.

31 Susan Tomkins, 'James I, 3rd Earl of Southampton and Beaulieu', *Beaulieu History Society Newsletter*, No.5, June 2007, 6.

BINDON ABBEY

1 This is an updated and expanded version of an account concentrating solely on the garden at Bindon, which first appeared in Timothy Mowl, *Historic Gardens of Dorset* (Stroud, 2003), 15-25.

2 John Hutchins, *The History and Antiquities of the County of Dorset*, 3rd edn, 4 vols (London, 1861), 1, 356.

3 Dorset Record Office, Dorchester, D-WLC/T3.

4 Quoted in Josephine M Bohs, *A Short History of Bindon Abbey, Dorset*, undated and unpaginated (Dorset Record Office, D1-OY/13).

5 Harold Brakspear drew a ground plan of the complex for his projected history of the Cistercian Abbeys in England (Wiltshire and Swindon History Centre, Chippenham, 2512/MS/340/1).

6 For Lulworth see Jean Manco, David Greenhalf & Mark Girouard, 'Lulworth Castle in the seventeenth century', *Architectural History*, vol. 34 (1991), 145-170.

7 For Cecil's garden at Theobalds see Paula Henderson, *The Tudor House and Garden: Architecture and Landscape in the Sixteenth and Early Seventeenth Centuries* (New Haven and

London, 2005), 85.

8 Quoted in Roy Strong, *The Renaissance Garden in England* (London, 1979), 53.

9 Dorset Record Office, D-WLC/P/76/1.

10 Dorset Record Office, D-WLC/P/76/2.

11 Hutchins, 353.

12 Dorset Record Office, D/WLC/AF27-32.

13 Dorset Record Office, Ron/17/2/1: Transcript of Weld Family Accounts concerning Bindon Abbey.

14 Hutchins, 353.

15 John Newman & Nikolaus Pevsner, *The Buildings of England: Dorset* (Harmondsworth, 1972), 94.

16 We are grateful to Joanne Jenner for allowing us access to the site.

BISHAM ABBEY

1 From: 'Parishes: Bisham', *A History of the County of Berkshire: Volume 3*, ed. PH Ditchfield and William Page, (London, 1923), 139-52.

2 Ibid.

3 Thomas Hoby, *The Travels and life of Sir Thomas Hoby [...].* ed. Edgar Powell (London,1906), xviii, xix.

4 Martin Heale, *The Abbots and Priors of Late Medieval and Reformation England* (Oxford, 2016), 294.

5 'Houses of Austin canons: The priory of Bisham', in *A History of the County of Berkshire: Volume 2*, ed. PH Ditchfield and William Page (London, 1907), 82-5.

6 Ibid.

7 Ibid.

8 ET Long, *Bisham Abbey, Berks* (pamphlet reprinted from three articles which appeared in the issues of *Country Life,* 12, 19, and 26 April, 1941), 4, 5.

9 'Parishes: Bisham', *A History of the County of Berkshire: Volume 3*, ed. Ditchfield and Page, 139-52.

10 Hoby, xviii, xix.

11 *Oxford Dictionary of National Biography,* http://www.oxforddnb.com/view/article/13413

12 Jonathan Woolfson, *Padua and the Tudors: English Students in Italy 1485-1603* (Cambridge, 1998), 246.

13 From: 'Parishes: Bisham', *A History of the County of Berkshire: Volume 3*, ed. Ditchfield and Page, 139-152.

14 From: 'Cecil Papers: 1553', *Calendar of the Cecil Papers in Hatfield House, Volume 1: 1306-1571*, (London, 1883), 106-34.

15 Woolfson, 246.

16 *Oxford Dictionary of National Biography,* http://www.oxforddnb.com/view/article/13413

17 *Oxford Dictionary of National Biography,* http://www.oxforddnb.com/view/article/13414

18 Edward Chaney, *The Evolution of the Grand Tour* (London and New York, 1998), 69.

19 Clare Howard, *English Travellers of the Renaissance* (London and New York, 1914), 24.

20 Hoby, x.

21 Long, 11.

22 Hoby, xi.

23 Ibid., xxi-xxii.

24 Nikolaus Pevsner, *The Buildings of England: Berkshire* (London, 1966; repr. 1993), 89.

25 Ibid.

26 Long, 8.

27 Pevsner, 89, 90.

28 Long, 9.

29 Hoby, xviii.

30 Piers Compton, *The Story of Bisham Abbey* (Maidenhead,

1973), 65.

31 Howard Colvin, *Essays in English Architectural History* (New Haven and London, 1999), 61.

32 From: 'Cecil Papers: 1557', *Calendar of the Cecil Papers in Hatfield House, Volume 1*, 138-46.

33 Hoby, 126.

34 Ibid.

35 James Lees-Milne, *Tudor Renaissance* (London, 1951), 53.

36 Long, 5.

37 Girouard, *Elizabethan Architecture, Its Rise and Fall* (New Haven and London, 2009), 138.

38 Pevsner, 89.

39 Hoby, 112.

40 Simon Thurley, *The Royal Palaces of Tudor England* (New Haven and London, 1999), 14, 15.

41 Ibid., 15.

42 Hoby, 121.

43 Ibid., 129.

44 For a discussion on rooftop turrets, see Paula Henderson, 'Life at the Top', *Country Life* (January 3, 1985), 6-9. Also see Henderson, *The Tudor House and Garden: Architecture and Landscape in the Sixteenth and Early Seventeenth Centuries* (New Haven and London, 2005), 213-4.

45 Girouard, 174.

46 Margaret Whinney, *Sculpture in Britain, 1530-1830* (Harmondsworth, 1964), 9.

47 Inscription, Hoby tomb, All Saints Church, Bisham, Berkshire.

BRUTON ABBEY

1 Information on Bruton Tower is taken from an unpublished report carried out for the National Trust by AHC Consultants, 2010.

2 This is illustrated in Colin Clark, *A Bruton Camera*, (Bruton, 1994), 13.

3 *A History of the County of Somerset*, Volume 2, ed. William Page (London, 1911), 134, citing Dorset Record Office, D/FSI, box 76.

4 Phyllis Couzens, *Bruton in Selwood: Some account of its history* (Bruton, 1972), 48.

5 *A History of the County of Somerset*, Volume 7, ed. CJR Currie and RW Dunning (London, 1999), 25.

6 From a report of a paper on Bruton given by JG Bord to the Somerset Archaeological and Natural History Society, published in their *Proceedings during the Years 1856-7*, vol. 7, p. 11.

7 *A History of the County of Somerset*, Volume 2, ed. Page, 135.

8 Ibid., 136.

9 Thomas Hearne ed., *The Itinerary of John Leland the Antiquary*, 9 vols (London, 1770), 1, 74.

10 The copy is held in Special Collections, University of Bristol Library, to whom we are grateful for their reproduction here. There are four further, larger-scale watercolours of the mansion at Stourhead House.

11 I am indebted to Christopher Francis and David Miller for sourcing this, and the following quotation and for help with the translations.

12 The *History of the County of Somerset*, Volume 2, 138, states: 'The house was certainly a house of scholars, five at least were graduates of the University of Oxford, two were Bachelors of Divinity (Harte and Dunster) and Wilton was an MA; Ely and Bishop were Bas.'

13 Wiltshire & Swindon History Centre, Chippenham (hereafter WSHC), 383/995 and 383/996: Letters Patent, 1546 and 1550.

14 *A History of the County of Somerset*, Volume 7, ed. Currie and Dunning, 25.

15 Somerset Record Office, Taunton, DD\BRU\7/1: Eighteenth-century Plan of the 'Mansion' copied from the Hoares' papers in WSHC.

16 WSHC, 383/142.

17 This accounts for the presence at Stourhead House of the four larger-scale watercolours.

18 WSHC, 383/143.

BUCKLAND ABBEY

1 J Brooking Rowe, 'The Cistercian Houses of Devon I Buckland in *Report and Transactions of the Devonshire Association,* Vol. VII (1875), 329- 366, 334.

2 *Buckland Abbey* (Swindon, 1991), 28.

3 Crispin Gill, *Buckland Abbey* (Plymouth, 1951), 16.

4 Bridget Cheery and Nikolaus Pevsner, *The Buildings of England: Devon* (New Haven and London, 2004), 228.

5 Rowe, 336.

6 Annie Bullen, *Buckland Abbey* (Swindon, 2018), 9.

7 *Buckland Abbey,* 30, 31.

8 Bullen, 9.

9 Cheery and Pevsner, 229.

10 Rowe, 339.

11 Ibid., 341-2.

12 Ibid., 342.

13 Ibid.

14 Ibid., 343.

15 National Archives, Kew, E318/510.

16 Joyce Youings, *The Dissolution of the Monasteries* (London,1971), 235.

17 *Buckland Abbey,* 34.

18 *Oxford Dictionary of National Biography,* https://doi.org/10.1093/ref:odnb/11493

19 Ibid.

20 Ibid.

21 Ibid.

22 Sir Walter Raleigh, 'The truth of the fight about the Isles of Azores …' in Richard Hakluyt, *Voyages and Discoveries* (Harmondsworth, 1972: repr. 1985), 355-60, 355-6, 360.

23 *Buckland Abbey,* 37.

24 Ibid., 18.

25 Cheery and Pevsner, 227.

26 Bullen, 24.

27 Ibid., 24, 25.

28 Cheery and Pevsner, 229.

29 *Buckland Abbey,* 37.

30 Joyce Youings, 'Drake, Grenville and Buckland Abbey'. *Transactions of the Devonshire Association,* Vol.112 (1980), 95-99, 95.

31 Ibid., 97.

32 Bullen, 31.

33 Historic England List Entry Number 1163369.

34 Cheery and Pevsner, 228.

35 Bullen, 35.

36 Alex Cumming, *Buckland Abbey* (Norwich, 1972), 6.

37 *Buckland Abbey,* 48.

BUILDWAS ABBEY

1 David M Robinson, *Buildwas Abbey* (Swindon, 2002), 31.

2 Shropshire Archives, Shrewsbury, 212, Box 452.

3 Shropshire Archives, 2089/1/2/2.

4 Ibid.

5 Shropshire Archives, 2089/1/2/3. The modern spelling for the family surname is Grey, but Gray is retained here to accord with the documentation.

6 Shakespeare Birthplace Trust, Stratford, DR 473/292: contemporary copy of document relating to the lordship of Powys and the estates of Edward Grey.

7 This is the interpretation made by David Robinson, 33.

8 Shropshire Archives, 2089/1/2/6.

9 Shropshire Archives, PR/2/76.

10 Shropshire Archives, 6344/B: 'A mappe of the Manor of Buyldwas being part of the lands & possessions of Sir William Acton knight & Baronett'.

11 Shropshire Archives, 2089/1/244.

12 Shropshire Archives, 2089/1/210.

13 John Britton, *Architectural Antiquities of Great Britain*, vol. 4 (London,1814), 74.

14 Ibid. Walter Moseley died in 1712.

15 Sabrina is Goddess of the Severn.

COMBE ABBEY

1 Historically the name was spelled 'Combe', but 'Coombe' has become the modern form.

2 'Houses of Cistercian monks: Abbey of Combe', in *A History of the County of Warwick: Volume 2*, ed. William Page (London, 1908), 73-5.

3 Ibid.

4 Warwick Rodwell, 'Combe Abbey: From Cistercian Abbey to Country House' in *Coventry: Medieval Art, Architecture and Archaeology in the City and its Vicinity, The British Archaeological Association Conference Transactions XXXIII,* Linda Monckton and Richard K Morris, eds (Leeds, 2011), 286-303, 292.

5 Ibid., 296.

6 Ibid.

7 Ibid., 293.

8 Ibid., 288-295.

9 'Houses of Cistercian monks: Abbey of Combe', in *A History of the County of Warwick: Volume 2*, ed. Page, 73-75.

10 Ibid.

11 Ibid.

12 'Letters and Papers: January 1539, 21-25', in *Letters and Papers, Foreign and Domestic, Henry VIII, Volume 14 Part 1, January-July 1539,* ed. James Gairdner and R H Brodie (London, 1894), 41-51.

13 'Houses of Cistercian monks: Abbey of Combe', in *A History of the County of Warwick: Volume 2*, ed. Page, 73-75.

14 'Letters and Papers: January 1539, 21-25', in *Letters and Papers, Foreign and Domestic, Henry VIII, Volume 14 Part 1, January-July 1539,* ed. Gairdner and Brodie, 41-51.

15 Ibid.

16 Rodwell, 288.

17 'Parishes: Combe Fields', in *A History of the County of Warwick: Volume 6, Knightlow Hundred,* ed. LF Salzman (London, 1951), 72-74.

18 *Oxford Dictionary of National Biography,* https://doi.org/10.1093/ref:odnb/15257

19 Rodwell, 288.

20 *Oxford Dictionary of National Biography,* https://doi.org/10.1093/ref:odnb/12327

21 Rodwell, 288.

22 Ibid.

23 Nadine Akkerman, ed. *The Correspondence of Elizabeth Stuart, Queen of Bohemia,* 3 vols (Oxford, 2011, 2015, -) I, 8, 19.

24 *Oxford Dictionary of National Biography,* https://doi.org/10.1093/ref:odnb/12327

25 Rodwell, 288.

26 Ibid., 298.

27 Ibid., 298-9.

28 Ibid., 288.

29 Ibid., 286.
30 Ibid., 288-97.
31 Ibid. 299.
32 Ibid., 288-98.
33 Ibid., 288-92.

COMBERMERE ABBEY
1 *A History of the County of Cheshire*, Volume 3, ed. CR Elrington and BE Harris (London, 1980), 151.
2 Ibid., 154.
3 Letters and Papers, August 1539, 16-31, in *Letters and Papers, Foreign and Domestic, Henry VIII,* Vol. 14, Part 2, ed. James Gairdner and RH Brodie (London, 1895), 16-34.
4 Nikolaus Pevsner & Edward Hubbard, *The Buildings of England: Cheshire* (London, 1971), 181.
5 Ibid.
6 Ibid.
7 Daniel & Samuel Lysons, *Magna Britannica*, Vol. 2, part 2 (London, 1810), 479.
8 Charles Hulbert, *Memorials of Departed Ages* (London, 1844), 40.
9 *A History of the County of Cheshire*, Volume 3, ed. Elrington and Harris, 155.
10 Peter de Figueiredo & Julian Treuherz, *Cheshire Country Houses* (Bognor Regis, 1988), 60.
11 Ibid.
12 John Martin Robinson, 'Combermere Abbey, Cheshire', *Country Life*, 6 January 1994.
13 RE Howard, RR Laxton & CD Litton, 'Tree-Ring Analysis of Oak Timbers from Combermere Abbey, Whitchurch, Cheshire', Centre for Archaeology Report 83/2003, English Heritage, 2003.
14 Ibid., figure 3.
15 *A History of the County of Cheshire*, Volume 3, ed. Elrington and Harris, 154.
16 The painting hangs on the staircase at Combermere. We are grateful to Sarah and Peter Callander Beckett for allowing us to reproduce an image of it here.
17 John Harris, *The Artist and the Country House* (London, 1979), plate 137.
18 These are similar in style to work by Robert Bakewell; see Ifor Edwards, *Davies Brothers: Gatesmiths* (Cardiff, 1977), 19.
19 Quoted in 'Combermere Abbey Design & Access the North Wing – An Assessment of the Chronology of its Construction and Alteration', Arrol Architects, 5 June 2002. We are grateful to Andrew Arrol for supplying us with this manuscript document and for an informed tour of the house.
20 Robinson.

FORDE ABBEY
1 Christian Tyler, *Forde Abbey – The Story Behind the Stones* (Wimborne, 2017), 36.
2 Ibid., 39.
3 Ibid.
4 Ibid., 50.
5 Ibid., 55.
6 Quoted in Tyler, 38.
7 For Prideaux's work see Timothy Mowl & Brian Earnshaw, *Architecture Without Kings – The rise of Puritan classicism under Cromwell* (Manchester and New York, 1995), 106-7.

HAILES ABBEY
1 Sir James K Fowler, *Hayles and Beaulieu, A Brief History and Guide to Hayles Abbey, A Daughter-House of Beaulieu* (London, 1928), 51.
2 Ibid.

3 Ibid.
4 Wellbore St Clair Baddeley, *A Cotteswold Shrine* (Gloucester, 1908), 121.
5 Ibid., 118.
6 *A History of the County of Gloucestershire*, Volume 2, ed. William Page (London, 1907), 98.
7 Ibid., 98.
8 St Clair Baddeley, 59.
9 Fowler, 51.
10 Ibid., 66.
11 Nicholas Kingsley, *The Country Houses of Gloucestershire, Volume One: 1500-1660* (Bognor Regis, 1989), 99.
12 Fowler, 30-1. Brakspear's plan is a lithograph taken from his own drawing preserved in a projected history of Cistercian sites in England: Wiltshire & Swindon History Centre, Chippenham, 2512/340/1MS.
13 Michael Carter, *English Heritage: Hailes Abbey*, (Swindon, 2017), 25.
14 National Archives, Kew, MF 1/59.
15 Christopher Morris ed., *The Illustrated Journey of Celia Fiennes c.1682-c.1712* (London, 1982), 54.
16 The watercolour is owned by the National Trust and on loan to the Cheltenham Art Gallery & Museum.
17 James Joel Cartwright ed., 'The Travels through England of Dr Richard Pococke', *Camden Society*, 2 vols (London, 1889), 2, 276.
18 Ibid.
19 Samuel Lysons, *A Collection of Gloucestershire Antiquities* (London, 1794) plate 54.

LACOCK ABBEY
1 The hallowing of the Abbey in 1232 was celebrated 700 years later on 3 September 1932 with the Lacock Pageant in which Miss Matilda Talbot, then in ownership and suitably dressed in mediaeval costume, took the part of Ela, Countess of Salisbury (Wiltshire & Swindon History Centre, Chippenham, 2664/2/2F /10BW). Ela is buried in the South Cloister, her remains having been transferred there from the Abbey Church.
2 The sketch is in the Royal Collection, RCIN 912241.
3 Wiltshire & Swindon History Centre, 2664/3/1H/49, no. 1.
4 Sharington's portrait hangs in the South Gallery.
5 A 'restored arrangement' of the tiled pavement is illustrated in J Alfred Gotch, *Early Renaissance Architecture in England* 2nd rev. edn (London, 1914), plates 37 & 38.
6 Harold Brakspear, 'Lacock Abbey, Wilts', *Archaeologia*, vol. LVII (1900), 125-158; 126.
7 Ibid., 127.
8 John Gough Nichols ed., 'History from Marble […] by Thomas Dingley', *Camden Society*, 2 vols (London, 1867-8) 2, cccciii.
9 Ibid., ccccv.
10 The map is held at Lacock: NT 1545624.
11 Harold Brakspear noted this similarity when he visited Dudley in 1906. His letter of 22 April of that year (Wiltshire and Swindon History Centre, 2664/3/1H/49, no. 27) to Charles Henry Talbot states: 'I have been to Dudley where, though Chapman's chimney piece does not exist, the work is most interesting & much of the character of Lacock in the proportion of the windows & the charming gallery that connected the wings at either end of the hall.'
12 This layout is recorded on a map of 1764 (W&SHC, 2664/1/ 2E/19L); it is discussed and illustrated in Timothy Mowl, *Historic Gardens of Wiltshire* (Stroud, 2004), 53-5.
13 Similar windows light the south wall of the former Frater. These features and their authorship by the mason John Chapman or, indeed, by Sharington himself are discussed by WG Clark-

Maxwell, 'Sir William Sharington's Work at Lacock, Sudeley and Dudley', *The Archaeological Journal*, Vol. 70 (1913), 175-182.

14 Nichols ed., cccccv.

15 Thelma E Vernon, 'Inventory of Sir Henry Sharington: Contents of Lacock House, 1575', *Wiltshire Archaeological & Natural History Magazine*, Vol. 63 (1968), 79-82.

16 Sir Anthony Mildmay of Apethorpe Hall, Northamptonshire, was Sir Henry Sharington's son-in-law, married to his second daughter, Grace.

17 The Sea-dog Table dates from about 1575 and is directly related to designs by Jacques Androuet du Cerceau; see Timothy Mowl, *Elizabethan & Jacobean Style* (London, 1993), 16-18.

18 The Table Fountain design is in the Kunstmuseum in Basel, Switzerland, and the drawing of Denny's Clocksalt is in the British Museum; both are illustrated in Susan Foister, *Holbein in England* (London, 2006), plates 90 & 83 respectively.

19 We are most grateful to Sonia Jones, Curator at Lacock, for bringing these to our attention.

20 See CH Talbot, 'On a Letter of Sir William Sharington to Sir John Thynne, June 25th, 1553', *The Wiltshire Archaeological and Natural History Magazine*, Vol. 26 (1892), 50-1.

21 David Adshead, 'Sir William Sharington's Tower: A tale of two tables at Lacock Abbey, Wiltshire', *National Trust ABC Bulletin* (Summer, 2013), 17-19; 17.

22 Quoted in Mark Girouard, 'The Development of Longleat House between 1546 and 1572', *Journal of the Royal Archaeological Institute*, Vol. 116 (1959), 201-25; 205. The full text of the letter is given in Talbot, 50-1.

23 Gotch gives an approximate date of between 1550 and Sharington's death in 1553 for the tiled pavement and, by inference, the two tables in Sharington's tower, possibly because he is incorrectly informed about the date of Sharington's marriage to his third wife Grace Paget. Both Mark Girouard, *Life in the English Country House: A Social and Architectural History* (London, 1978), 106, and David Adshead follow this dating, while it is clear that Sharington married Grace in 1542 and is likely to have celebrated the union in the furnishing of his tower.

24 Adshead, 17-19.

25 Nikolaus Pevsner, *The Buildings of England: Wiltshire* rev. edn. (Harmondsworth, 1975), 287.

26 Holbein's design for a chimneypiece for Henry VIII is in the British Museum; the Erasmus portrait is in a private collection; both are illustrated in Foister, plates 102 & 12 respectively.

27 Mark Girouard, *Elizabethan Architecture Its Rise and Fall: 1540-1640* (London, 2009), 150.

LEEZ PRIORY

1 'Houses of Austin canons: Priory of Little Leighs', in *A History of the County of Essex: Volume 2*, ed. William Page and J Horace Round (London, 1907), 155-7.

2 A. W. Clapham, 'The Augustinian Priory of Little Leez and the Mansion of Leez Priory' in *Transactions of the Essex Archaeological Society*, Vol. XIII (3) (1901), 200-217; 206-7.

3 Ibid., 207-8.

4 Ibid., 206.

5 Ibid., 209.

6 Ibid., 207.

7 Ibid., 210.

8 'Houses of Austin canons: Priory of Little Leighs', in *A History of the County of Essex: Volume 2*, ed. Page and Round, 155-7.

9 Ibid.

10 Ibid.

11 Ibid.

12 *Oxford Dictionary of National Biography*,

https://doi.org/10.1093/ref:odnb/23491

13 Ibid.

14 Ibid.

15 Ibid.

16 Ibid.

17 Clapham, 211.

18 Ibid., 214.

19 Historic England: List Entry Number 1013148.

20 Clapham, 214-5.

21 Mary Hill Cole, *The Portable Queen: Elizabeth I and the Politics of Ceremony* (Amherst MA, 1999), 181.

22 'Little Leighs', in *An Inventory of the Historical Monuments in Essex, Volume 2, Central and South west* (London, 1921), 157-62.

23 Clapham, 206.

24 Historic England: List Entry Number 1112814.

LEWES PRIORY

1 Helen Poole, *Lewes Priory: The Site and its History* (Lewes, 2000), 12.

2 Graham Mayhew, *The Monks of Saint Pancras: Lewes Priory, England's Premier Cluniac Monastery and its Dependencies 1076-1537* (Lewes, 2014), 11.

3 Poole, 7.

4 Ibid., 13.

5 Mayhew, 56.

6 Poole, 15.

7 Mayhew, 58.

8 Ibid., 82.

9 Ibid., 61.

10 WH St John Hope, 'The Cluniac Priory of St. Pancras at Lewes' in *Sussex Archeological Collections relating to the History and Antiquities of the County* Vol. XLIX (Lewes, 1906), 82.

11 Ibid.

12 Mayhew, 59.

13 Ibid., 74.

14 Ibid., 72.

15 Ibid.

16 Ibid.

17 Ibid., 59.

18 Ibid., 427.

19 Joyce Youings, *The Dissolution of the Monasteries* (London, 1971), 65.

20 'Henry VIII: February 1538, 21-28', in *Letters and Papers, Foreign and Domestic, Henry VIII, Volume 13 Part 1, January-July 1538*, ed. James Gairdner (London, 1892), 124-42.

21 Mayhew, 436.

22 http://www.histparl.ac.uk/volume/1509-1558/member/cromwell-gregory-1516-51

23 St John Hope, 74.

24 Ibid., 75.

25 Ibid.

26 Ibid., 77-8.

27 Ibid., 79-80.

28 Mayhew, 440.

29 St John Hope, 87.

30 Ibid.

31 Mayhew, 80.

32 St John Hope, 87.

33 East Sussex Record Office. ACC 2187.

34 St John Hope, 81.

35 Mayhew, 79.

36 Ibid., 440.

37 Edward Town, *A House Re-edified: Thomas Sackville and the transformation of Knole 1605-1608* (unpubl. DPhil thesis, Univer-

sity of Sussex, 2010), 67-9.
38 Mayhew, 443.
39 Ibid.

LONDON CHARTERHOUSE

1 'Religious Houses: House of Carthusian monks', in *A History of the County of Middlesex: Volume 1*, ed. JS Cockburn, HPF King and KGT McDonnell (London, 1969), 159-69.
2 Ibid.
3 Ibid.
4 Julian Luxford, 'Carthusian Monasticism and the London Charterhouse', in *Revealing the Charterhouse*, ed. Cathy Ross (London, 2016), 42.
5 Stephen Porter, *Charterhouse: The Official Guide* (Stroud, 2010), 19.
6 'Religious Houses: House of Carthusian monks', in *A History of the County of Middlesex: Volume 1*, ed. Cockburn, King and McDonnell, 159-169.
7 Ibid.
8 Ibid.
9 Ibid.
10 Ibid.
11 Ibid.
12 Ibid.
13 'Henry VIII: April 1545, 26-30', in *Letters and Papers, Foreign and Domestic, Henry VIII, Volume 20 Part 1, January-July 1545*, ed. James Gairdner and R H Brodie (London, 1905), 278-329.
14 *Oxford Dictionary of National Biography*, https://doi.org/10.1093/ref:odnb/20300
15 http://www.histparl.ac.uk/volume/1509-1558/member/north-edward-1504-64
16 *Oxford Dictionary of National Biography*, https://doi.org/10.1093/ref:odnb/20300
17 http://www.histparl.ac.uk/volume/1509-1558/member/north-edward-1504-64
18 *Oxford Dictionary of National Biography*, https://doi.org/10.1093/ref:odnb/20300
19 Ibid.
20 Porter, *Charterhouse: The Official Guide*, 38.
21 Ibid.,19.
22 Stephen Porter, 'The Courtyard House' in *Revealing the Charterhouse*, ed. Ross, 69.
23 Porter, *Charterhouse: The Official Guide*, 22.
24 Philip Temple, *The Charterhouse: Survey of London Monograph 18* (New Haven, CT, 2010), 199, 200.
25 Ibid., 203, 204.
26 Porter, 'The Courtyard House', 71.
27 Ibid., 77.
28 Temple, 222.
29 Ibid., 201.
30 Porter, *Charterhouse: The Official Guide*, 40.
31 Porter, 'The Courtyard House', 77.
32 Ibid.
33 Ibid., 73-81.
34 Porter, *Charterhouse: The Official Guide*, 12.

MALMESBURY ABBEY

1 There were two other churches either in or close to the precinct: St Andrew, where the Saxon abbots were buried, and St Laurence.
2 John Allen Giles, *William of Malmesbury's Chronicle of the Kings of England* (London, 1846), 140; see also Sarah Foot, *Aethelstan The First King of England* (New Haven and London, 2012), 188.

3 'House of Benedictine monks: Malmesbury Abbey', in *History of the County of Wiltshire: Volume 3*, ed. RB Pugh and Elizabeth Crittall (London, 1956), 210-231.
4 Joyce Youings, *The Dissolution of the Monasteries* (London, 1971), 240; the November Letters Patent grant is held at Wiltshire & Swindon History Centre, Chippenham, 88/1/25A. Stumpe's purchase might be connected with Sir Edward Baynton's expedition to France in the same year – he made his will on 8 July – in which he died on 27 November.
5 http://www.historyofparliamentonline.org
6 Ibid.
7 Thomas Hearne, *The Itinerary of John Leland the Antiquary*, Vol. 2 (London, 1744), 26.
8 Ibid.
9 A reproduction of this aerial view can be seen at the Athelstan Museum.
10 Hearne, 26.
11 The plans for this addition are in the Wiltshire & Swindon History Centre, 2512/320/75.
12 Ibid. These are drawn on blue paper.
13 Thomas Fuller, *The History of the Worthies of England*, Vol. 3 (London, 1840), 337.
14 See Mark Child, *Abbey House & Gardens, Malmesbury* (Stroud, 2011); in 1994 Ian planted a yew hedge to pick out the line of William of Colerne's lost Lady Chapel according to Harold Brakspear's plan.
15 We are most grateful to Rufus and Kristen Pollard for allowing us access to Abbey House and its gardens.

MILTON ABBEY

1 Arthur Oswald, *Country Houses of Dorset* (London, 1959), 108; the seal is illustrated in John Hutchins, *The History and Antiquities of the County of Dorset*, 3rd edn, 4 vols (London, 1861-74; re-publ. London, 1973), 4, 391.
2 Oswald, 109.
3 Maurice Howard, *The Early Tudor Country House – Architecture and Politics 1490-1550* (Eastbourne, 1987), 28.
4 Hutchins, 392-5.
5 James Joel Cartwright, 'The Travels through England of Dr Richard Pococke', *Camden Society*, 2 vols (London, 1889), 2, 143.
6 Vardy's drawings for Milton Abbey are in the RIBA Drawings Collection. The alternative schemes are illustrated in Roger White, 'John Vardy, 1718-65 – Palladian into Rococo', in Roderick Brown ed., *The Architectural Outsiders* (London, 1985), plate 56.
7 Dorset Record Office, Dorchester, D919/5.
8 White, 72.
9 Oswald, 111.
10 Quoted in Arthur Oswald, 'Milton Abbey, Dorset: IV', *Country Life*, 21 July 1966.

MOTTISFONT PRIORY

1 Hampshire Record Office, Winchester, 13M63/3.
2 Quoted in Christopher Currie, 'An archaeological and historical survey of the Mottisfont Abbey Estate, near Romsey, Hampshire' Report to the National Trust (Southern Region), July 1999, Appendix 2.
3 Gervase Jackson-Stops, Mottisfont Abbey (Swindon, 1978), 6.
4 Christopher Hussey, 'Mottisfont Abbey, Hampshire – I', *Country Life*, 29 April 1954.
5 H Avray Tipping, 'Mottisfont Priory, Hampshire', Country Life, 19 November 1921.
6 Hampshire Record Office, 13M63/4.
7 Annie Bullen, Mottisfont, Hampshire (Swindon, no date), 10.
8 Henry VIII: August 1538, 21-25, in Letters and Papers, Foreign

and Domestic, Henry VIII, Volume 13, Part 2, August-December 1538, ed. James Gairdner (London, 1893), 57-73; partly quoted in Hussey, Country Life, 29 April 1954.

9 Victoria County History: Hampshire, volume 4, plate opposite 504.

10 Tipping, Country Life, 19 November 1921.

11 Hussey, Country Life, 29 April 1954.

12 Ibid.

13 Ibid.

14 Ibid.

15 Quoted from Leland's Itinerary, vol. 4, 11, by Jackson-Stops, 8.

16 Ibid., 8-9.

17 Hampshire Record Office, 13M63/420.

18 Jackson-Stops, Mottisfont Abbey, 9.

19 Hampshire Record Office, 13M63/58.

20 Currie, 17.

21 Ibid.

22 Hampshire Record Office, 13M63/446, fol. 35.

23 The inventory is in the Rutland Papers at Belvoir Castle. We are grateful to Peter Foden for his help with this and to George Roberts for making a transcript available to study.

24 Bullen, 11.

25 Hampshire Record Office, 31M57/643.

26 James Rothwell, personal information.

27 Bullen, 11.

NETLEY ABBEY

1 WS Lewis ed., *The Yale Edition of Horace Walpole's Correspondence*, 48 vols (New Haven CT, 1973-83), 35, 251.

2 John Hare, 'Netley Abbey: Monastery, Mansion and Ruin', *Proceedings of the Hampshire Field Club and Archaeological Society:* Vol 49 (February 1993), 207-27; 207-8.

3 Ibid., 208-10.

4 Ibid.

5 A Hamilton Thomson, *English Monasteries* (Cambridge, 1913; repr. 2011), 14-6.

6 Mick Aston, *Monasteries in the Landscape* (Stroud and Charleston SC, 2000), 85.

7 Hamilton Thomson, 15.

8 Ibid., 16-18.

9 Hare, 211.

10 'Parishes: Hound with Netley', in *A History of the County of Hampshire, Volume 3*, ed. William Page (London, 1908), 472-8.

11 Hare, 213.

12 Ibid., 211.

13 'Houses of Cistercian monks: Abbey of Netley', in *A History of the County of Hampshire: Volume 2*, ed. H Arthur Doubleday and William Page (London, 1903), 146-9.

14 Hare, 212.

15 'Houses of Cistercian monks: Abbey of Netley', in *A History of the County of Hampshire: Volume 2*, ed. Doubleday and Page, 146-9.

16 Hare, 212.

17 Ibid.

18 'Parishes: Hound with Netley', in *A History of the County of Hampshire: Volume 3*, ed. Page, 472-8.

19 Hare, 216.

20 'Houses of Cistercian monks: Abbey of Netley', in *A History of the County of Hampshire: Volume 2*, ed. Doubleday and Page, 146-9.

21 *Oxford Dictionary of National Biography*, https://doi.org/10.1093/ref:odnb/21622

22 John Nichols, *The Progresses and Public Processions of Queen Elizabeth*, 3 vols (London, 1823), 3, 87 fn.1.

23 Hare, 220.

24 https:// www.historyofparliamentonline.org/volume/1509-1558/member/paulet-sir-william-1488-1572

25 Mary Hill Cole, *The Portable Queen: Elizabeth I and the Politics of Ceremony* (Amherst MA, 1999), 180.

26 Hare, 217.

27 'Parishes: Hound with Netley', in *A History of the County of Hampshire: Volume 3*, ed. Page, 472-8.

28 Hare, 218.

29 'Parishes: Hound with Netley', in *A History of the County of Hampshire: Volume 3*, ed. Page, 472-8.

30 Ibid.

31 https://www.historyofparliamentonline.org/volume/1509-1558/member/paulet-sir-william-1488-1572

32 Robert Naunton, *Fragmenta Regalia* (London, 1641), 12.

NEWSTEAD PRIORY

1 Colin Briden, 'The Augustinian Priory *c.* 1163-1539', in Rosalys Coope and Pete Smith, eds, *Newstead Abbey, A Nottinghamshire Country House: Its owners and Architectural History 1540-1931* (*Thoroton Society record Series Volume 48*) (Nottingham, 2014), 1.

2 'Houses of Austin canons: The priory of Newstead', in *A History of the County of Nottingham: Volume 2*, ed. William Page (London, 1910), 112-7.

3 Ibid.

4 Briden, 1.

5 Ibid.,6.

6 'Houses of Austin canons: The priory of Newstead', in *A History of the County of Nottingham: Volume 2*, ed. Page, 112-7.

7 Ibid.

8 Briden, 2.

9 Ibid., 3.

10 Ibid., 4.

11 Ibid., 7.

12 Ibid.

13 Ibid.

14 Ibid., 8.

15 'Houses of Austin canons: The priory of Newstead', in *A History of the County of Nottingham: Volume 2*, ed. Page, 112-7.

16 Briden, 2.

17 http://www.historyofparliamentonline.org/volume/1509-1558/member/byron-(beron)-sir-john-148788-1567

18 Ibid.

19 Ibid.

20 Rosalys Coope, 'The Byrons' Acquisition and Transformation of the Priory 1540-1640', in Rosalys Coope and Pete Smith, eds, *Newstead Abbey, A Nottinghamshire Country House: Its owners and Architectural History 1540-1931* (*Thoroton Society record Series Volume 48*) (Nottingham, 2014), 9.

21 Ibid.

22 Ibid., 11.

23 Ibid.

24 Ibid., 12.

ST OSYTH'S PRIORY

1 Houses of Austin canons: Abbey of Chich or St Osyth's', in *A History of the County of Essex: Volume 2*, ed. William Page and J Horace Round (London, 1907), 157-62.

2 Historic England List Entry Number 1002193.

3 Houses of Austin canons: Abbey of Chich or St Osyth's', in *A History of the County of Essex: Volume 2*, ed. Page and Round, 157-62.

4 'St. Osyth', in *An Inventory of the Historical Monuments in Essex, Volume 3, North East* (London, 1922), 195-206.

5 Ibid.

6 Ibid.

7 Ibid.

8 Ibid.

9 Houses of Austin canons: Abbey of Chich or St Osyth's', in *A History of the County of Essex: Volume 2*, ed. Page and Round, 157-62.

10 Ibid.

11 Somerset de Chair, *St Osyth's Priory* (Derby, 1971), 18.

12 Houses of Austin canons: Abbey of Chich or St Osyth's', in *A History of the County of Essex: Volume 2*, ed. Page and Round, 157-62.

13 de Chair,18.

14 http://www.histparl.ac.uk/volume/1509-1558/member/darcy-sir-thomas-1506-58

15 *Oxford Dictionary of National Biography*, https://doi.org/10.1093/ref:odnb/70579

16 Ibid.

17 http://www.histparl.ac.uk/volume/1509-1558/member/darcy-sir-thomas-1506-58

18 Ibid.

19 St Osyth, in *An Inventory of the Historical Monuments in Essex, Volume 3, North East*, 195-206.

20 Ibid.

21 Ibid.

22 Ibid.

23 de Chair, 18, 20.

SYON ABBEY

1 *Oxford Dictionary of National Biography*, http://www.oxforddnb.com/view/ article/25159

2 Simon Thurley, *Somerset House: The Palace of England's Queens 1551-1692* (London, 2009), 3.

3 Ibid., 4-5.

4 *Oxford Dictionary of National Biography*, http://www.oxforddnb.com/view/ article/25159

5 Marjorie Blatcher, ed., *Report on the Manuscripts of the most Honourable the Marquess of Bath preserved at Longleat,* Vol. 4 (London, 1968), 376.

6 Thurley, 8.

7 Ibid., 6.

8 RW Dunning, 'The Building of Syon Abbey', *Transactions of the Ancient Monuments Society*, Vol.25 (1981) 16-26, 16-7.

9 Samuel Fanous, 'Becoming the Theotokos: Birgitta of Sweden and Fulfilment of Salvation History', *Motherhood, Religion and Society in Medieval Europe, 400-1400*, ed. Conrad Leyser and Lesley Smith (Farnham, 2011: repub. London and New York, 2016), 262.

10 Dunning, 17.

11 Ibid., 22.

12 Ibid., 18.

13 Ibid., 21.

14 Barney Sloane, 'Syon House, Syon Park, Hounslow, October 2003: An Archaeological Evaluation of a Bridgettine Abbey and an Assessment of the Results' (Ref: 52568.05, The Trust for Wessex Archaeology Limited, 2003), Paras. 1.1.9., 3.4.1., 7, 14.

15 Dunning, 17.

16 Ibid., 17-20

17 Ibid., 20-1.

18 Ibid., 17-21.

19 Ibid., 20-1.

20 Sloane, Para.1.1.3., 6.

21 Charles Wriothesley, *A Chronicle of England during the Reigns of the Tudors from A.D. 1485 to 1559*, ed. William Douglas

Hamilton (London, 1875), 109.

22 *A History of the County of Middlesex: Volume 3, Shepperton, Staines, Stanwell, Sunbury, Teddington, Heston and Isleworth, Twickenham, Cowley, Cranford, West Drayton, Greenford, Hanwell, Harefield and Harlington*, ed. Susan Reynolds (London, 1962), 97-100.

23 Historic England List Entry number TQ 17 NE 69.

24 Thurley, 25.

25 Ibid., 17.

26 Sloane, Appendix 1

27 Thurley, 5.

28 Malcolm Airs and Mark Girouard, *The Tudor and Jacobean Country House: A Building History* (Godalming: Bramley Books, 1995; repr. 1998), 58.

29 Thurley, 6.

30 Gordon Batho, 'Syon House: The First Two Hundred Years', *Transactions of the London and Middlesex Archaeological Society*, Vol.19 (1958), 1-17, 13.

31 Thurley, 8.

32 Batho, 12.

33 Sloane, Paras.1.2.10 and 3.4.2.,11, 14.

34 Ibid.

35 English Heritage: NMR Number TQ 17 NE 69.

36 Anon. *The Life of Edward Seymour, Duke of Somerset, Lord General and Lord Protector of the Realm* (London, 1713), 12.

37 John Cloake, *Palaces and Parks of Richmond and Kew: Volume I, The palaces of Shene and Richmond* (Chichester: Philimore, 1995), 101, 102.

38 Thurley, 8.

39 Cloake, 103.

40 Thurley, 8, 20.

41 Ibid., 5, 6.

TITCHFIELD ABBEY (PLACE HOUSE)

1 'Parishes: Titchfield', in *A History of the County of Hampshire: Volume 3*, ed. William Page (London, 1908), 220-33.

2 G.W. Minns, 'Titchfield Abbey and Place House', *Proceedings of the Hampshire Field Club and Archaeological Society* Vol. 3.3, 317-38, 318-9.

3 Ibid., 332-3.

4 Ibid., 334.

5 'Houses of Premonstratensian canons: Abbey of Titchfield', in *A History of the County of Hampshire: Volume 2*, ed. H Arthur Doubleday and William Page (London, 1903), 181-6.

6 'Henry VIII: December 1537, 15-25', in *Letters and Papers, Foreign and Domestic, Henry VIII, Volume 12 Part 2, June-December 1537*, ed. James Gairdner (London, 1891), 430-43.

7 Minns, 325.

8 Ibid., 326-7.

9 *Oxford Dictionary of National Biography*, https://doi.org/10.1093/ref:odnb/30076

10 Ibid.

11 Ibid.

12 *John Goodall, The English Castle* (New Haven and London, 2011), 426.

13 WH St. John Hope, 'The Making of Place House at Titchfield, Near Southampton, in 1538', *Archaeological Journal* Vol. 63 (December 1906), 231-43.

14 Ibid., 235.

15 Ibid., 233.

16 Ibid., 242.

17 Ibid., 233.

18 Ibid., 233-5.

19 Ibid., 233.

20 Ibid., 236.

21 Ibid., 237.

22 Ibid., 236.

23 Ibid.

24 'Henry VIII: April 1538, 10-15', in *Letters and Papers, Foreign and Domestic, Henry VIII, Volume 13 Part 1, January-July 1538*, ed. James Gairdner (London, 1892), 277-91.

25 St. John Hope, 237.

26 Ibid., 238.

27 'Parishes: Titchfield', in *A History of the County of Hampshire: Volume 3*, ed. Page, 220-33.

28 St John Hope, 235.

29 John Leland, The Itinerary of John Leland in or about the Years 1535-1543, Parts I-III, ed. Lucy Toulmin Smith (London, 1907), 281.

30 'Parishes: Titchfield', in A History of the County of Hampshire: Volume 3, ed. Page, 220-33.

31 St John Hope, 233.

32 Susan M Youngs, John Clark and Terry Barry, 'Medieval Britain and Ireland in 1984', *Medieval Archaeology*, Vol. 29 (1985), 158-230, 182.

33 Nikolaus Pevsner and David Lloyd, *The Buildings of England: Hampshire and the Isle of Wight* (Harmondsworth, 1967), 629.

34 *Oxford Dictionary of National Biography*, https://doi.org/10.1093/ref:odnb/30076

35 http://m.english-heritage.org.uk/daysout/properties/titchfield-abbey/history-and-research/

TORRE ABBEY

1 Historic England List Entry Number 1009302.

2 Michael Rhodes, *Devon's Torre Abbey: Faith, Politics and Grand Designs* (Stroud, 2015), 9.

3 Historic England List Entry Number 1009302.

4 Jane Palmer, *Torre Abbey* (Peterborough, 2015), 31.

5 Rhodes, 20.

6 Historic England List Entry Number 1009302.

7 Ibid.

8 John Leland, *The Itinerary of John Leland in or about the years 1535-1543, Parts I-III*, ed. Lucy Toulmin Smith (London, 1907), 223.

9 Rhodes, 51.

10 'Letters and Papers: February 1539, 21-25', in *Letters and Papers, Foreign and Domestic, Henry VIII, Volume 14 Part 1, January-July 1539*, ed. James Gairdner and RH Brodie (London, 1894), 129-44.

11 Rhodes, 53-4.

12 https://www.historyofparliamentonline.org/volume/1604-1629/member/seymour-edward-1563-1613

13 https://www.historyofparliamentonline.org/volume/1604-1629/member/ridgeway-sir-thomas-1566-1631

14 Ibid.

15 Ibid.

16 Ibid.

17 Rhodes, 60.

18 Ibid., 61.

19 Ibid.

20 Palmer, 32.

VALE ROYAL ABBEY

1 Peter de Figueiredo and Julian Treuherz, *Cheshire Country Houses*, (Chichester, 1988), 189.

2 This summary of the abbey is taken from R McNeil & RC Turner, 'An Architectural and Topographical Survey of Vale Royal Abbey', *Journal of the Chester Archaeological Society*, Vol.

70 (1988), 51-79.

3 Ibid., 66.

4 Cheshire Archives & Local Studies, Chester, DDX 3: 'Vale Royal Abbey, grant of the estate', 1544.

5 de Figueiredo and Treuherz, 190.

6 histparl.ac.uk: The History of Parliament, Member Biographies

7 McNeil and Turner, 66-7.

8 Ibid., 67.

9 de Figueiredo and Treuherz, 191.

10 Cheshire Archives & Local Studies, D 4460/1: 'Survey of Vale Royal Manor House and Estate', 1616. Lady Cholmondeley was the widow of Sir Hugh Cholmondeley and heiress of Christopher Holford of Holford Hall. The house remained with the Cholmondeleys, afterwards earls of Delamere, until 1947.

11 McNeil and Turner, fig. 23.

12 Ibid., 56.

13 Ibid., fig. 7.

14 Ibid., 68.

15 de Figueiredo and Treuherz, 193.

WALDEN ABBEY (AUDLEY END)

1 *Audley End, Essex* (London,1958), 3.

2 Houses of Benedictine monks: Abbey of Walden, *A History of the County of Essex,* Volume 2, ed. William Page and J Horace Round (London, 1907), 111.

3 Ibid.,112.

4 Ibid., 114.

5 Richard Neville, Lord Braybrooke, *The history of Audley End and Saffron Walden* (London,1836), 66.

6 *Audley End, Essex*, 3.

7 *Oxford Dictionary of National Biography,* https://doi.org/10.1093/ref:odnb/896

8 William Addison, *Audley End* (London, 1953), 11-12. The quote is taken from Thomas Fuller's *Worthies of England*.

9 english-heritage.org.uk: 'History of Audley End House and Gardens'.

10 PJ Drury and S Welch, 'Walden Abbey into Audley End', CBA Research Report 45, ed. S R Bennett: Saffron Walden: excavations and research 1972-80, 1982, 94-105.

11 Maurice Howard, *The Early Tudor Country House – Architecture and Politics 1490-1550* (London, 1987), 204.

12 The Winstanley view is illustrated in Paul Drury, *Audley End* (Swindon, 2010), 42-3.

13 Drury and Welch, 104.

14 Addison, 12.

15 Nikolaus Pevsner and Enid Radcliffe, *The Buildings of England – Essex* (Harmondsworth, 1965), 333.

WENLOCK PRIORY

1 Victoria & Albert Museum, London, E.1308.79-2001.

2 Shropshire Archives, Shrewsbury, 1037/20/134; Julie Pinnell, *Wenlock Priory* (Swindon, 1999), 22.

3 Milburge (Mildburh, Milburga or Milburgh) died in 727 and was supposedly endowed with the gift of healing and restored sight to the blind.

4 MR James, *Abbeys* (London,1925), 99 remarks that it was 350 feet long.

5 Royal Academy, London, Object Number 03/243.

6 Anthony Emery, *Greater Medieval Houses of England and Wales, Vol. II, East Anglia, Central England and Wales 1300-1500* (Cambridge, 2000), 593.

7 John Britton, *Architectural Antiquities of Great Britain*, Vol. 4 (London,1814), 63.

8 Ibid., 63-4.

9 Ibid., 64.

10 Thomas Hudson Turner, *Domestic Architecture in England* (Cambridge, 1859), plates between 366-71.

11 Ibid. 368, 370.

12 Ibid. 367-8. The reading desk is shown in a photograph of 1981, just before the property was bought by Miss Gabrielle Drake and Mr Louis de Wet: Shropshire Archives, PH/M/23/9/219. It does not appear in photographs taken in 2011 for a *Country Life* article on the house (1 June 2011).

13 Turner, 371.

14 *Country Life*, 1 June 2011; see also *In the Gaze of the Medusa – The Restoration of a Mediaeval Priory by the Contemporary Artist Louis de Wet*, a film by Gavin Bush.

WILTON ABBEY

1 'Wilton: Early History', *A History of the County of Wiltshire: Volume 6*, ed. RB Pugh and Elizabeth Crittall (London, 1962), 7-8.

2 Adam Nicolson, *Arcadia: The Dream of Perfection in Renaissance England* (London & New York, 2009), 46.

3 'Houses of Benedictine nuns: Abbey of Wilton', in *A History of the County of Wiltshire: Volume 3*, ed. R B Pugh and Elizabeth Crittall (London, 1956), 231-42.

4 Jenni Butterworth, *Monastic Sites and Monastic Estates in Somerset and Wiltshire in The Middle Ages: A Regional Perspective* (Unpublished PhD Thesis, University of Bristol, 1999), 52.

5 Nicolson, 47

6 'Houses of Benedictine nuns: Abbey of Wilton', in *A History of the County of Wiltshire: Volume 3*, ed. Pugh and Crittall, 231-42.

7 Ibid.

8 Ibid.

9 From: 'Henry VIII: Appointments to Offices', *Letters and Papers, Foreign and Domestic, Henry VIII, Volume 17: 1542*, ed. James Gairdner and RH Brodie (London, 1900), 690-705.

10 From: 'Henry VIII: January 1544, 26-31', *Letters and Papers, Foreign and Domestic, Henry VIII, Volume 19 Part 1: January-July 1544*, ed. James Gairdner and RH Brodie (London, 1903), 28-45.

11 Wiltshire & Swindon History Centre, Chippenham, 1501/2.

12 Nicolson, 52.

13 Ibid., 52-4.

14 Ibid., 55-6.

15 From: 'Index: P', *Calendar of State Papers Foreign; Edward VI: 1547-1553*, ed. William B Turnbull (London, 1861), 385-7.

16 Sidney Charles Herbert, 16th Earl of Pembroke, *Wilton House* (London, 1974), 3.

17 From: 'Venice: September 1556, 16-20', *Calendar of State Papers Relating to English Affairs in the Archives of Venice, Volume 6: 1555-1558* ed. Rawdon Brown (London, 1877), 620-37.

18 John Heward, 'The Restoration of the South Front of Wilton House: The Development of the House Reconsidered', *Architectural History,* Vol. 35 (1992) 78-117, 80.

19 Herbert, 3.

20 Charles R Straton, ed., *Survey of Lands of William First Earl of Pembroke*, 2 vols (Oxford, 1909), I, p.xl.

21 Ibid., Roll III, 2, trans. by author: The aforesaid Earl of Pembroke holds the whole capital Mansion as his own, with all and each of the houses, buildings, gardens, orchards and yards within the entire site, the surroundings, enclosures, areas and precincts of the same house, containing in total by estimation four acres which have not been valued because they are reserved in the hands of the Lord. And the aforesaid Earl made from new all houses, gardens, orchards and all belonging to the same, to his great cost, viz. ten thousand pounds and more.

22 Ibid., I, 2.

23 Heward, 87.

24 Ibid., 88.

25 Ibid., 89.

26 John Bold with John Reeves, *Wilton House and English Palladianism: Some Wiltshire Houses* (London, 1988), 32.

27 Ibid.

28 Ibid., 71, 77-8.

29 Mark Girouard, *Elizabethan Architecture: Its Rise And Fall, 1540-1640* (London, 2009), 149.

30 Bold with Reeves, 32.

31 Girouard, 150.

32 Lieutenant Hammond, 'Relation of a Short Survey of the Western Counties' (1635) in *The Camden Miscellany* Vol. XVI, 3rd Series, 52, ed. LG Wickham Legg (London, 1936), 66.

33 Heward, 92.

34 Ibid., 90.

35 Ibid., 80.

36 Ibid.

37 Ibid., 115.

38 Ibid., 91.

39 Straton, I, xlv.

40 Historic England: NMR number SU 03 SE 32.

41 Straton, I, 12, trans. by author: There is a large grange called Washerne Barne containing ten bays roofed with tiles for storing corn and hay, and also various separate stalls constructed of tiles in the same way, in which eighty horses are able to stand.

42 Ibid., Roll III, 2.

43 Ibid.

44 Nicolson, 17.

45 Straton, Roll III, 13.

46 Ibid.,14.

47 Ibid.

48 Girouard, 106.

49 Straton, I, xxx-xxxi.

50 Mary Hill Cole, *The Portable Queen* (Amherst MA, 1999), 187.

51 Extract from an unpublished MS. written in 1578, taken from John Nichols, *The Progresses and Public Processions of Queen Elizabeth,* 3 vols (London, 1823), I, 409.

52 Ibid.

List of Illustrations

Acknowledgements

I would like to particularly thank Professor Timothy Mowl for all his encouragement and contribution to the writing of this book.

I would also like to acknowledge the great help provided by
Andrew Arrol, Neil Bailey (www.nsbailey.com), Sarah Callender
Beckett, Thomas Brakspear, Marian Brooks, Alex Denman,
Maisie Hill (www.maisiehill.co.uk), Joanne Jenner, Sonia Jones,
Georgy Kantor, Alice Kennard, Laura Mayer, Rufus and Kristen Pollard
Simon Raeburn (www.simonraeburnphotography.com),
Michael Richardson, Michael Riordan, Jim Riseley, Lisa and Mark
Roper, David Rymill, James Watson and Gabrielle de Wet.

Index

A